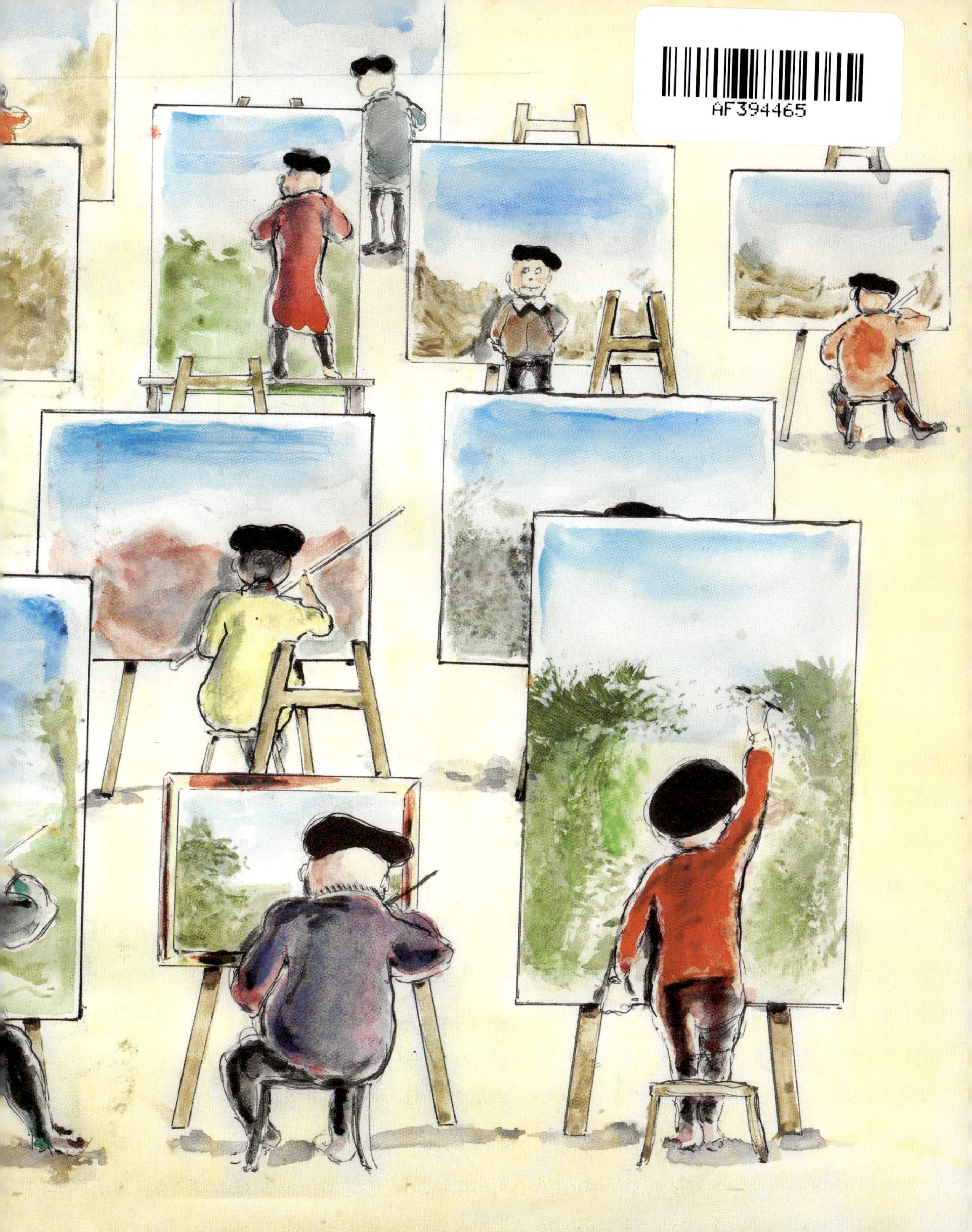
AF394465

The Little Book of Art History
for Children and Curious Grown-Ups

The Li[brary]
Book
Histor[y]

Peter Michael Hornung

ttle
of Art
y

for Children and Curious Grown-Ups

Strandberg Publishing

A short introduction

The American artist Philip Guston once said that it's okay to laugh at his paintings. And his compatriot Claes Oldenburg didn't mind if you smiled when you saw one of his sculptures either. When it comes to experiencing art, frown lines aren't always better than dimples.

However, art has, for the most part, been a serious matter. And not only does it demand a lot from the artist who creates it, but it also requires something from the people who want to get to know it better.

It is for these people, big and small, young and old, children and adults alike, that *The Little Book of Art History for Children and Curious Grown-Ups* was conceived. The purpose of the book is to provide everyone – regardless of age – with an easily accessible introduction to the history and evolution of art. In my opinion, this is best achieved by downplaying the aspects of art that may deter many first-time visitors by seeming solemn, demanding, or simply unfamiliar.

In contrast to countless books on art history, this book is only illustrated with drawings specifically created for this purpose. The hope is that these drawings will familiarize the reader with the most important artistic styles and expressions in an enjoyable and educational manner. The text is written to complement these drawings and place them in a slightly broader context.

The book has two purposes. Firstly, in a relaxed manner, to teach the young or slightly older reader about some facts and aspects of the art world. And secondly, to provide these readers with tools to seek out art in the real world.

Should the reader encounter one of the original works one day, there may be, besides perhaps the joy of recognition, a sense of relief that it is so much more art with a capital A.

The book was first published in Danish in 2014. In this first English edition, the selection of works has been made more international, and a number of new examples of works of significance to what is happening in art today have been added. Additionally, the glossary has been updated. All the entries listed there are highlighted in red.

Enjoy!

Peter Michael Hornung

Content

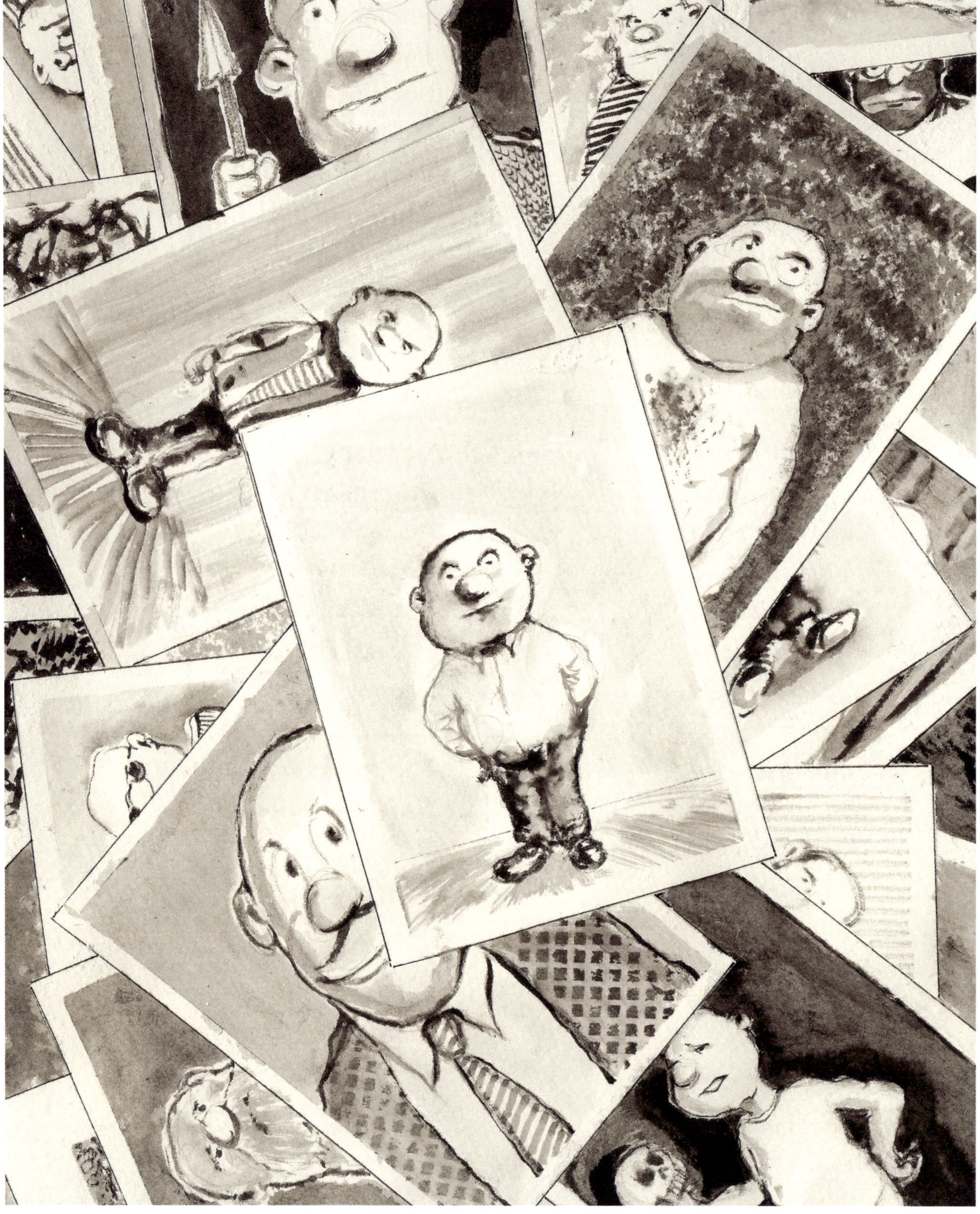

Our guide in art

The image presents a glimpse of what could resemble a photo album, where the photographs are scattered among each other. But one figure is recurring. You can see that the person is small and has a round head. You can also see that the person appears in various disguises. But regardless of the disguise and the role he plays, you can almost always recognize him when you encounter him on the following pages.

It is this person who will bring a bit of order to the chaos. For you will follow him as art evolves and becomes increasingly modern.

He is your guide. We could call him the all-time guide, for he is present in all the times in art history that are covered. He is there in the cave paintings from the earliest Stone Age, in Egypt, in ancient Greece, and in ancient Rome. And he does not abandon you, even as you leave the past, which there is a lot of in art history, and move closer to the present. Sometimes he becomes part of a work. Other times he stands outside it and may even wonder about it, as many others have done. And one should not wonder about this wonder. It is natural.

For when it comes to art, things that no one could have expected often happen. But usually, there is at least one good reason why it happens. In this book you will learn more about what happens, how it happens, and perhaps even why it happens.

Is art something exalted?

Throughout most of its many thousands of years of history, visual art has been tightly intertwined with the societies it has been part of. They are connected, and one can always debate whether it is time that has influenced art or if art has left its mark on time. It is only in the last couple of hundred years that art has begun to carve its own path. Or so it may seem.

Initially, art was created solely for religious reasons, to honour, exalt, or worship the deity it either symbolised or stood in place of. For art was often a kind of surrogate. For a long period in Europe's ancient history, the church was the main patron and commissioner of art. But the church was also a most demanding employer of art. Later, the nobility and monarchy took over alongside the church, and in the last 200 years, it has been ordinary people who have kept art alive.

However, it is not only us who keep art alive. For art also contributes to keeping us alive. We do this, among other things, thanks to the discoveries that art provides us and because of the discussions that new art prompts.

Art is no longer just for the mighty, powerful, refined, and noble. Today, art does not need to be more exalted than you want it to be. And you can always find a beautiful cross-section of it in art museums.

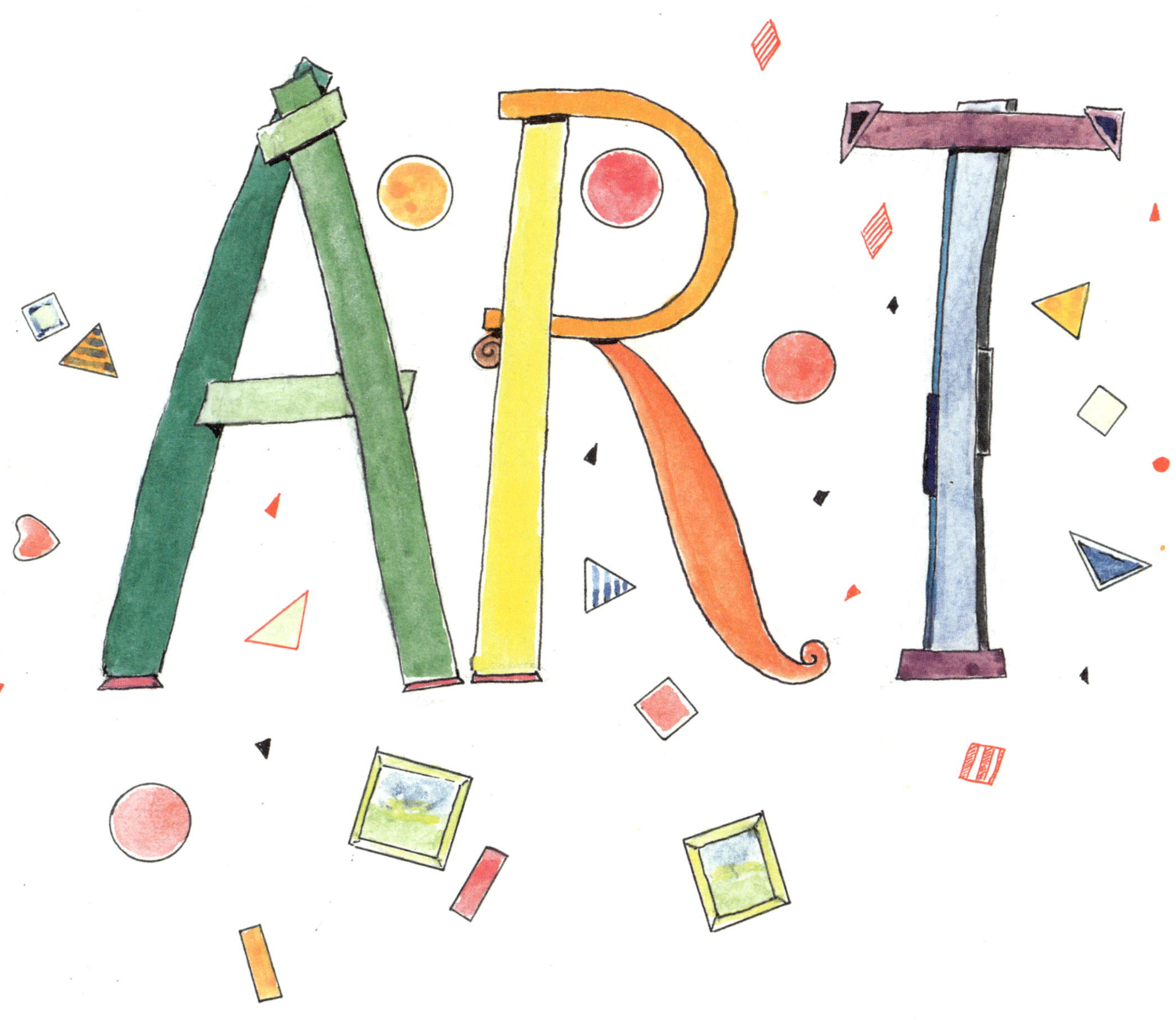

Can art be dangerous?

At first glance, approaching art should be easy. It is not intimidating in the same way as the creature in the picture. It could perhaps harm your finances if you buy it too expensively. And it can also offend and provoke you. Modern art has done this many times throughout its history, sometimes without intending to. In doing so, it has not only pushed your boundaries but also the boundaries of what art is usually allowed to do. But remember: if the artists who create art had never occasionally crossed the boundaries of what they were allowed to do, art would not have had the opportunity to evolve. It would have always stayed the same throughout time, and that might have been rather dull in the long run.

The rule that applies to individuals who want to attract attention also applies to works of art. If a work of art reminds you too much of something

you already know, you will not be surprised to see it, and you may not find it particularly original. The artist who we notice, and perhaps look up to, is usually an explorer in the possibilities of artistic expression and does not stop merely because they are leaving behind traditions and conventions. They continue to evolve and believe that the development of art is never truly complete.

Previously – and right up to the end of the 19th century – it was rare for women to pursue a career as an artist, mainly because, for women, this path was paved with prohibitions, obstacles, and a lot of inherited intolerance. Thankfully, the world has changed and improved in this regard.

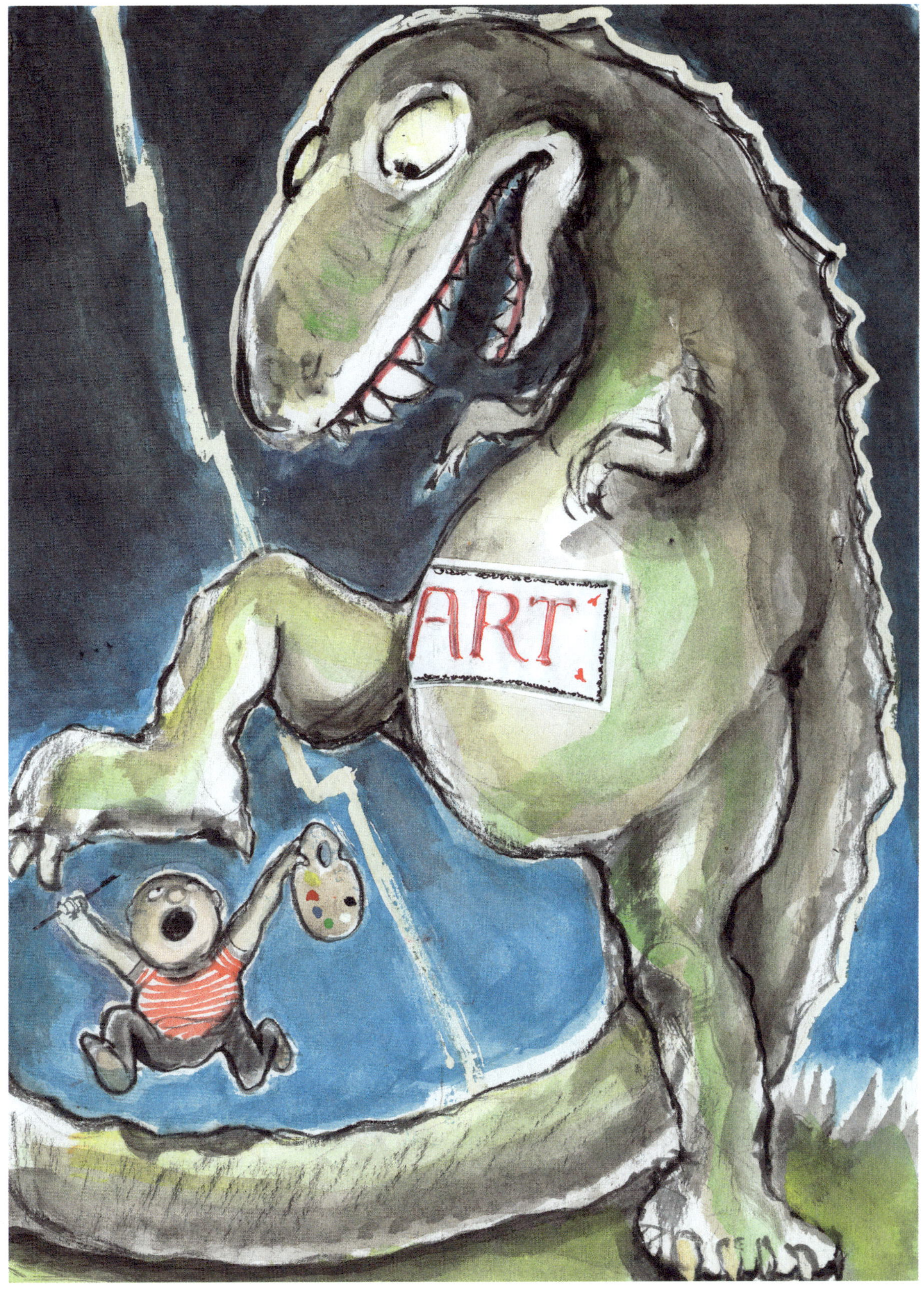

ART

Art History Timeline

Ancient Greece

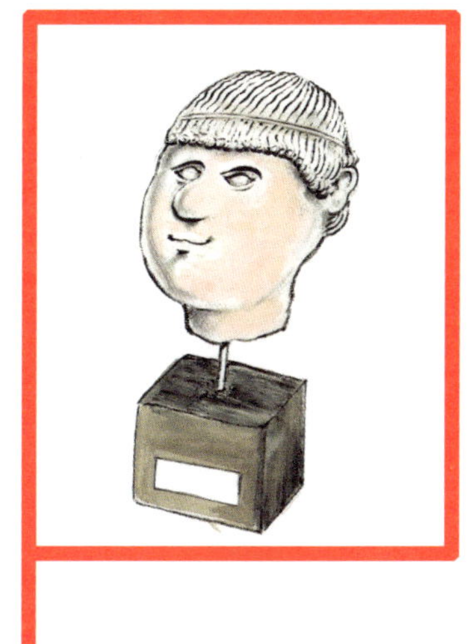

Viking Age

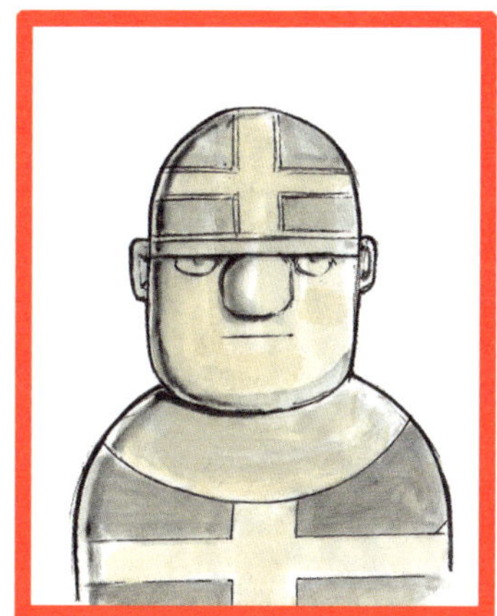

Ancient Rome

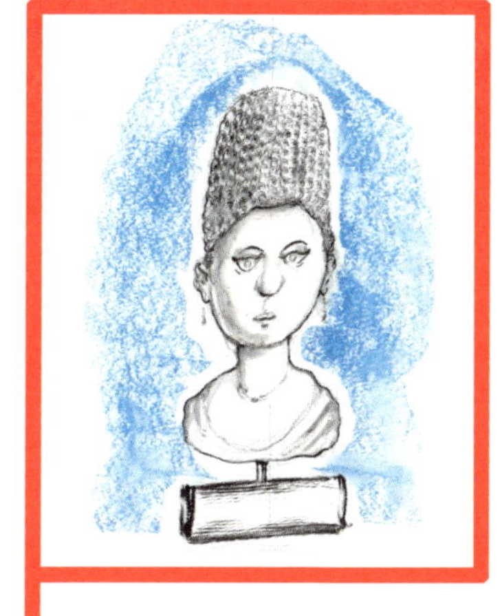

1000—400 BCE

500 BCE—500

700—1100

Renaissance

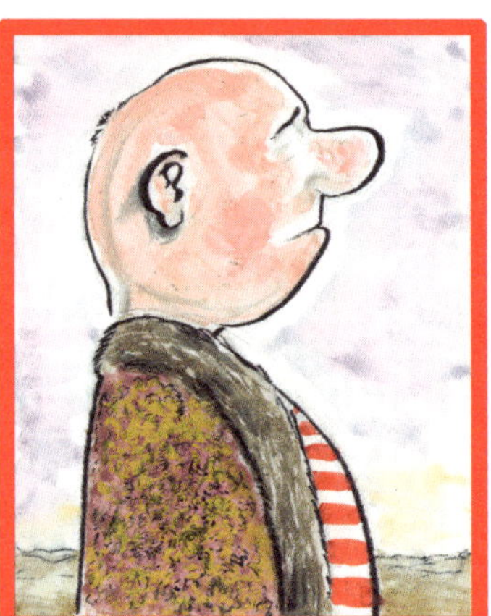

Romanesque art

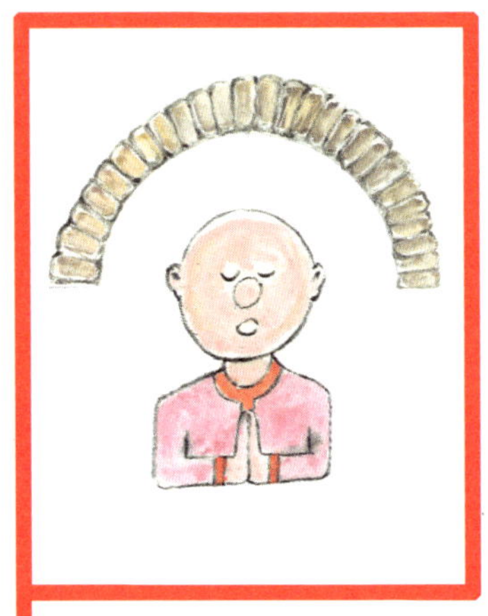

Gothic art

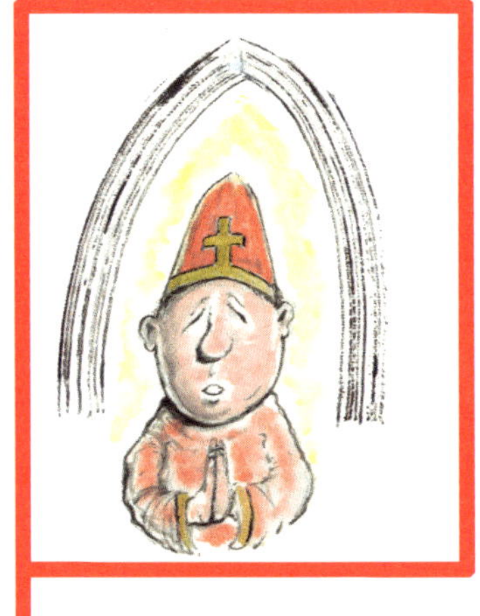

1000—1200

1150—1500

1400

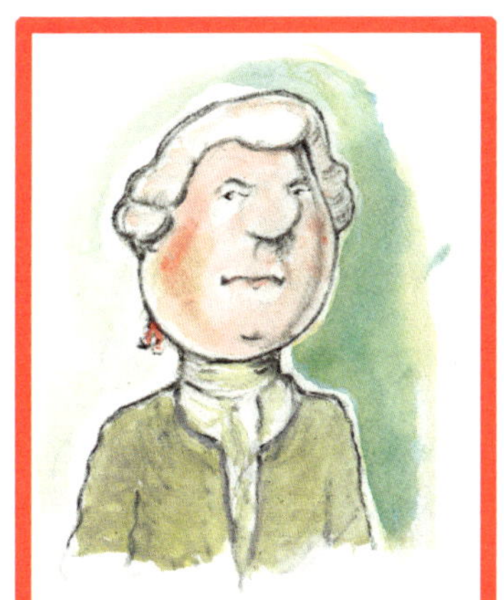

Rococo

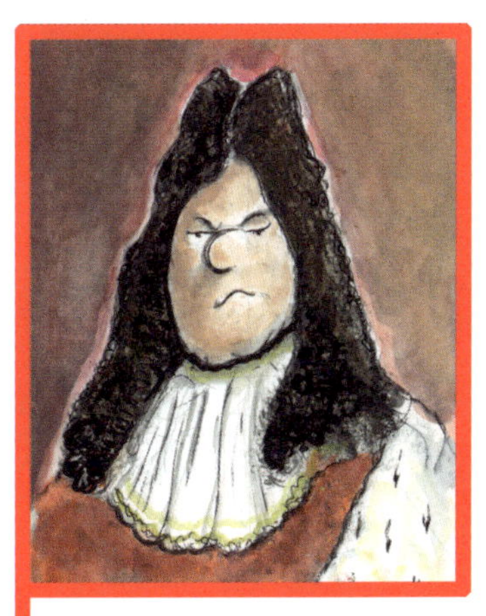

Baroque

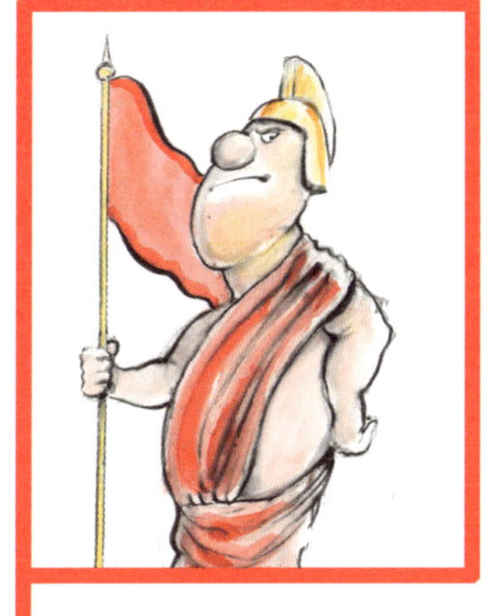

Neoclassicism

1600 1700 1800

Realism

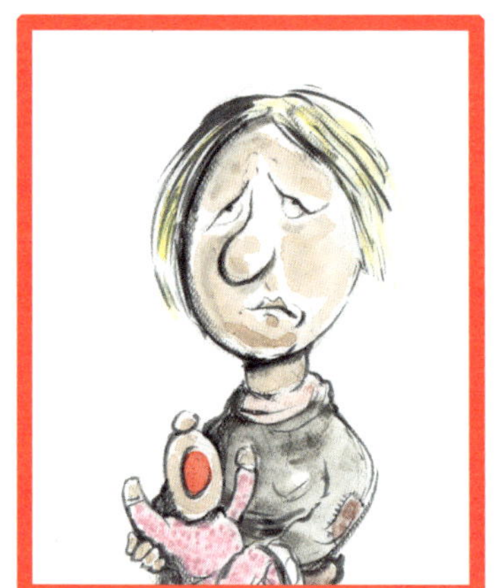

Romanticism

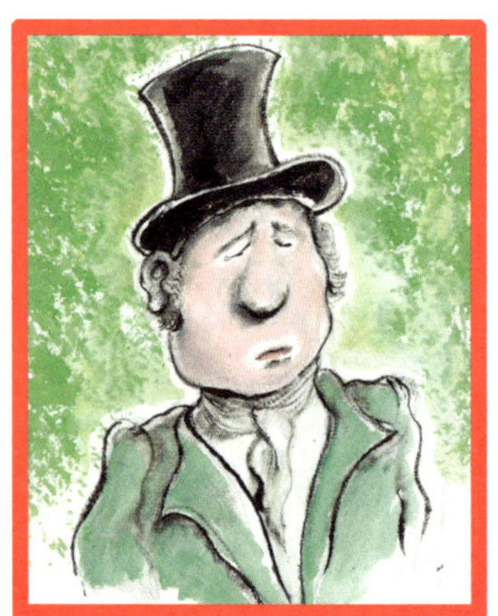

Impressionism

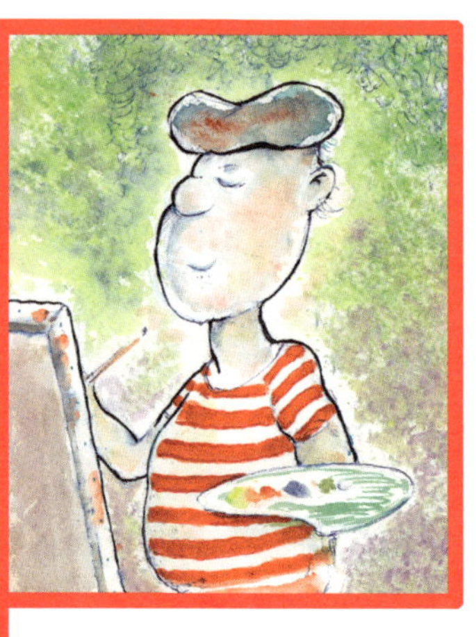

1800

1850

Expressionism

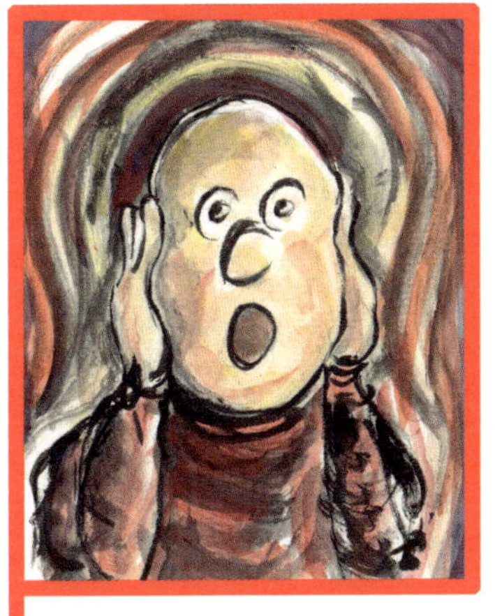

Surrealism

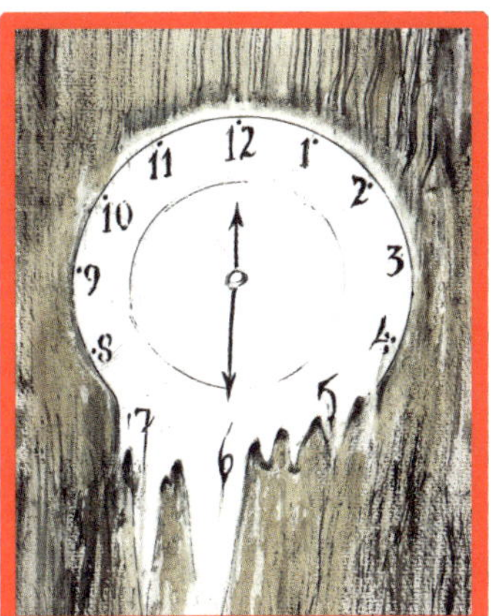

Cubism

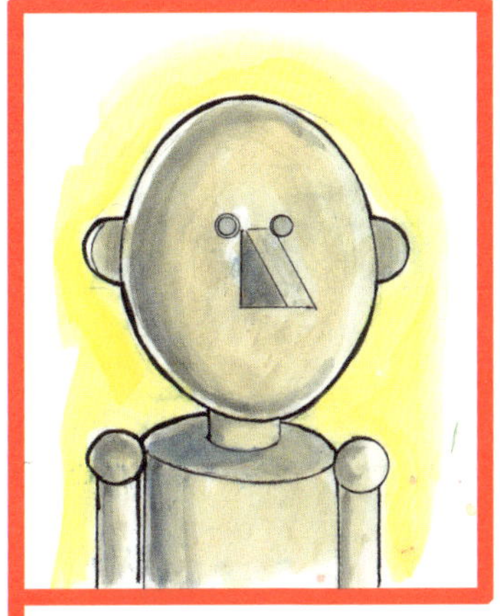

Figurative art

Abstract art

Pop Art

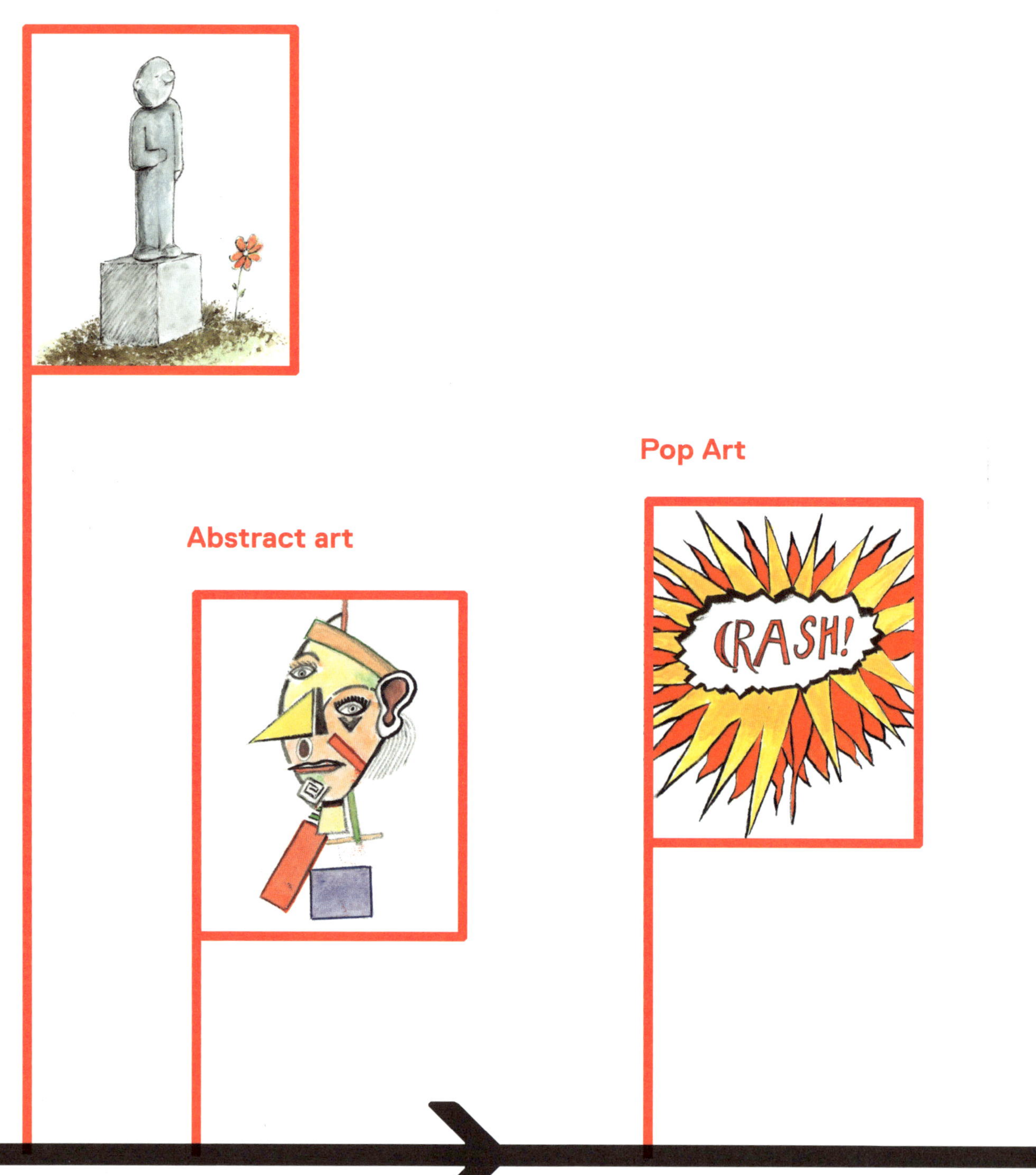

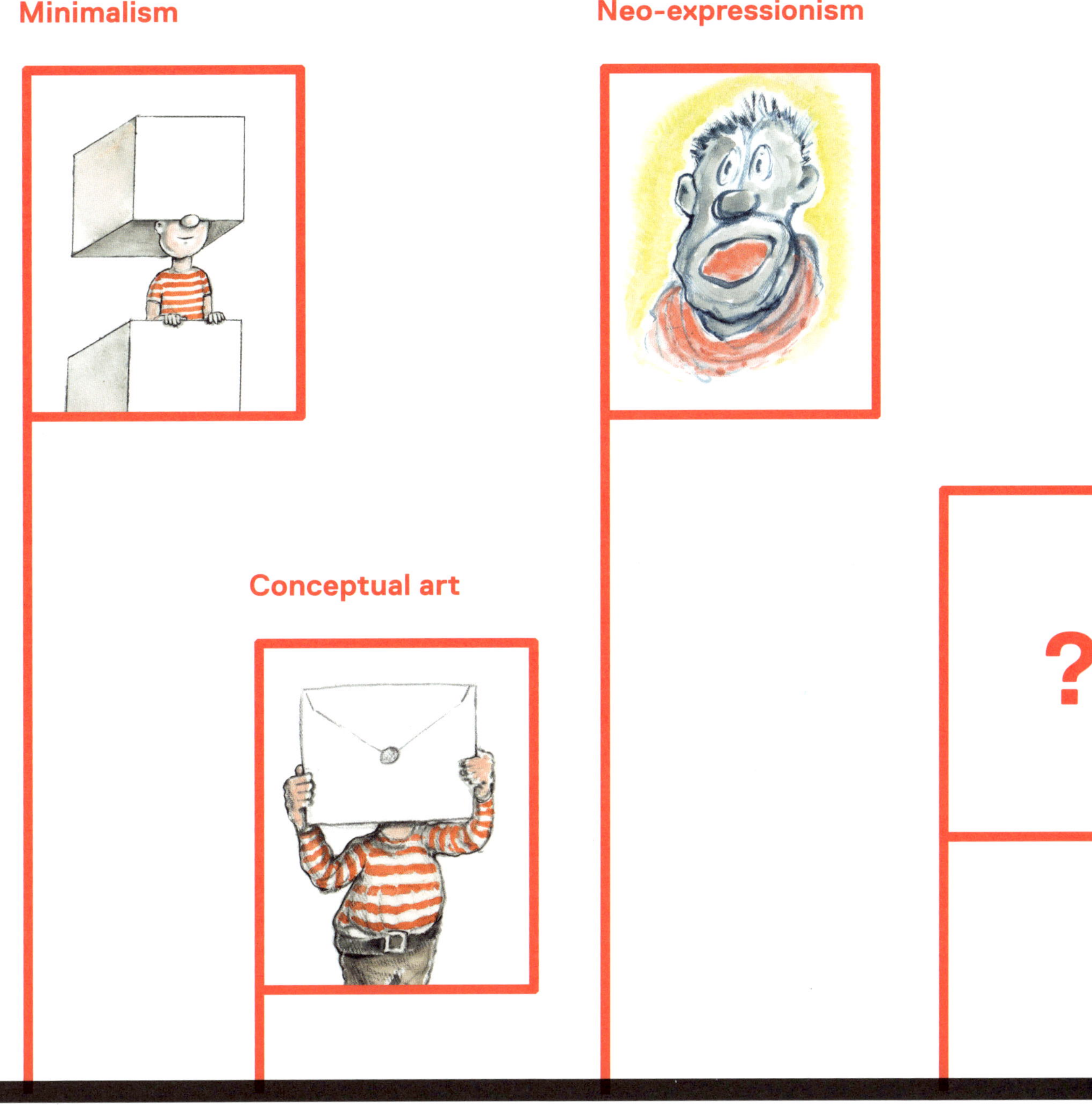

Minimalism
Neo-expressionism
Conceptual art
?
1960
1970

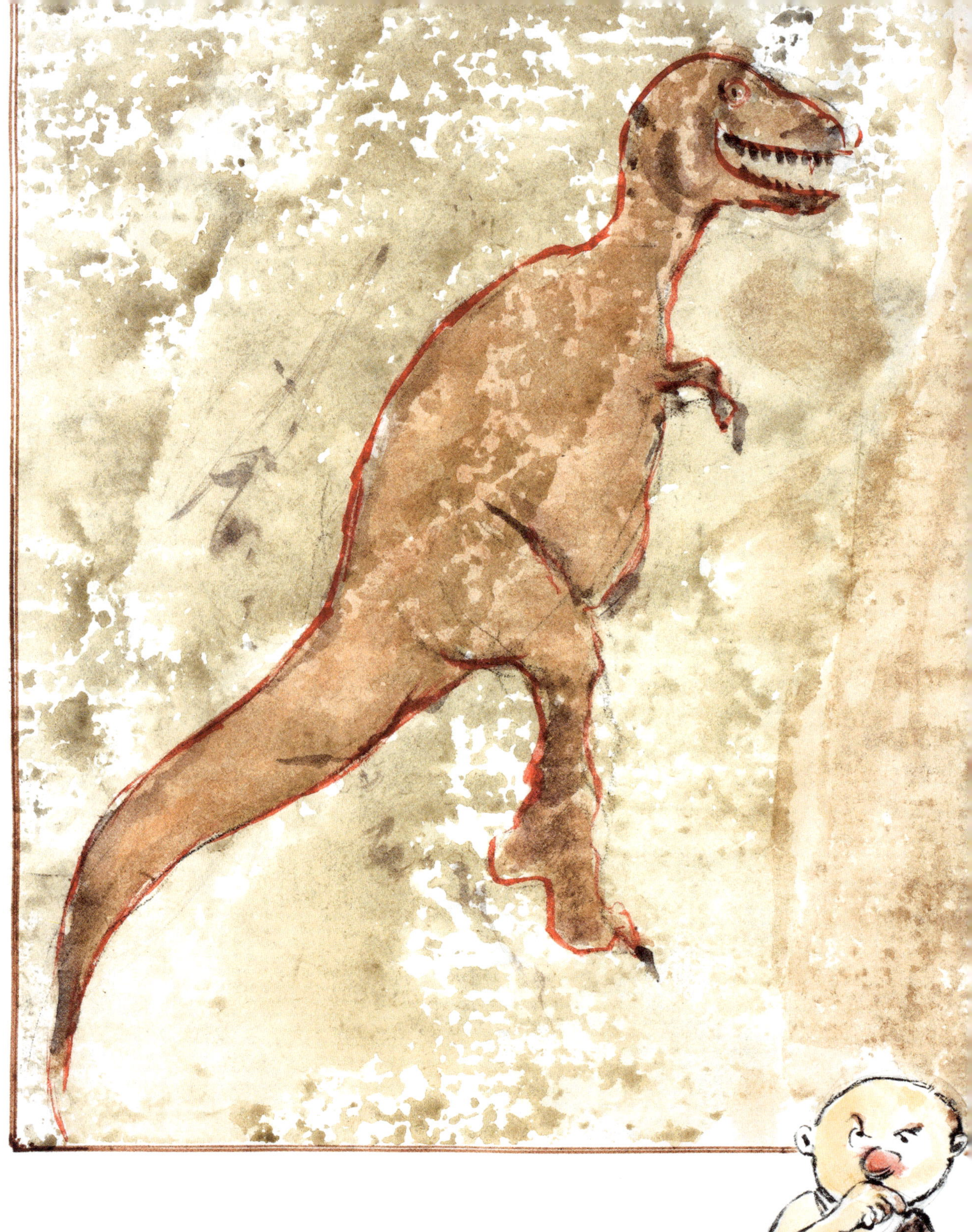

Dino pictures – authentic and fake

Prehistoric cave paintings are the oldest artworks created by humans. That is, the oldest paintings that we *know of.* For art history is largely a history of the works of art that have been preserved, which we can still seek out or see representations of.

The cave paintings depict animals such as horses, bison, mammoths, and deer. It is somewhat miraculous that the artists were able to create them, as they were painted deep inside caves where daylight cannot reach. They were executed using natural pigments directly on the cave walls, so it is also quite a technical marvel that they have retained so much of their vibrancy to this day.

When the first cave paintings in Altamira, northern Spain, were discovered over 130 years ago, some scientists believed them to be a hoax. Their view was that prehistoric cave dwellers were too primitive to create such beautiful and lifelike depictions of animals. But the paintings were indeed authentic.

However, if one of the paintings had shown a Tyrannosaurus rex, the doubters would have been right. It would have been a forgery, the very first of many in the long history of art.

Because dinosaurs lived over 66 million years before our time. And that is long before the first artists in art history. So our primitive ancestors could not have painted living dinosaurs, as in the drawing on the next page. But in principle, a situation as dangerous for the artist as this one is not entirely implausible. Real artists have rarely been afraid to push boundaries and put their reputation on the line.

If they had come up with a good motif like the one we see in the picture, more than just fear and fright would be needed to hold them back. They often continued what they had started, regardless of the cost. Here, a person from ancient times is painting the sharp teeth of a lizard so they resemble an abstract motif.

Our distant ancestors painted their pictures around 10,000–15,000 years before our time. Back then, humans had walked the Earth for four million years. Even in prehistoric times, it seems one had to go through a lot to become an artist. That is, the people who painted these animals were not at all aware that they had created something that much later would be called 'art'. For they had no idea what the word 'art' meant. The concept of 'art' only emerged many thousands of years later. They also did not know that they were a kind of artist. However, we know that they could not resist creating images. Making pictures of what interests us as human beings is, in other words, a very ancient impulse.

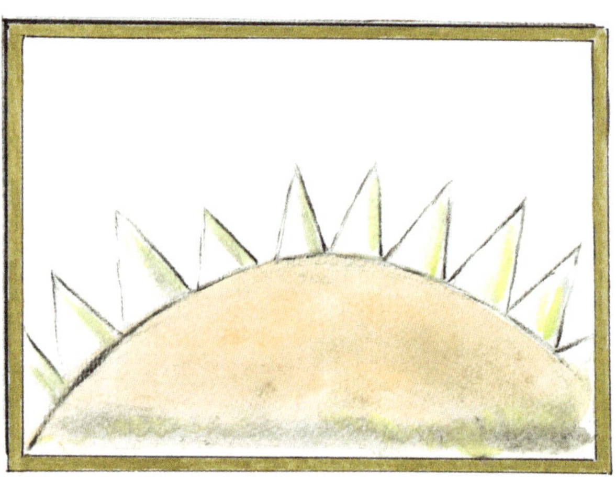

However, we do not know why our distant ancestors began to paint animals on the walls where they resided. We know that they lived as hunters, and perhaps the depiction of animals was part of a sacred hunting ritual. Maybe they believed that by creating lifelike images of the animals, they would gain special power over them. It is also possible that they hoped it would attract more prey. Or perhaps they simply revered the animals because they relied on them for survival.

The paintings were made inside caves that were difficult to access, so one should not imagine that cave dwellers were outdoor painters, sitting on a rock and depicting wild animals face to face with nature. A situation like this one certainly never took place

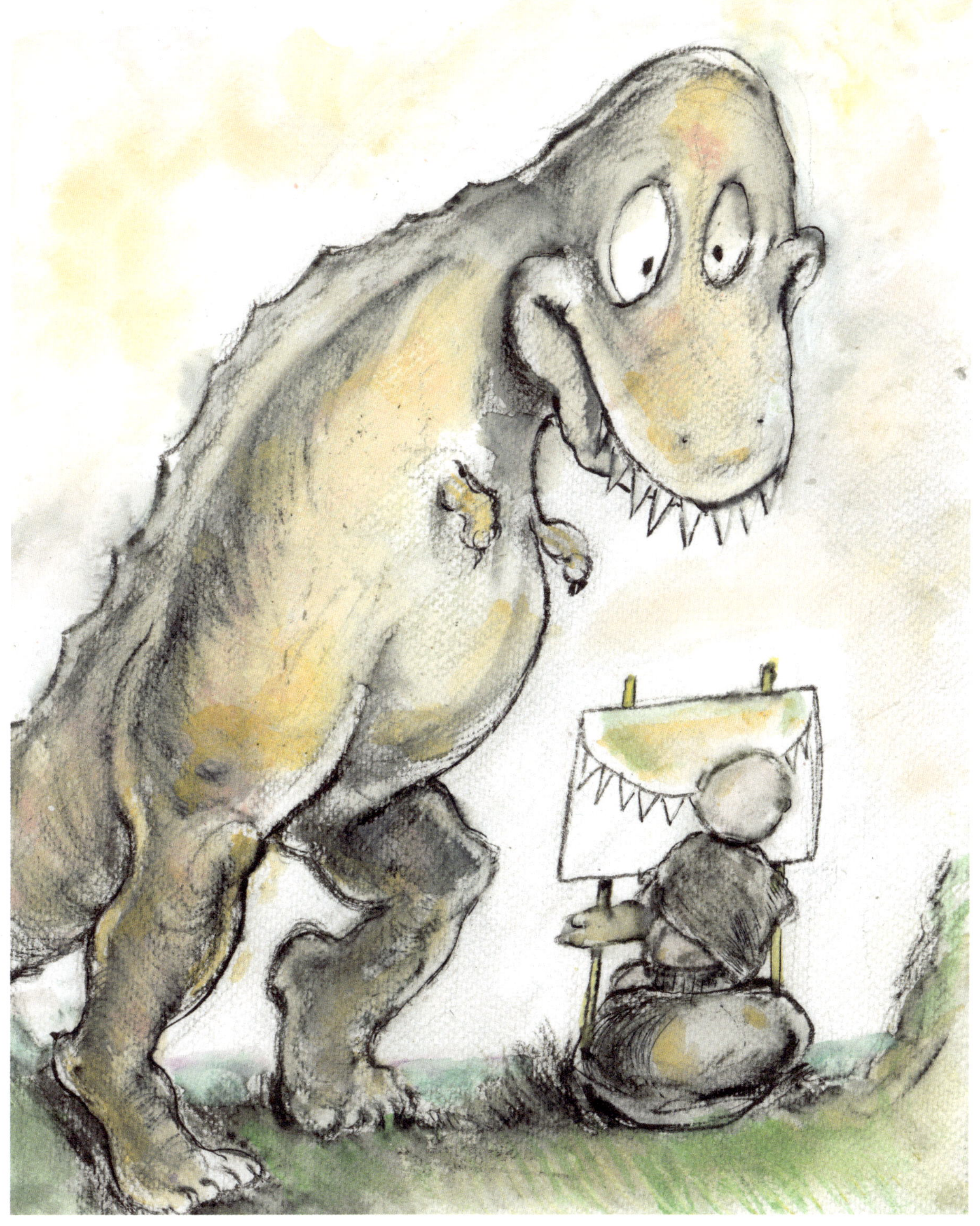

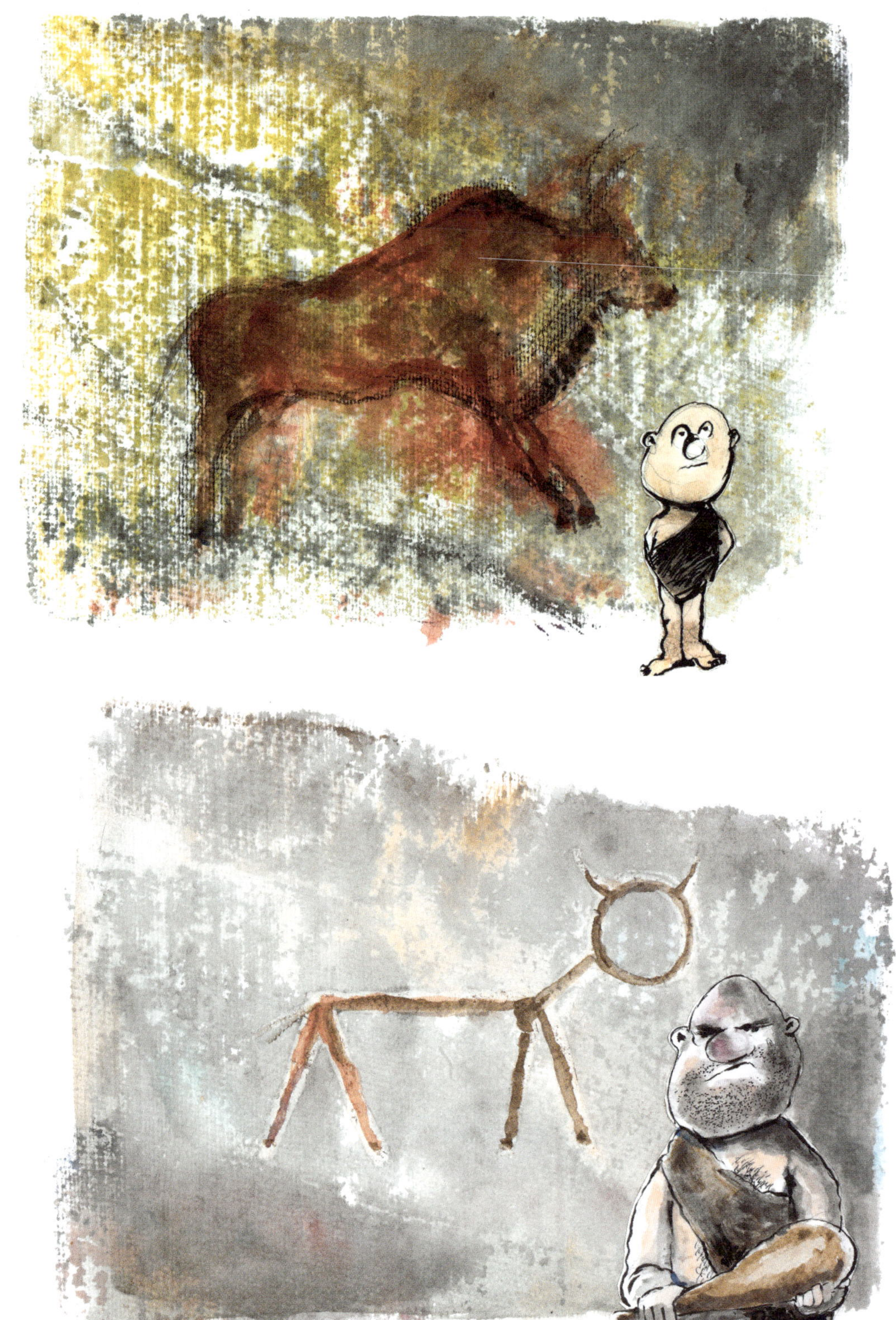

(especially not with an ancient lizard!). But that does not mean one cannot draw or paint an animal upon the safe return to the cave. It is simply done from memory. Or using one's imagination, as has been done countless times in art.

We do not know if there was one or several people involved in creating each cave painting. Nor do we know if it was the men or women in a community who executed them. We only know that the quality of what has been preserved is remarkably high. And if a work is successful enough, the need and desire to preserve it for posterity are correspondingly greater.

Perhaps in a tribe, there was someone who was particularly skilled at drawing and painting, and therefore was assigned the task. But as far as we know, they never attempted to paint their self-portrait. This did not happen until many thousands of years later. In fact, we have to take a leap forward in time to the Renaissance before artists become self-aware enough to start painting themselves.

However, the prehistoric human who painted pictures of animals in deep caves actually has quite a lot in common with the artists working and exhibiting today. Nobody had asked them to do what they did. But they did it anyway. Because it was far too exciting for them to resist.

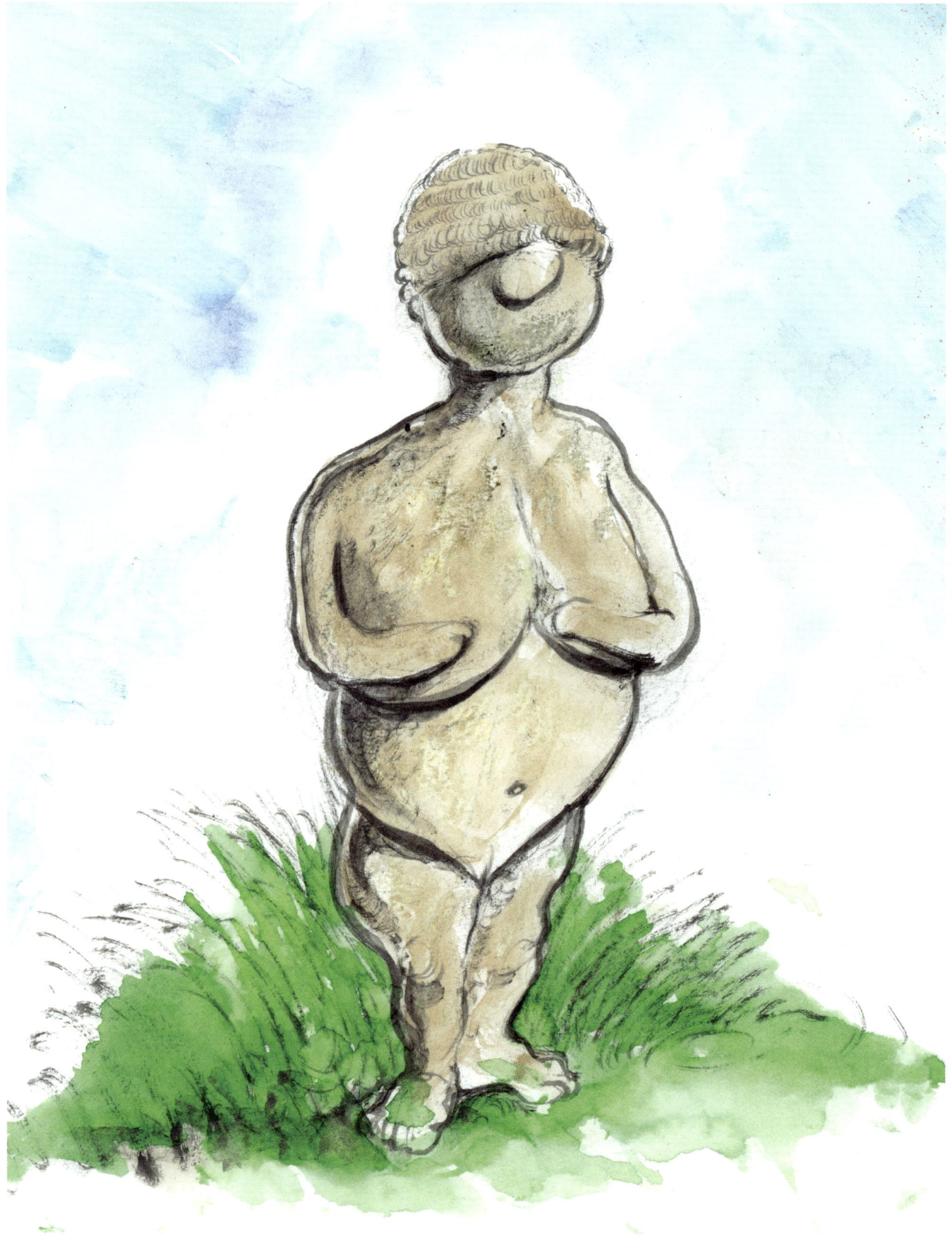

Venus of Willendorf – and of Vienna

Venus of Willendorf is an elderly lady, possibly the oldest in all of art history. She dates back to between 28,000 and 25,000 BCE. Despite her small size – she is only 11 cm tall – her voluptuous body may have been a symbol of prosperity and success.

It is likely that the figure symbolized fertility or a natural force that could assist in bringing children into the world, which is why we call her 'Venus'. According to the ancient Greeks, who are not nearly as old as the little figurine, Venus is the goddess of love.

'Venus' was discovered in Austria, at a Stone Age settlement near Willendorf. Hence her name. But we could also call her 'Venus from the Natural History Museum in Vienna', because this is where she can be seen today.

With the exaggerated portrayal of bodily forms, this 'Venus' may have inspired many modern sculptors who sought to move beyond the norms of beauty and perfection. She was discovered in 1908, just as Modernism was about to revolutionize art, so it is no exaggeration to say that she embodies the concept of fertility.

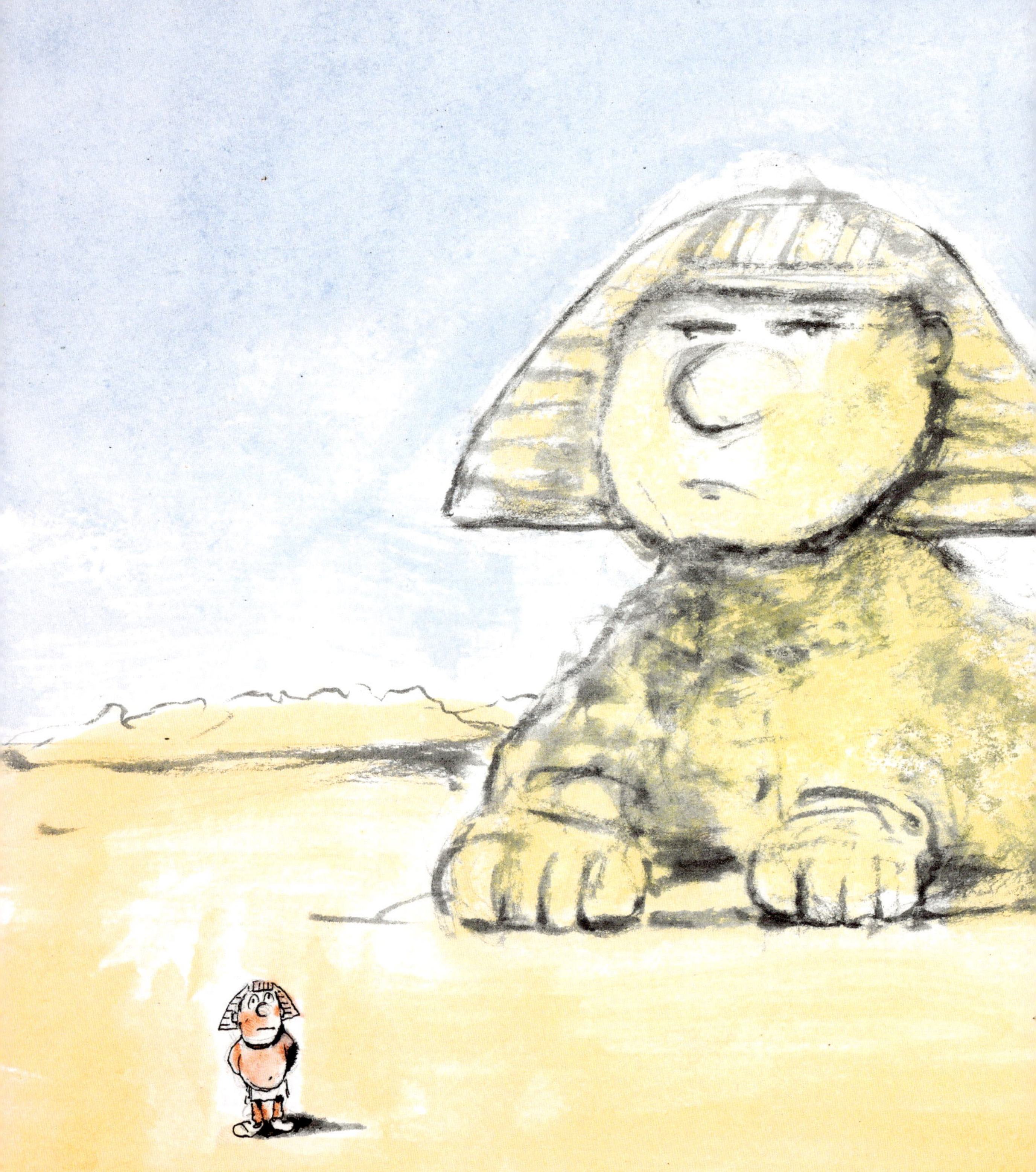

3,000 years without losing face

3,000 years span from the earliest pharaohs (the Egyptian kings) to Cleopatra, the last queen of the Nile. This is a long period compared to all other periods we will be dealing with. If we were to allocate space for Egyptian art in our brief art history, considering its duration, there wouldn't be many pages left for the rest.

Oddly enough, Egyptian art did not change much throughout this lengthy period. It always revolved around the same theme: glorifying the pharaoh, both in this life and the next. Egyptians believed in an afterlife, and both the monumental architecture and its artistic embellishments were guided by their religion and the belief in an extra life.

Egyptian art does not seem to have been very open to influence from neighbouring cultures. On the other hand, Egyptian art influenced early Greek art.

So it is not entirely off the mark to say that their art behaved like the great Sphinx which to this day lies unyielding in Giza in Lower Egypt, guarding over Pharaoh Khafre's pyramid. With a height of 20 meters and a length of 73 meters, this cross between a lion and a human is as monumental as when it was carved out of rock outcrop 2,500 years BCE. Originally, the Sphinx bore Khafre's facial features, but wind and weather have eroded much of it.

Of mud and marble

During the time of the ancient Egyptians, or even a bit earlier, another great empire emerged in Mesopotamia – present-day Iraq, between the rivers Euphrates and Tigris. As early as the 4th millennium BCE, the Sumerians created what is perhaps the oldest high culture in world history. Yet, we do not know this culture very well. While the Egyptians knew how to make large, sturdy stone constructions, the Sumerians could only build with mud, dried and hardened in the sun.

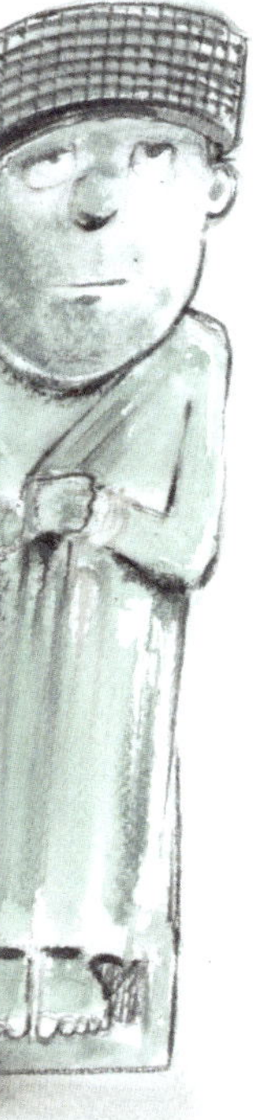

However, the rain could not destroy the medium-sized statues of limestone and marble that this ancient people erected in their temples. These statues were not depictions of the gods themselves but rather divine agents or representatives, recognizable by their very large eyes, perhaps expressing clarity and wisdom. Although they did not actually squint at each other, as in the drawing, it could indeed happen that, as city-states in the same area, they waged war against each other. One of the most stable of the regions was Lagash, where Gudea ruled around 2500 BCE. About twenty statues of him, seated or standing, with folded hands, have been preserved. These statues can teach us about the Sumerians, as they are sometimes adorned with a special form of cuneiform script.

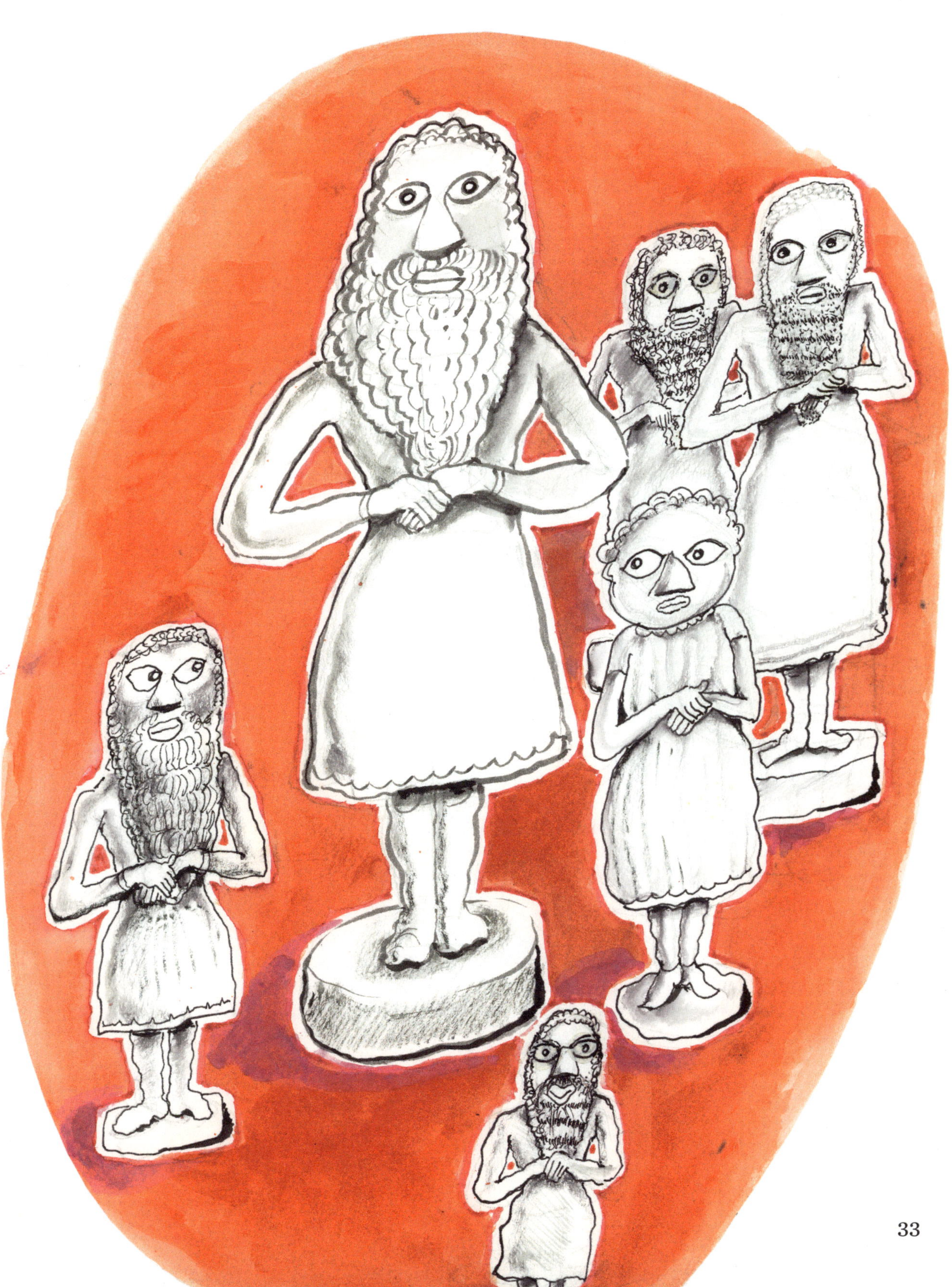

Goddesses gather

There is not much information available about this statuette (small statue) of a snake goddess or priestess from the Middle Minoan period, dating back to around 1600 BCE. It was during this period that the Minoan Mediterranean culture flourished the most. It is uncertain whether the figure depicted here was a priestess, a goddess, or a woman used in religious rituals. The reason for her holding a snake in each hand is also not entirely clear, as there were not many snakes on the Greek island of Crete, where the remains of the great palace complex at Knossos, the centre of Minoan civilization, were discovered.

However, our 'goddess' is depicted with bare breasts, indicating her likely association with a local fertility cult. Yet, no other similarly exposed goddesses have been found during excavations at Knossos. Instead, some smaller gods or goddesses, slightly older, have been discovered. There might have been a connection between them, as they are depicted similarly, with both arms raised, as if invoking higher powers.

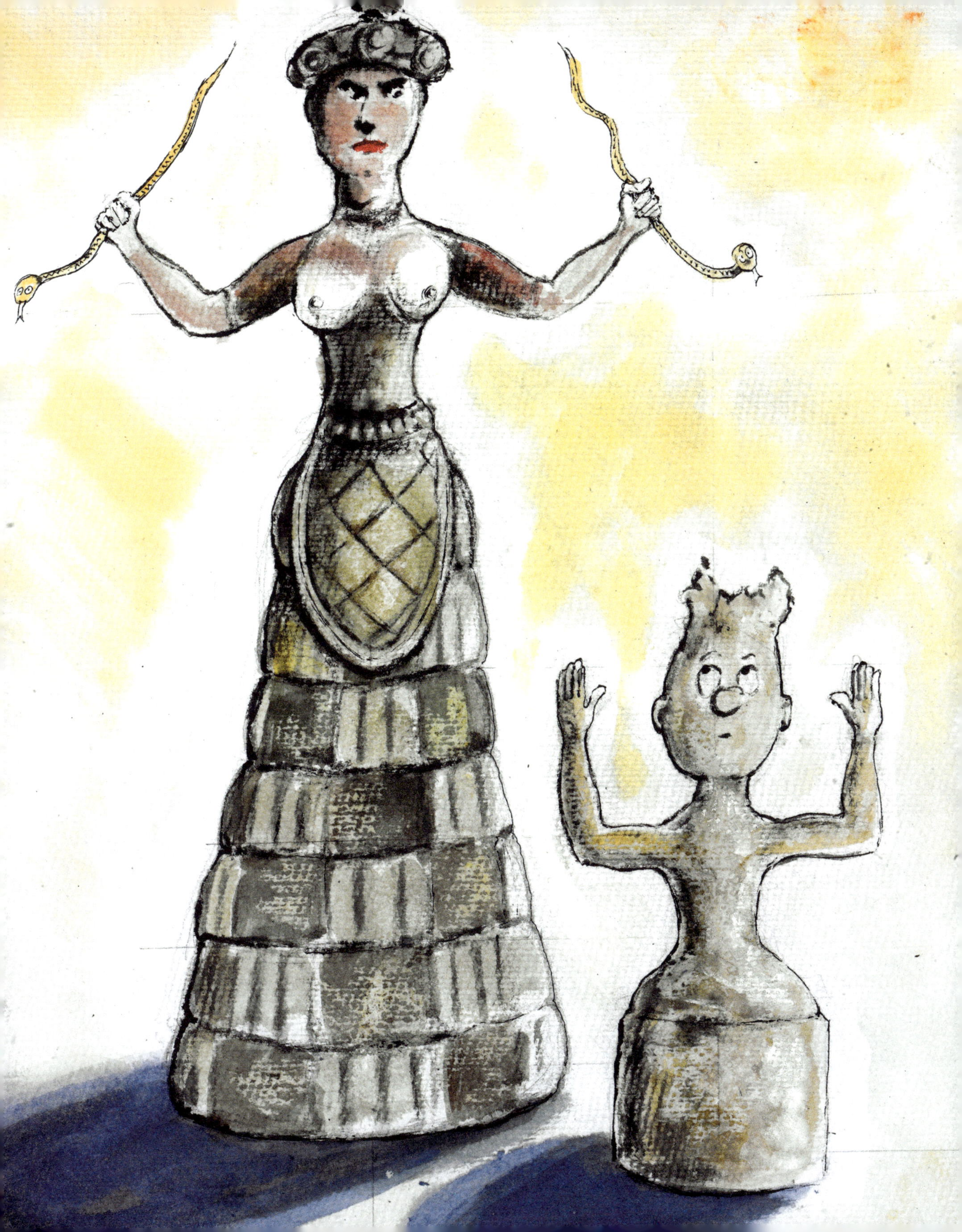

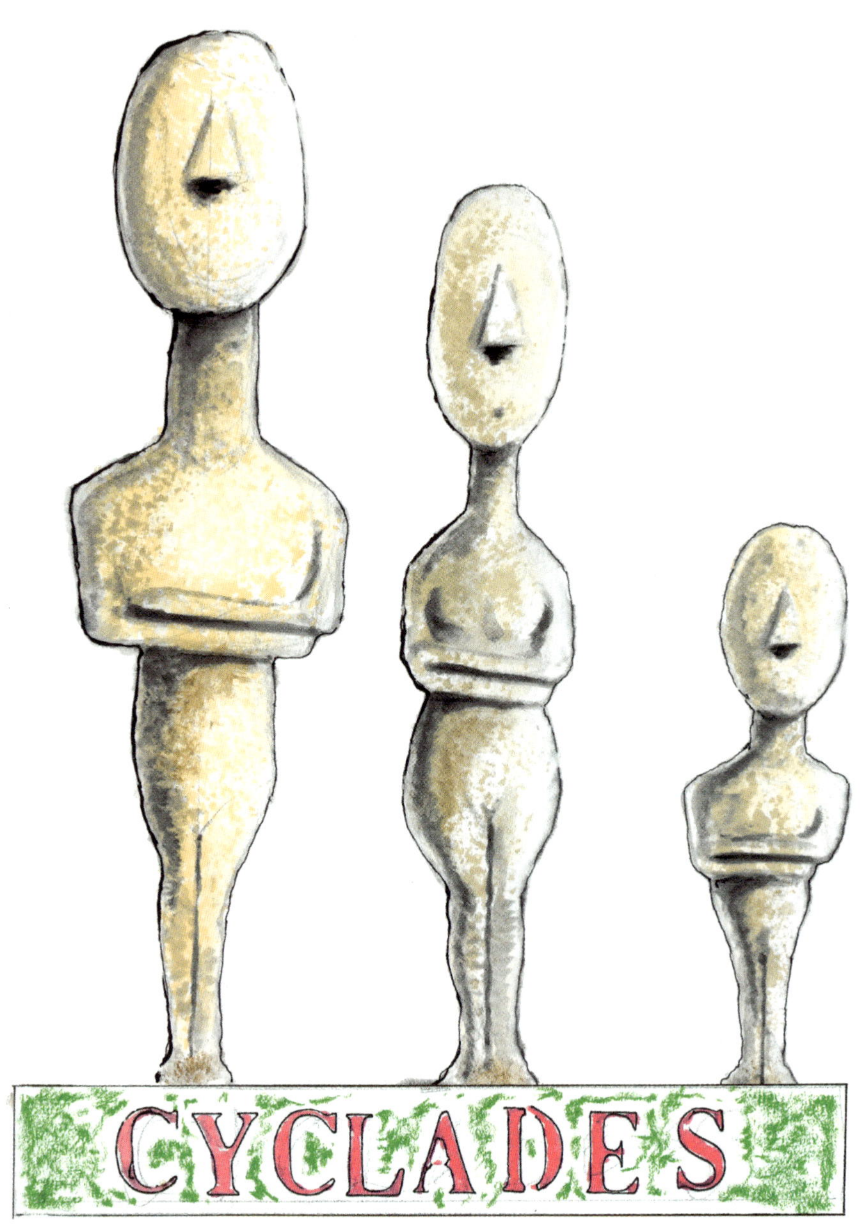
CYCLADES

Cycladic art

Idols with breasts and small noses

Sometimes, very ancient sculptures can appear so simple, or abstract even, that they could easily be mistaken for modern art. This is true for these small statues from the Cyclades. The Cyclades are a cluster of Greek islands in the Aegean Sea, where today wine, olives, wheat, and cotton are produced. But a couple of thousand years before our time, the inhabitants also worshipped their own special gods, which they created some rather unique divine images of.

At least two of the figures in the picture – the man and the child – are entirely incorrect. Why? Well, all the Cycladic figures we know of are actually female. For example, you can see that they have breasts. This suggests that they were likely associated with a fertility cult, as breasts were symbols of fertility at that time. But otherwise, not much attention has been paid to the shape of the figures, and the faces are so simple that they resemble pure Cubism. These small statues are dated to between 2600 and 2000 BCE.

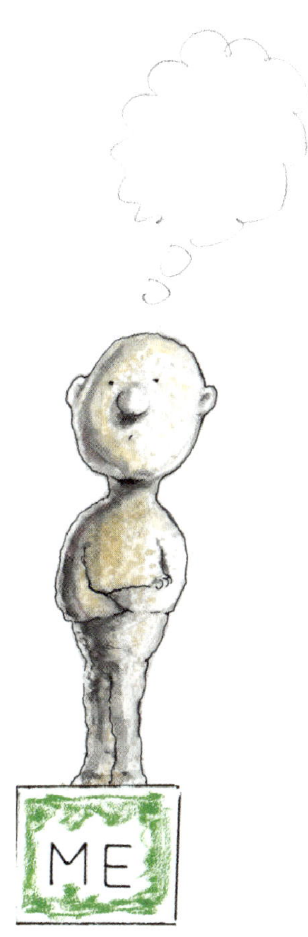

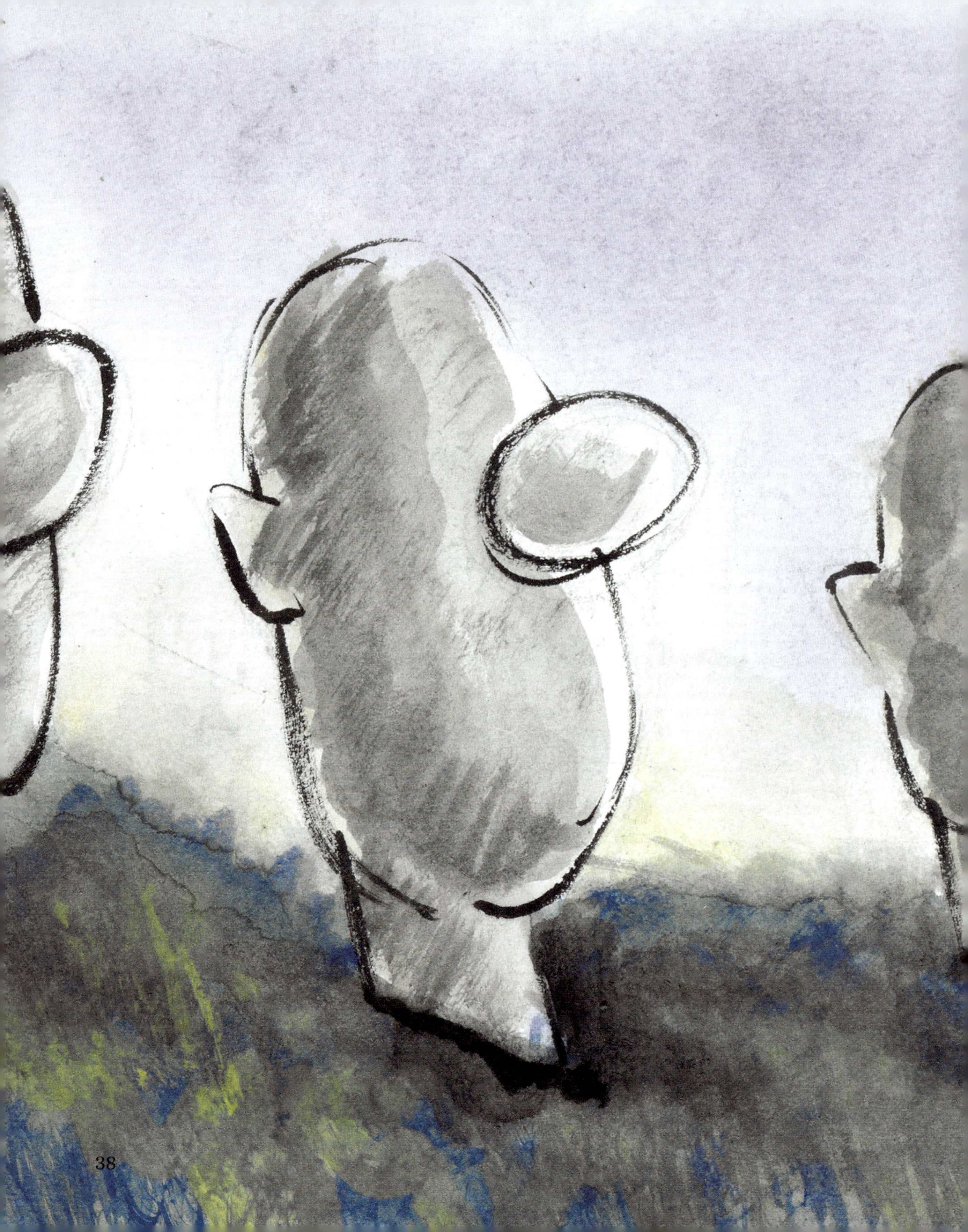

Planted in the ground

Things in the world of art can often resemble each other, even if there are thousands of years and kilometres between them. The purpose of the much larger and later figures on Easter Island in the South Pacific, 3,600 km west of Chile, remains unclear, but historians suspect they have something to do with burials. Easter Island is part of the Polynesian archipelago, located in the middle of the Pacific Ocean. Here, in the 20th century, an explorer discovered just over 500 giant statues, dating back to around the year 1000 CE. They were carved from tuff (a volcanic stone) and appeared to be firmly planted in the ground, with only the heads visible. But there was more beneath, it was simply hidden. With their simplified facial features, they bear a resemblance to the figures from the Cyclades. In both cases, we are far from the style that prevailed on the mainland during the same period. Such unique features are often found in isolated communities, such as island societies.

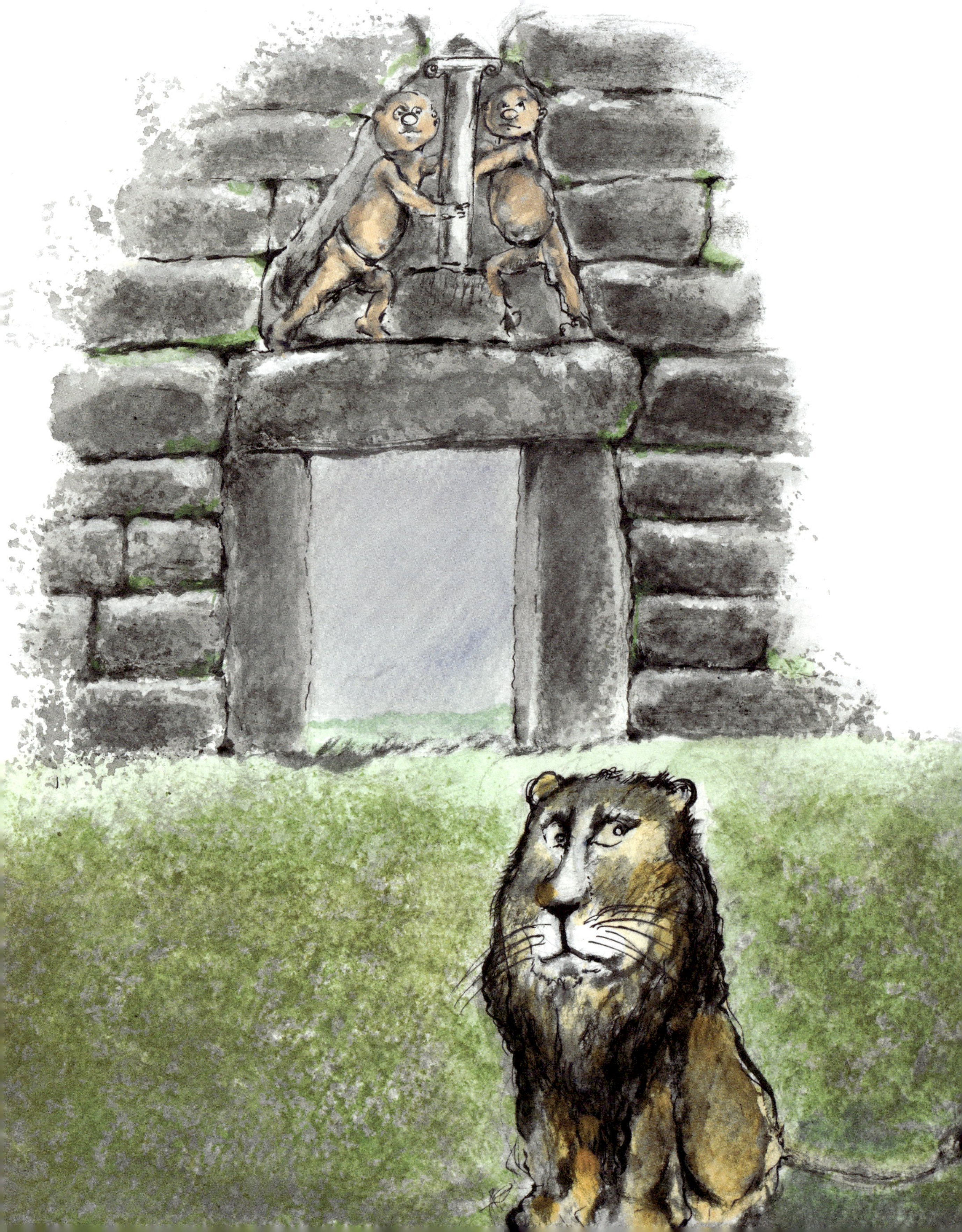

Everyone is afraid of a pair of lions

The fact that the Mycenaeans – an ancient people who lived on the Peloponnese in southern Greece – could afford to lay masks of gold over the faces of the deceased when burying them, tells us that gold was not exactly in short supply. Still, gold is precious. Therefore, this wealthy ancient people surrounded their fortress with a ring wall, with walls up to ten meters thick. However, there had to be a way in, and that was through the so-called Lion Gate, dating from 1250 BCE. It is called that because two lions adorn the triangular relief above the large lintel. Such animals serve the same function as guard dogs; they are meant to scare off intruders.

If, in imagination, one was to free the lions and let two small bald men take their place, the ornamentation would not have the same deterring effect, and grave robbers and other unwelcome guests might not hesitate to enter. Lions symbolized courage and strength, even if they were carved in limestone, and have also been used as guardian figures in other cultures.

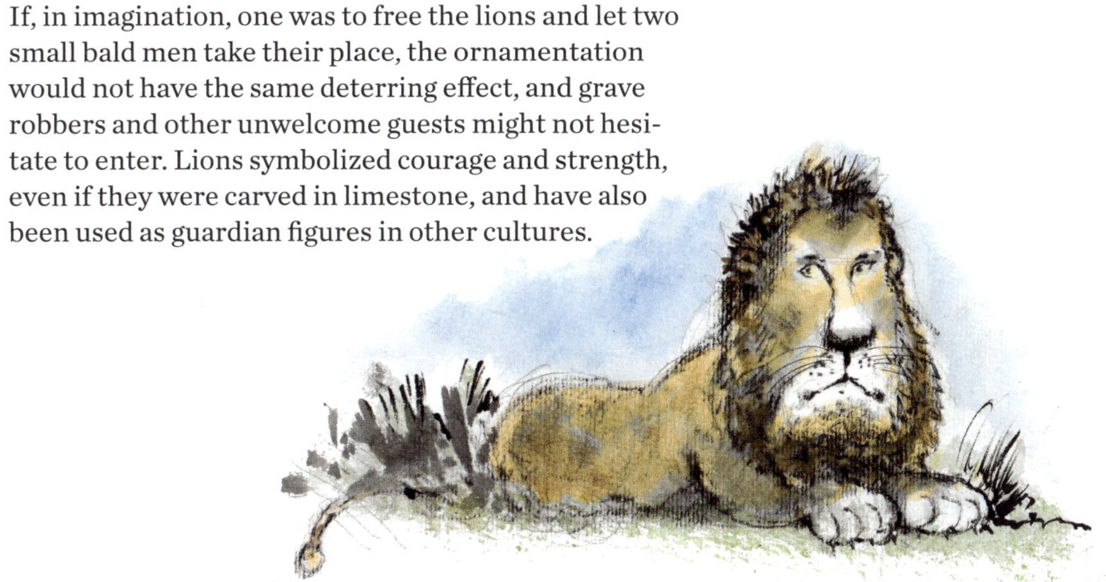

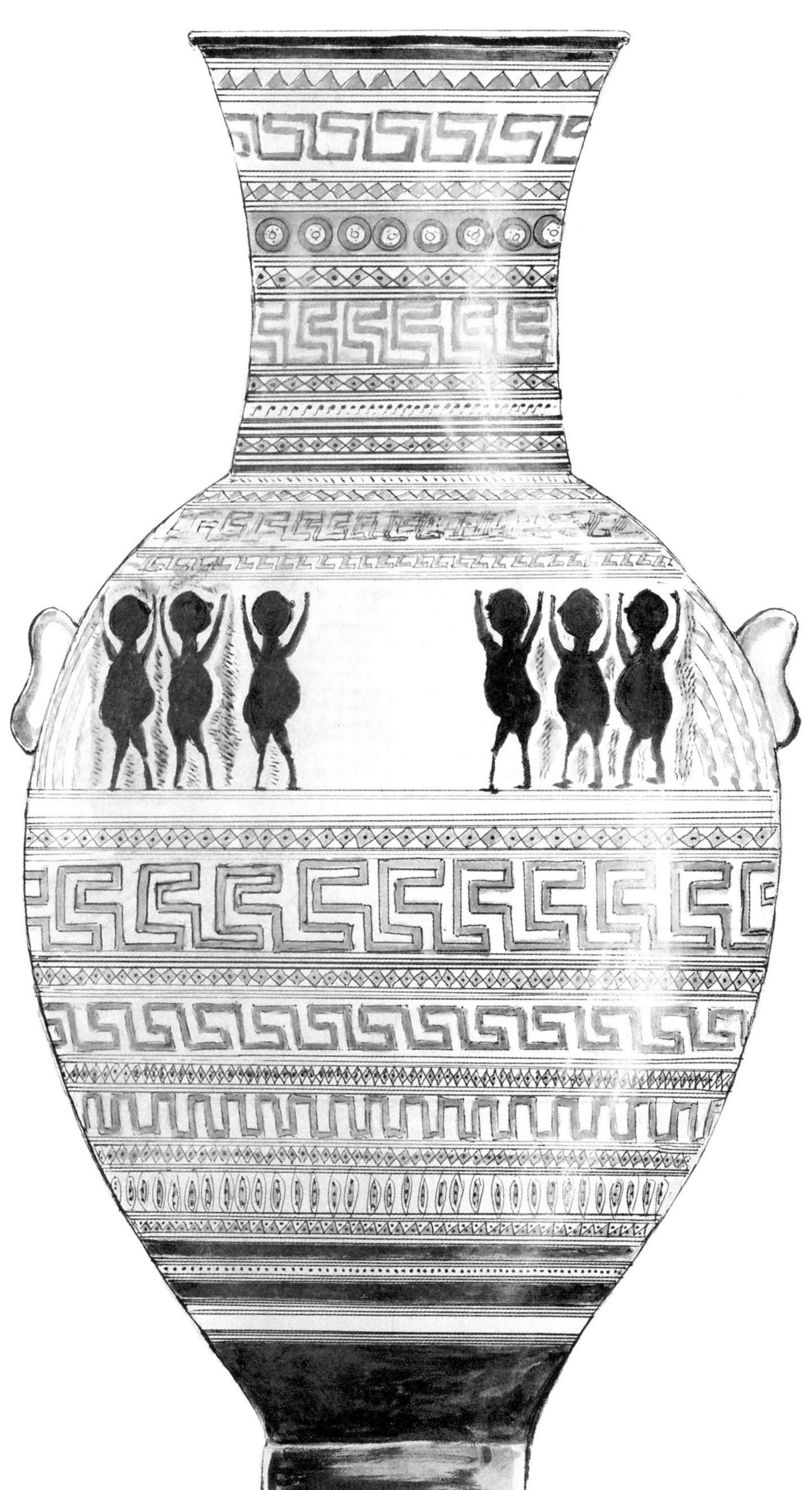

Wine for the dead

We don't know much about
the people who decorated
the vases in Greek art, but
we *do* know a few things
about the painter in this
case: he must have been
really good at his job. Because such
decoration work requires skill and time. He was
a true master at painting geometric patterns of all
kinds and combining them in a beautiful and harmonious
way.

In the art of ancient Greece, there existed in the 9th and 8th centuries
BCE a style called the geometric style. This was not only very strict, as if
everything was drawn with a ruler, it was also very beautiful and decorative. The vase here is called an amphora, and it was quite a special vase,
because it had a hole at the bottom. It was meant to be placed on a grave,
and the idea was that oil and wine could be poured down to the deceased
buried beneath the vase. That way, the Greeks believed, one could also
have some pleasure in the afterlife.

You could not overlook such amphorae. Because they could measure
up to one and a half meters in height and did not have a single spot
on them that was not decorated – a phenomenon known as 'hor-
ror vacui', which means: fear of empty space. There had to be
patterns everywhere. In our rendition, there is actually a
space just below the vase's neck that is not decorated.
There usually is a burial scene right here. But funerals
are not particularly uplifting to look at, so we left
the space empty.

Perhaps you can come up with a more
cheerful motif.

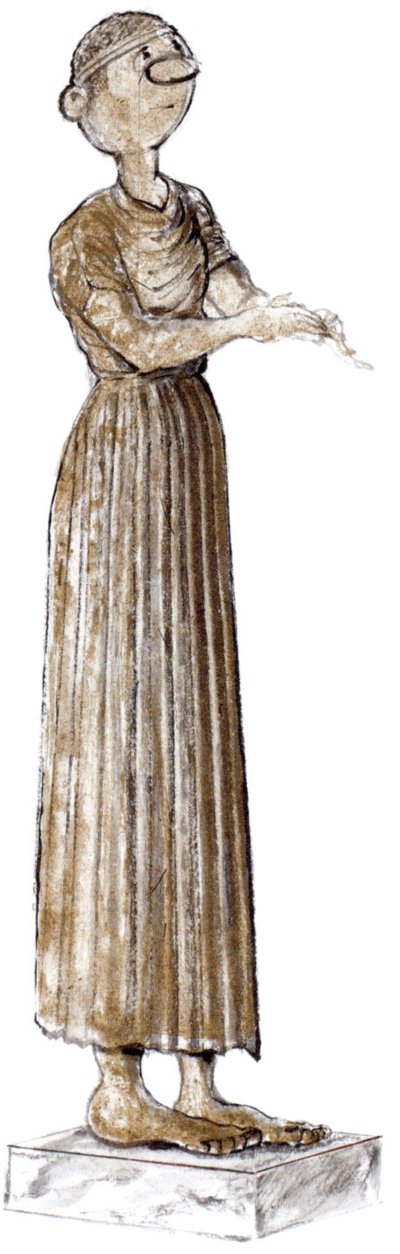

Greek art – classical style

... or the story of the perfect human

Without classical art in ancient Greece, we would not have had Roman art either, or if we did, it would have looked very different. And we definitely would not have had the Renaissance, Baroque, or Neoclassicism as we know them. European art academies would have lacked something to teach their students for generations. Not to mention what the field of classical studies would have lacked. They are all indebted to the Greeks.

Until Modernism truly emerged in the early 20th century, classical Greek art was the foundation of all art. The way the Greeks depicted the human body was how the body was supposed to look. They had their own theory of beauty, and the consideration of beauty always took precedence, as that is how the gods originally must have envisioned it. Art was there to improve upon nature's flaws.

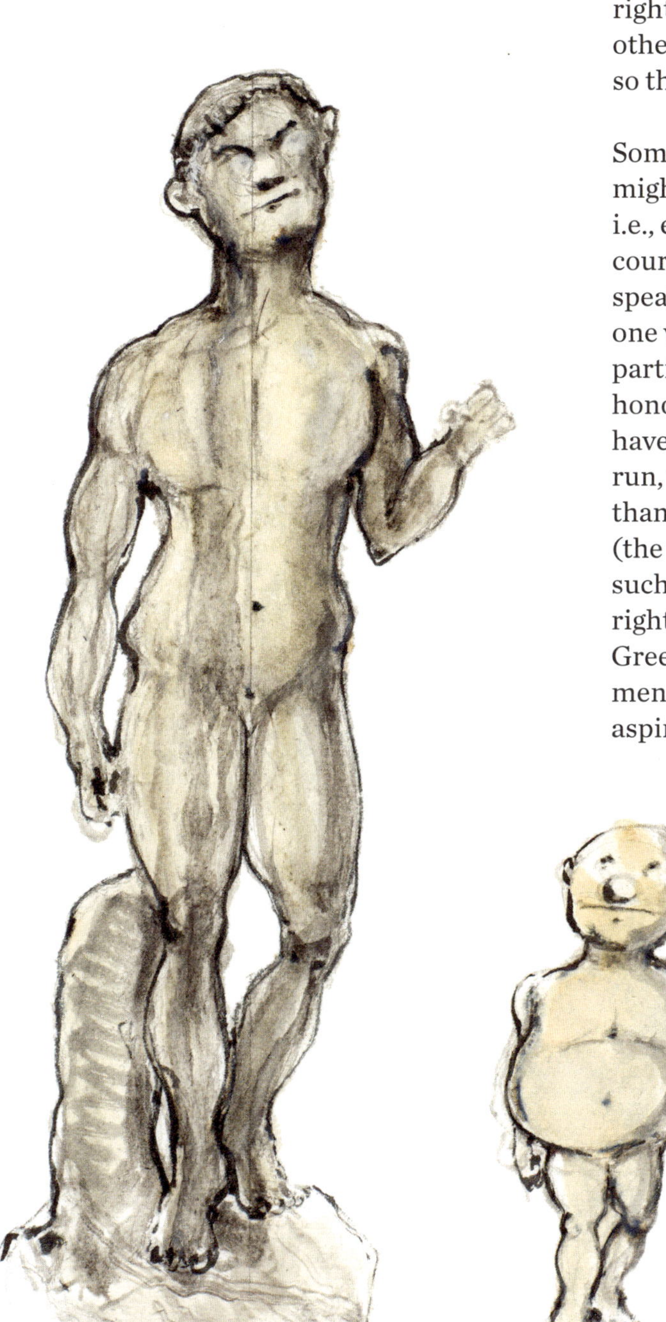

The Greek sculptor Polykleitos published a
'Canon', where he recommended specific
poses and proportions, or measurements,
for sculptures. His famous masterpiece,
'The Spear Bearer' from the 5th century
BCE, is a prime example of how to strike the
right balance in an athletic figure. Among
other things, the weight is only on one leg,
so the figure appears to be in motion.

Someone once claimed that a Greek statue
might not engage in intellectual discourse,
i.e., express itself very wisely. Statues, of
course, cannot speak. But if they instead of
speaking could engage in Olympic sports,
one would imagine that Greek statues, in
particular, could win plenty of medals and
honours. They often depict athletes who
have done just that, proving that they can
run, throw a javelin, wrestle, etc., better
than anyone else. 'The Charioteer of Delphi'
(the tall one on the left) is presumably
such a Greek athlete who has earned the
right to be a role model for all others, as the
Greek artists created art so their countrymen could have something to admire and
aspire to.

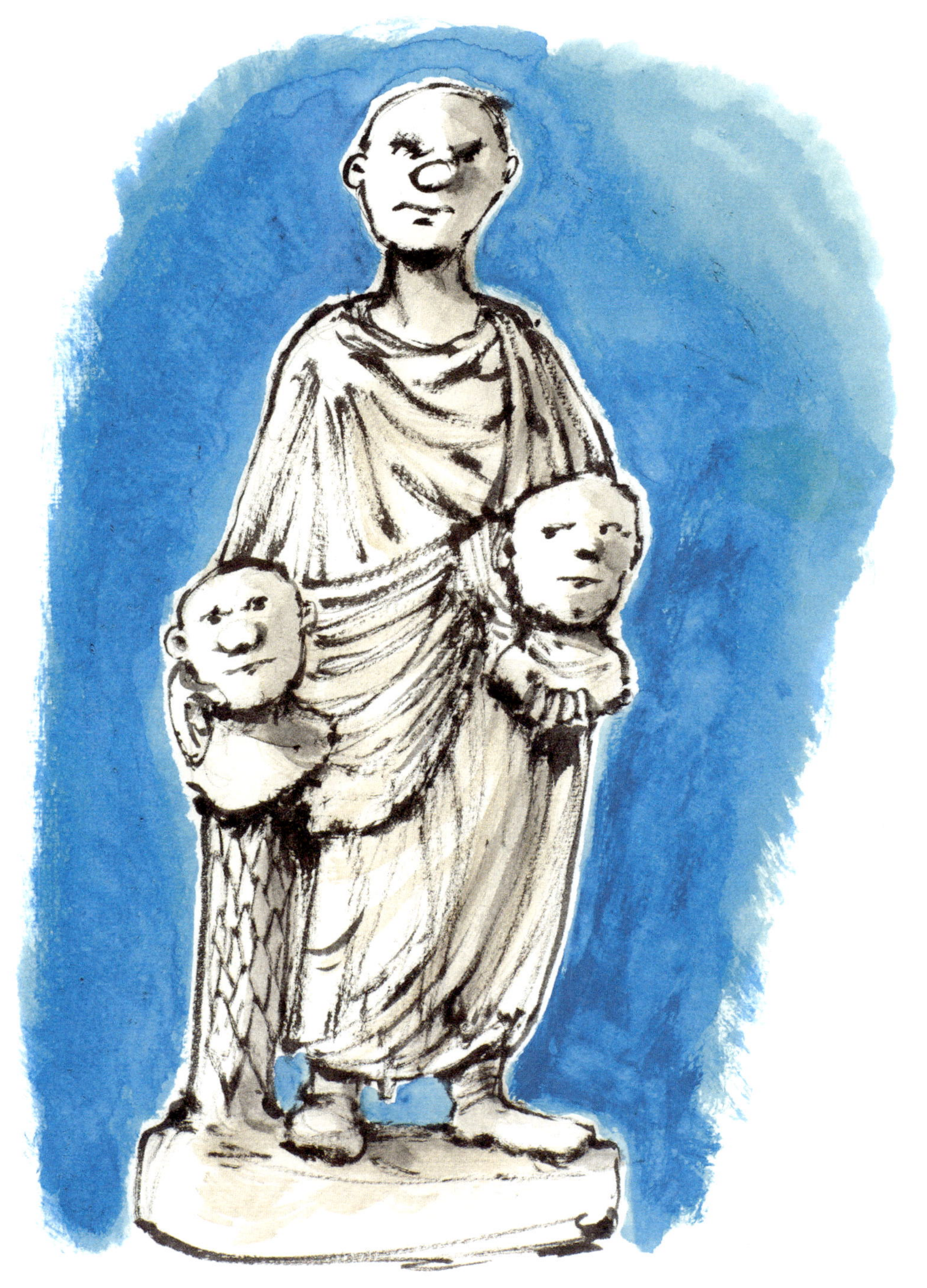

Roman art

Mostly masks and people

The Roman Empire existed from around 200 years BCE to 300 years CE. In this half-millennium, the Romans, being a warrior people, worked to expand their empire. In addition to conquering most of the known world at the time, the Romans excelled in architecture, reliefs, mosaics, and more. They built temples for their gods, made triumphal arches and erected columns to commemorate their military victories but also found time to construct theatres, baths, and aqueducts to transport fresh water over long distances.

In art, the Romans were influenced by the classical Greeks, whose works they collected and whose style they emulated. However, while the Greeks in their sculpture had a penchant for idealism – art was meant to be a human ideal – the Romans were more practical and down-to-earth, and they were particularly strong in realistic portraiture. High-ranking Romans wanted to be remembered for posterity, and there is hardly a better reminder of a citizen's importance than a lifelike statue or portrait bust in an enduring material like marble. Thanks to the many sculptors, we have an idea of how these Romans may have looked – or wanted to look. But the artists who made them famous are now unknown. And if we have difficulty recognizing the immortalized emperor, archaeologists can usually turn to the coins that these Roman emperors had minted.

Whenever a wealthy and influential Roman attended a funeral or official ceremony of some kind, he would bring along deceased members of his family. This was

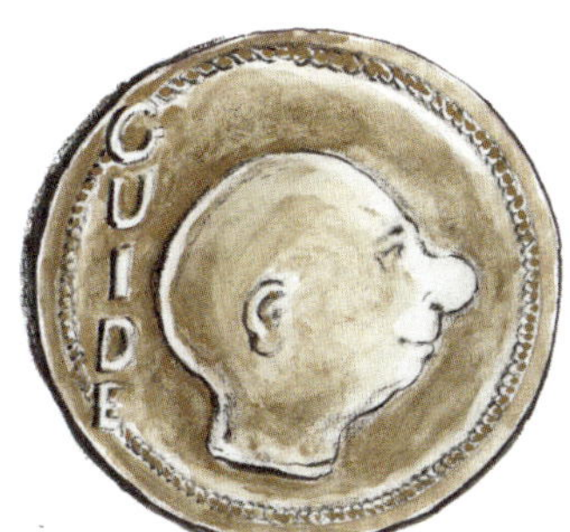

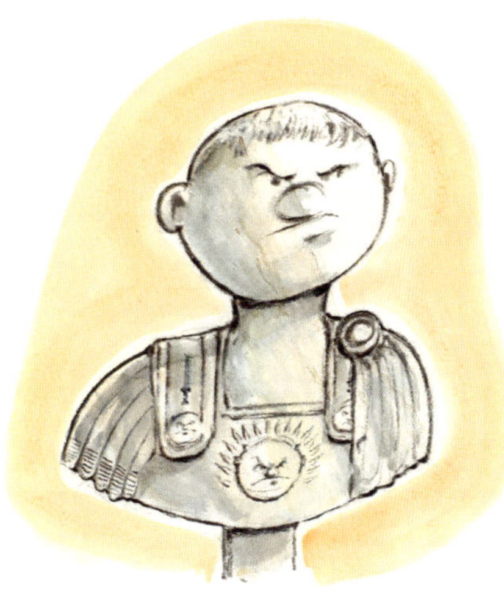

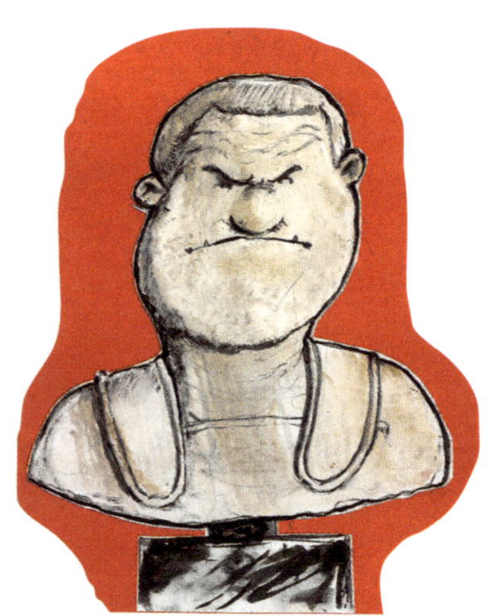

possible if he had timely made wax casts of their faces. A statue of such a Roman is preserved, on the preceding spread accompanied by his predecessors – or rather: their faces. It's somewhat akin to having photographs of our closest family members on the desk these days.

Not all Roman rulers were equally sensible and exemplary, and especially towards the end of the empire's long history, there were more and more who certainly weren't. The so-called soldier-emperors could resemble modern day dictators. They used every means imaginable to gain power and equally terrifying means to retain it. Therefore, only a few managed to die of old age. They were often murdered by their equally tyrannical successors. The violent and turbulent events is reflected in the art left behind by these rulers. What initially seemed like an influence from ancient Greece's idealized and harmonious art was replaced by coarser methods. As if the development of art suddenly regressed.

Back when one empire had four emperors

About 1,700 years ago, in the 3rd century of our time, the Roman Empire was falling apart at the seams. The empire had become too large and complex for one ruler to hold it all together. Therefore, it was divided among four emperors, each responsible for overseeing their own quarter. It was bound to end badly.

One of the best-preserved relics from this tumultuous period is this group portrait of the emperors from the tetrarchy (*tetra* is Greek for four). In the original, found in Venice on the facade of the San Marco Church, the four rulers maintain their composure. In reality, the four were competing to seize power over the entire Roman Empire for themselves, and in our rendition of the scene, they step on each other's toes and scowl.

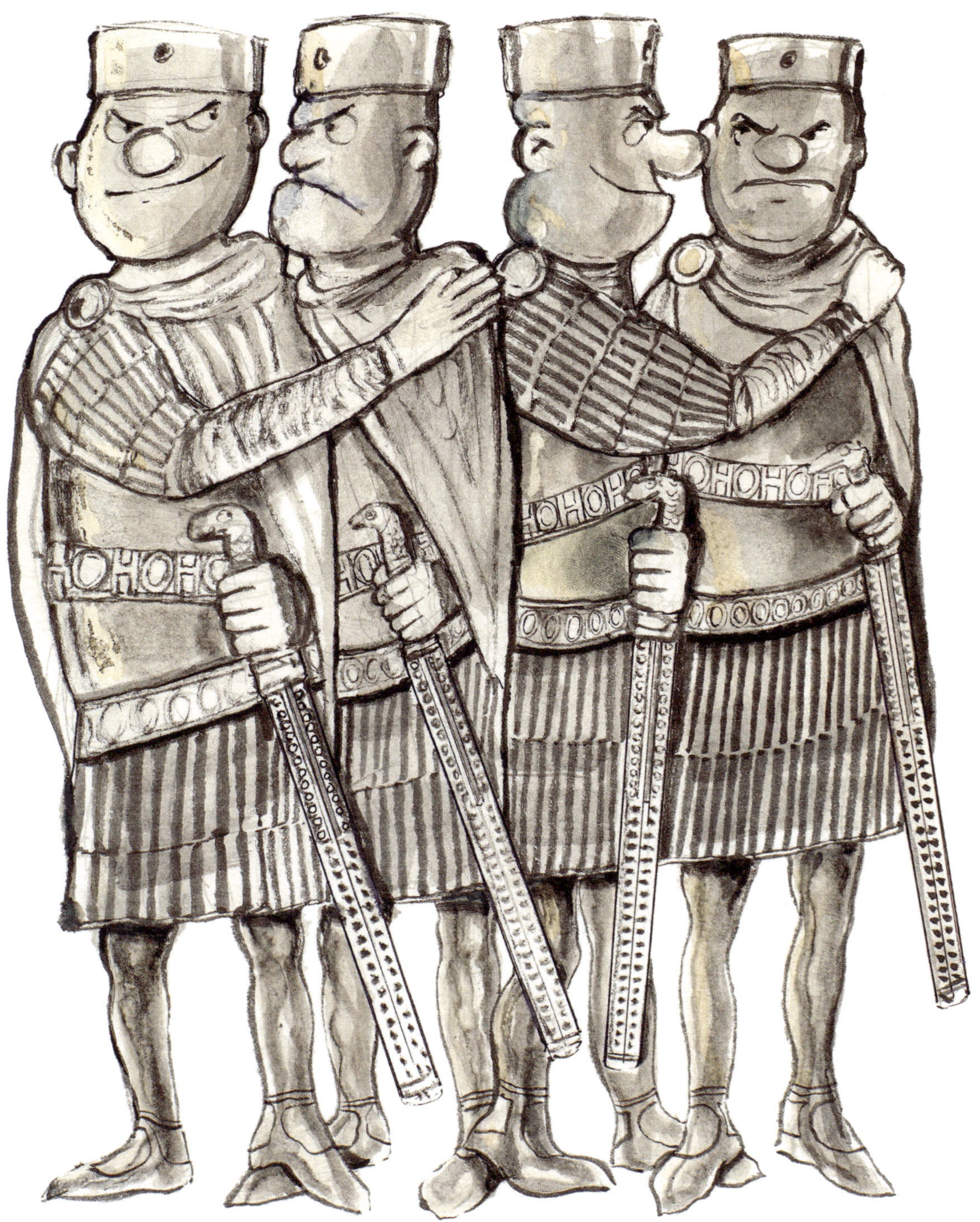

HOHOHO
HOHOHO
HOHOHO

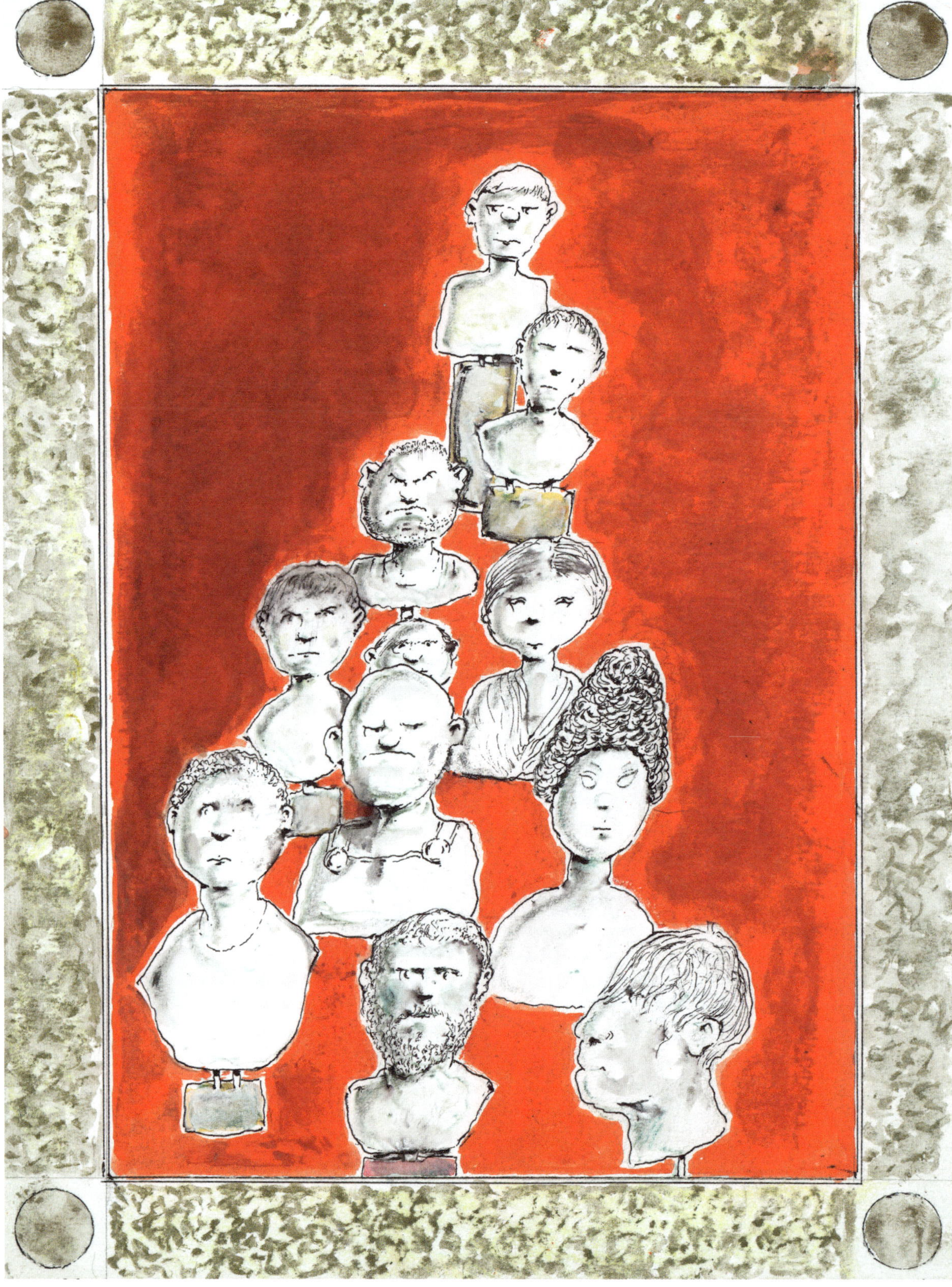

Roman art evolved as the empire came into contact with other peoples and cultures, and the classical influence that art had during Rome's heyday gave way to something more primitive. It was the influence from the east that became prevalent.

Roman art did not go unaffected when the Roman Empire began to crumble. Having remained true to Greek and Hellenistic ideals for centuries, it now started to change, assuming new forms and expressions. Late Roman Emperors were often depicted on a monumental scale – some of the statues were as large as houses! – and the model's proportions were not as correct either, or true to life, as they used to be in ancient Athens. What mattered to these people was not so much *how* things were represented, but *what* was represented, and what they themselves believed.

When Christianity, the new faith, knocked on Rome's gates, it caused a shock that sent tremors through every part of society. This happened already in the first century. Things were kept secret at first, as the new faith was strictly forbidden, and its followers risked persecution. However, as time passed, it emerged triumphant into the light, and soon it was leaving its unmistakable mark on both art and architecture. Where there used to be temples for Roman gods in the Empire's heyday, new church buildings were now erected, enabling devout early Christians to meet and hold their services without interference.

When the Vikings raided the others

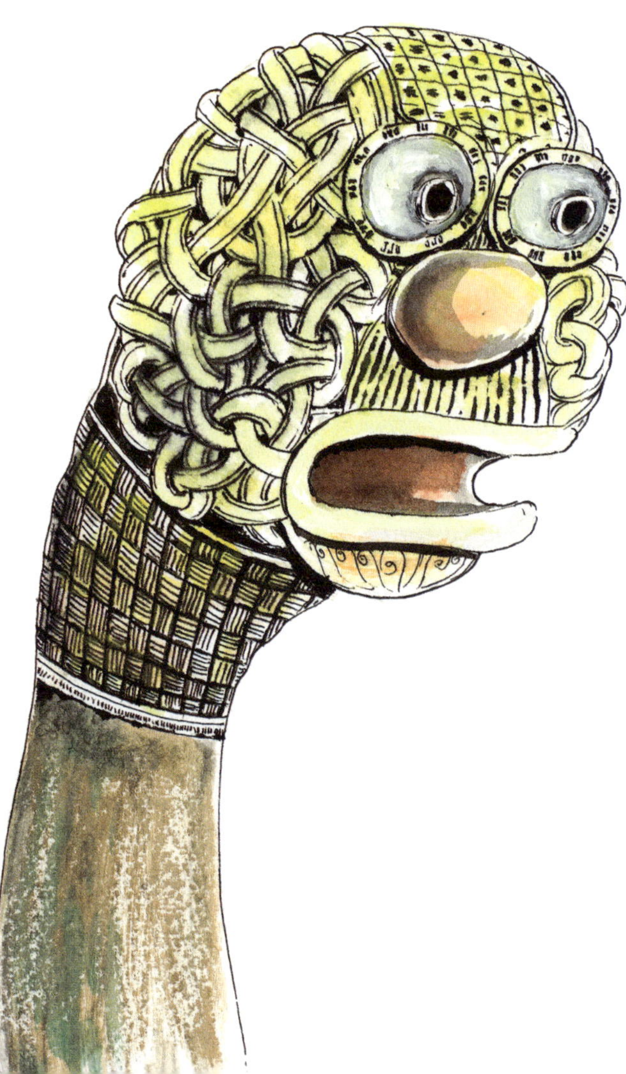

Once upon a time, it was said that the Nordic Vikings incessantly plagued, plundered, and raped any West European people they could reach with their longships. We tend to forget that these Norsemen also traded with other peoples, and as time passed, they were culturally influenced by them. Eventually, the Vikings were converted to Christianity, and only then did they become – more or less – as civilized as everyone else.

But in fact, they – the most artistically gifted among them – were experts in woodcarving. This can be seen in the Viking ships that have been preserved to this day. It is truly incredible how they could carve intricate patterns into the heads of animals or dragons, winding in and out of each other, much like you would see in an old-fashioned carpet beater.

For a long time, wood was the preferred material. It wasn't until the Norsemen replaced the god Odin with Christ that they began to use stone when building a house or erecting a monument that could withstand the test of time. The breakthrough of Christianity here in the North can be dated to around the year 965.

From this period dates the rune stone that King Harald Blue-tooth had erected in Jelling in Denmark to commemorate his parents Gorm and Thyra. It was only many hundreds of years later that it was discovered that the figure on one side of the relief did not actually depict the king himself, but rather the new god he prayed to: Christ.

On the stone's other side, a large animal with a forked tail entwined with a snake could be seen. Possibly, the creature was supposed to be some kind of lion. Nordic artists from the early Middle Ages were not experts in depicting lions as they, for many, many years, never had a model to look at.

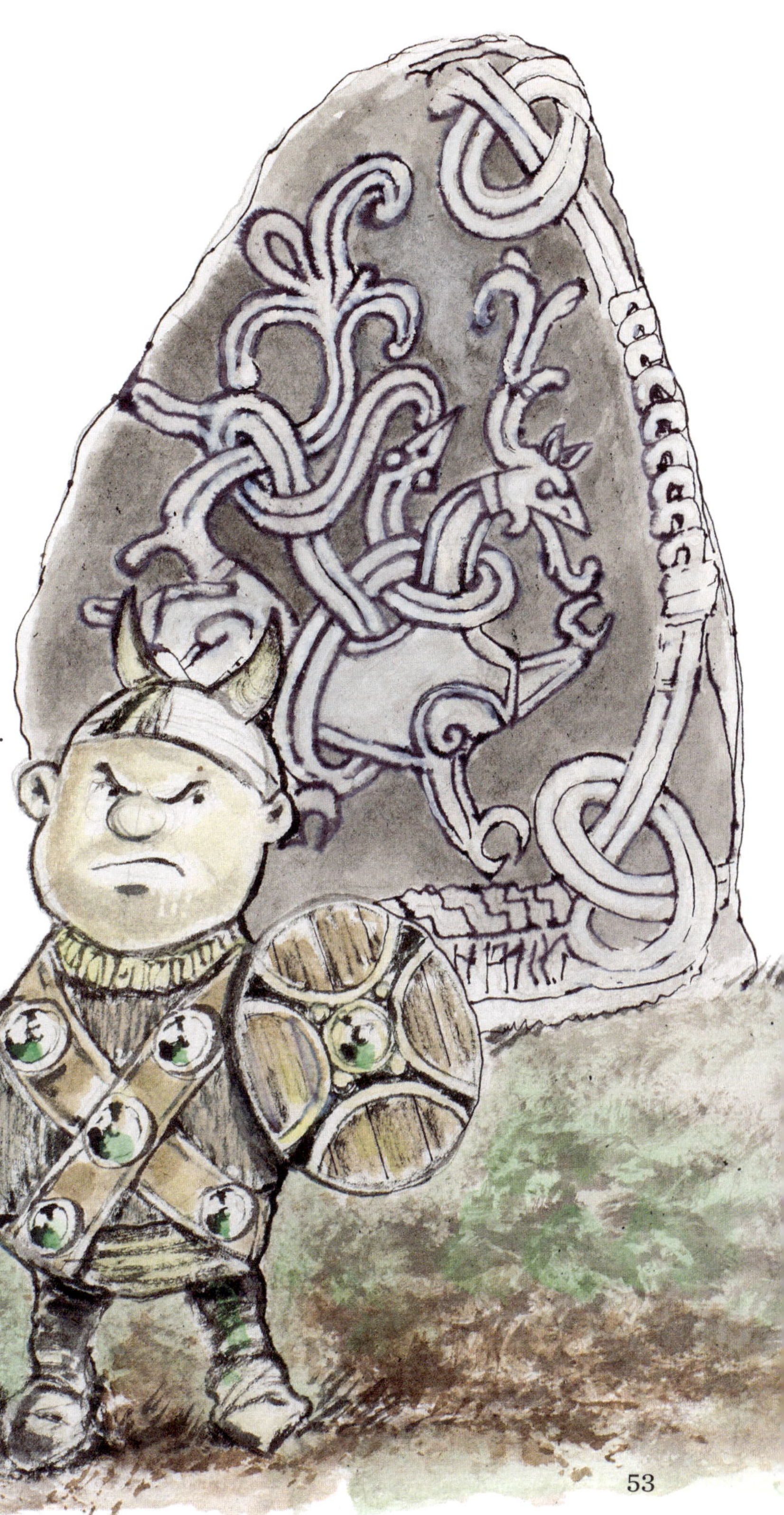

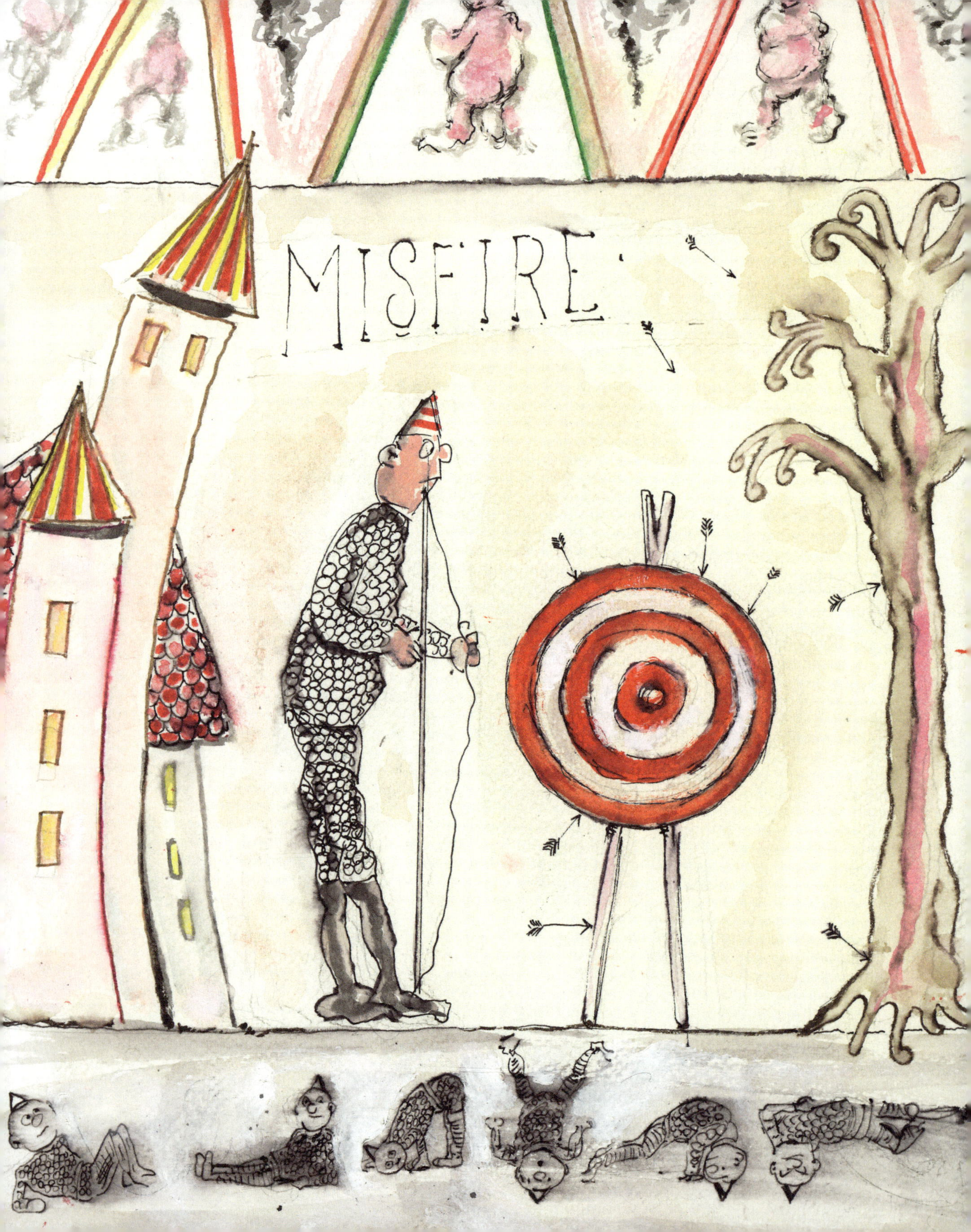

MISFIRE

Embroidered battle

The Bayeux Tapestry is unusual for the early Middle Ages as it depicts a historical event that had just taken place. In 1066, the Normans sailed from France and triumphed in a decisive battle over the Anglo-Saxons, thereby seizing power in England. And the Bayeux Tapestry was not actually a tapestry at all, but a wall hanging, embroidered on linen canvas with wool yarn in several different colours. Bishop Odo – a half-brother of the victorious leader from Hastings, William the Conqueror –commissioned the work, and presumably it was William's wife, Queen Matilda of Flanders, and her ladies-in-waiting who embroidered the approximately 70-meter-long and half-meter-high masterpiece, which is now housed in the museum in Bayeux.

The Bayeux Tapestry not only depicts the battle itself but also the preparations for it. In one illustration, we see a scene that probably never took place where a soldier practices shooting a bow and arrow, but he is evidently a poor marksman, as all he manages to do is hit another soldier in the rear.

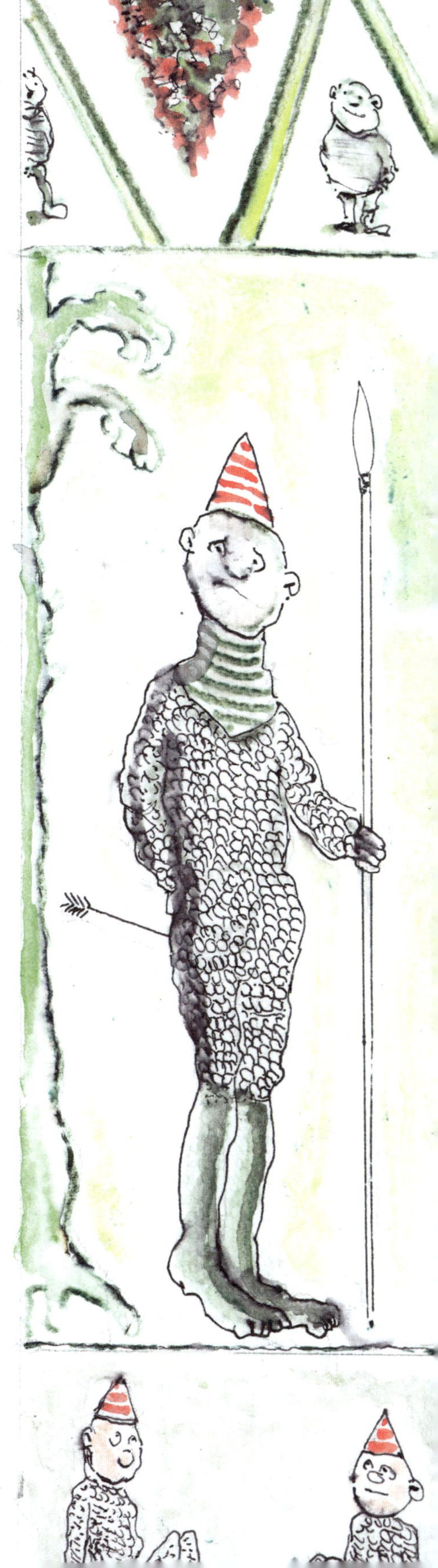

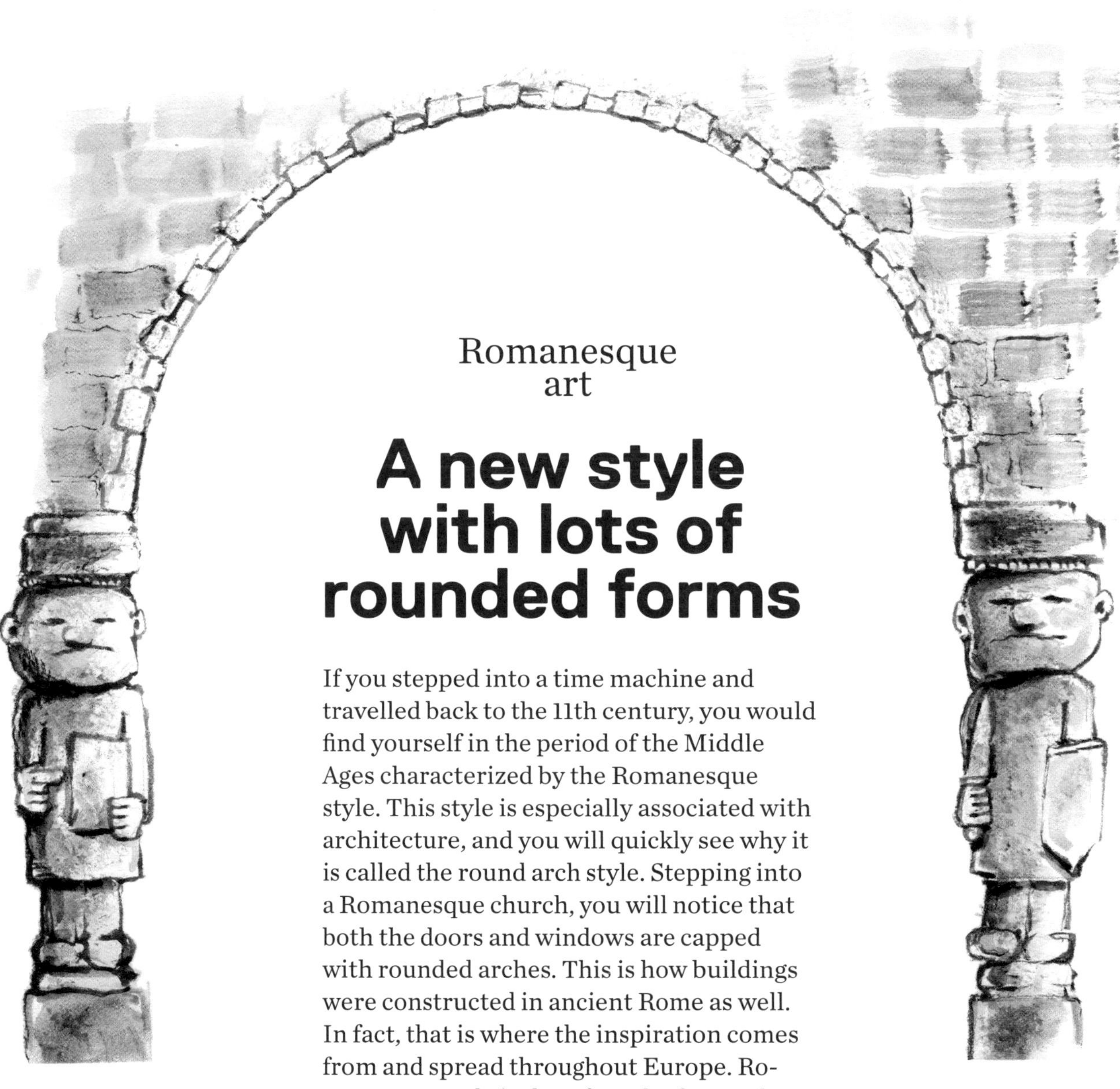

A new style with lots of rounded forms

If you stepped into a time machine and travelled back to the 11th century, you would find yourself in the period of the Middle Ages characterized by the Romanesque style. This style is especially associated with architecture, and you will quickly see why it is called the round arch style. Stepping into a Romanesque church, you will notice that both the doors and windows are capped with rounded arches. This is how buildings were constructed in ancient Rome as well. In fact, that is where the inspiration comes from and spread throughout Europe. Romanesque style is therefore the first style that can be considered international.

Not much light enters the room as the windows in Romanesque churches are small. But we can still see that the walls are adorned with motifs, and if you know a bit about the Bible, you will recognize that these motifs relate to the topics preached by the priests. For example, it might depict a scene from the New Testament, such as the Three Wise Men kneeling before Mary with the infant Jesus, who has just come into the world.

Figures claim our attention everywhere we look in the Romanesque church. Even the baptismal font, typically made of granite, is often adorned, but always in a highly simplified, stylized manner. The entire church speaks to us through images that calmly and majestically narrate Christianity. Only the ceiling does not say much, especially in early Romanesque churches. Here, a flat beam ceiling was mostly preferred. It was not until later that vaulted ceilings were introduced.

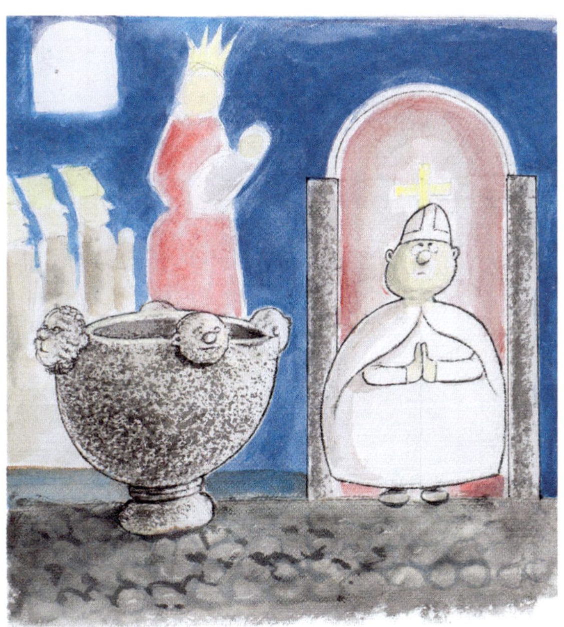

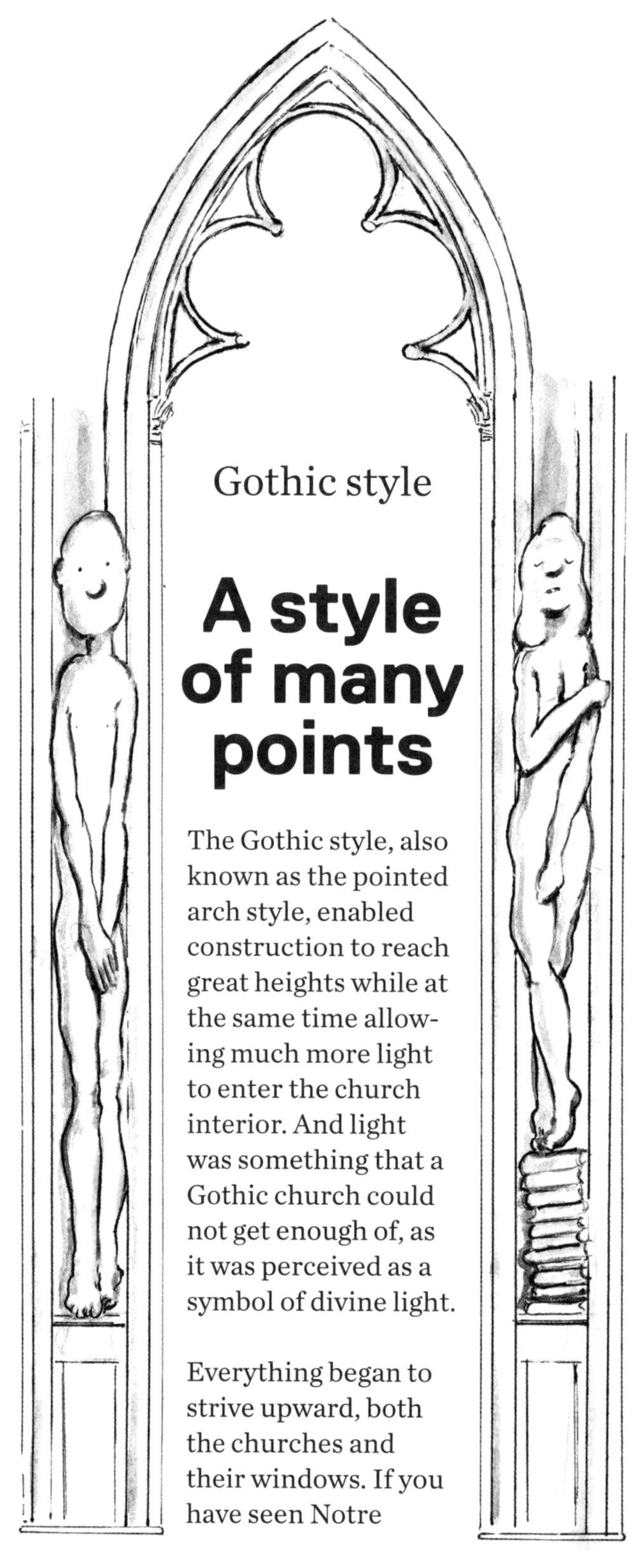

A style of many points

The Gothic style, also known as the pointed arch style, enabled construction to reach great heights while at the same time allowing much more light to enter the church interior. And light was something that a Gothic church could not get enough of, as it was perceived as a symbol of divine light.

Everything began to strive upward, both the churches and their windows. If you have seen Notre

Dame in Paris or the Gothic cathedrals in Chartres, Reims, or Amiens, you might be a little disappointed if you visit the St. Denis church, just outside the centre of Paris.

But it was here it all began around the year 1140. Every style is like a living organism. And, like all living organisms, styles must learn to crawl before they can walk. From France, the Gothic style spread to the rest of Europe. But back then, the spread of new ideas was not as swift as today. An idea could only travel accompanied by craftsmen and artists who were so familiar with the style that they could work with it. However, once the Gothic style had taken root in the 14th century, round arches were out and pointed Gothic arches started shooting up everywhere possible. Many Romanesque churches were made up-to-date and modern by inserting so-called 'false' vaults into the rooms. The churches became brighter and taller. Even the figures you see in artworks changed and shot up, thus matching the architecture they were meant to adorn.

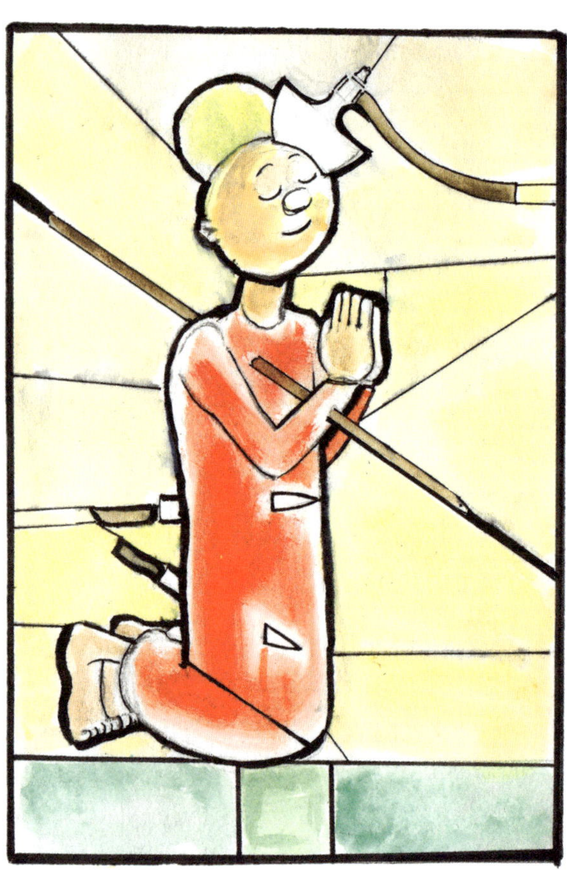

Portrait of a cool saint

A saint is a holy person who, after their death, has been canonized (i.e., made a saint) by the Catholic Church. Saints had the advantage over ordinary mortals of being highly visible in the art found on walls and vaults of churches, on baptismal fonts, in stained-glass windows, or in hand-painted books.

There was just one catch to becoming a saint. Saints had to suffer for their faith. And real saints were more than willing to do so. They allowed themselves to be stoned, crucified, beheaded, impaled, or roasted over a slow fire. For example, Saint Sebastian was pierced by arrows, while Saint Lawrence was laid on a burning grid-iron. After lying on the gridiron for a while, Lawrence is said to have remarked, "Turn me over! I'm done on this side." Perhaps that's why he became the patron saint of cooks. And comedians.

Saints could even smile blissfully while enduring the most gruesome things, as shown in the picture on the left. For their minds were focused on far greater things than their own well-being, namely God and the heavenly kingdom. This applies to the kneeling saint you see here in the stained glass. Nothing fazes him. Today, you would say that he was cool.

Artistic terms in the Middle Age

Working as an artist in the Middle Ages could be challenging in a way that is difficult for us to imagine today. For at least five hundred years, the church was the overwhelming patron and user of artistic decorations. However, the art that the church desired was not art in our very liberal sense of the word. When an artist created a work for the church, it was for the glory of God, not for the artist's own sake, and it mattered less whether the work was fantastic. In fact, it was preferred that it was not too innovative. More important was that it adhered to the tradition inherited from earlier times and approved by the powerful church.

Therefore, we do not even know the names of the masters who decorated the walls, vaults, and ceilings of churches from the introduction of Christianity and well into the 1500s. They were anonymous. It was not made any easier by the fact that many of these painted decorations were whitewashed or covered up after the Reformation, perhaps because church authorities found the motifs morally offensive. Only in modern times have they been uncovered again.

Since the correct names of these master painters are often unknown, in order to describe them, nicknames have often had to be used. So, the artist was named after a motif they were known for, or a place where they had worked.

When artists were long seen simply as craftsmen who specialized in making images, it was due to the workflow. For it was a priest or a bishop who determined the programme for the images with absolute authority. For a long time, those were the conditions in Northern Europe. But south of the Alps, especially in Renaissance Italy, artists were given more status. They had become their own masters.

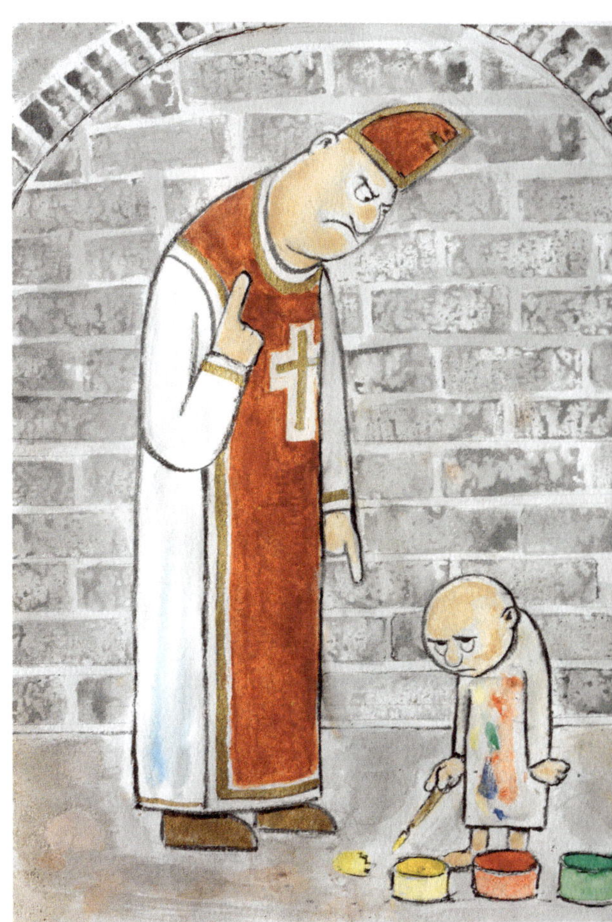

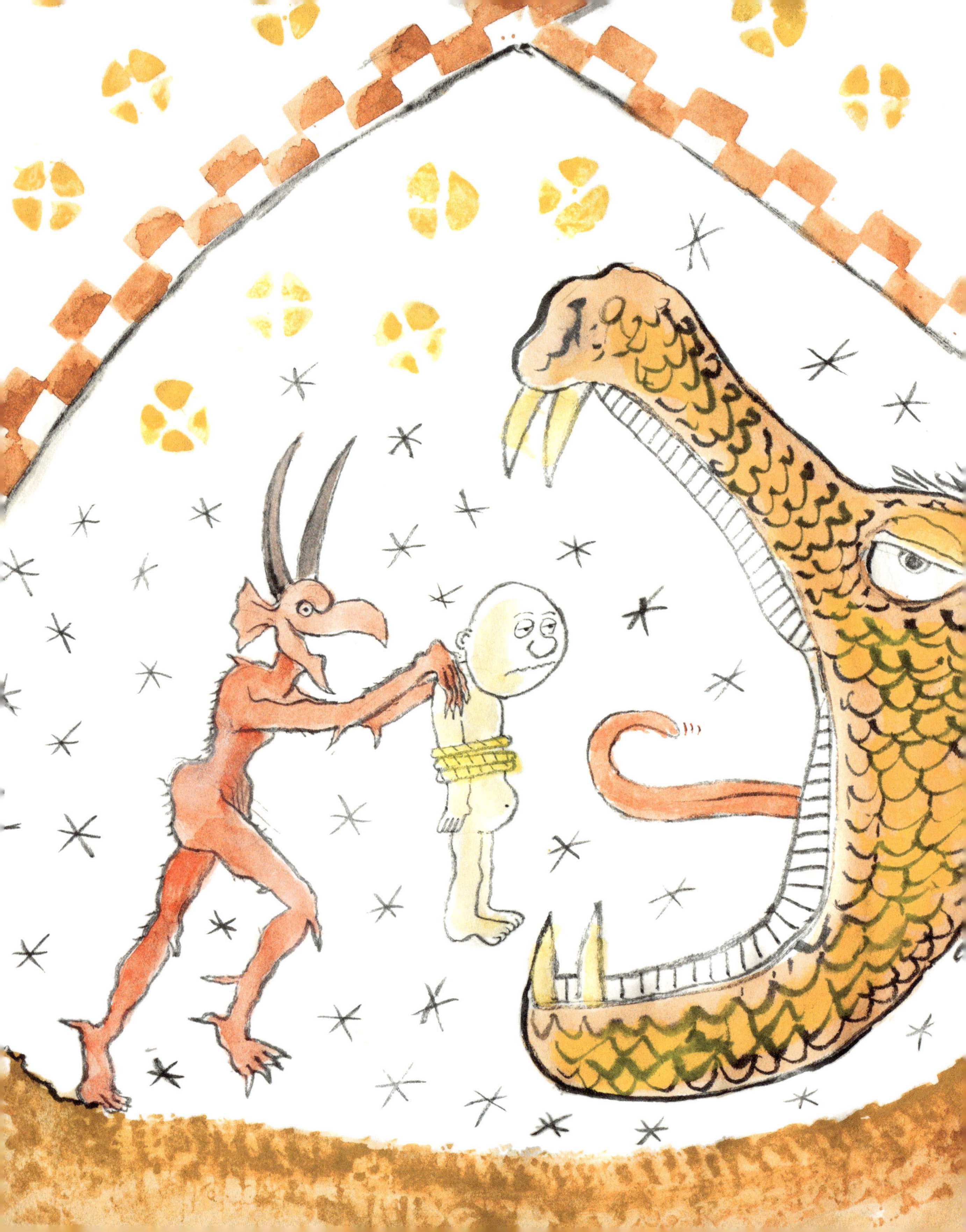

Judgment Day

In the Middle Ages, it was not a great shame to be illiterate, meaning one who cannot read or write. It was a skill reserved for priests and very few others. Since the printing press had not yet been invented (and wasn't until 1440), books were a rarity for a long time. There was also no formal schooling. The vast majority of a church's congregation could not read, for example, the account of how the world was created or why it would eventually come to an end, and it was especially the latter that medieval church art focused on.

Despite being much more devout than today, people did not own a Bible. Therefore, the priest had to read the text to them. But the priest and the congregation did not always speak the same language. So the broader congregation had to learn about faith by studying the images in the church. Looking up, they could see, among other things, what awaited those who had not behaved properly. For them, the devil and purgatory awaited.

The happy giver

Knowing the right people, people with power and money, has always been a good idea if you plan to build a new church or decorate an old one.

Today, there are large foundations for such purposes. When a foundation contributes, it likes to be visible. Lords in the old days had the same attitude. It

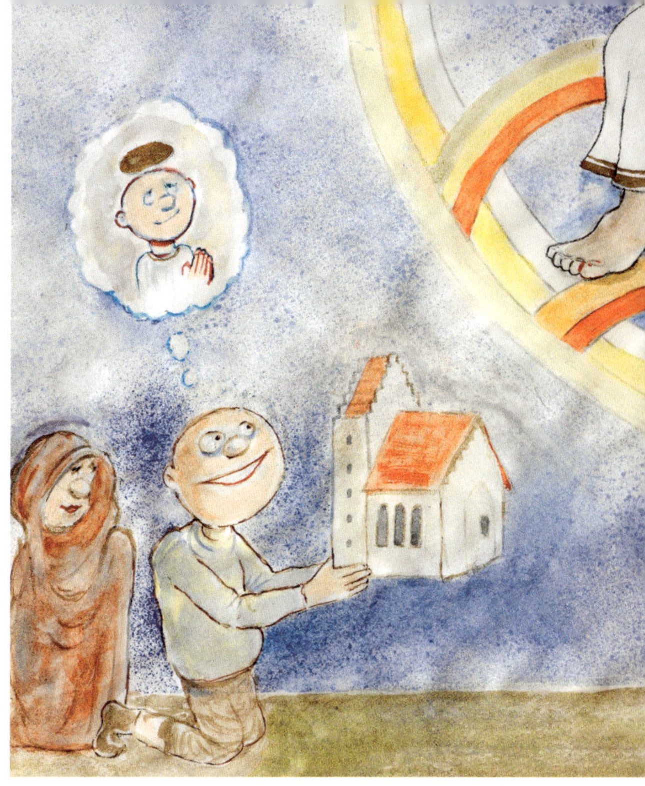

happened that they, for example, asked the local artist to depict them kneeling in front of a representation of Christ or the Virgin Mary on the wall of the church they had funded. Being portrayed like this could even be part of the conditions for their gift. It is this kind of happy giver that we see here.

Of course, the giver has an ulterior motive with their gift. They want to share in the bliss and be rewarded in heaven. But that was not always easy. Taking the Bible literally, it was harder for a wealthy person to enter heaven than for a camel to pass through the eye of a needle, which is why donating money to the church could be a good idea.

Being pious is important

During the early Renaissance in Northern Europe, painting continued its moral preaching where the Gothic frescoes left off. The raised finger of admonition was particularly felt north of the Alps. Whether a picture was painted on the church wall, on a wooden panel, or on canvas, one of the most important tasks of the artwork was to influence you to live a better life. If the artwork was a portrait, the person depicted would want to convince those around him that he lived a life where he behaved properly, resisted temptation, and in general did everything he could to deserve to go to heaven. He was sensible, especially with money matters, but he wasn't greedy.

Religion and the church's commandments meant more to these people of the 15th century than we in the 21st century might imagine. While the people portrayed look out on us, their fellow human beings, their thoughts are with the Savior, that is, with Christ, who has suffered on the cross for the sake of humanity. They knew that everything – except heaven – is fleeting and ephemeral, and the wait here on Earth is not always pure joy. As for the many temptations, a good Christian always had to renounce them.

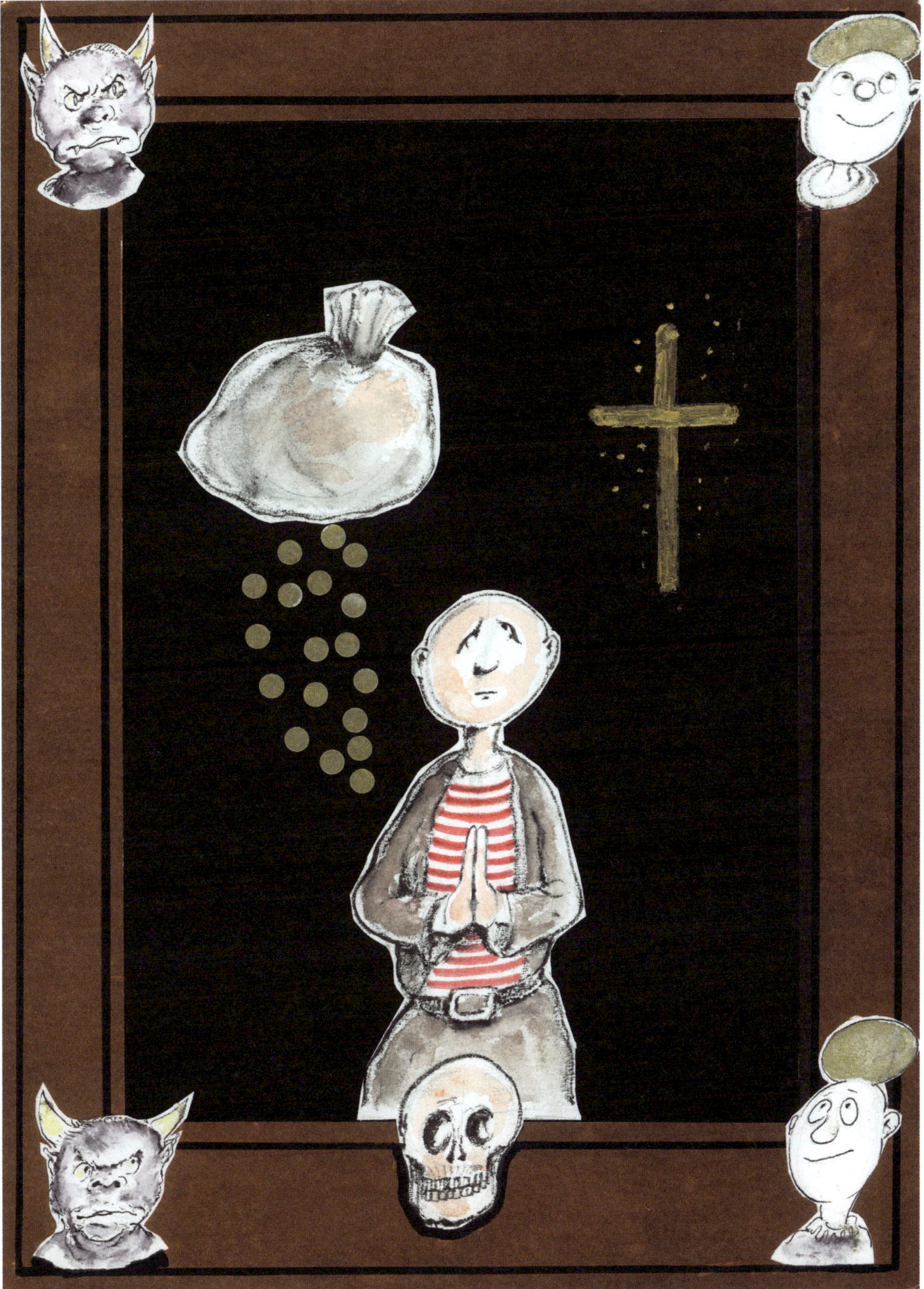

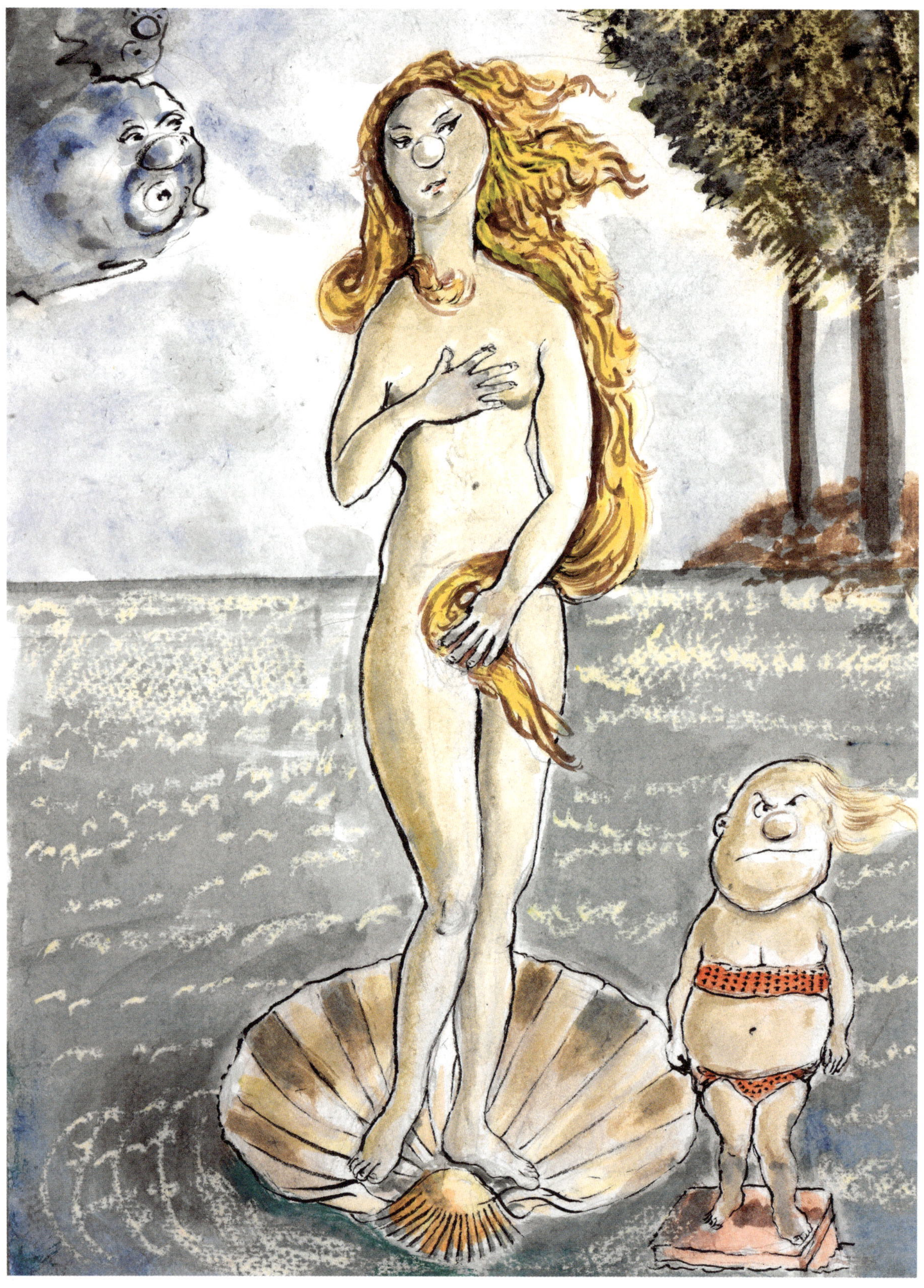

Italian Renaissance

Renaissance means rebirth. What was reborn in the early 15th century was the interest in antiquity – including the interest in comprehending and describing the world. It's difficult to imagine this cultural revival without considering the economic boom in the Italian city-states of the 15th century. The concept of the Renaissance is therefore especially associated with Italy. However, the interest in investigating and understanding the world's configuration gradually spread to the rest of Europe.

Now it wasn't just the church summoning the artist, but also princes and a wealthy and enlightened bourgeoisie. While intellectual life and cognition in the so-called Dark Ages had been hindered by ecclesiastical bans and dogmas, it now became easier to satisfy one's thirst for knowledge. A new freedom gave painters better opportunities to follow their own minds. They explored their surroundings and learned, among other things, to depict both space and spatial objects on a flat surface using a new practical invention: linear perspective. With this, a painter could precisely calculate how people and objects would appear on the picture surface as they moved into the distance.

The artists of the Renaissance looked forward to greater freedom. Still, they did not forget to look back at the ancient models. That's why the Italian Renaissance artist Botticelli (1445–1510) quoted a Greek Venus statue when he painted his Venus rising from the foam. She was tall, slender, and had long legs – exactly as the Greek ideal dictated. Our little guide is here trying to copy Venus but looks somewhat dissatisfied.

Leonardo disguised as Mona Lisa – or vice versa

Everyone knows what Mona Lisa looks like. The painting of her must be the world's most photographed artwork. Not quite as many know what the creator of Mona Lisa looked like. But here we have him, Leonardo da Vinci (1452–1519) with the big white beard (because he probably had one), sitting in the same pose as his most famous model.

There is so much about Leonardo da Vinci we don't know. But we *do* know that he was an extraordinary talent in virtually every field that an artist and scientist could engage with in the transition between the 15th and 16th centuries. This universal genius made himself noticed not only as a painter but also as an engineer and architect, but watch out, here comes a bunch of difficult words. These are the terms for all the sciences that Leonardo was familiar with. We know this from his thousands of drawings – and from his notes (which, by the way, he wrote in mirror writing).

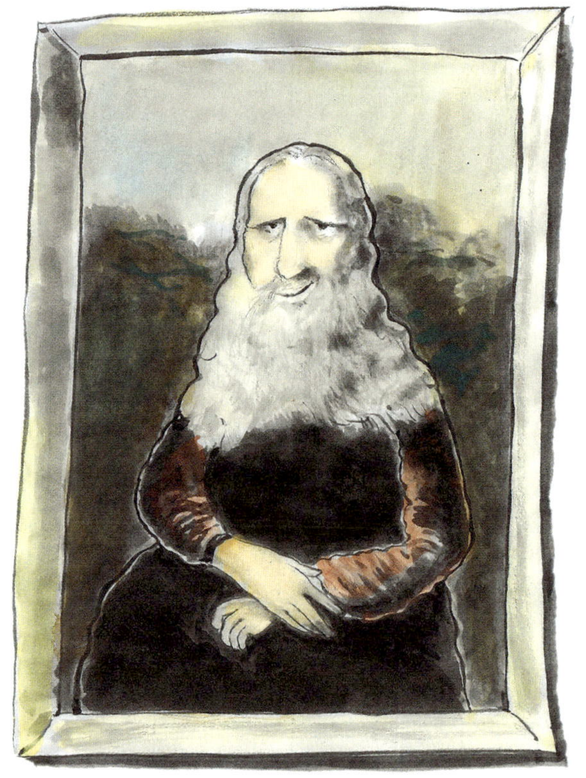

They are: biology, anatomy, physiology, hydrodynamics, mechanics, and aeronautics. The latter term means the study of flight, and it gives us an idea of how far ahead of his time this Renaissance man was. Only on one point did he lag behind his colleagues, and that was in the technical and craftsmanship field. Leonardo couldn't help but experiment without any certainty about the outcome of his experiments. More than one of his masterpieces has been lost or almost lost for that reason.

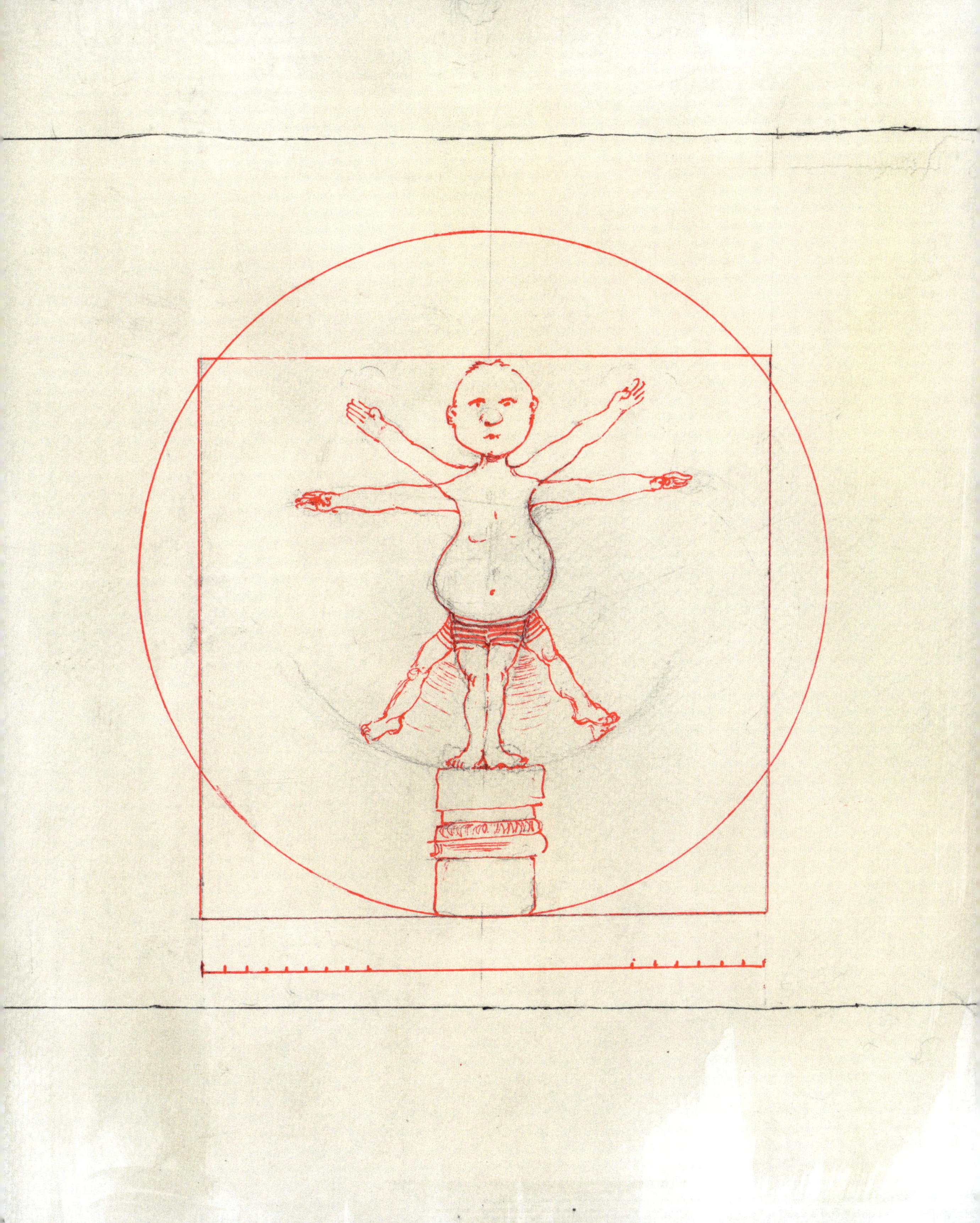

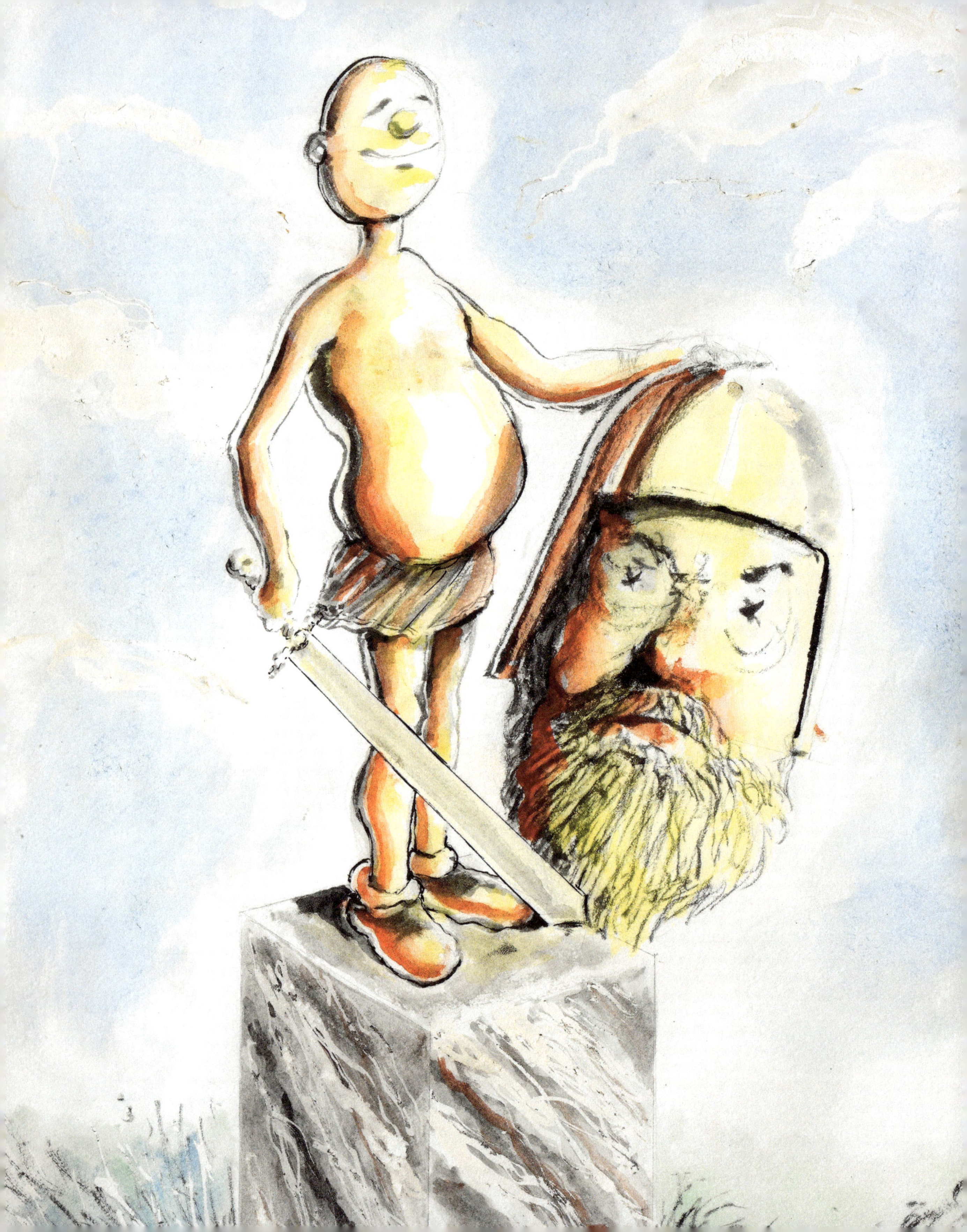

Michelangelo

To triumph over a giant is a giant triumph

If a Renaissance artist were to illustrate a historical event or a human achievement, the many stories of the Bible were always a close inspiration.

David's battle with the giant Goliath was one of the period's most popular subjects, and three of the its greatest sculptors: Donatello (c. 1386–1466), Verrocchio (1435–1488), and Michelangelo (1475–1564) each provided their version of this dramatic motif from the Old Testament.

Here is a fourth version where David's enormous opponent is made even larger than in the well-known depictions to emphasize the uneven battle. Despite all odds, it is still the slender David who emerges victorious, now standing with Goliath's severed head.

In a country like Italy, which was divided into several city-states or republics, any state would find such a motif appealing as it could show that in a war, it was not always the size of a city that mattered but the courage and righteousness of those who fought.

The figure hidden within

In every block of marble – even if it's bigger than a good-sized
fridge with a built-in freezer – there might be a figure waiting to
be carved free. The art is to be able to see it. Michelangelo was
skilled enough to both see the figure in the marble and then to
subsequently carve it free from the stone, piece by piece. That's
how his so-called 'Slaves' were made. They were to adorn a tomb
for an important Roman pope.

Here, both the stone and the artist determined how the finished
figure would look, because the figure could obviously not be larger
than the material available. But it also required a great artist to see
the possibilities hidden in the form of the stone.

If you ask the author of this book, he will tell you that he – not the
author, but Michelangelo – was one of the greatest artists who ever
lived. It was also Michelangelo who single-handedly adorned the
ceiling of the Sistine Chapel in the Vatican between 1508 and 1512.
The Pope in Rome was the most important and powerful employer, and because Michelangelo was both the greatest architect,
sculptor, and painter of his time, there were no limits to what the
Pope would have him do. He didn't manage to achieve everything,
but what he accomplished in all fields with his incredible energy
and fabulous talents made him the most significant – and imitated
– artist of the Renaissance.

He also designed the dome of St. Peter's Basilica in Rome, the
world's largest church. It is impossible to do justice to this great
man in such a small drawing, so we better stop here.

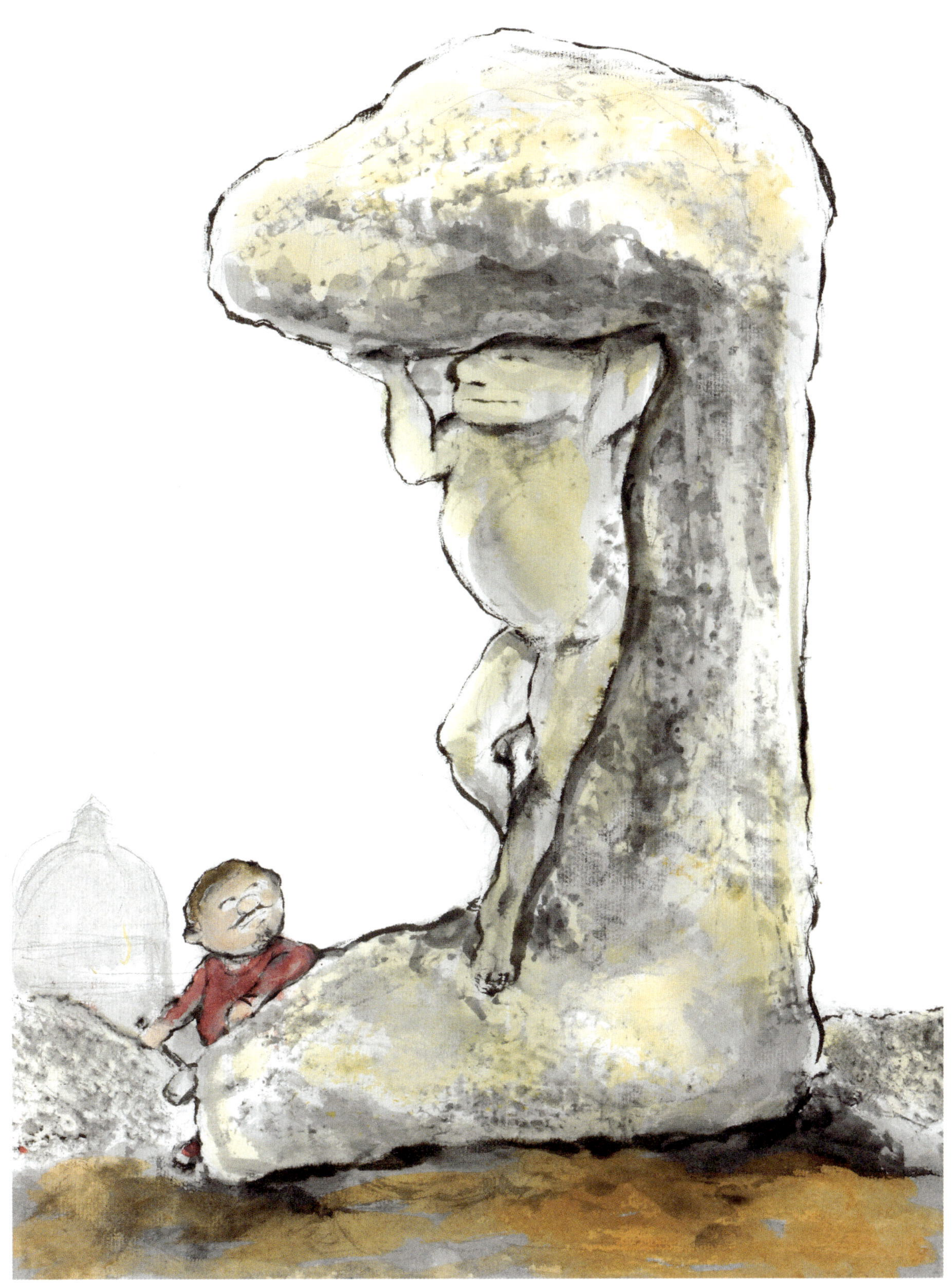

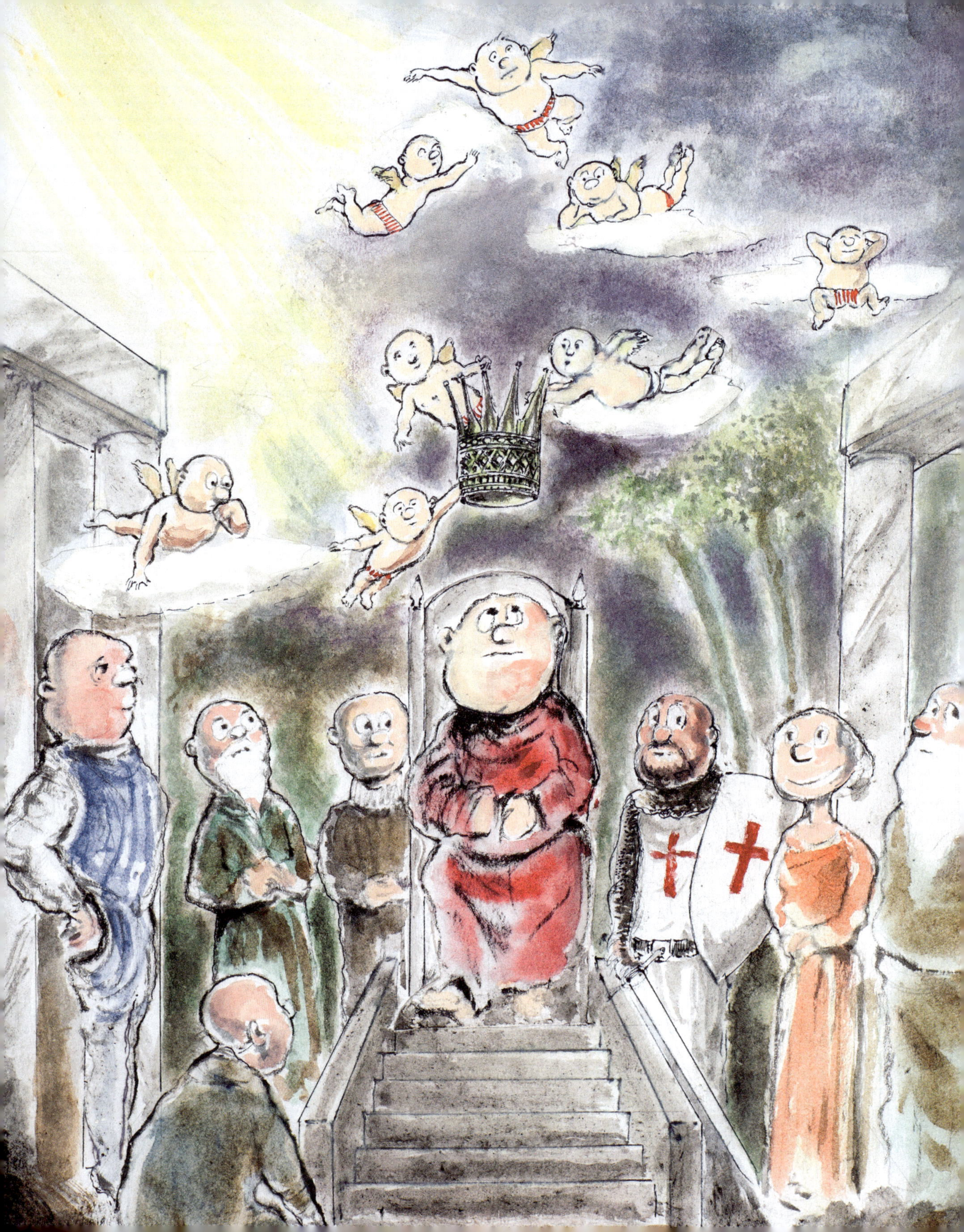

An assembly of even more saints

If there were many saints in the Middle
Ages (as we have seen), there were even
more during the Renaissance. A Renaissance artist had to be able to depict saints.
They could have their own chapel dedicated
to them, or even have a whole church named
after them. They had special tasks or areas
that they managed, and each of them had
their own story to tell. But it was the artists
who did it for them – on altarpieces. The
most depicted saints were the Virgin Mary,
Saint Peter, Saint Paul, John the Baptist,
John the Evangelist, Saint Francis of Assisi,
etc. They each had their characteristic
features so they could be recognized.

Here you see an entire assembly of saints.
Such depictions, where they gather, almost
as if they are invited to a party, are called
'holy conversations', in Italian: *sacra conver-
sazione*. And you find plenty of such holy
conversations among saints in Renaissance
art. Most of the time it is the Virgin Mary
who sits in the centre. Here our guide in art
has momentarily taken centre stage and is
about to be crowned by angels.

A new style comes knocking

Why does art suddenly change its style? Well, Mannerism didn't just appear out of nowhere. After the three geniuses of the Italian High Renaissance – Leonardo da Vinci, Raphael, and Michelangelo – had shown their compatriots what art should look like at its greatest and deepest, some painters and sculptors in the early 16th century went in a different direction. The figures they painted or sculpted became very tall and slim, their faces like beautiful masks, and the colours on the artist's palettes shifted into soft harmonies and broken colours, such as ice blue, lemon yellow, and rose pink.

Linear perspective, which Italian artists had cultivated with great strictness and precision just a few generations before, could be downright hard to spot in the most typical images of Mannerism. The architecture could become entirely impossible. What once had been clear and evident was replaced by a perception of space that was more decorative and anything but realistic.

But what was the reason for this upheaval, which in parts of Italy lasted until the powerful Baroque style emerged? Was it Rome's conquest and plunder in the year 1527? It was certainly an event that shook the values of the High Renaissance. For the capital of the Papacy had been the stronghold of the High Renaissance. The Reformation was now gaining momentum. It was the beginning of a transformation that also left its mark on the fine arts and, in many eyes, made them less beautiful but perhaps, with the arrival of the Baroque, more true.

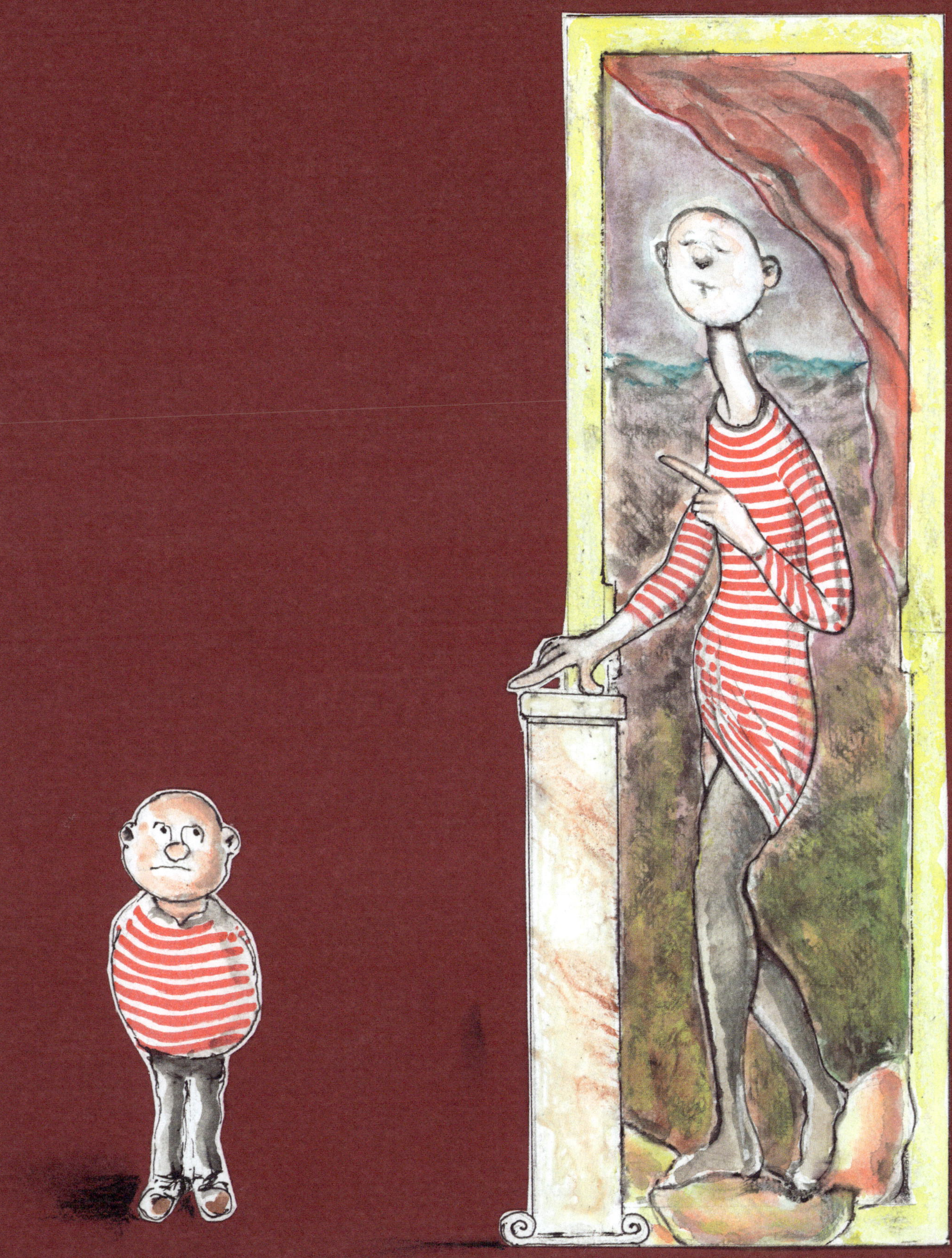

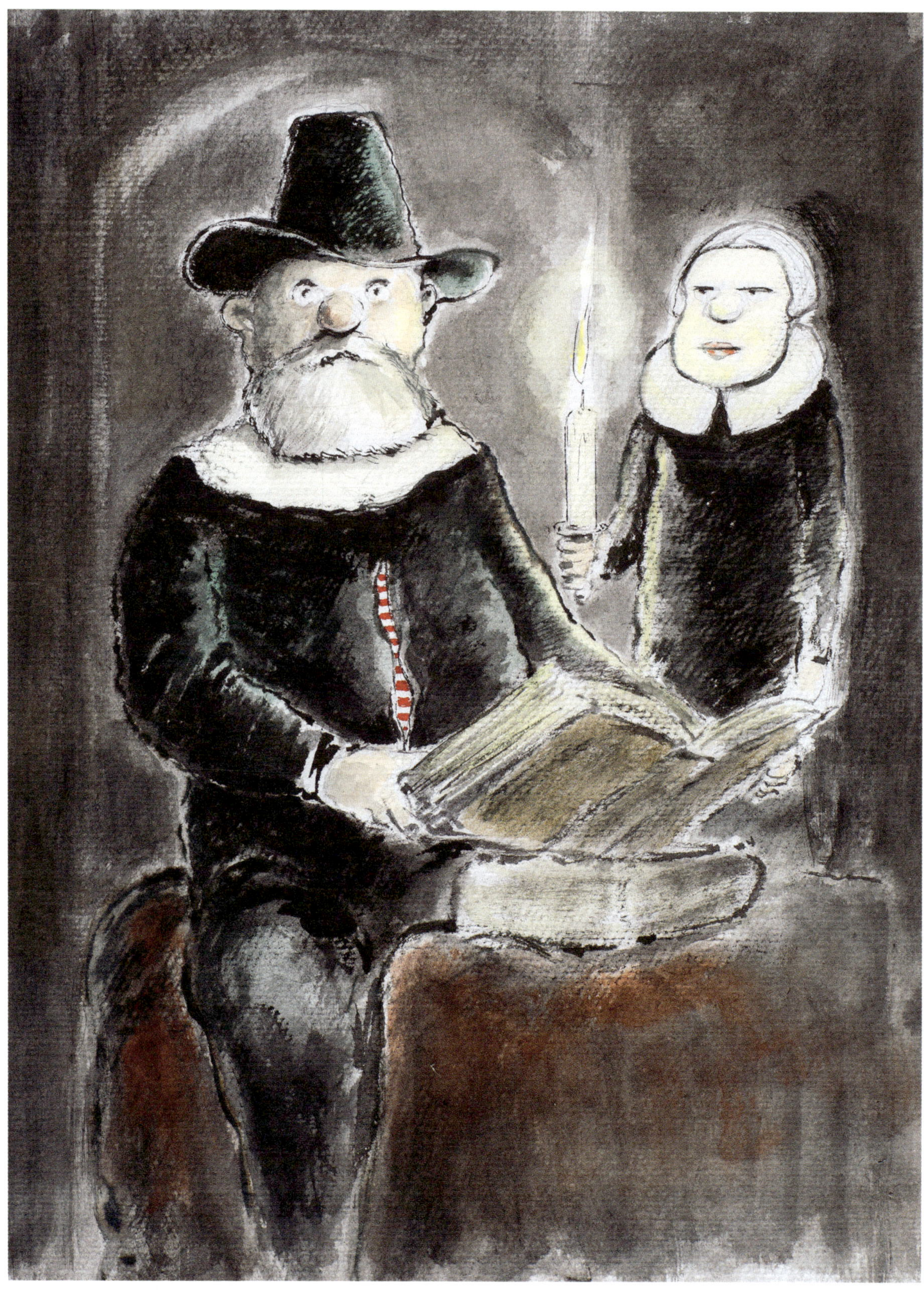

Art for the home

Having someone tell you what to do all the time, including who you can pray to, is more than most people can bear. And that's how the northern provinces in the Netherlands – present-day Holland – felt too. So they broke away from Catholic Spain and, over the course of the 17th century, developed into Europe's leading power in both trade and painting. Never has such a small country – and Holland wasn't particularly large even then – employed so many great painters and created so much significant art. Rembrandt (1606–1669) is the greatest and most famous among them. But there were many others across various genres. The wealthy Dutch in the new republic had an eye for good art and the means to buy it for their homes. Churches were cleared of pictures. Instead, they spread everywhere else.

Collecting fine paintings even became a status symbol, and the depiction of reality – what we call Realism – had its first heyday here. The reality painted included people, landscapes, cityscapes, church interiors, moralizing images, and still lifes. The common thread in all these different genres was a love for the society that the Dutch had built through hard work, courage, struggle, and stubbornness.

One thing you don't come across so often in Dutch art is typical Catholic motifs such as, for example, the Virgin Mary with the baby Jesus. For the Dutch were Calvinists, a particular form of Protestants.

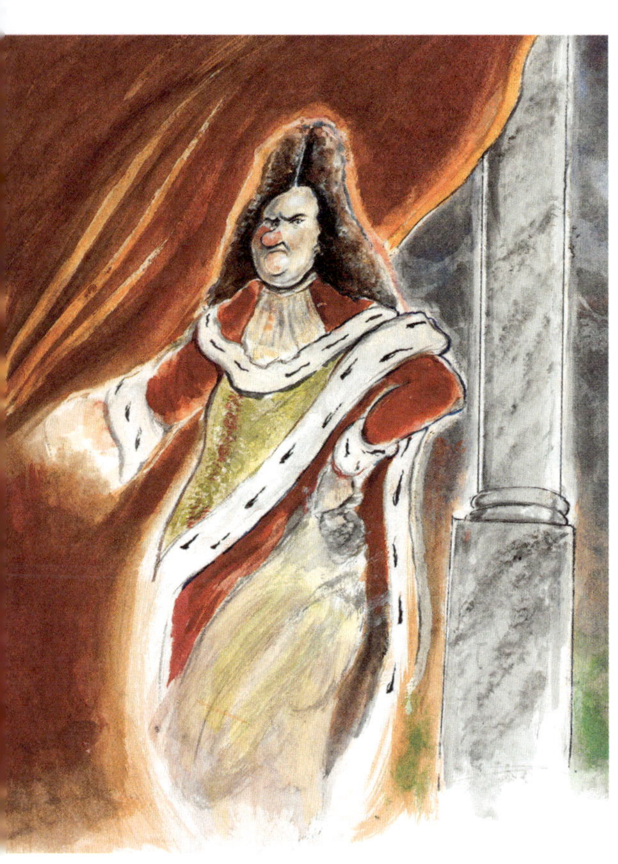

A master in armour with his dog

Look at the dog looking at his master. The painting is, of course, not so much a portrait of the dog as it is of its master. But still, the dog is important. It tells us about its special qualities: loyalty, devotion, and submissiveness. These are precisely the qualities that a ruler's portrait should inspire, not only in his dog but also in his subjects.

The master in armour is indeed a ruler. He has power, and he is ready to fight, as evidenced by his helmet lying on the table right in front of him. You can see his confidence in the way he stands. We can call it his body language. His body speaks to us as if it were a language. One hand is tucked into our prince's side, so that his body takes up more space. The other hand rests on a globe. It could also rest on the books below. Both the globe and the books are symbols of power and wisdom.

Behind him, a landscape is visible. In this kind of painting, we often see rulers placed as if they are both outdoors and indoors. If it were today, they might have been painted standing in their conservatory. But here, the message is more symbolic: to let us know that the prince's power and influence are limitless. They extend outdoors as well.

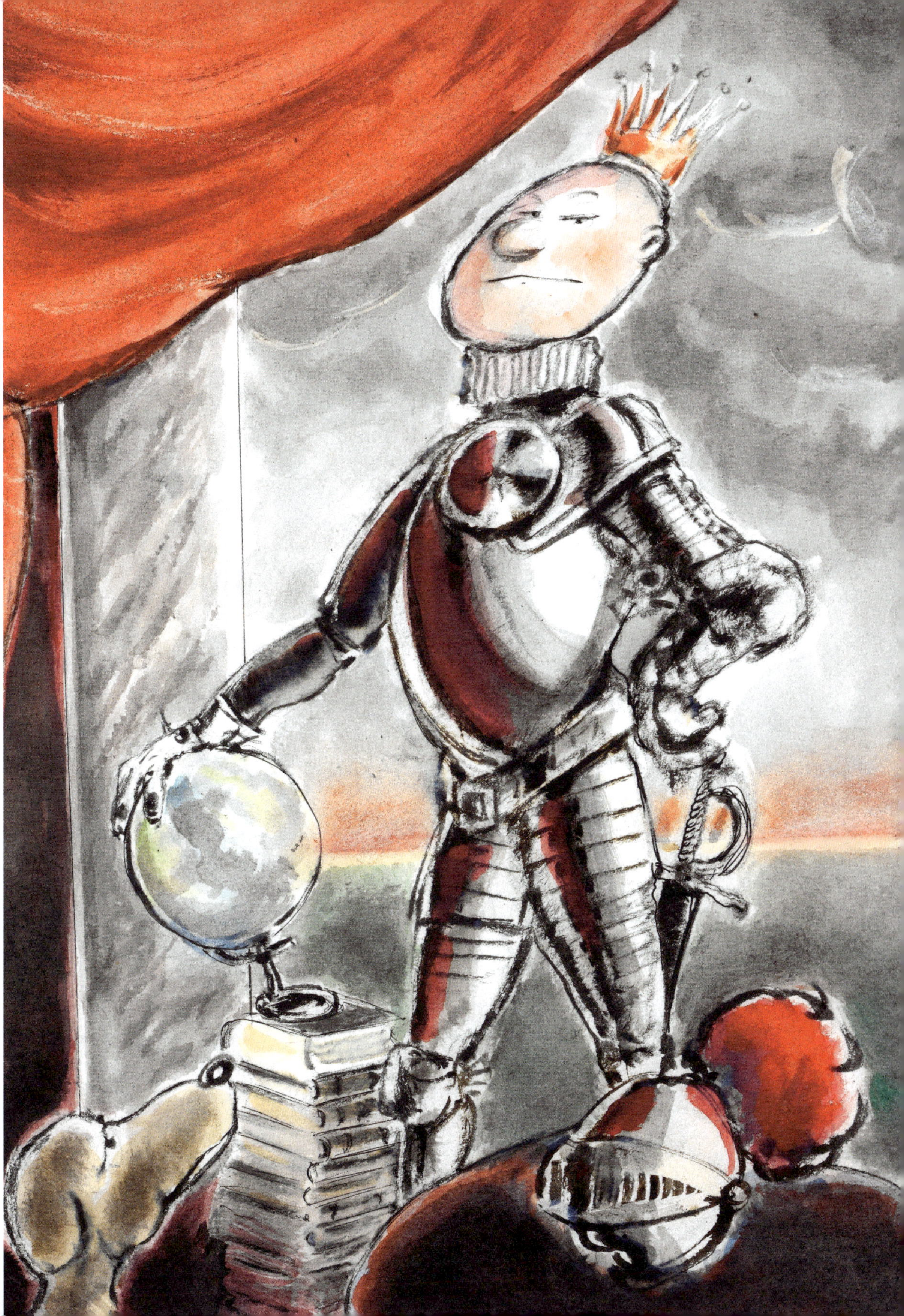

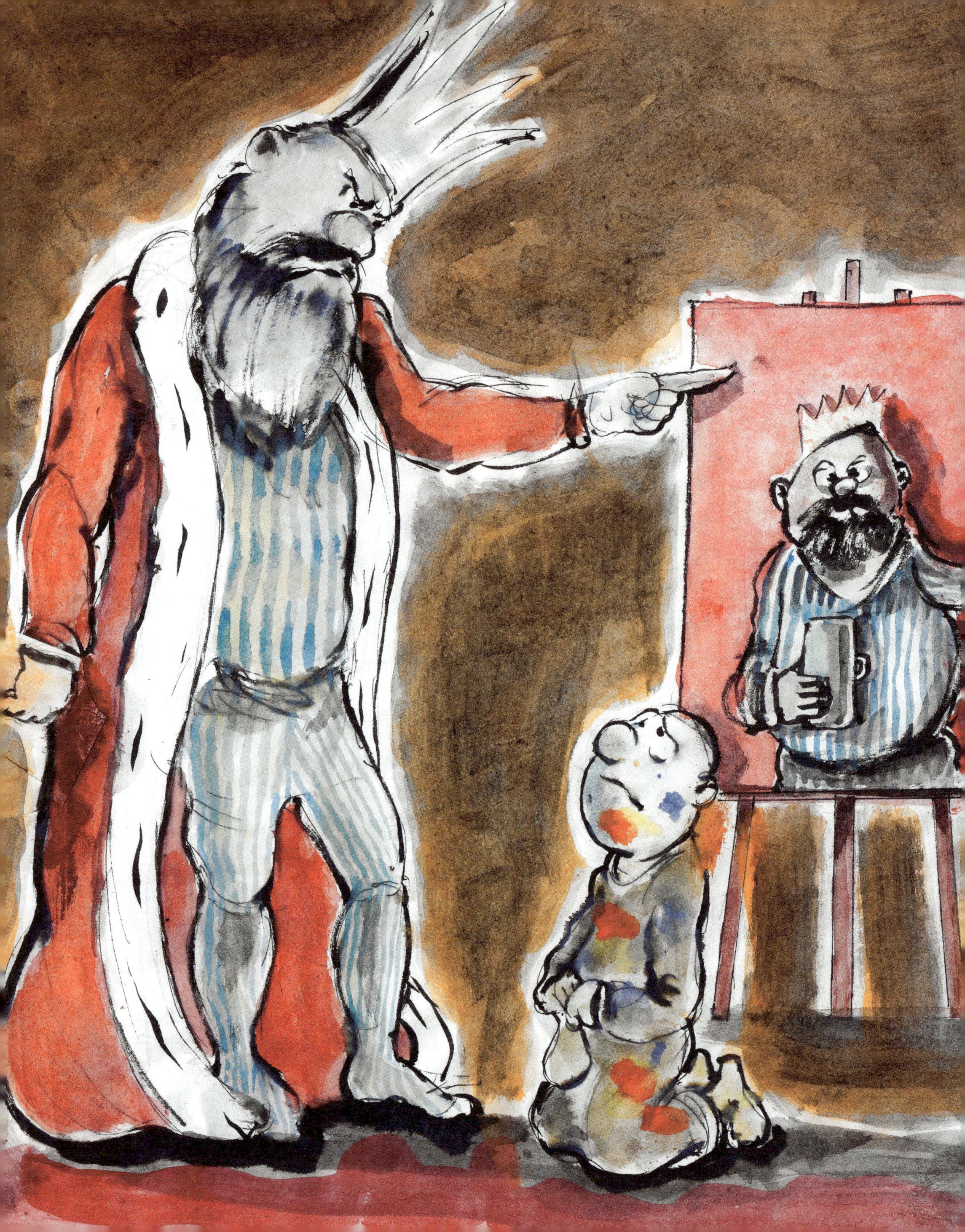

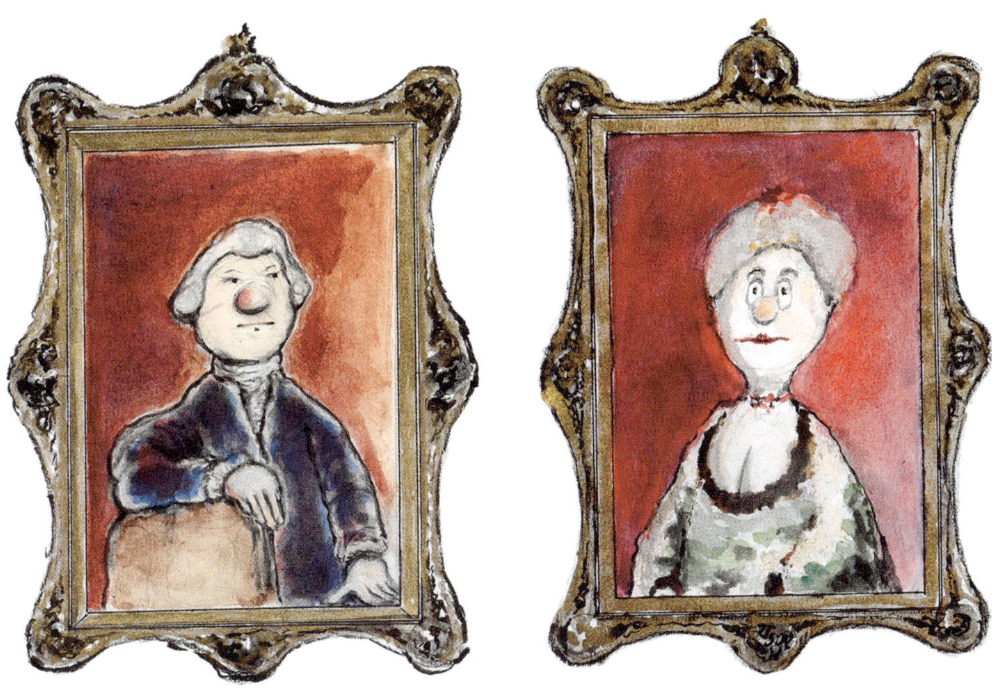

Portrait painters cross all borders

Imagine being noble or a member of a royal family and wanting to have your portrait painted by a portrait painter who ideally should be as famous as yourself. For this purpose, the second half of the 18th century would probably be the best period. Here, outstanding painters who specialized in this genre travelled around Europe to paint portraits of noble and powerful individuals.

For such a painter to be successful, he not only had to be good at his job, he also needed to keep his customers happy. The most popular portrait painters knew how to make their clients look more beautiful and noble than they perhaps were in reality. Never have so many embellishing pictures been painted in art history as in the period leading up to the French Revolution. This desire to embellish everything ended with naturalism.

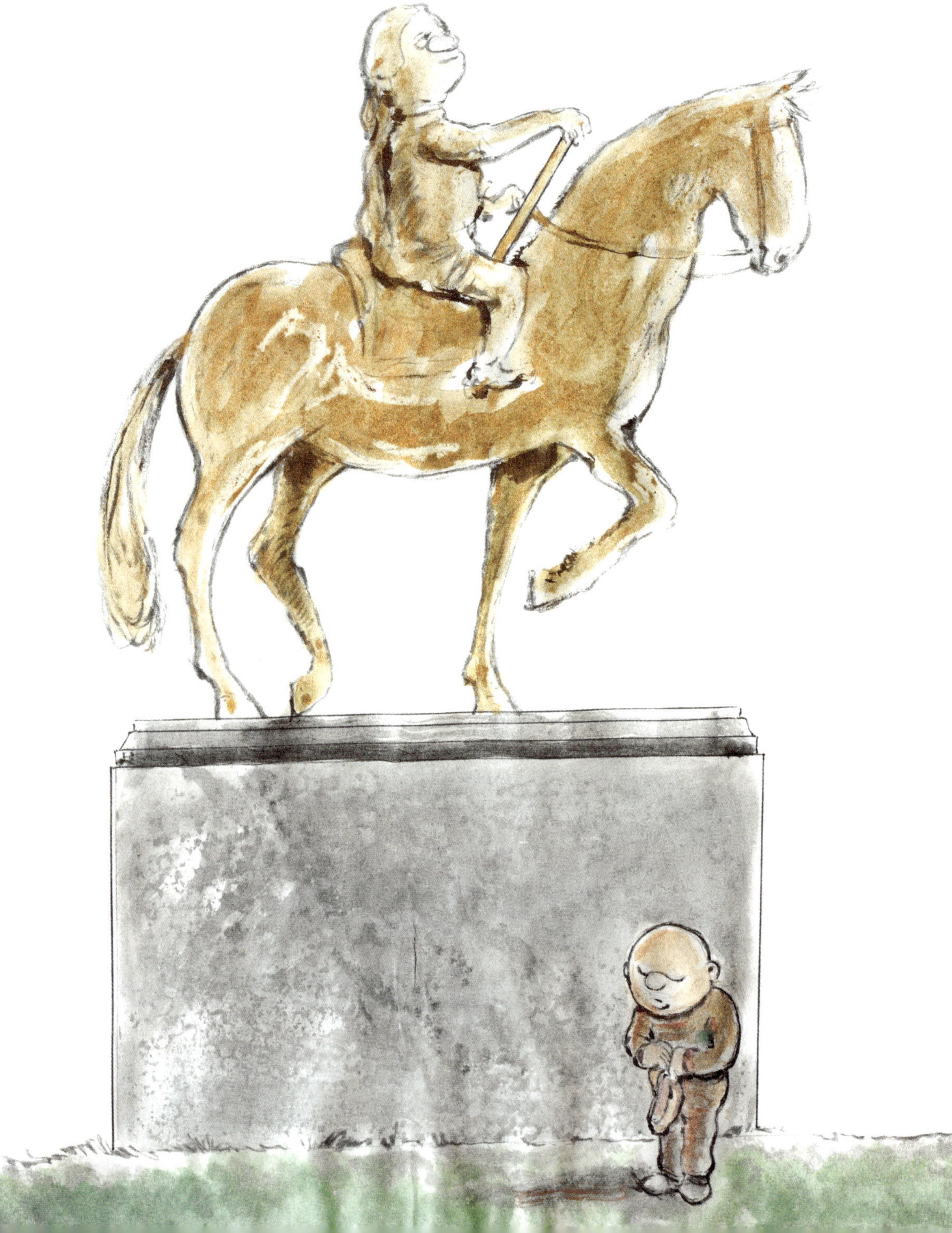

Ruler on horseback

Bronze equestrian statues are for the princes who couldn't settle for having their portrait painted in oil. Ancient Rome was the model for such monuments, where a monarch sits high on horseback on a pedestal and looks impressive. Particularly inspiring was the Roman Emperor Marcus Aurelius, whose statue stands on the Capitol in Rome. Therefore, many more modern princes are dressed as Roman generals, even if they lived much later.

As a form of political art, such equestrian monuments lead an uncertain life. For during major political upheavals, the otherwise sturdy bronze may prove fragile. The French Revolution in 1789 took a toll on a famous equestrian statue of King Louis XV. It disappeared! The material can indeed be melted down and used for much more than glorifying a ruler who has since faced the judgment of history. Therefore, such monuments have become rare in Europe over time.

Moreover, it's mostly kings who have come to horseback in this manner. In Denmark, there is only one equestrian statue of a queen: sculptor Anne Marie Carl-Nielsen's (1863–1945) monument to Margaret I. It was unveiled in 2006, almost 600 years after the model's death and 61 years after the artist's death.

Equestrian statues are cumbersome to move around. The one of King Frederik V, which today stands in Amalienborg Square in Frederiksstaden, Copenhagen, weighed 22 tons, and took 200 sailors to drag it to its place.

A famous French sculptor, Jacques-François-Joseph Saly (1717–1776), was summoned to Denmark to execute this monument for the 100th anniversary of the introduction of absolute monarchy. (Absolute monarchy means that one ruler decides everything). He took his time. For the monument was almost 19 years in the making and was not unveiled until 1771. By then, the king himself had been dead for five years. Absolute monarchy in Denmark did not last long either. It was abolished in 1849 and did not reach its 200th anniversary. But the monarchy endured.

A memory buried beneath lava

Living next door to a volcano can be dangerous – something the inhabitants of Pompeii, a city in southern Italian, learned for themselves when their houses were buried under layers of volcanic lava in 79 CE. It wasn't until 1748 when excavation began on the vanished ancient city, that temples, theatres, houses, and decorations in the classical Roman style emerged. This marked the beginning of Neoclassicism, bringing the ancient style back into fashion. Now, forms were to be simple and strict, contrasting with the decorative and curved lines of the Rococo era. Marble became once again the material of choice for construction.

The crouching figure is meant to represent the wounded Philoctetes. He was a renowned archer tasked with helping his countrymen, the Greeks, conquer the legendary Troy. Along the way, he was bitten by a snake, and when the wound became foul-smelling, the Greeks abandoned him on a deserted island so he wouldn't bother anyone. Except perhaps

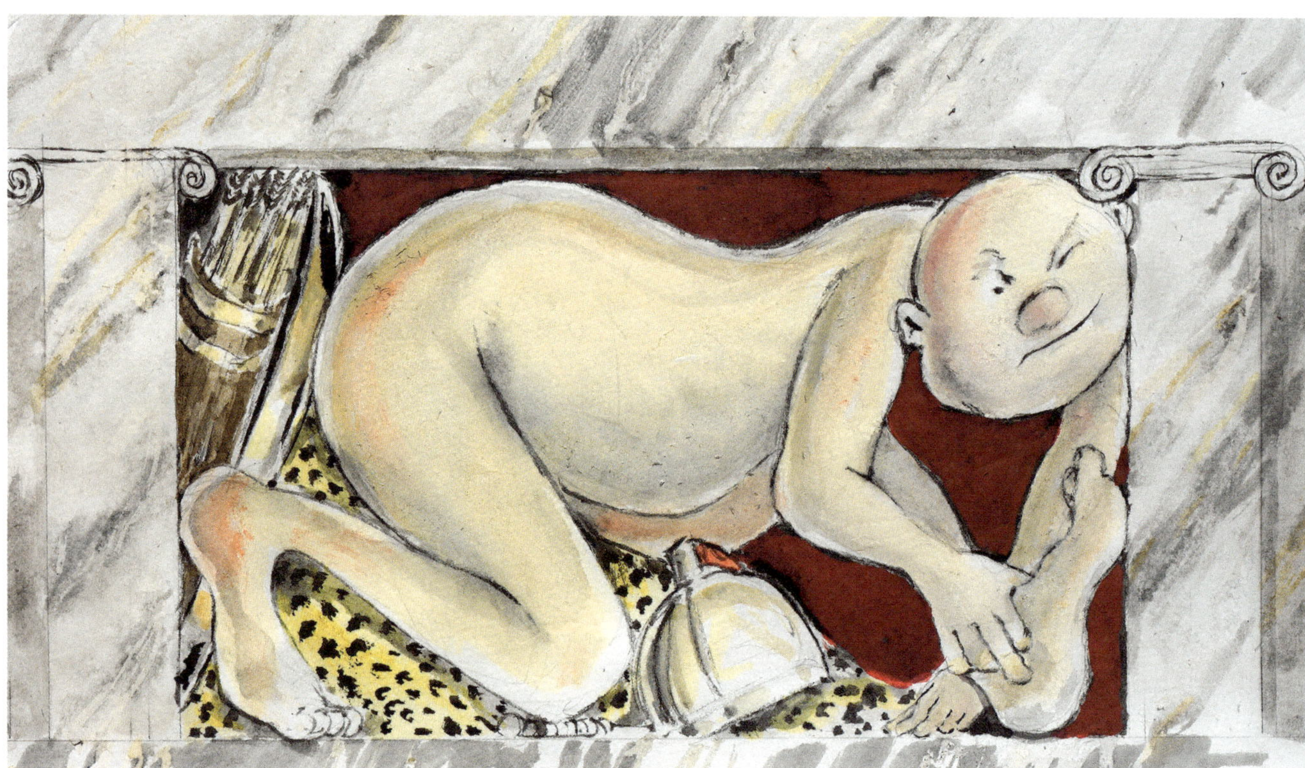

the birds, which he hunted with his bow.
He had to survive somehow. Here,
Philoctetes is almost encapsulated in
marble. The most famous depiction of
him was made by Nicolai Abraham
Abildgaard (1743–1809), a neoclassicist
painter.

When Jason outsmarted the never-sleeping monster

Jason is the young man standing on the
pedestal, looking somewhat overwhelmed. He is almost naked, as was
customary for sculptures of heroes
during Neoclassicism. However, he is not
quite as athletic as most other heroes of
the period. The neoclassical ideals of the
body were inspired by those of ancient
Greece.

Perhaps this Jason hasn't fully recovered
from his encounter with a monster with a
hundred eyes. But he did manage to
obtain the golden fleece from the monster that guarded it. With the help of a
potion given to him by his lover, the
sorceress Medea, he put the monster,
which never slept, into a slumber. Only
when the creature had closed all hundred
eyes did Jason steal the fleece, which may
not be the most heroic act.

Danish artist Bertel Thorvaldsen (1770–
1844) also benefited from the golden
fleece. As a young sculptor, shortly
after his arrival in Rome, he created the
most famous depiction of Jason. He
became so sought after because of the
statue that he didn't return home until
nearly 40 years later when his countrymen offered to build a museum for his
extensive collections.

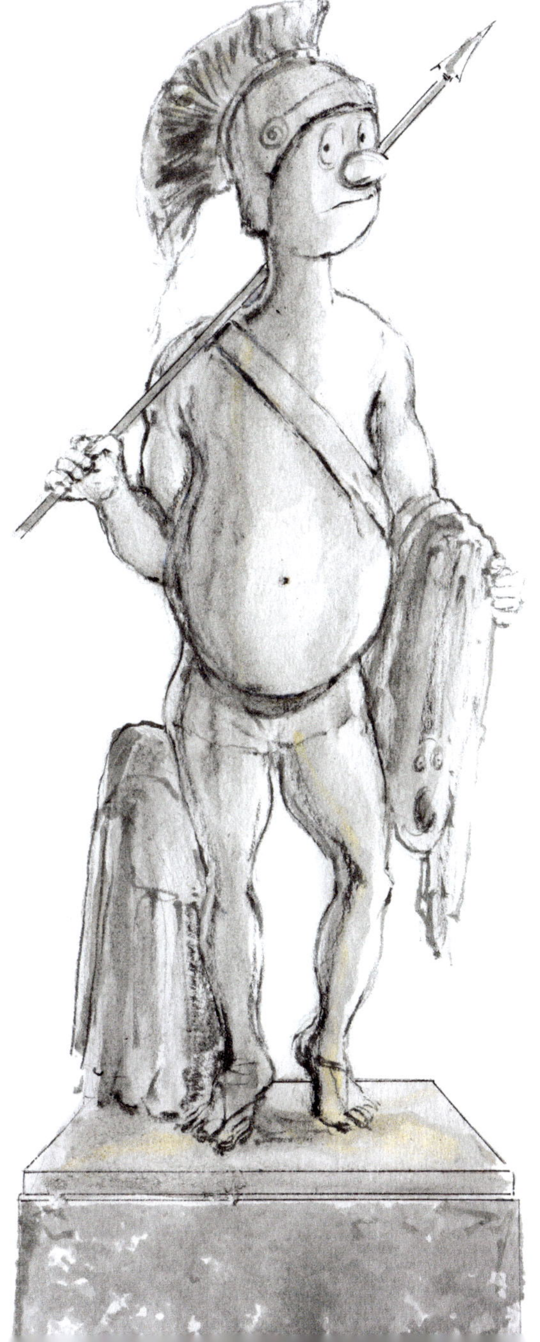

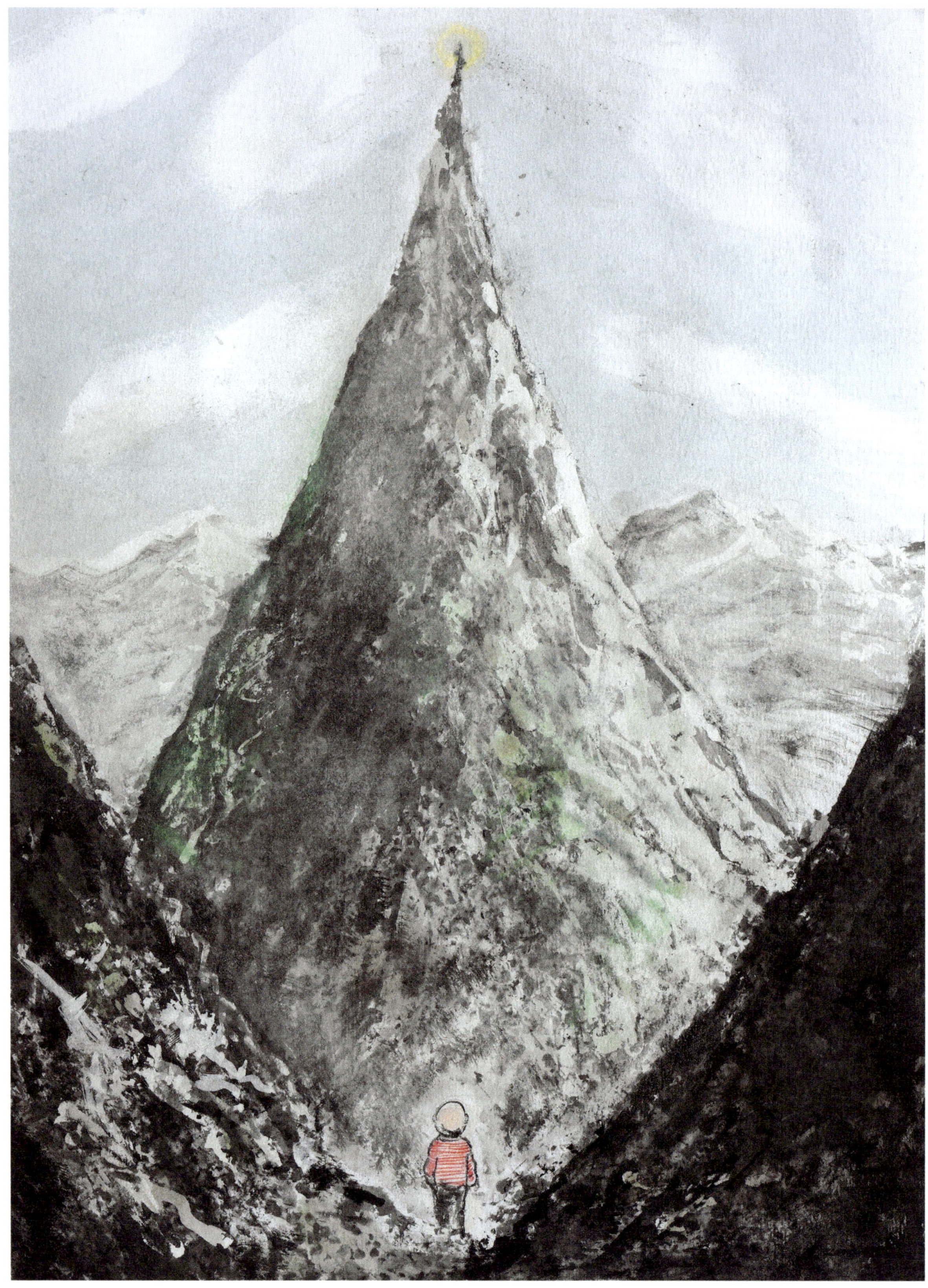

Encountering something greater than oneself

It's difficult to make a clear distinction between Neoclassicism and the subsequent Romanticism. Both styles strongly appeal to emotions. However, while neoclassical artists prioritized collective human ideals, such as sacrificing oneself for society and grappling with great moral questions, Romantics focused more on the individual and their relationship with nature, which always felt greater than the individual. This can be seen in the works of the German Romantic painter Caspar David Friedrich (1774–1840). Between 1770 and the mid-19th century, he and other artists set a new agenda in painting: they gave the landscape a leading role.

The Romantic experience can have multiple causes, but one thing remains constant: it revolves around overwhelming experiences. When we encounter something vast, something that shakes us and makes us feel small, we are inspired. In nature, superhuman forces rule. Perhaps this is why we venture into nature – to seek experiences that are greater than ourselves.

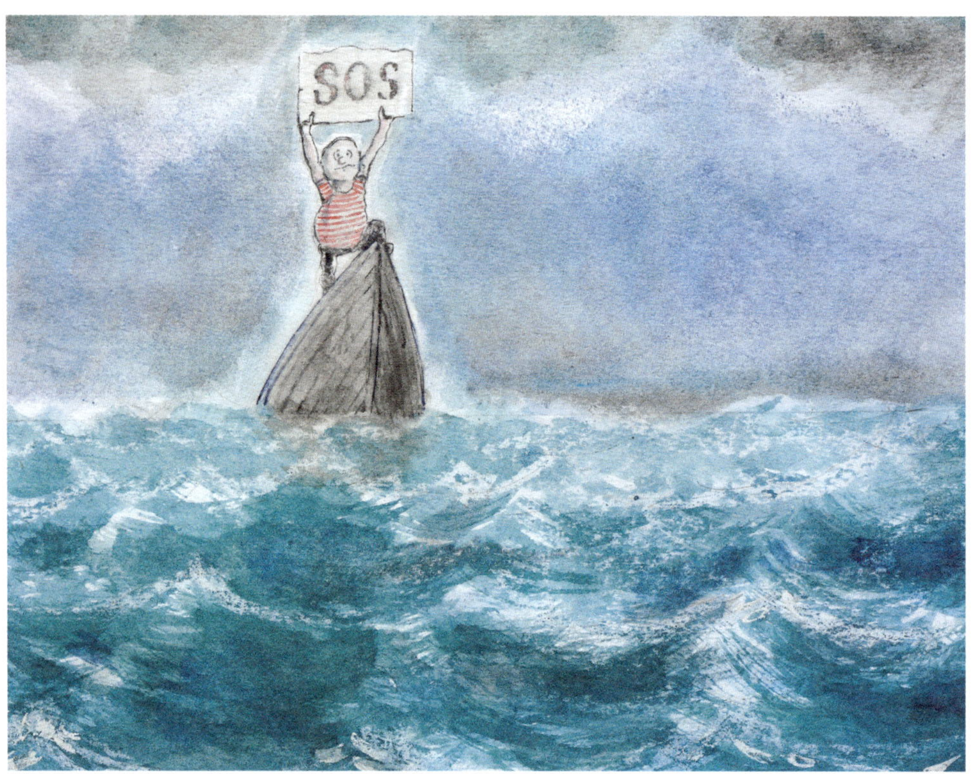

This happens when we stand amidst a raging sea and are no longer masters of our own destiny. We think: will the ship sink – and take us down with it? And will we survive? Regardless, it's an overwhelming experience.

The same occurs when we stand before a towering mountain landscape. We may feel threatened, overwhelmed by mighty natural forces, or imbued with the eternal mystery of nature. Or perhaps we simply sit in the forest, among tall trees, thinking of something that makes us feel similarly warm inside: our loved one at home?

For the Romantic painter, the most important thing is to show us that humans don't always have control over things, and that our reason and other abilities have limitations. This happens when we face the great, sublime nature.

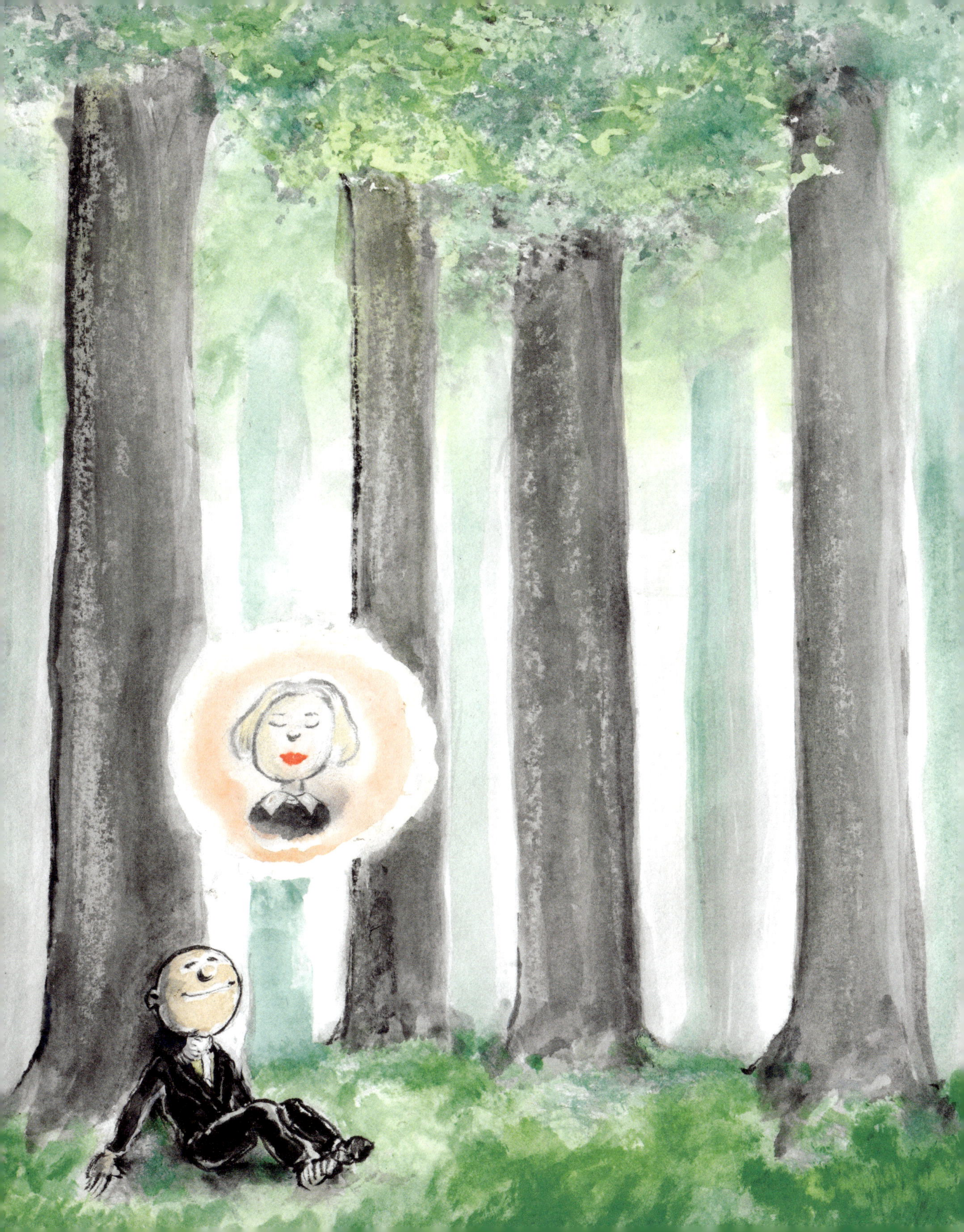

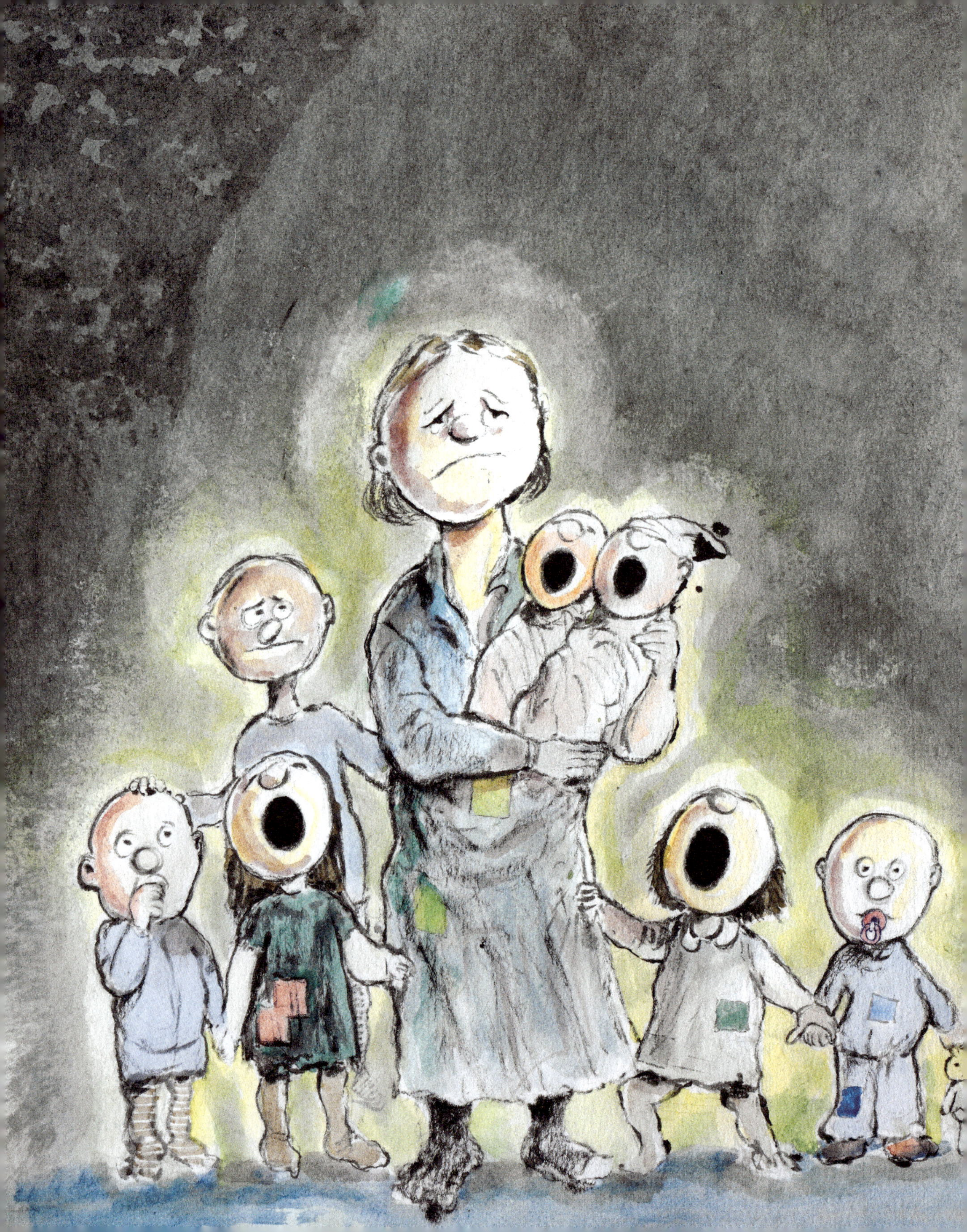

Moving closer to reality

Realists are known for not embellishing reality when depicting it. It's only the pure, unadulterated truth they aim to convey on the canvas, even though it's not always popular. Throughout art history, it has happened more than once that artists have got up close to reality. It happened in ancient Rome, in Renaissance Italy, in the Netherlands before the Reformation, in Holland, and so on.

Realism took over after Romanticism in the mid-19th century. It was France, with the painter Gustave Courbet (1819–1877), that wiped the slate clean and banished anything idealized or staged from its pictures. The typical realist had no qualms about delving into society's shadows. They could paint the poor and the outcasts, all those who suffered. It could be a poor mother burdened with too many children. For Realism – at least a part of it – sought to expose society's flaws, in the hope that it would improve. It was a beautiful dream that required time to become something more.

Realism had its breakthrough in the same decades as photography. The invention of

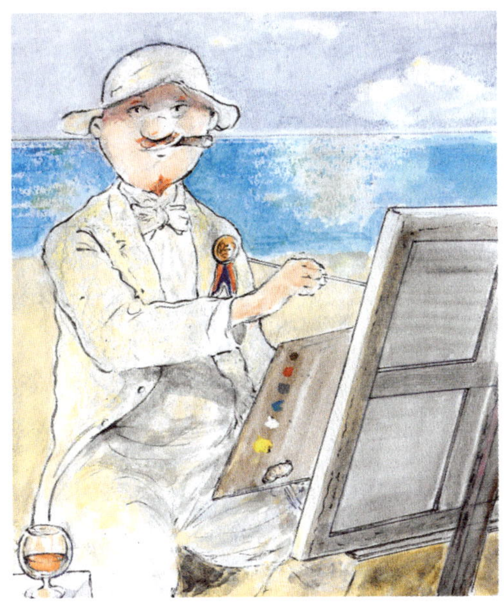

photography didn't immediately lead to the death of painting, as some artists feared. Instead, it became a new crutch for painting. Those artists who had the means – and the money – utilized photographs as aids. A good photograph could render a perhaps troublesome model unnecessary, and the Danish painter P. S. Krøyer (1851–1909), who was successful and financially secure, wasted no time in acquiring a camera. When we compare the photographs he took – or had others take – with the paintings he created, we can see that even the realist embellished reality a bit.

The painter in the picture bears some resemblance to Krøyer. The picture is supposed to be a self-portrait of the artist painted on the beach. Added are a cigar, a well-poured cognac, and one of the exhibition medals that the artist received a couple of.

Art with red flags

You need to pay close attention to spot the difference between social Realism and socialist Realism. The difference is in the intention, rather than the appearance. Social Realism is an honest depiction of a world the artist has seen with their own eyes. The purpose may be to showcase the social disparities and injustices that can afflict the weak in society. Thus, it's a socially critical art with hidden agendas for societal improvement.

On the other hand, socialist Realism is politically controlled art, most often found in the former Soviet Union. The tone is more heroic because the aim of socialist Realism is to advertise the ruling social order positively, often commissioned directly by the political regime itself.

In European art, Realism – a close, yet aesthetically pleasing depiction of surroundings – gradually transitions into a more critical perception of the reality the artist lives under. Subjects like the one in the drawing here are a prime example of art when it wants to be political. Here, we see a speaker addressing his party and advocating for a better society. Some citizens gather around him to listen to what he says. To the right, the sun rises as a symbol that a new system and society may be emerging. In the red flags fluttering over the podium, one might expect to find political symbols like a hammer and sickle. However, some would say this is too old-fashioned. Instead, we've shown an example of something more modern: product placement. Product placement occurs when a company seeks to draw attention to itself, or when someone wants to highlight the company.

(By the way, the 's' on the spine of this book doesn't stand for socialism. It stands for the publisher, Strandberg Publishing, who has released the book.)

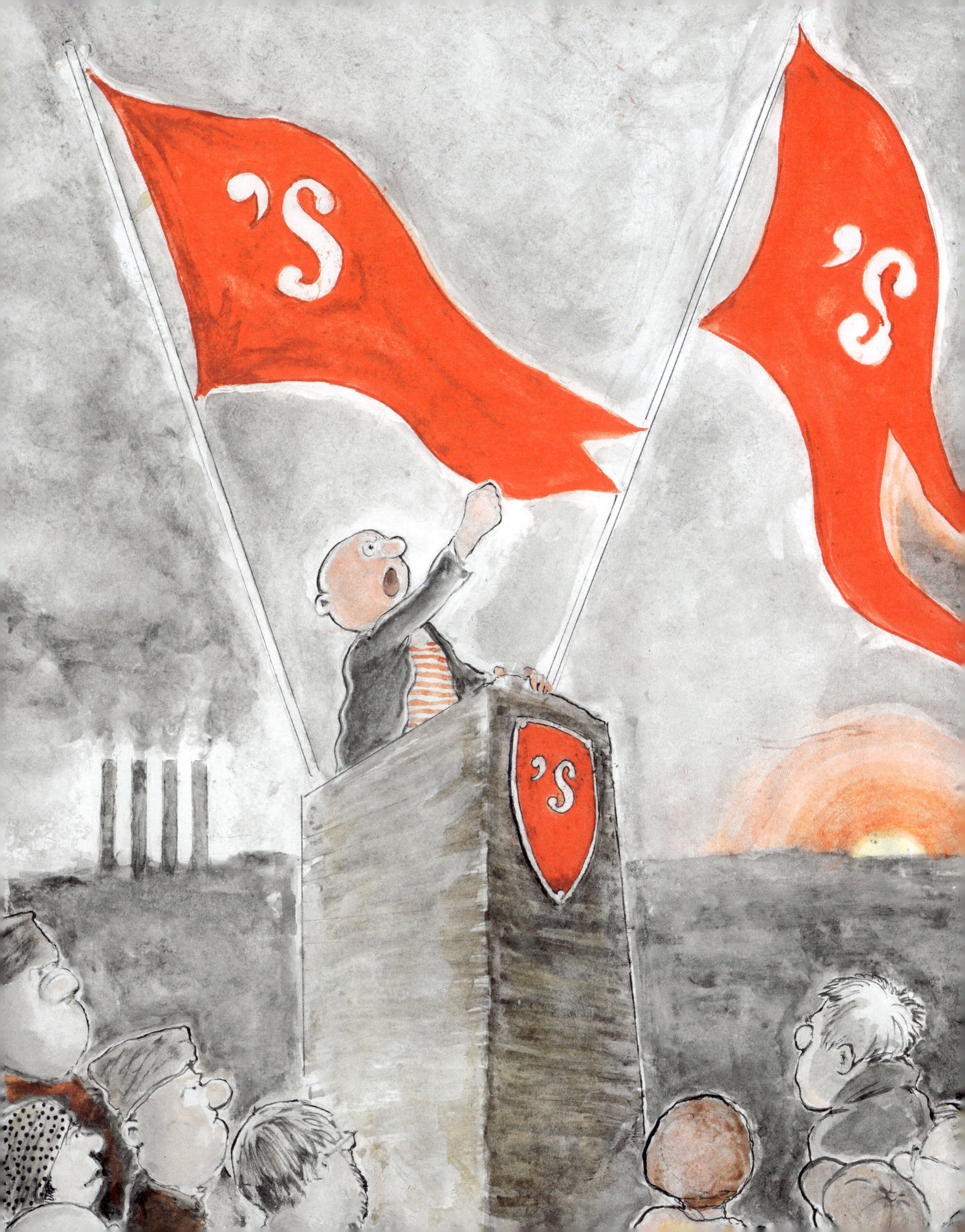
'S
'S
'S

Landscape à la Turner

If you want to paint a landscape like the English painter Joseph Mallord William Turner (1775–1851) did in his later years, remember to skip the details. Because if there are too many small particulars – and there typically were in 19th-century paintings – they will steal attention from the more painterly qualities: the light and colour. Above all, it was light and colour that Turner wanted to highlight in his paintings, and a landscape was almost his excuse to do so.

Without aiming for it, Turner created some of the prerequisites for modern art. When he died in 1851, the French impressionist Claude Monet (1840–1926) was only ten years old. But Turner's paintings were already ahead of what the impressionists would first create a score of years later. He had started as a quite traditional romantic landscape painter, but as the years went by, his view of nature became more and more emotional and glowingly romantic.

Turner travelled extensively for his time and made a wealth of sketches in countries like France, Switzerland, and Italy. He did this to have something to rely on when translating his observations into finished paintings. Over the years, he became a bit odd. The same happened to his art, and it ended up standing out from everything else painted in the same period. In the end, only the light and colour remained. Nothing is truly in focus, and the paintings can seem entirely abstract. When experiencing one of them today, you almost begin to wonder if you forgot to put your glasses on.

First hated and reviled, then loved and praised

Nearly one hundred and fifty years after its first exhibitions – in the 1870s – Impressionism remains the most popular of all art movements. If a museum struggles with visitor numbers, all it needs to do is organize an exhibition featuring Impressionism. It's not hard to understand why. The impressionists painted natural scenes that are bright, poetic, beautiful, and above all, recognizable.

These are pictures that depict life as it was lived on the streets of Paris, by the Seine, or at the popular excursion spots in the Parisian outskirts. Today, everyone loves these paintings. But in the beginning, there weren't many who did. Some were even outraged by them. They couldn't understand why anyone would paint, for example, trains at a railway station when they could just as well paint a Greek god. But for these painters, the most important thing was to depict their own time.

When the impressionists opened their first exhibition on April 15, 1874, in the former studio of the photographer Nadar on boulevard des Capucines in Paris, they didn't call themselves impressionists at all. They were simply called: 'La Société anonyme des artistes,

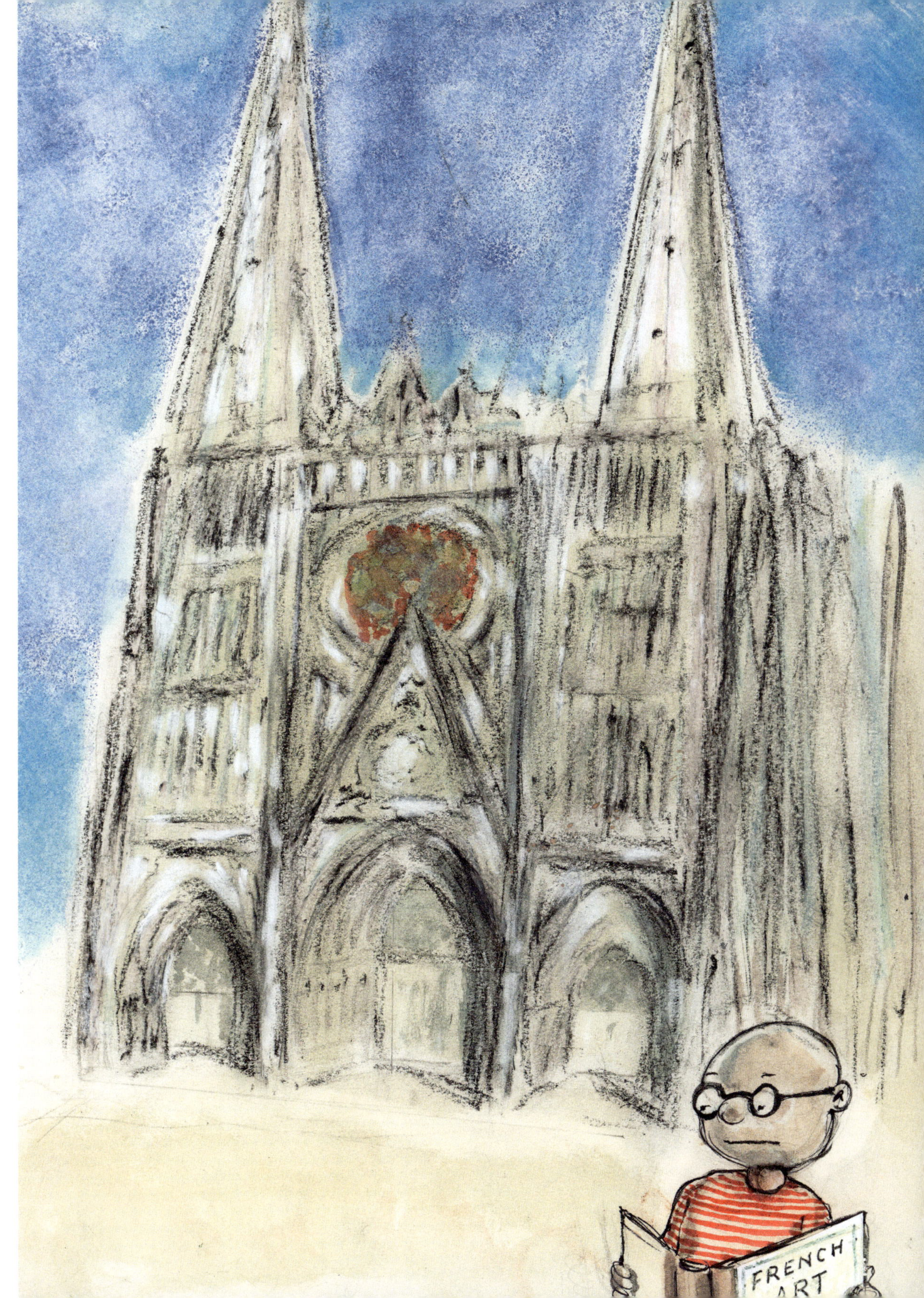
FRENCH
ART

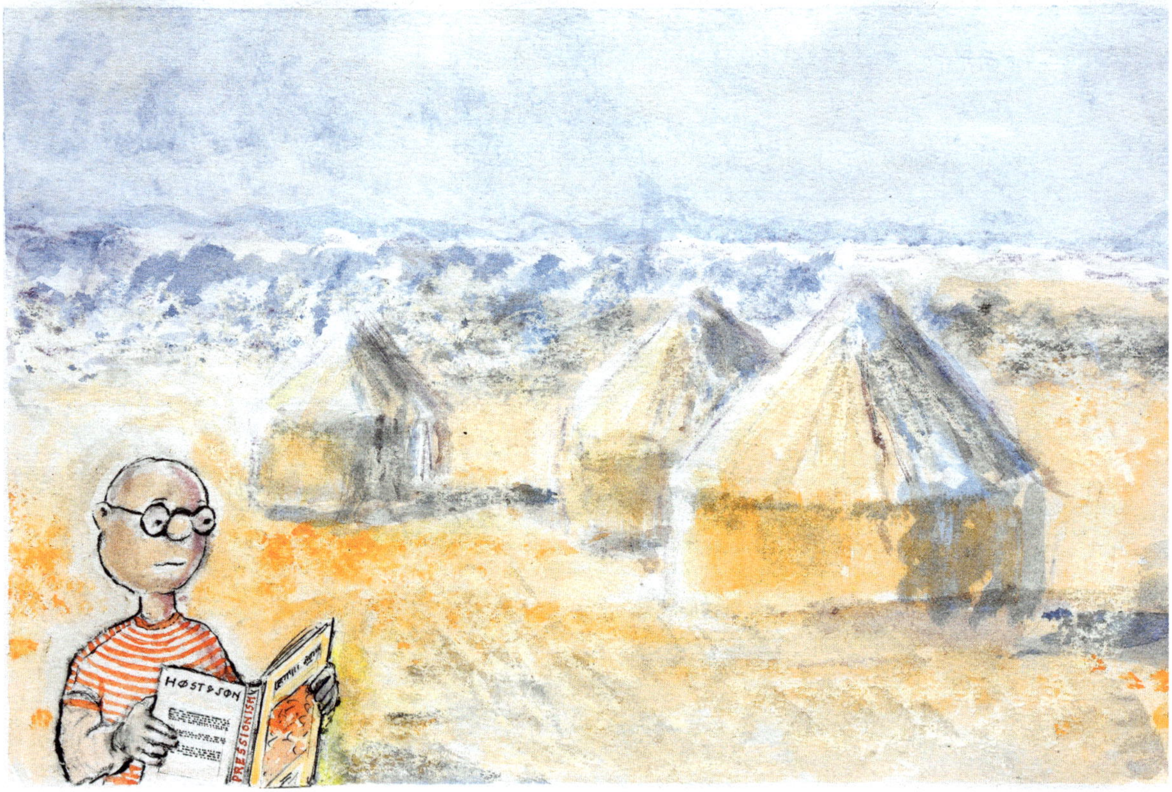

HØST & SØN
PRESSIONISM

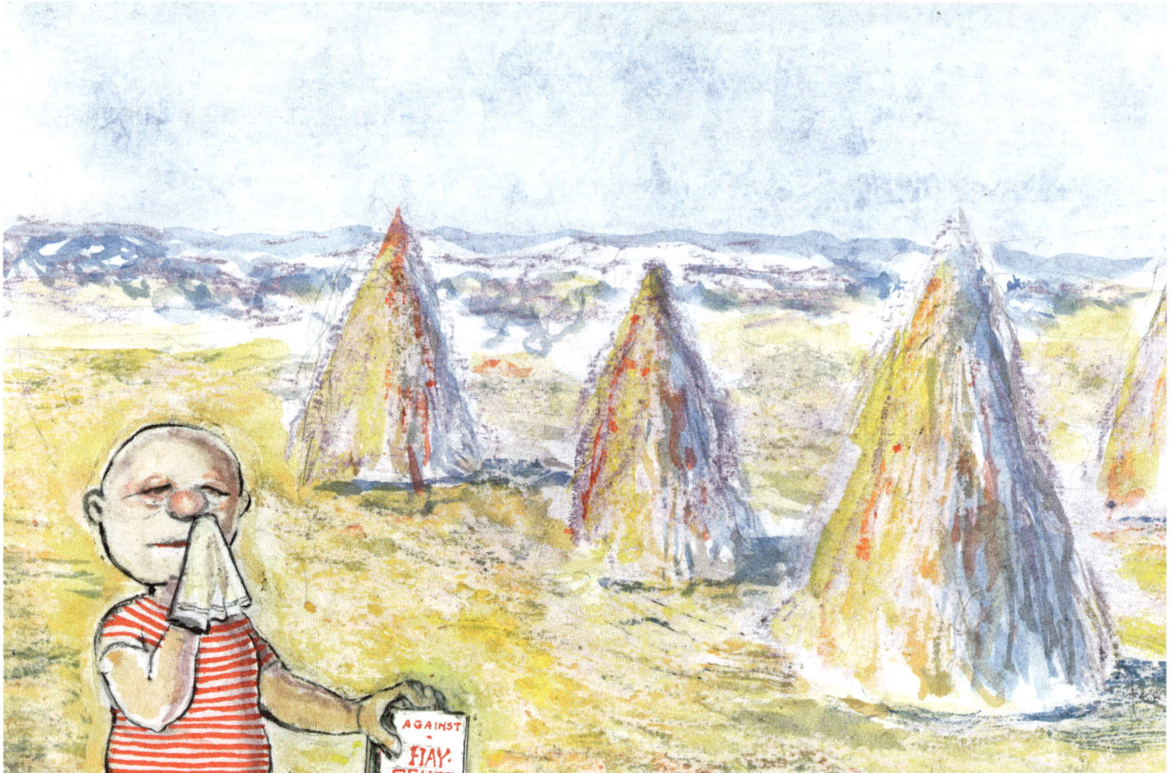

AGAINST
HAY-
FEVER

peintres, sculpteurs etc', which roughly translates to: 'The Anonymous Society of Artists, Painters, Sculptors, etc'. Ten days after the opening, the exhibition was visited by a critic from the satirical magazine *Charivari*. It was this critic who coined the term 'Impressionism', which the movement has been known as ever since. But the word was not meant kindly. Like many others, he made fun of this new way of painting, because, he believed, the pictures were not painted properly. Some blobs on a canvas were supposed to pass for a depiction of nature. He was not used to seeing this at the large, curated exhibitions, where everything was meticulously finished. Even a wallpaper draft would be more finished than one of these paintings, he wrote. After all, they were just 'impressions'.

But the way of painting was not the only thing new. The impressionists painted their own time. They did not look back in time to celebrate France's history, antiquity, the Bible, or Greek and Roman mythology, as their older colleagues did. It could happen, however, that they painted a Gothic cathedral, but then it was for the sake of light and colour, not for the architecture itself.

They sought to capture and preserve the light as it appeared at a specific place at a specific time of day. Such a painting should always be done in a moment, and the nature in the painting should be the same as that surrounding the artist when he worked on his picture. Thus, the impressionists became the first to depict the modern world.

Haystacks could also be part of this modern world. At the top, you see the haystacks as they could appear in France and in paintings by Claude Monet (1840–1926). Below, you have the stacks in the Scandinavian version. In both cases, it is the impressionist Monet whom our guide in art has followed out into nature and the fresh air.

Sailing up the river

If an impressionist and an expressionist were to sail down the same river in the same weather, they wouldn't experience the same thing. Instead, they would react completely differently to what was around them.

The impressionist would float along, sensing how the sunlight and the trees on the bank reflect in the water's surface. Throughout the journey, he would be in harmony with the nature around him. The expressionist, on the other hand, might already feel seasick from the start, afraid of drowning or fearing a storm. Because he always has something to struggle with. If it were not so, he would lack inspiration.

To simplify, Impressionism captures what is seen in the moment. In nature, the light changes with the time of day. If the sun is shining, for example, the leaves on the trees have a different green colour than if it is overcast. The clouds filter the light. As the light changes, so does the colour. That's why you sometimes need to rush more when painting impression-istically than if you were to paint in the old realistic style.

You also place more emphasis on getting the colour, light, and air right than on getting all the details. The air and atmosphere are what lie between you and nature.

If it's windy, you need to soften the forms a bit to better illustrate that something is trembling in the wind.

As far as impressions go, a quick sketch can often be more truthful than a large painting. The large painting requires much more time to complete because it is the sum of many moments of observation and work, whereas a sketch is more suitable for capturing the single moment. However, the boundaries between Impressionism and Expressionism are fluid; Monet's late works of the water lilies at Giverny contain elements of both.

Expressionism is what the painting tells about what is felt in the moment. And you best express your feelings by intensifying the colour and changing the forms. That way, the painting also tells us something about yourself. Only by bringing yourself and your temperament into the painting can you express your personal experience of the subject and the mood you were in when you painted your picture.

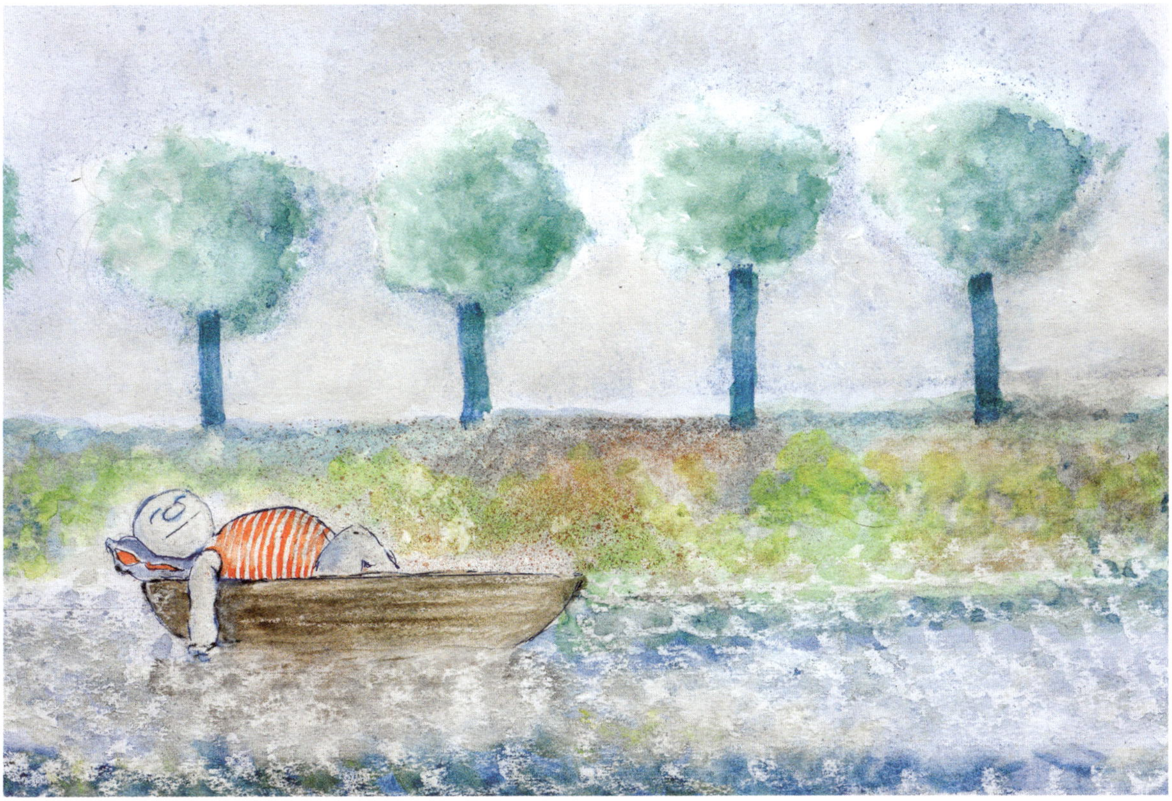

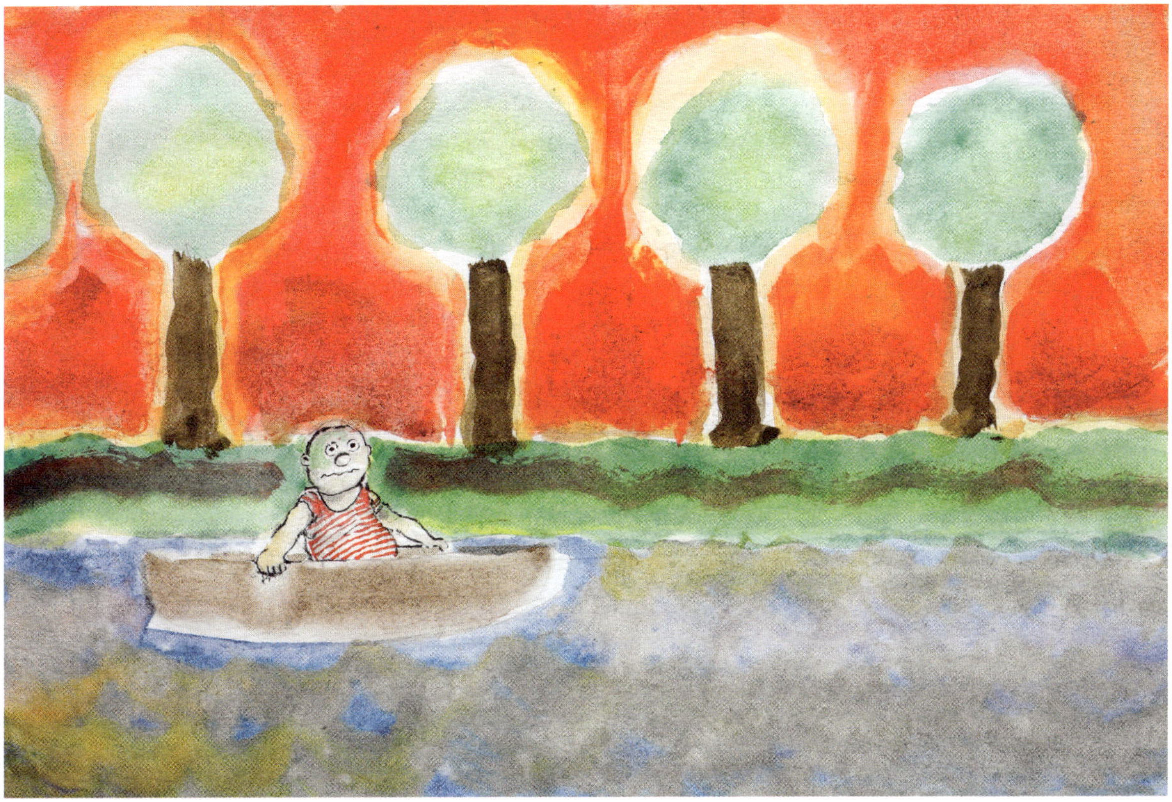

Vincent van Gogh

A star on the rise

As a unified movement, Expressionism first broke through in the early 20th century. By that time, the colours on the most important expressionist paintings had long dried. The Dutch painter Vincent van Gogh (1853–1890) became one of the great tragic figures of painting.

His short life was full of personal crises. While he lived, he only sold one painting. But just a few years after his death, his star began to rise, and continued to do so. Twenty-five years ago, one of his portraits, of Dr. Gachet, was sold at auction for approximately $67. If van Gogh had had any idea that it would go that way, his life might have looked very different.

In his work, van Gogh was not a typical expressionist, as he never painted from pure imagination. It was necessary for him to have the subject in front of him. His subjects were landscapes, places, people, flowers, and objects that he had a special connection to. It could be his old worn-out boots, some sunflowers, or himself. But he didn't copy what he saw. He transformed it, so the strong colours took on a special flowing quality. Van Gogh took a long time to realize that he should be an artist. But once he got started, his energy and intensity were unparalleled. Over the course of just ten years, he completed about 800 paintings and just as many drawings.

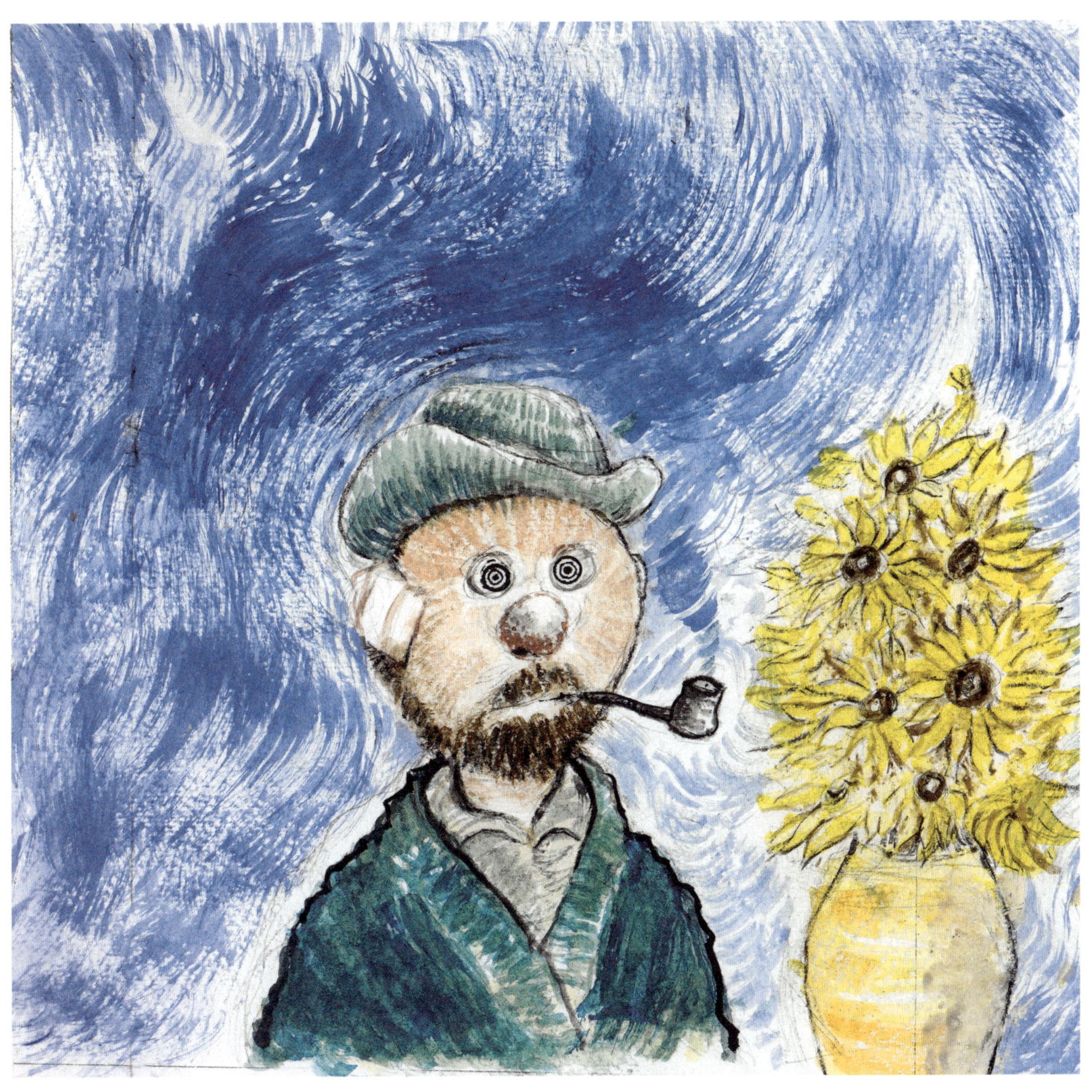

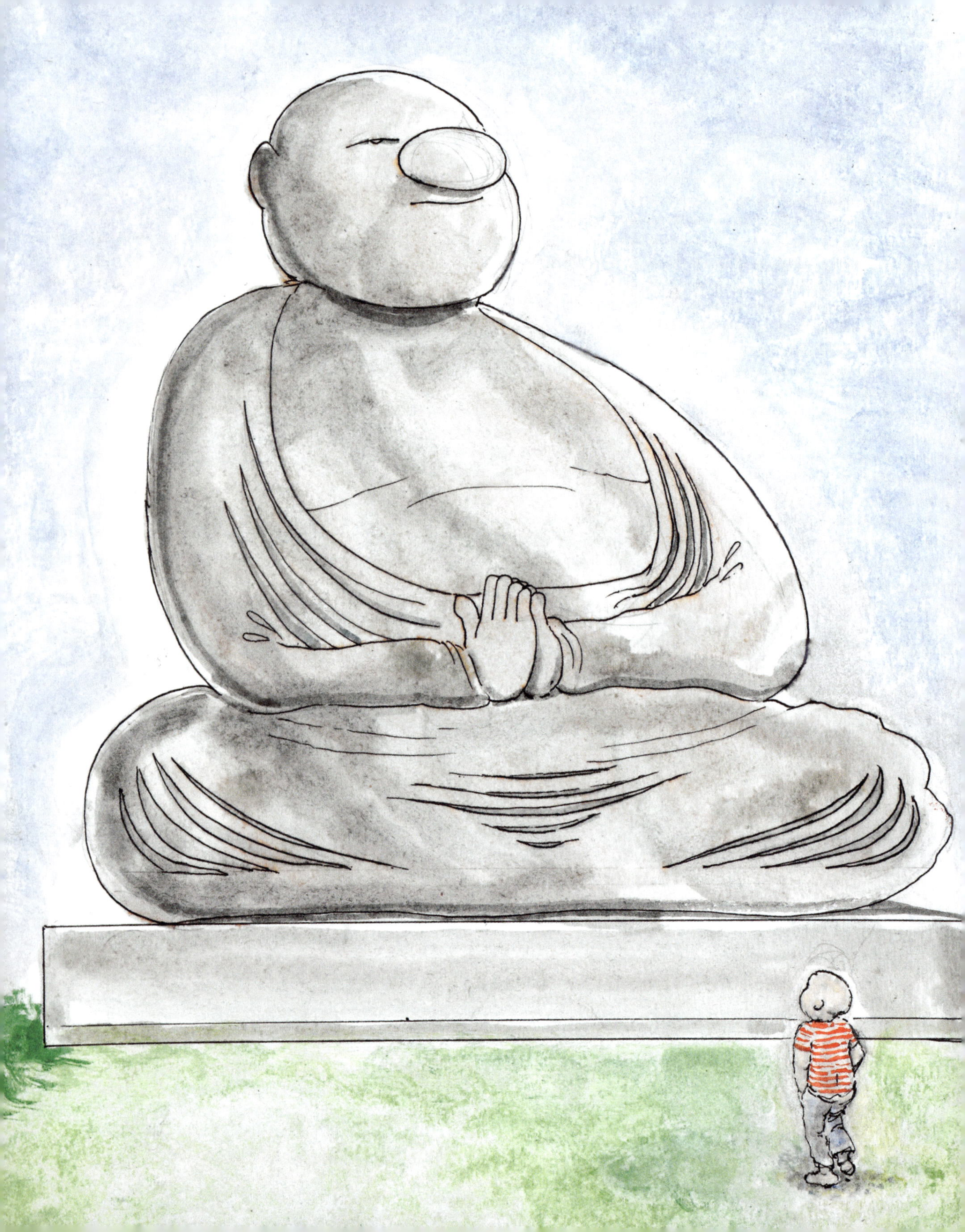

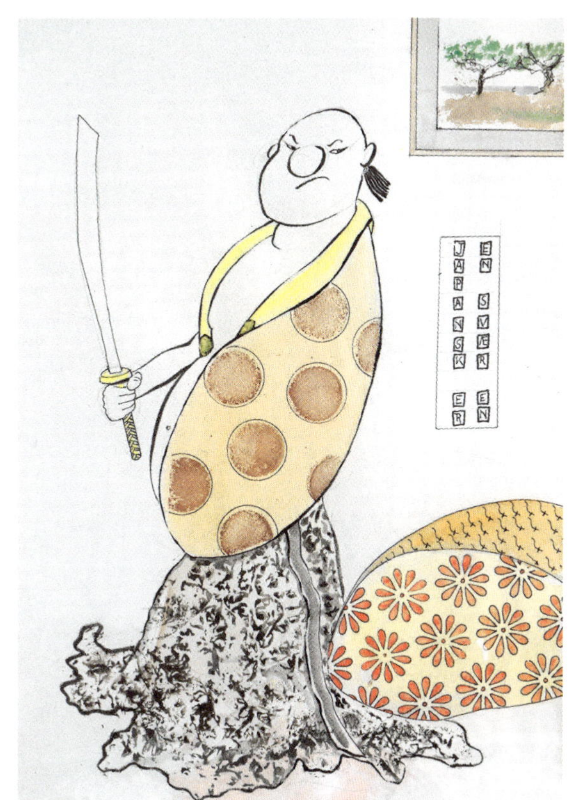

Japanese art

The great
Buddha figure

Sculptures in stone or bronze don't travel as easily as works on paper, and if they're really large, they don't move from their place at all. To experience a figure like the fifteen-meter-high Buddha from Kamakura, dating back to 1252, one must travel to Japan. In the 19th century, very few European artists – if any – had the opportunity to do so. If they knew such works, it could only be through photographs. However, Japanese drawings and woodcuts came to Europe in large quantities, where young artists collected them and were inspired by their unique expression.

The Japanese didn't focus much on perspective, and their way of drawing a figure wasn't like what European artists learned at art academies in Europe. The Japanese emphasized the decorative aspect. But the French impressionists learned from their unique use of the picture plane, and so did van Gogh. For a picture could be beautiful as an ornament. It didn't need to pretend to be spatial when it was flat anyway.

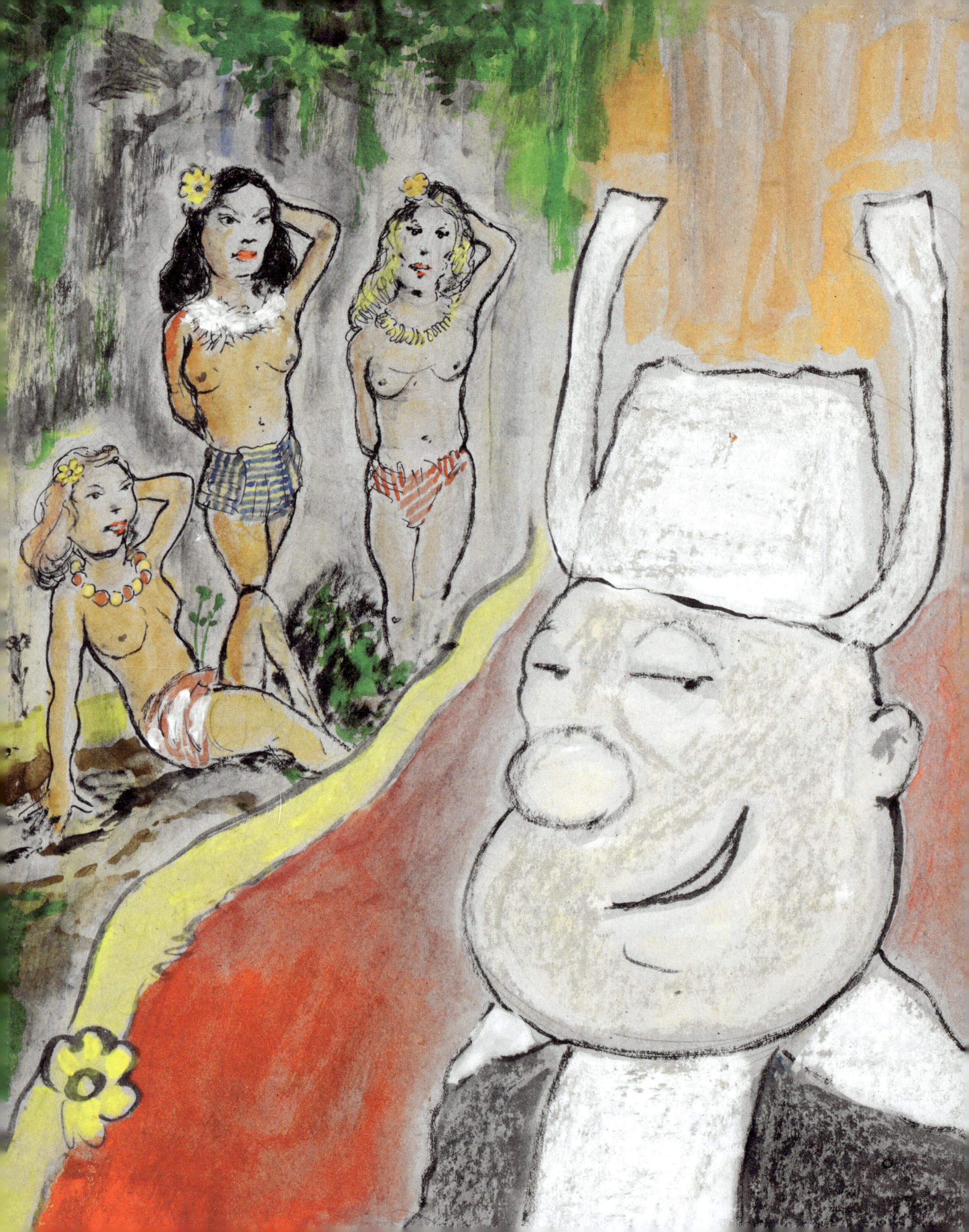

Paul Gauguin

Goodbye Europe and European art

Do you know the story of the artist who gives up everything – family and friends, and homeland – in order to realize what is most important to him: his art? This story fits the French painter Paul Gauguin (1848–1903), who cut all ties to become a completely innovative artist. He started as a stockbroker in Paris and married a Danish woman named Mette Gad. But as Gauguin became more convinced that he should be an artist, he left everything behind to seek new challenges. His attitude was: to find the path to a new and true art, one had to leave Paris, the capital of classical art with all its conventions and traditions. Therefore, he first settled in Brittany.

The strange hat worn by the man in the picture is inspired by the local headgear in this French region. Later, Gauguin decided to seek inspiration in so-called primitive art – a term previ-

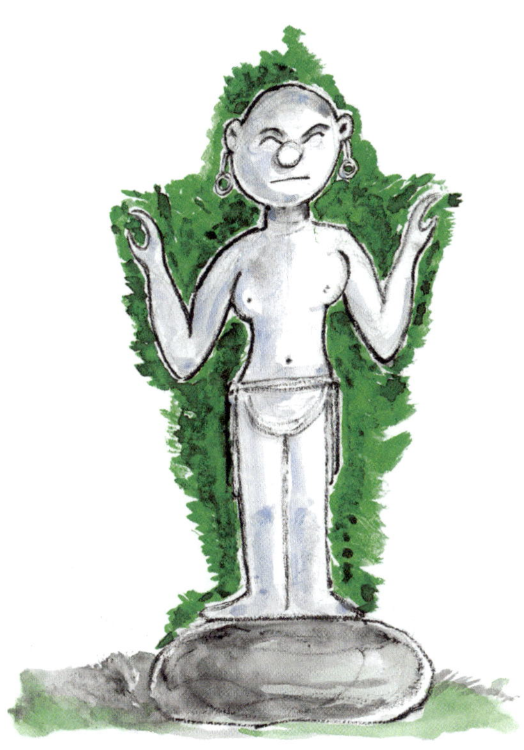

ously used to describe very old Western art and art from non-Western societies – and he therefore travelled as far from France as he could, including to Tahiti and the South Seas. As one can guess from many of Gauguin's motifs, women played a significant role in his life. He depicted them not only in the exotic surroundings where he might have been the only Frenchman but also portrayed their beliefs – and superstitions. For he wanted to live – and be – like a native among other natives.

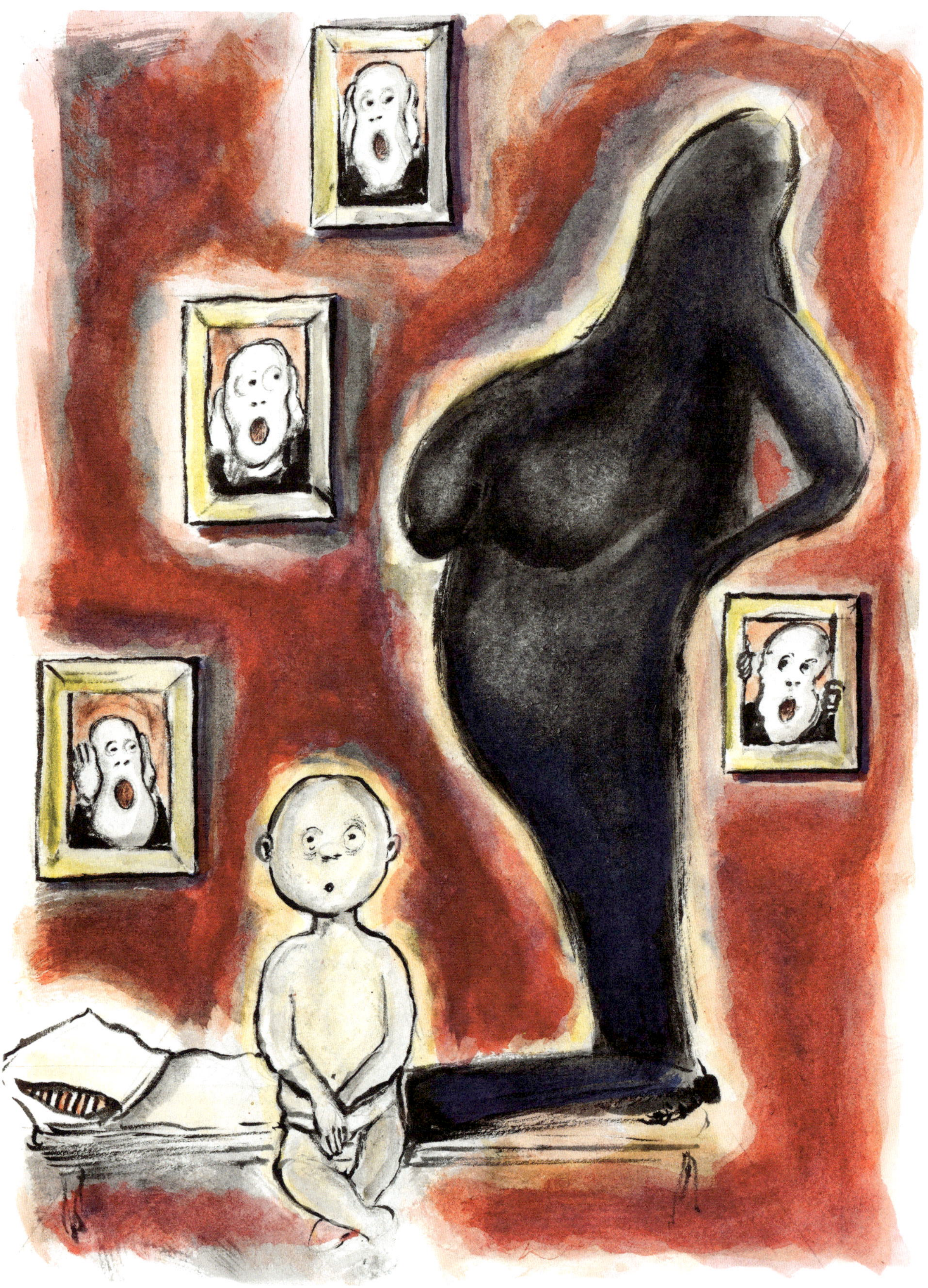

Edvard Munch

A master of depicting anxiety

The expressionist creates art of expression. When an expressionist wants to depict nature, it is the human inner nature that he seeks to express. For the expressionist is both in close combat with his own nature and with the great nature surrounding him. At no time does he seem more exposed and fragile than when darkness falls, and he is alone with his thoughts and imaginings. Then anxiety begins to take hold. That is why the Norwegian painter Edvard Munch (1863–1944), in picture after picture, focuses on the evening moods and summer nights, where nature becomes like a projection screen. It is a screen that mirrors the melancholic emotional life of humans.

If the expressionist is afraid of passion and love, his anxiety can take the form of a large woman overshadowing him. With the expressionist, anxiety and passion are always visible. It is evident both in the colouration and the forms he describes using colours. That's how we see anxiety depicted here. And that's also how we see anxiety depicted in Munch's work. He is perhaps the most important artist in the Nordic region. And he is one of those artists whose work lends itself to a biographical approach. That is, the idea that by learning about Munch's life, we understand his art better. When he was very young, he lost his mother, and only a few years later his older sister, then his father and his brother. He was left to himself and the fear of death and the world surrounding him. It is this anxiety, more than anything, that he has depicted in his paintings.

The entire family on a vase

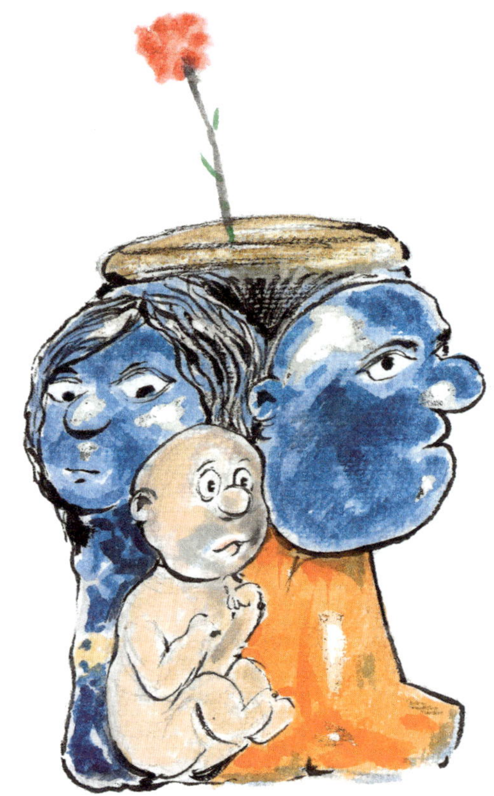

In art, every new 'ism' arises as a reaction to an older 'ism' that has had its heyday. This was the case with Neoclassicism, which followed after the Baroque and Rococo periods, and with Realism, which followed after Romanticism. And so it was with Symbolism, which emerged right after Realism.

The new style broke with the notion that art could only depict what the artist had seen or felt themselves. That was too unimaginative. With Symbolism, it wasn't enough for an artwork to simply show something. It also had to mean something.

Put another way: a symbolist work must by no means resemble a police report. In such a report, the description must be as close to the event as possible. Instead, an artwork could be like a poem. It had to embody an idea, and that idea could reflect the artist's stance on art and life. Lines, shapes, and colours shouldn't just describe something recognizable. It was much more important that they formed a cohesive whole and had their own significance.

This meant that the artist had to imbue the forms with symbolic meaning. Furthermore, they had to ensure that these forms were staged in a decorative manner. In 'Family Vase' from 1891, the Danish artist J. F. Willumsen (1863–1958) freely imagined his own family. It consists of the mother, Juliette Meyer (Willumsen's first wife), the father, who is Willumsen himself – and between them, the child, here shown as our guide in art. Only the child is depicted in full figure and has a colour resembling skin. He is portrayed realistically, unlike the mother and father. You can't see anything of them other than a part of the lower body. Of the father, you can barely discern an orange foot. And they both have blue faces. The parental couple has been stylized to the point that they don't even look like they belong to the same family as the child.

The art of contemplation

The figure sitting here pondering has been doing so for over 100 years. Because of this contemplation, the sculpture has become very popular. There is always a good reason to ponder things. 'The Thinker' was created by the French sculptor Auguste Rodin (1840–1917), and he was influenced by Michelangelo, at least when he made this sculpture. Originally, it was supposed to be one of the

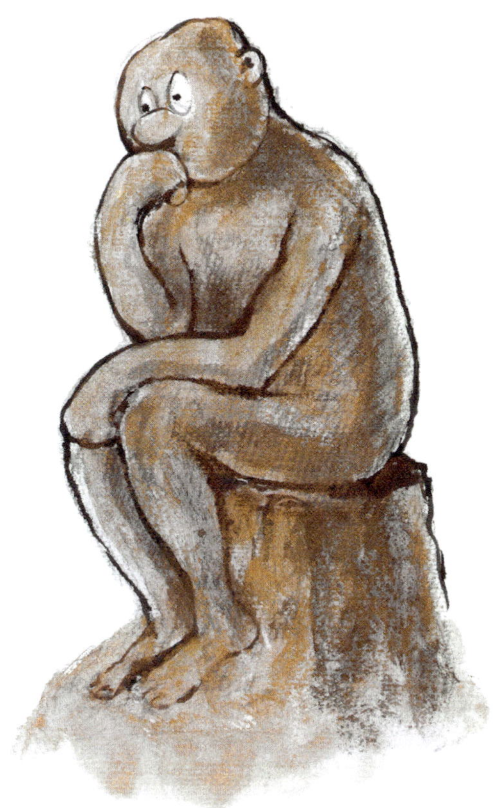

many figures in 'The Gates of Hell'. But then Rodin, like his figure, pondered carefully and decided that he also wanted to create his figure as a free-standing sculpture, which was a good idea. Today, there are 28 large versions of Rodin's statue, placed all over the world. This is the 29th edition, and it only exists on paper in this book. Our guide in art is also lost in thought, perhaps about the future of art or just his own.

The expulsion from Paradise

Because Symbolism had grown weary of
Realism and its depictions of a reality only
visible to the naked eye, it drew its motifs,
for example, from history, mythology, or
the Bible. Much of the earlier art had also
drawn inspiration from these sources since
medieval times. Therefore, the symbolists
were not afraid to delve into the past. And
they didn't shy away from telling a moralizing story. One was always allowed to learn
from the older artists. But the symbolists
took it a step further than the ancients and
placed extra emphasis on the decorative
aspects.

With the 'Expulsion from Paradise', a motif
that many artists have painted over time,
and which could be represented like this, we
are as close to the Bible as one can get. For
the story unfolds at the beginning of the Old
Testament, just after Earth, the animals,
and Adam and Eve have been created. It
tells of how God had forbidden the first
humans in the Garden of Eden to eat from
the Tree of Knowledge. And what did they
do? They ate from the tree. First, the serpent tempted Eve to do so, and then Eve
tempted Adam to do the same. We don't
know how much they ate. Judging by the
picture, it was more than one fruit. But we
know from the Bible that they could not
hide their sin. Therefore, they were both
expelled from the Garden of Eden by a
cherub, which is an angel with a flaming
sword. That's what we see in the picture
here. But the serpent was not expelled. It
was only commanded to crawl on the
ground and eat dust all its days.

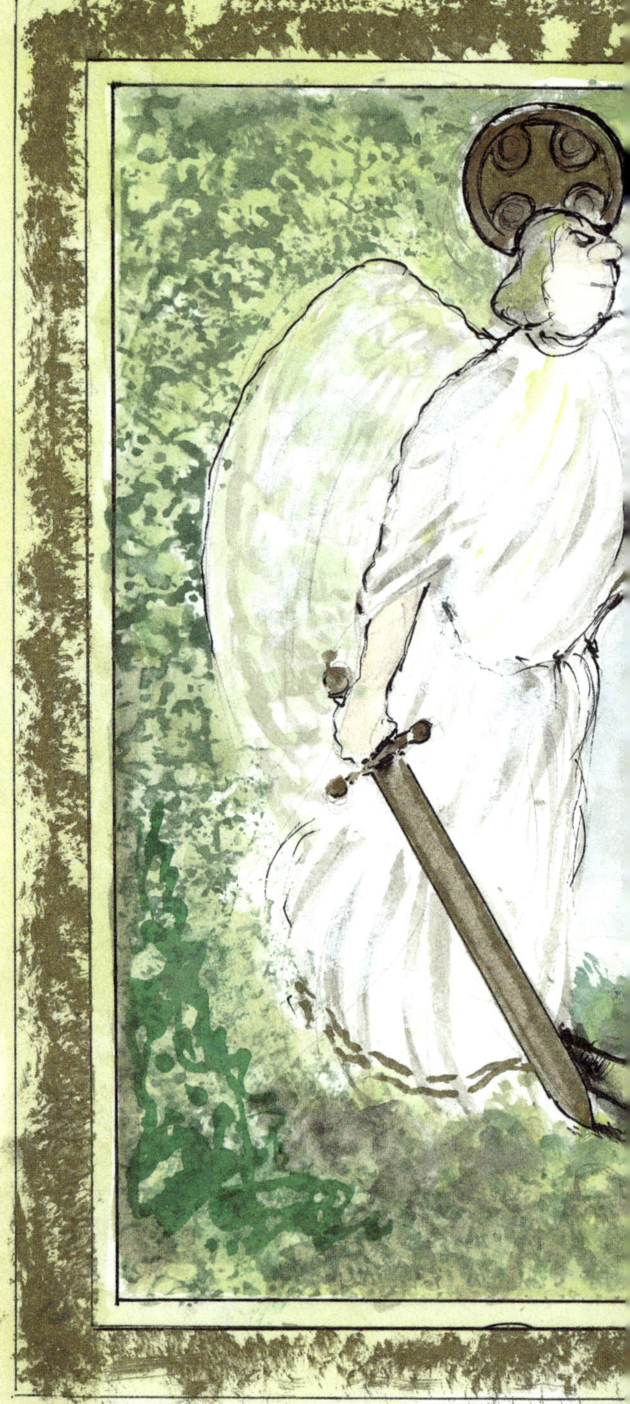

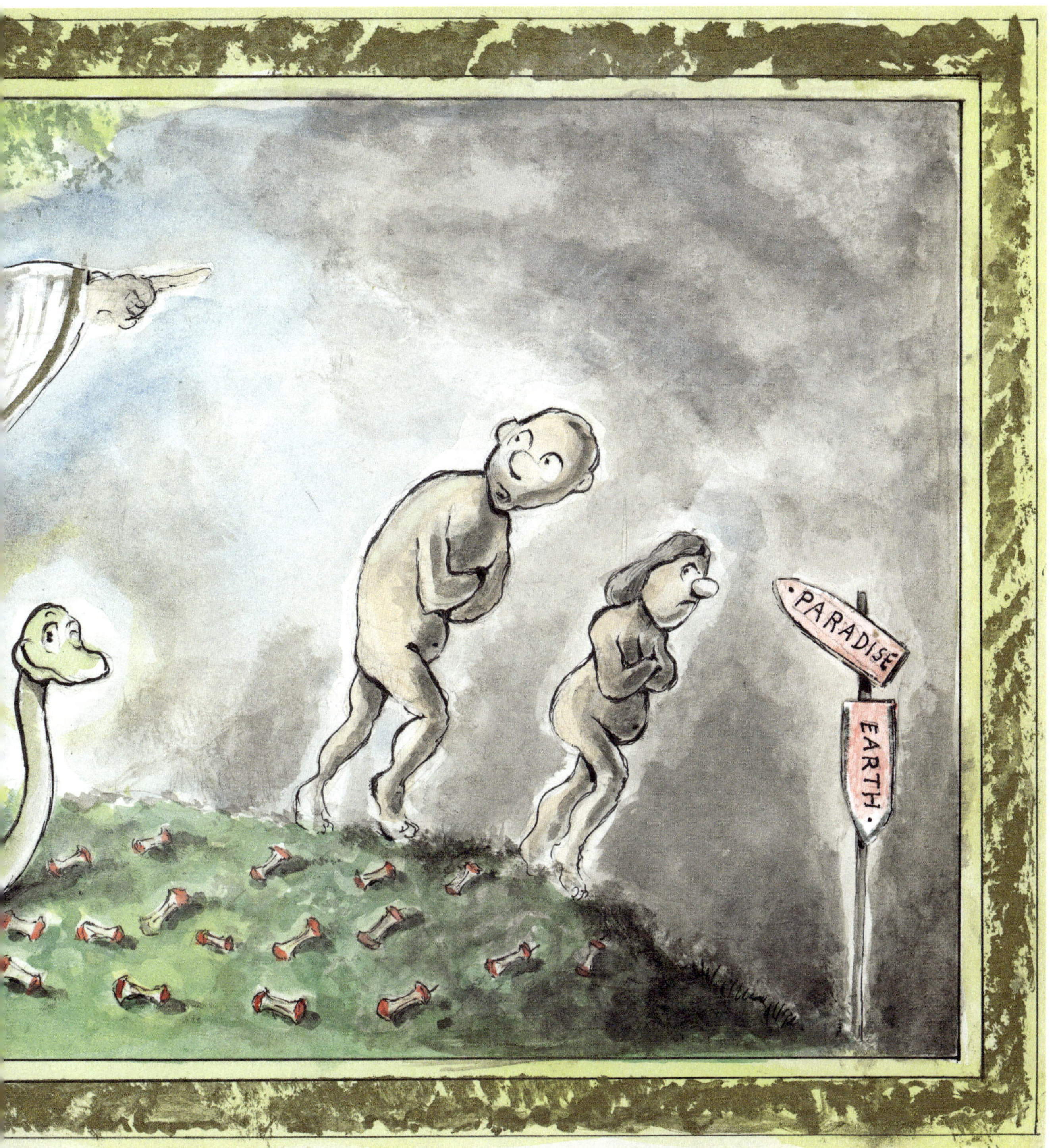

PARADISE
EARTH

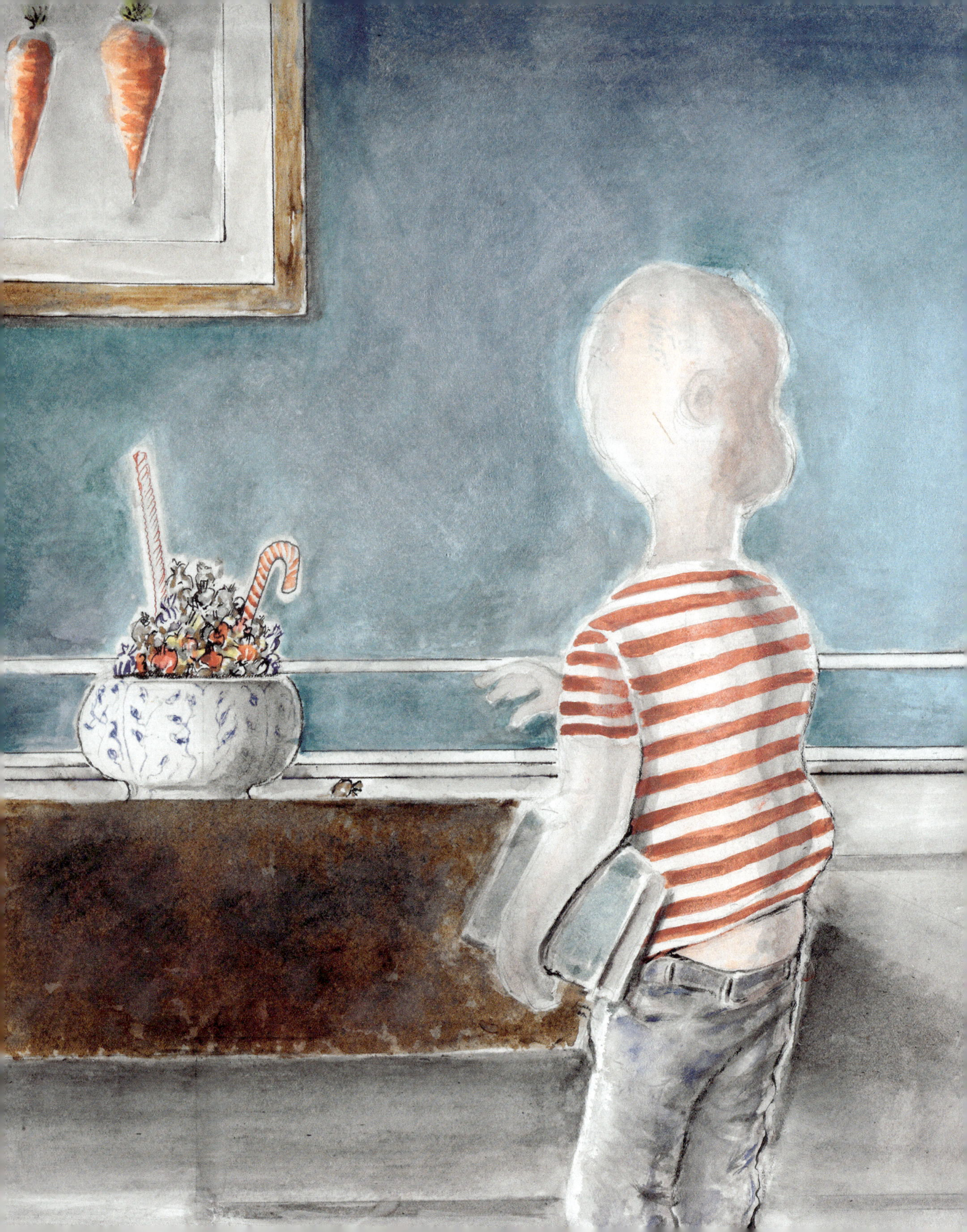

Vilhelm Hammershøi

Does a painting have to be about something?

The painter of quiet interiors, as Danish Vilhelm Hammershøi (1864–1916) is often called, was quiet about everything. He minded his own business – and his painting – and wasn't swayed by anyone or anything.

When he had the chance to gain attention abroad, he wasn't interested. Other things mattered more to him. We simply can't know for sure what this was as he managed to destroy all the letters and documents that could have given us insight into his personal life and the secrets that his paintings themselves don't reveal. For example, art historians can't agree on how much symbolism is hidden in Hammershøi's motifs. The only thing they can agree on is that his paintings don't resemble anyone else's. Their colour scheme is subdued and more limited than other contemporary artists', dominated by shades of grey. There aren't always people present in his paintings either. And when there are, they often have their backs turned to us.

His paintings aren't meant as portraits. In fact, it's hard to say for sure what they're about, or if they're about anything other than lines, planes, and the balance between different objects, much like some of the abstract painters such as the contemporary Wassily Kandinsky (1866–1944).

If Hammershøi had seen the painting to the right of this text, he would have shaken his bearded head, because it shows a boy trying to sneak some candy from the candy bowl on the table, but he looks around before doing so. So, it *is* about something.

You can try comparing it with a very similar composition, 'Interior with a Young Woman Seen from Behind'. The painter of quiet interiors would never paint something as mundane as stealing candy. He also didn't paint children. The reason wasn't just that he and his wife, Ida Hammershøi, whom he often used as a model, didn't have children themselves. No, he was only interested in drawing and painting figures that could stand as still as statues in the interiors where he lived.

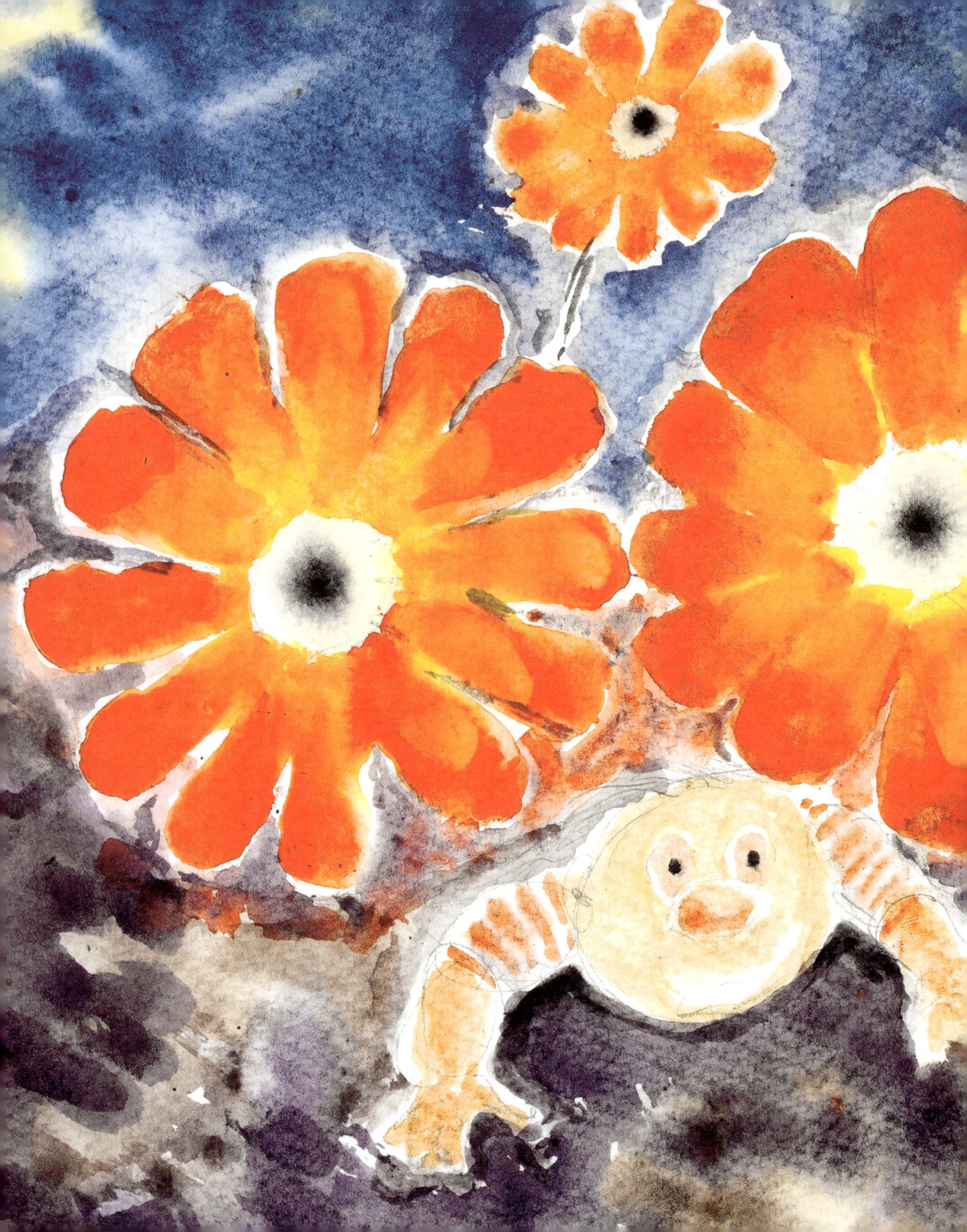

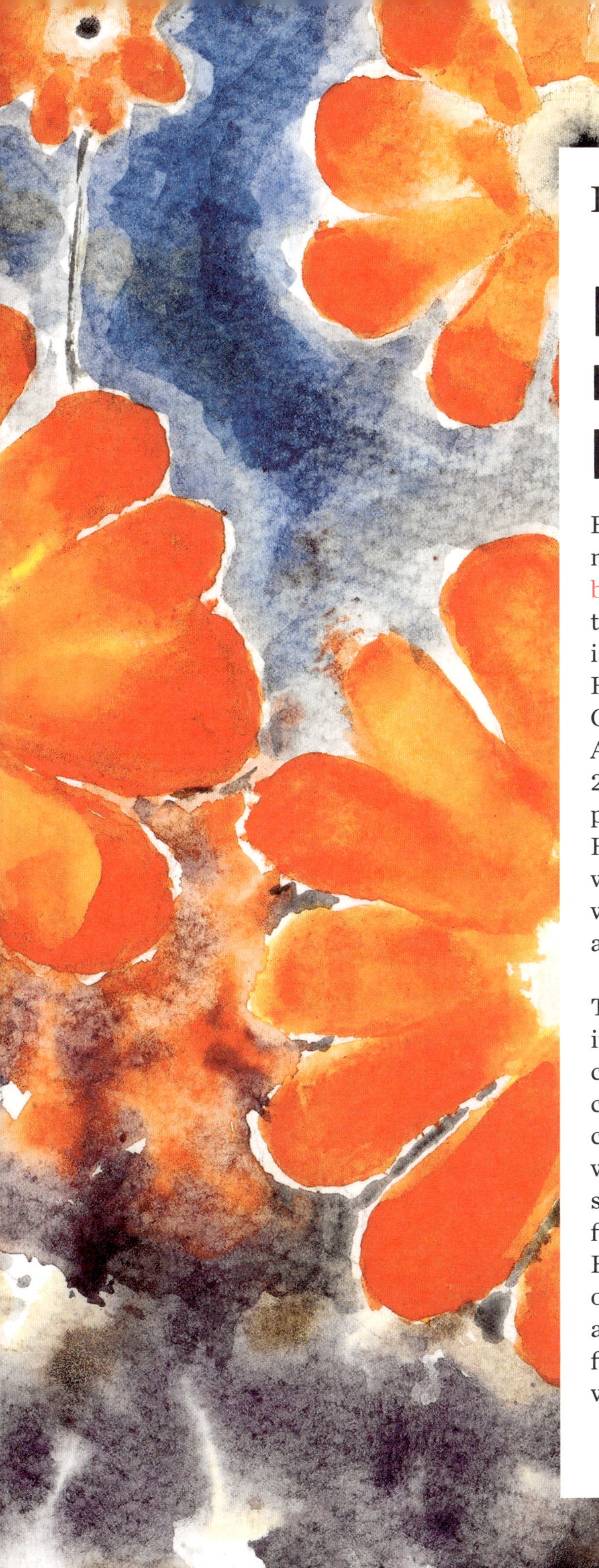

Back to the raw form and pure colour

Emil Nolde (1867–1956) painted many religious motifs. However, that didn't make him a symbolist. He was very much an expressionist, one of the last great ones. What also characterizes Nolde is his fascination with non-Western peoples' art. He had seen this kind of art when travelling from Germany, where he lived, to, among other places, Asia and the South Seas (Oceania) in the early 20th century. These travel impressions didn't push our artist to a place he hadn't been before. He was already somewhat of a primitive, an artist who hadn't received much formal training and who worked directly and roughly with form and colour.

The experience confirmed Nolde in his belief that if great passions were to fill a painting so that it could be seen and felt, one must not skimp on colours. The colours and shapes shouldn't recount what one had seen and observed, but rather what one had felt upon observation. This expressionism was later applied by the artist to his flower motifs, initially executed as watercolours. Here too, it was the colour that set the agenda. If one were a bit timid by nature, like our guide in art, one could become quite frightened by Nolde's flowers. For they were – and still are – overwhelming.

Paul Cézanne

Sphere, cone, cylinder

At the forefront of the
picture stand three shapes: a
sphere, a cone, and a cylinder, three figures
from solid geometry. According to the stern man
behind these forms, Paul Cézanne (1839–1906), one cannot create space in a painting without them. And without
Cézanne, the stylistic movement known as Cubism would hardly
have existed. He has also been called the father of 20th-century
modern art.

It wasn't because he hung out with the impressionists. He didn't have much
regard for the fleeting and restless manner in which they painted their surroundings. He exhibited with them only twice. He also didn't live in Paris but
kept to himself in Aix in south-eastern France. There, he painted the same
motifs over and over again, to delve deeper into their secrets. Drawing inspiration from nature, he sought structure and solid composition, which he could
only find in classical art displayed in major art museums. Therefore, he said,
'I want to make something solid and lasting out of Impressionism – like
the art in museums.' The young artists admired him from a respectful
distance, especially in the last decade of his life. For Cézanne was not
one to socialize. He also didn't sell many paintings during his
lifetime. But when you're the son of a wealthy banker, that
doesn't matter much. Cézanne was completely independent. But not just financially. He was artistically independent, and that was his
greatest strength.

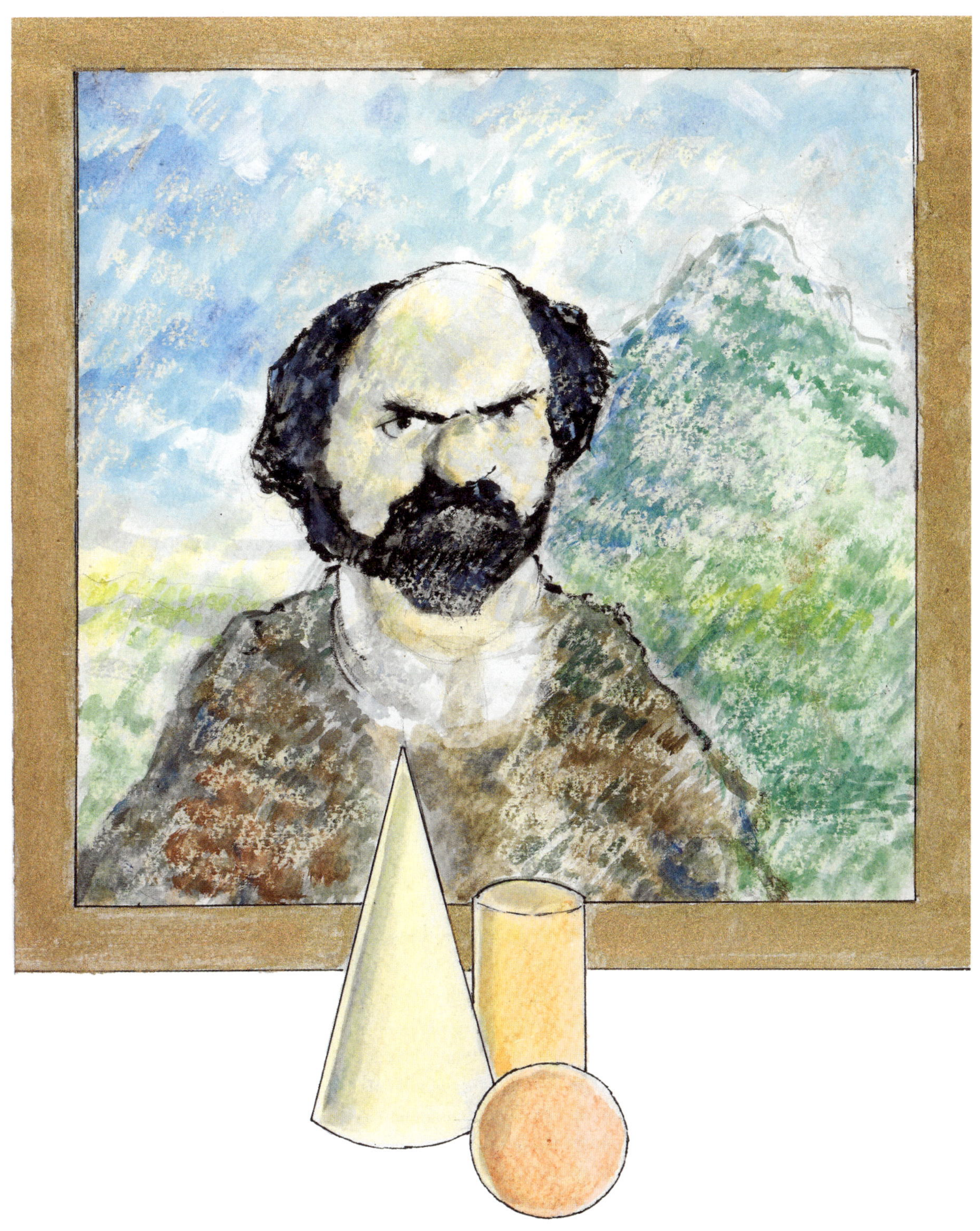

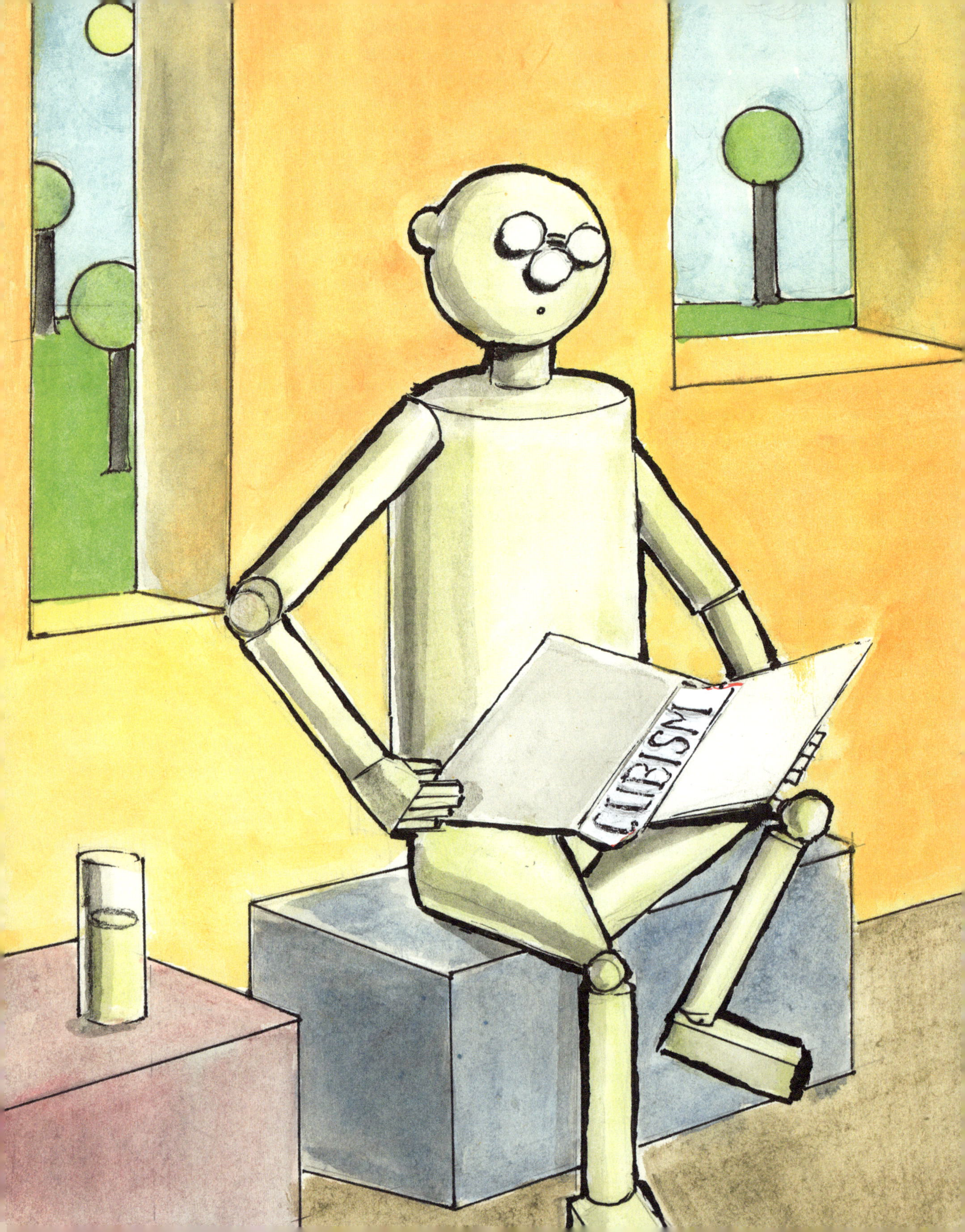

CUBISM

With arms like drainpipes

Just a year after Cézanne had closed his marvellous eyes, the two artists Pablo Picasso (1881–1973) and Georges Braque (1882–1963) noticed how they could further develop Cézanne's way of painting. The result was Cubism.

And Cubism was a completely new way of thinking about painting. Unlike the impressionists and the expressionists, the cubists didn't paint what they saw or felt when encountering nature, but rather what they knew about the forms of nature. For example, that these forms could be simplified into simple spatial things, as you see in the picture to the left: Instead of trying to paint something resembling reality, the man's body and his surroundings are simplified into geometric shapes.

The cubists also didn't pay much attention to linear perspective, which had influenced almost all art since the Renaissance, because linear perspective required the artist to stand still while painting their subject. The cubists, on the other hand, constantly moved around and showed in their paintings that in a modern painting, an object could often be seen from multiple angles. For if one knew how both the front and back of a thing looked, why shouldn't both be shown?

Pablo Picasso

The man who mastered all styles

The Spanish artist Pablo Picasso once asserted that every child is an artist, by which he meant that as children, we still possess a special spontaneity and immediacy. And then he added, 'The problem is how to remain an artist once we grow up.'

Because when the typical artist grows up, they want to improve and learn from others. But when one insists on learning from others, one can become rigid or stagnant. Picasso had his own personal solution to the problem, and that solution couldn't be copied by others. It consisted of him painting better, more ingeniously than almost any academy-trained artist, even as a child. It was only as an adult that Picasso consciously turned towards his own beginnings and developed his intuitive or 'childlike' style. After this early period, he was influenced by the artists who either followed the

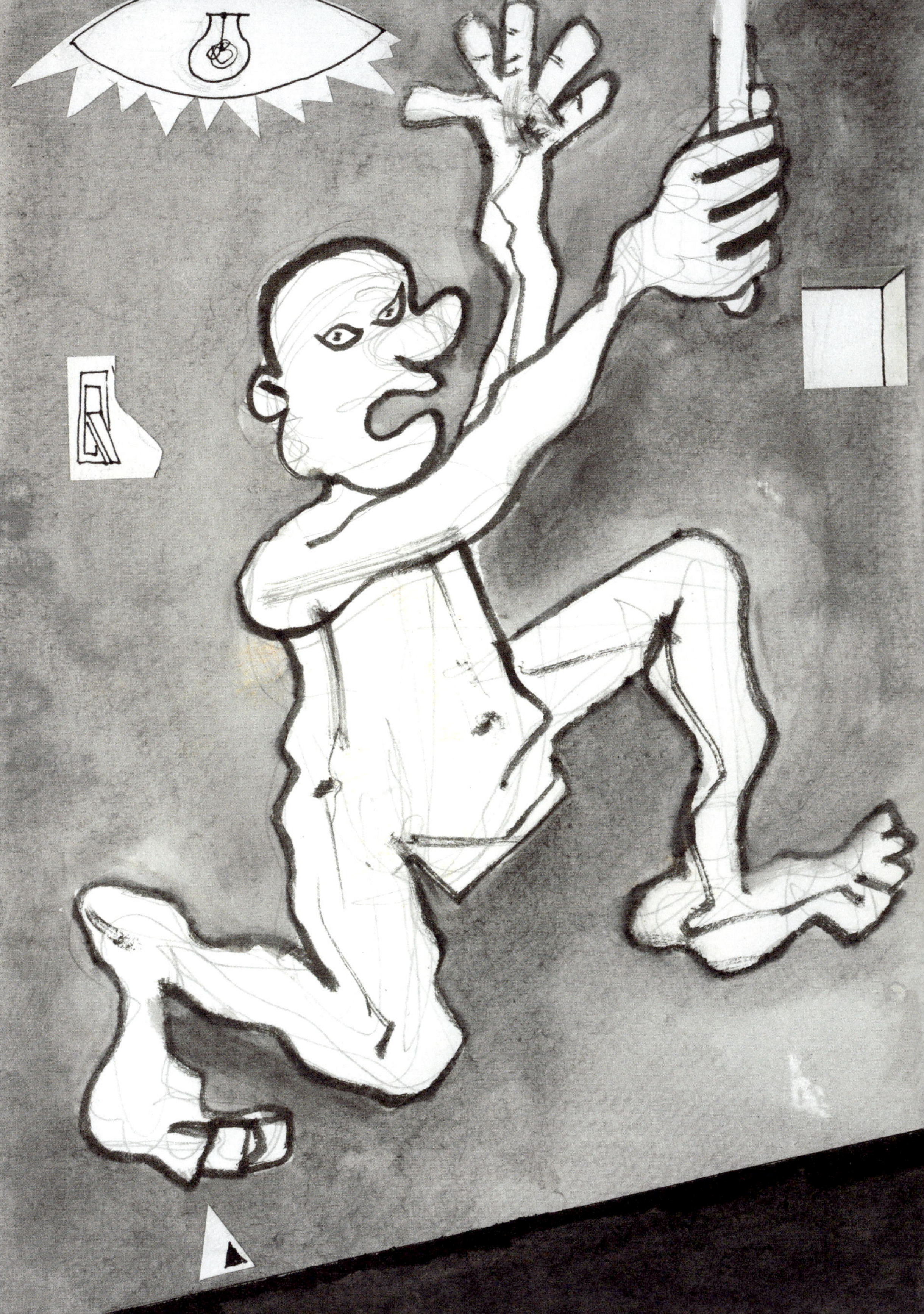

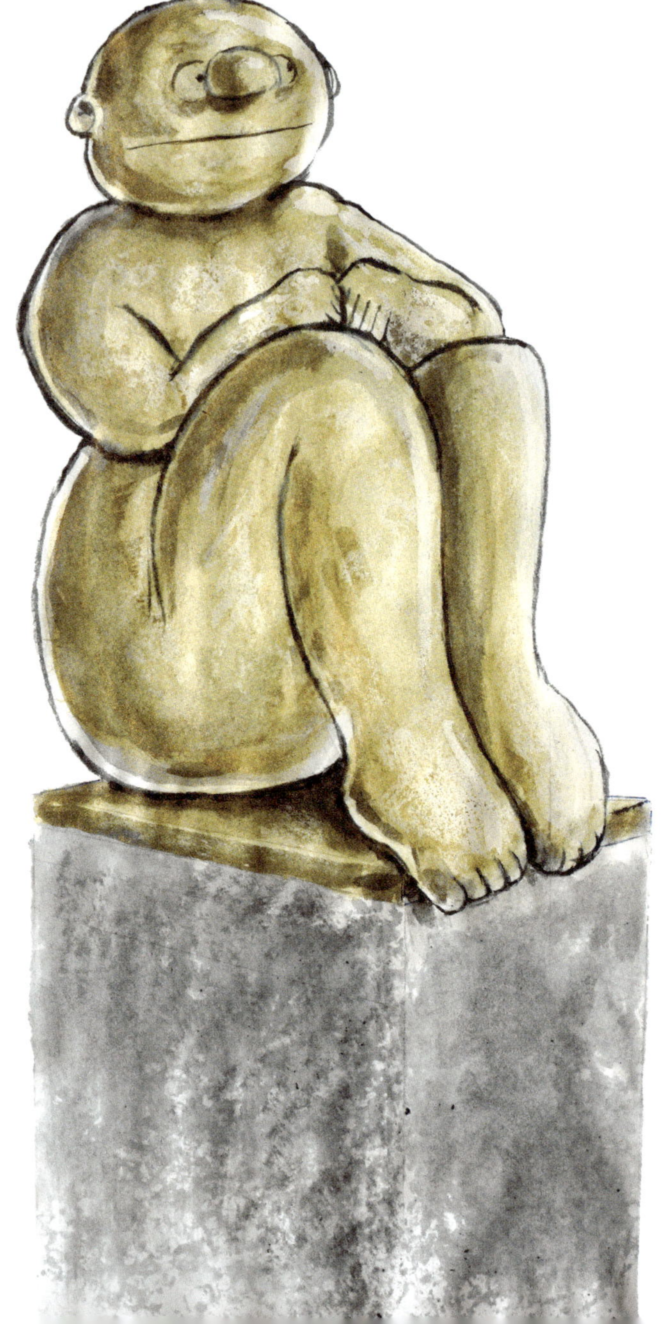

impressionists or reacted against what they stood for. Then came his so-called blue period, then his rose period, and finally his cubist phase, which gave him his first major breakthrough.

Here, he merged his own fragmented perception of space with inspiration from African masks: 'I paint objects as I imagine them, not as I see them'.

Picasso kept evolving until he almost couldn't anymore. 'For I always do that which I cannot do, in order for me to learn how to do it'. All in all, he became the most dominant artist of the 20th century, mastering most of its styles.

In contrast to Henri Matisse (1869–1954), whom you can read about later in this book, Picasso never opened a painting school. Nevertheless, his art has had enormous significance. From the beginning of his career, he became a role model and a beacon for an entire era.

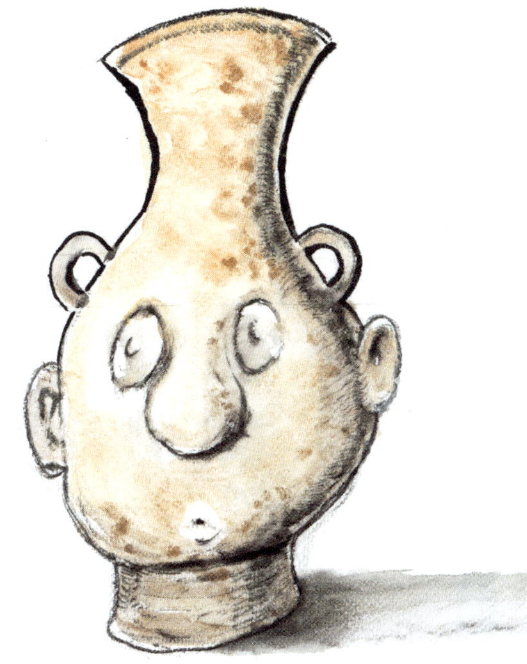

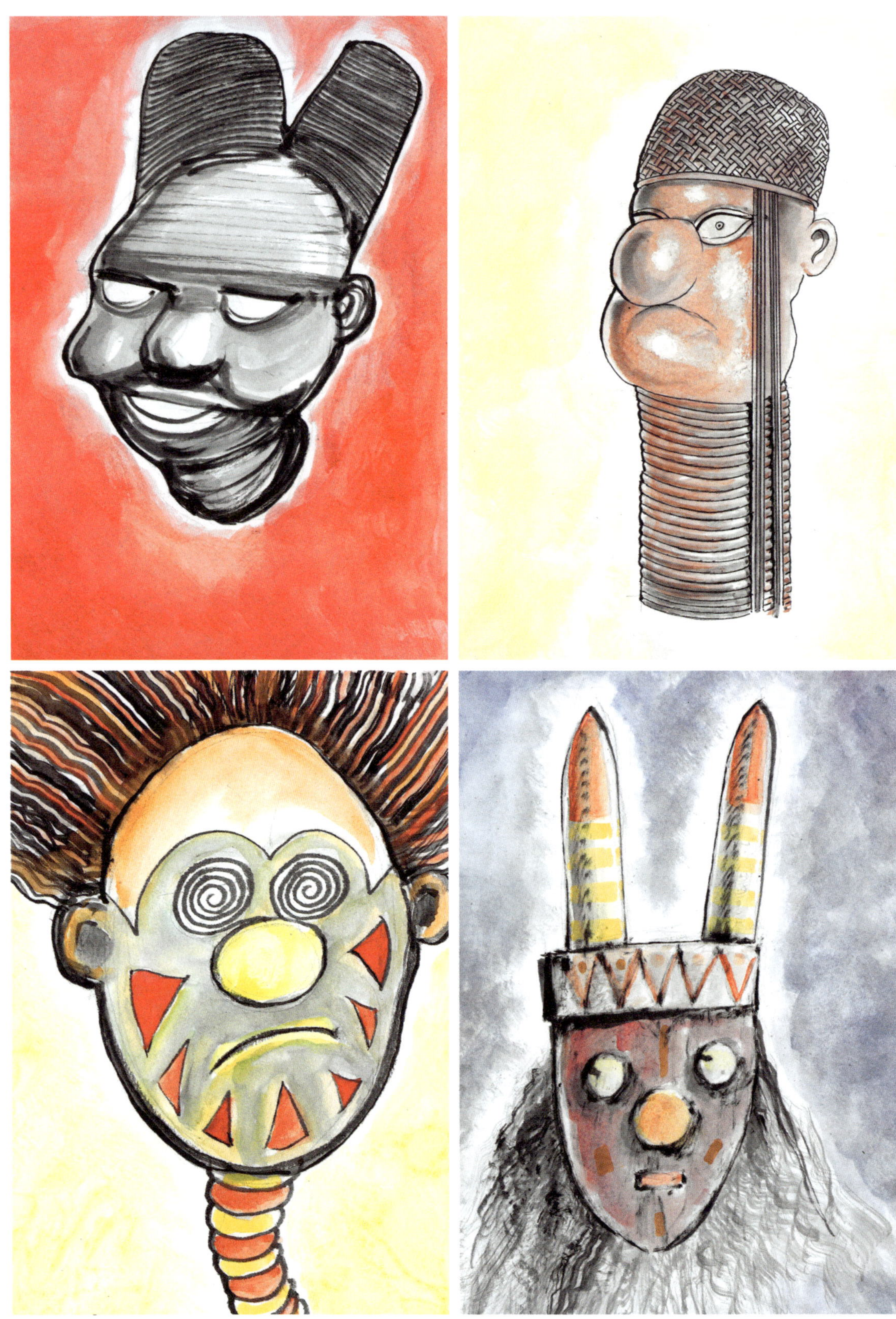

Lots of masks

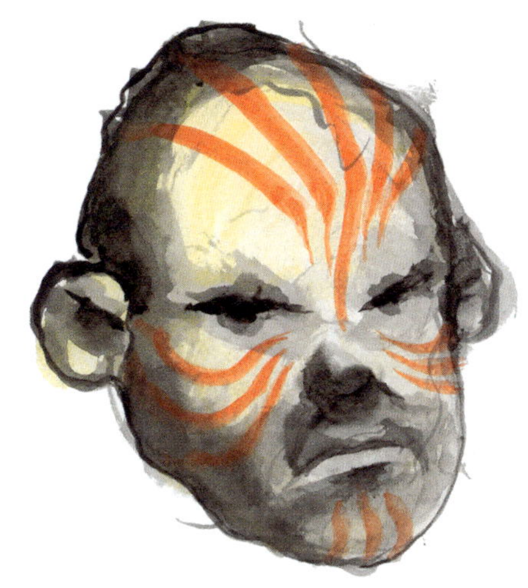

Much of 20th-century European art would have looked different if it weren't for the art created outside of Europe. Take African art, for example. If it hadn't been for African mask art, Cubism – and Picasso's breakthrough at the beginning of the century – would have missed its most important source of inspiration. The same goes for the movement we call Cobra, which emerged forty years after Cubism.

It wasn't until the end of the 19th century and the beginning of the following century that some artists became aware that other parts of the world, such as the African continent, also had a rich production of art.

Modernists were inspired by the different visual language, which didn't resemble anything one was used to seeing in European art museums. Yet, few knew the function and significance of the African masks and figures. African artefacts can be found in ethnographic museums, and it was here and in a few scattered private collections that artists sought them out to learn from these 'artists' who had never attended any academy.

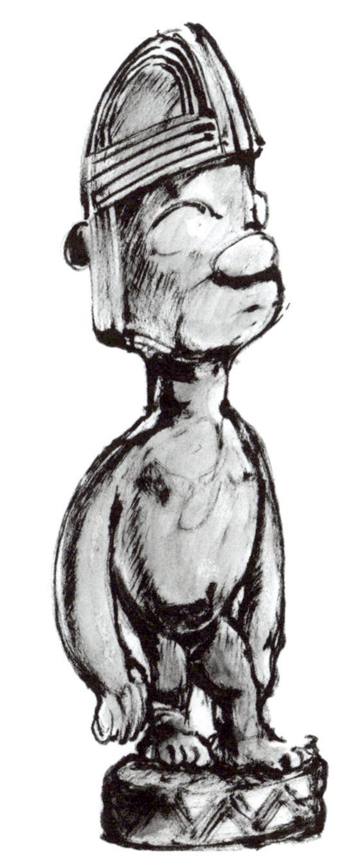

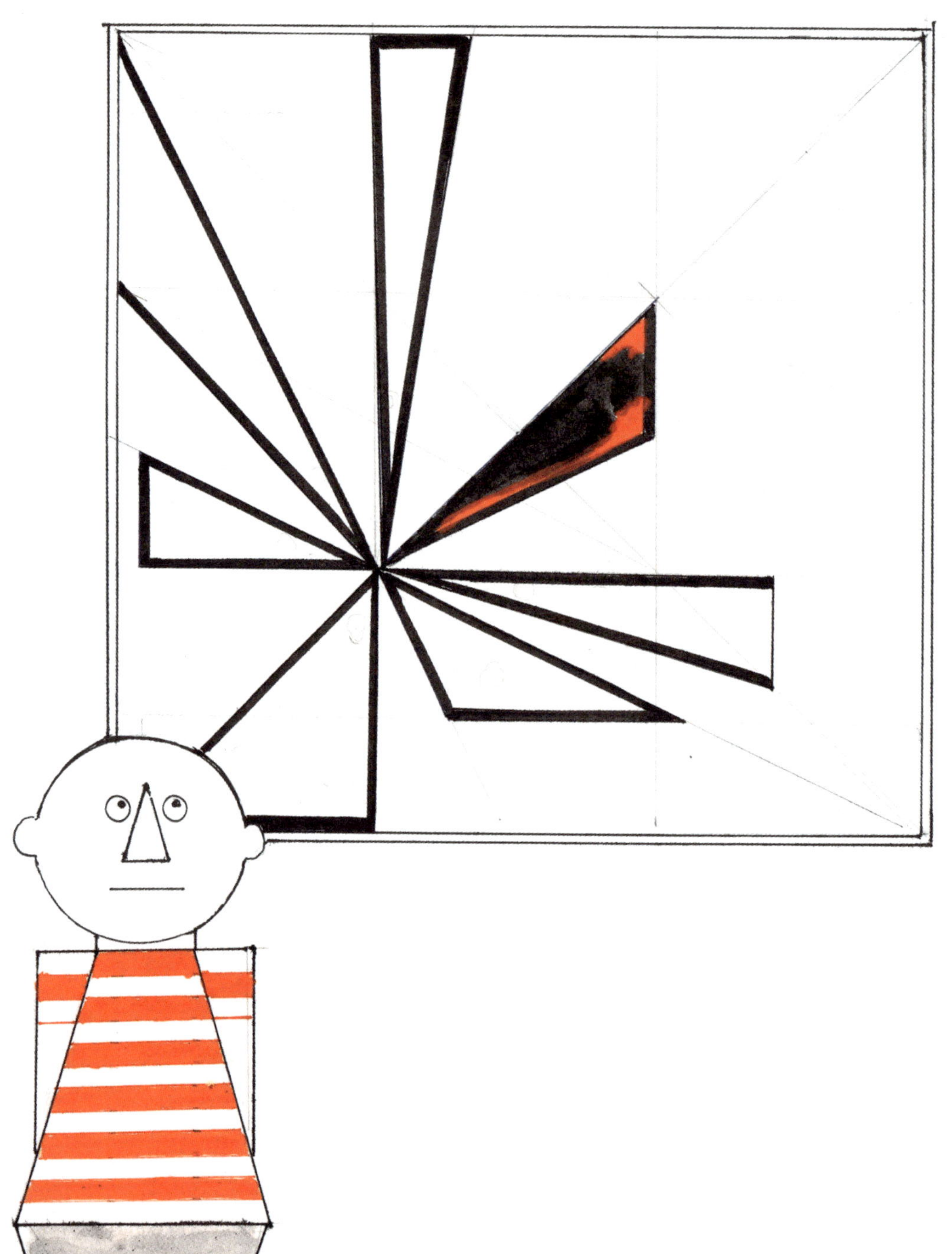

Who took the first step?

Determining who painted the first abstract painting in the history of art requires more than a snapshot and a stopwatch. There were a couple of earlier attempts. The Englishman J. M. W. Turner came close in the 19th century, although it was never his intention to break free from what he saw. The great Swedish author and occasional painter August Strindberg (1849–1912) also came close in some paintings. But in the first decades of the 20th century, several different artists began to seriously explore how to paint a picture that didn't depict anything.

The Russian Wassily Kandinsky painted a rather abstract painting as early as 1910, so he could be considered the first. But his compatriot Kazimir Malevich (1878–1935) and the Dutchman Piet Mondrian (1872–1944) were right on his heels.

Striking a balance

Wassily Kandinsky (1866–1944) was once destined for a promising career in law, but in 1896, he interrupted his studies and began painting instead.

When Kandinsky encountered some works by the French painter Claude Monet during a trip to Munich, he was transformed. From Impressionism, he journeyed through Expressionism to Fauvism, until around 1910, Kandinsky came to the realization that the form and colour in a painting don't necessarily need to depict something real and tangible. It was much more impactful if a painting was completely liberated and only concerned with itself: with form and colour, lines and planes. Kandinsky was deeply interested in music and, because music also doesn't represent anything, believed that the form and colour in a painting could be compared to the rhythm and harmony in music. Instead, it is expressive in itself. He believed, the same should apply to painting. For Kandinsky, abstract painting was a spiritual liberation. But it required that everything within the frame should harmonize and be in balance simultaneously.

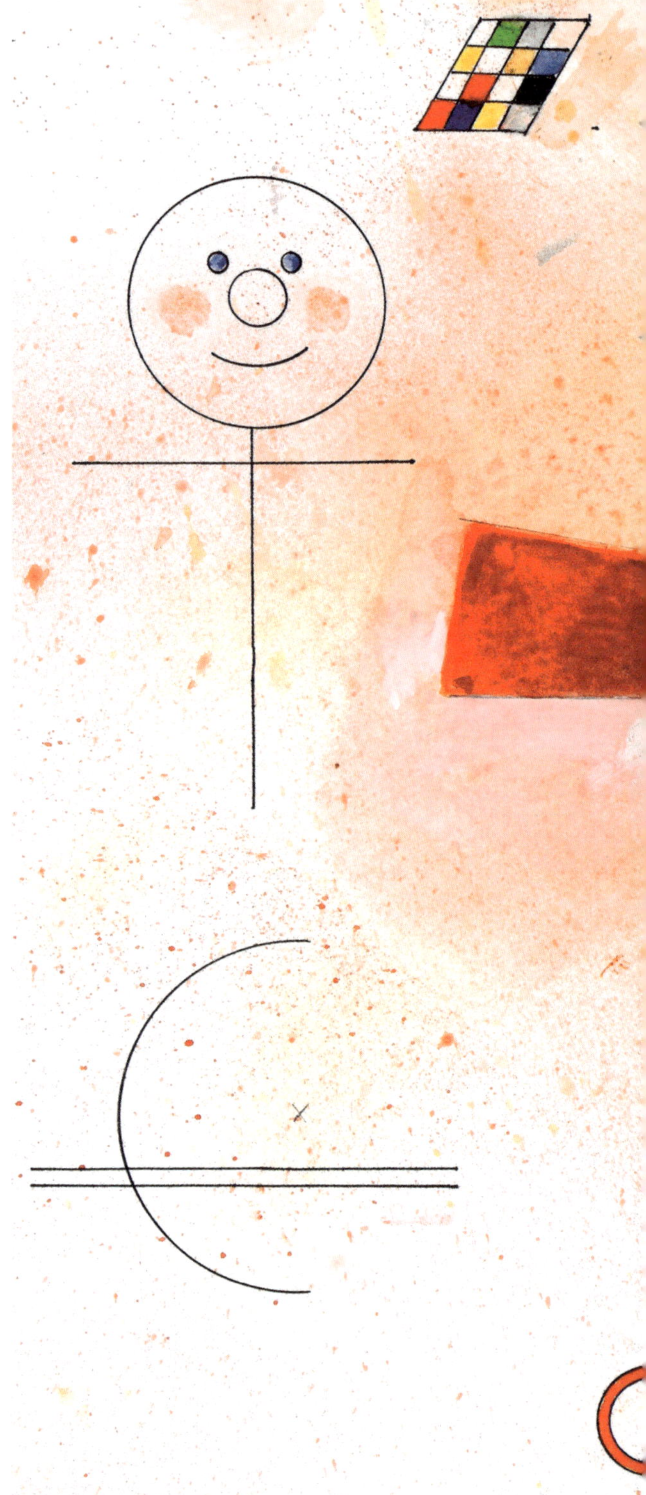

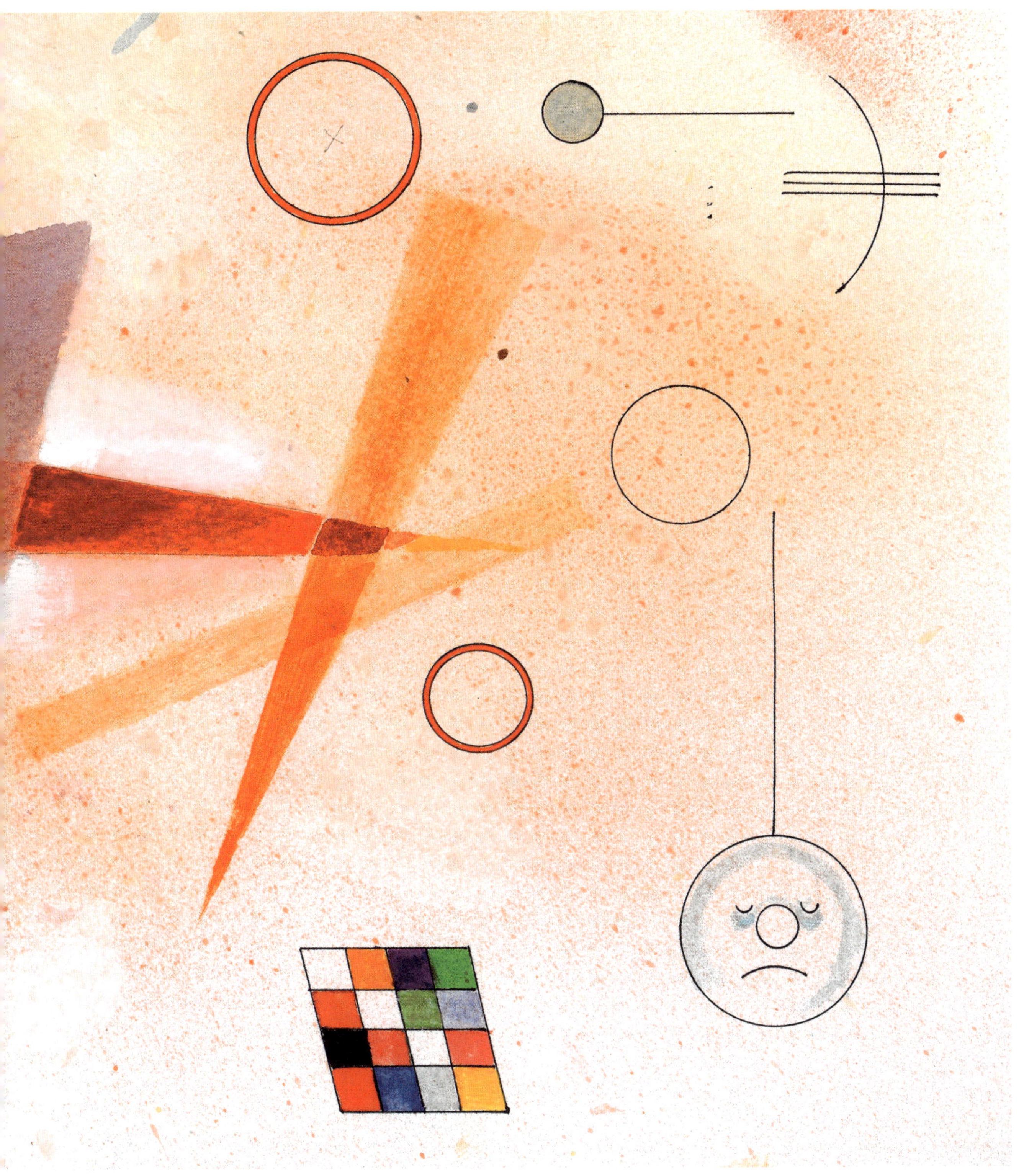

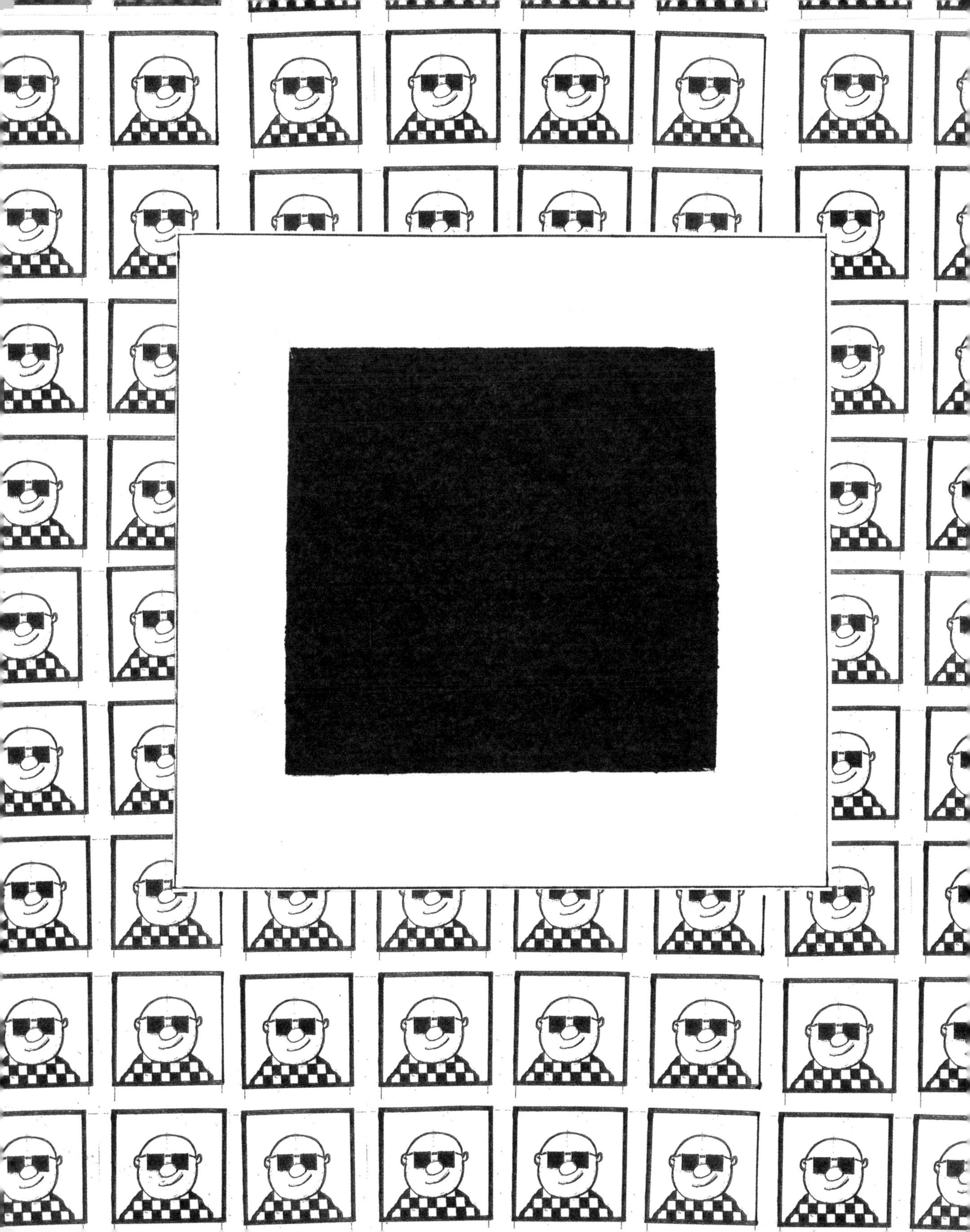

Kazimir Malevich

It doesn't get any simpler than this

In 1913, the Russian artist Kazimir Malevich (1879–1935) painted a picture that was so simple and bold that he didn't dare to show it publicly. At least not right away, which is understandable because it consisted of only a black square on a white background.

Malevich called his style Suprematism and stated that with this painting, he had liberated art from the burden of the subject. Now a painting could just be a painting without depicting anything. Five years later, he took it a step further and created a series of paintings showing a white square on a white background. It brought him art historical fame in the long run. But in the short term, he had painted himself into a corner.

Unable to progress further with abstract painting, meaning painting that didn't depict anything, he turned instead to writing, teaching, and building models. Eventually, he returned to the genre he originally came from: figurative painting. Malevich thereby demonstrated that it's never too late to start over if one aims to achieve something entirely new.

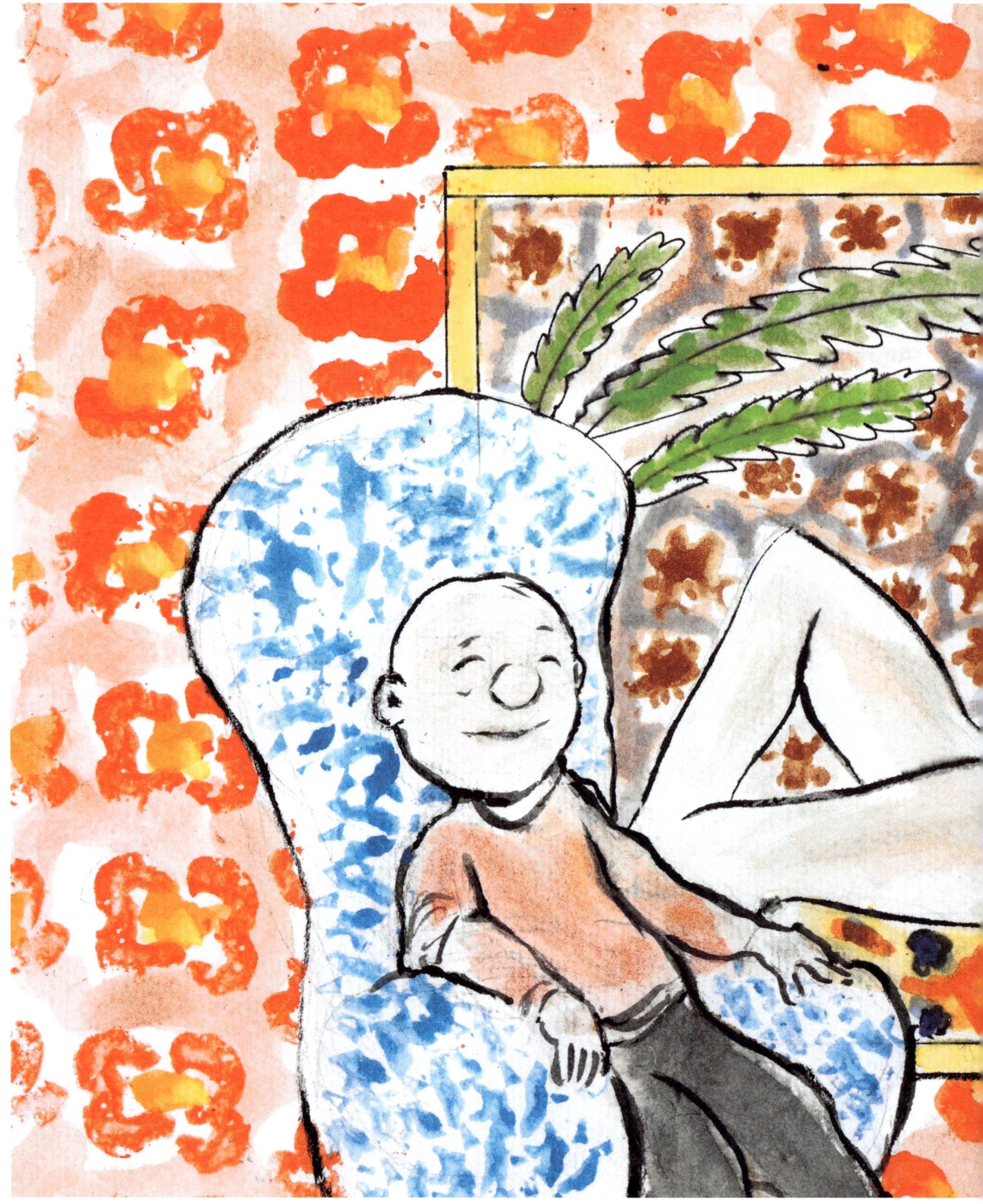

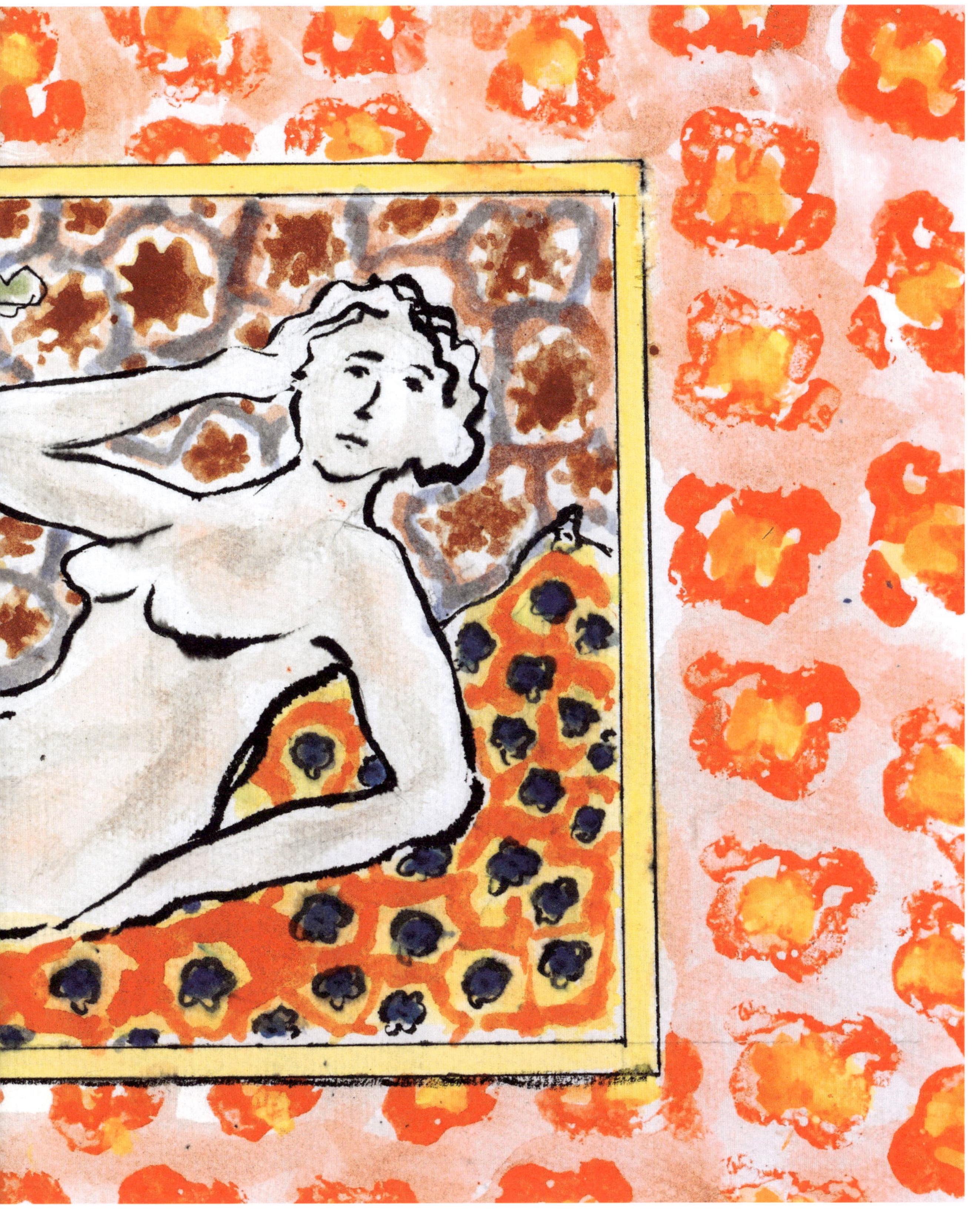

Is there anything better than a comfy armchair?

Some artists aspire to revolutionize the world with their art. Others dream of changing art history with what they create. And then there's the French painter Henri Matisse (1869–1954). He simply wanted to create something that was beautiful and pleasant to look at. Once, he compared his art to a good armchair, where the weary businessman or literary person could relax after a hard day's work. He believed that art should be devoid of anything that could cause problems or put one in a bad mood.

Matisse knew what he was talking about when he spoke of problems. He lived through two world wars. But no conflicts were allowed to influence his work. For the most important aspect of a painting was that it was clear and in perfect balance, both in terms of colour and form. It should be like an eternal spring. For the sake of balance, all colours should harmonize with each other. And he was not afraid to use the strongest and purest colours he could find on his palette.

What these colours might remind other people of was not crucial to Matisse. He said that when he used green, it was not to depict grass, and when he painted with blue, it was not a sky. For the painting was not about the reality outside the frame. Creating a painting was the same as arranging something beautiful, where everything found its rightful place in a whole. What could not be used in this entirety was therefore removed as it was damaging to the painting. The crucial thing was that the result was decorative in itself. That's how Middle Eastern and North African art was too, and it became a great inspiration for Matisse. And in 1911–12, he visited Morocco for the first time.

Of the painters who constituted Fauvism, Matisse was the most important. Just as with the impressionists, it was a critic who ended up giving the new artists their name. This happened at their breakthrough exhibition in 1905. The critic called them 'Les fauves', which means 'the wild beasts', and it was not meant as a compliment. To him, these painters' handling of colour seemed wild and uncivilized. They could paint tree trunks blue and noses green. But the name stuck and became 'Fauvism', the French version of Expressionism.

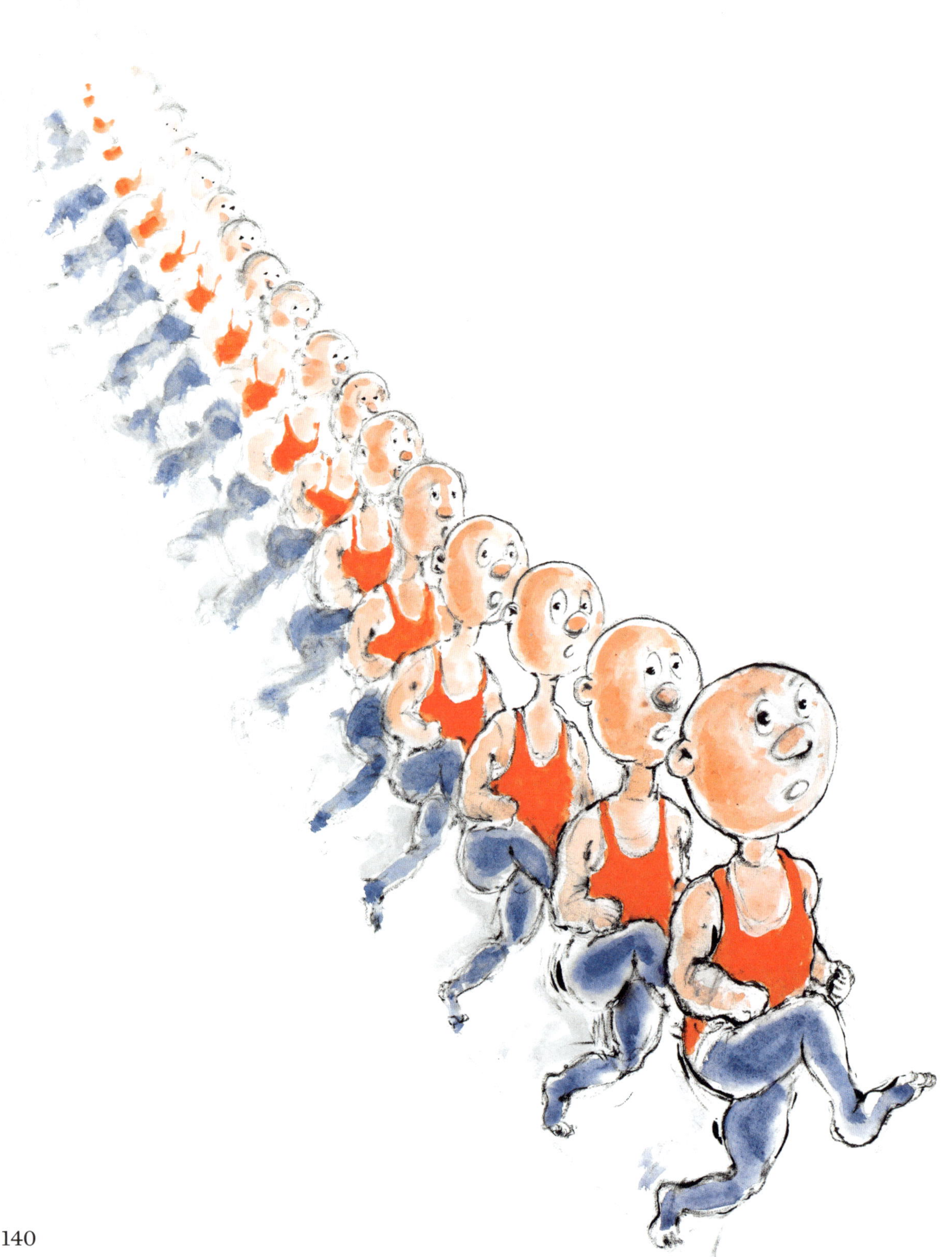

Full speed ahead!

The figure in the picture is in motion. Perhaps he's wearing Nike shoes, the famous sports brand named after the victory goddess. 'Nike of Samothrace' is one of the most famous ancient statues in the world, including the Louvre, Paris' largest art museum, where it stands with outstretched wings.

Nevertheless, in 1909, a poet claimed that a roaring car speeding like a machine gun is more beautiful than even this world-famous victory goddess. The poet was the founder of Futurism, the Italian Filippo Tommaso Marinetti (1876–1944), and there probably never existed a more speed-loving poet than him. Futurism was supposed to be a tribute to speed and movement – and to war! Because, accord-ing to Marinetti, war was the best means to cleanse the old so that something new could emerge. In this respect, Futurism and Dadaism were opposites. But in other areas, such as their relationship to mu-seum art, they resemble each other, as their supporters didn't like visiting museums, where people revered the art of the past.

The word Futurism is derived from the Latin word for future. The first futuristic manifesto came in 1910, but as an artistic movement, it didn't have much of a future, as it didn't survive World War I, which ended in 1918.

Before that, however, Futurism managed to provide a recipe for how an apparently static medium like a painting could still depict movement. Initially, the task seemed as difficult as portraying space on a two-dimensional surface. But the futurists came up with the idea that movement in a painting could be shown by depicting a figure in different posi-tions. Just like if you took a picture every second of a running man and then stacked all the pictures on top of each other. That way, you could clearly see that he was in motion.

Marcel Duchamp

It doesn't get more daring than this

People often call Marcel Duchamp (1887–1968) the most significant artist of the 20th century, alongside Picasso. He certainly was the most daring. Ironically, as the years went by, he became more interested in playing chess than producing art. He never became a world chess champion, but he was quite good at the game, and even represented his country – France – at four different Chess Olympics. And in 1917, he came close to putting art in checkmate.

That year, Duchamp helped organize an open exhibition in New York. In an open exhibition, anyone can submit works without censorship, meaning there's no committee deciding which works should be included in the exhibition – and which should not.

For his contribution to the exhibition, Duchamp chose a white enamelled urinal (!), which he had bought from an ordinary plumber in New York. When he had brought home the urinal, he turned it upside down and signed it: 'R. Mutt' with the year '1917', and then submitted it to the exhibition.

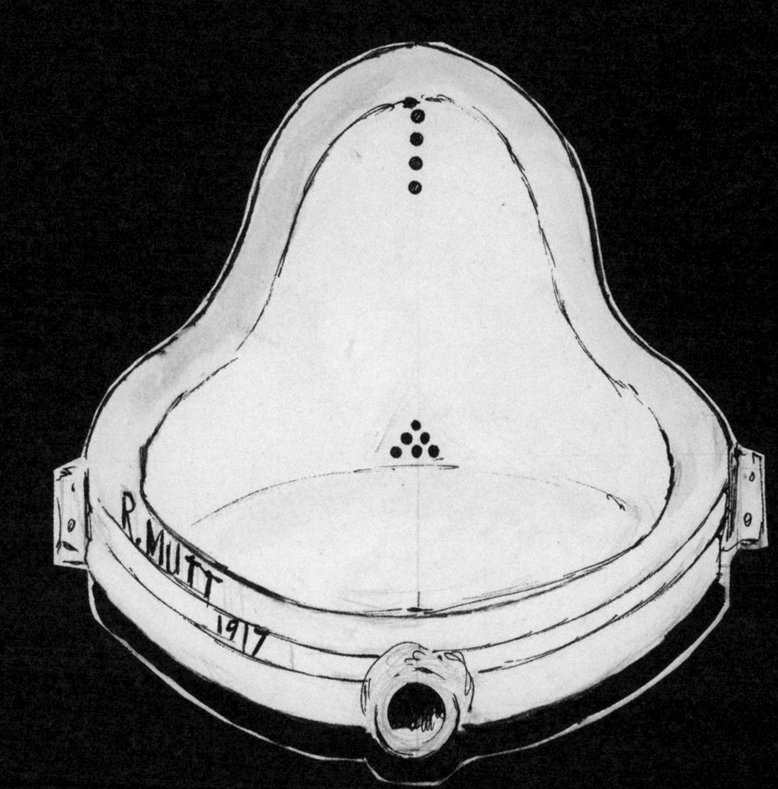

R.MUTT
1917

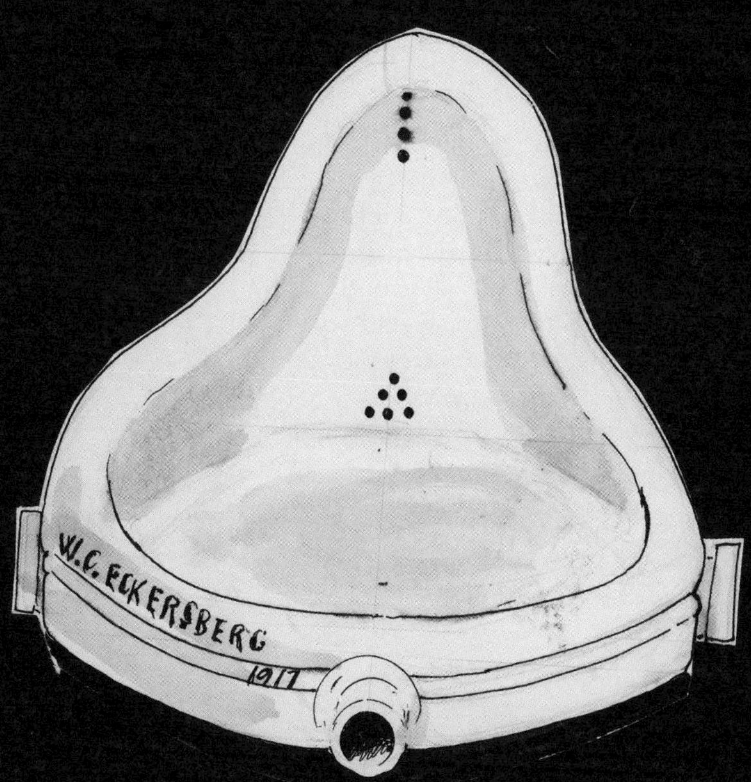

W.C.ECKERSBERG
1917

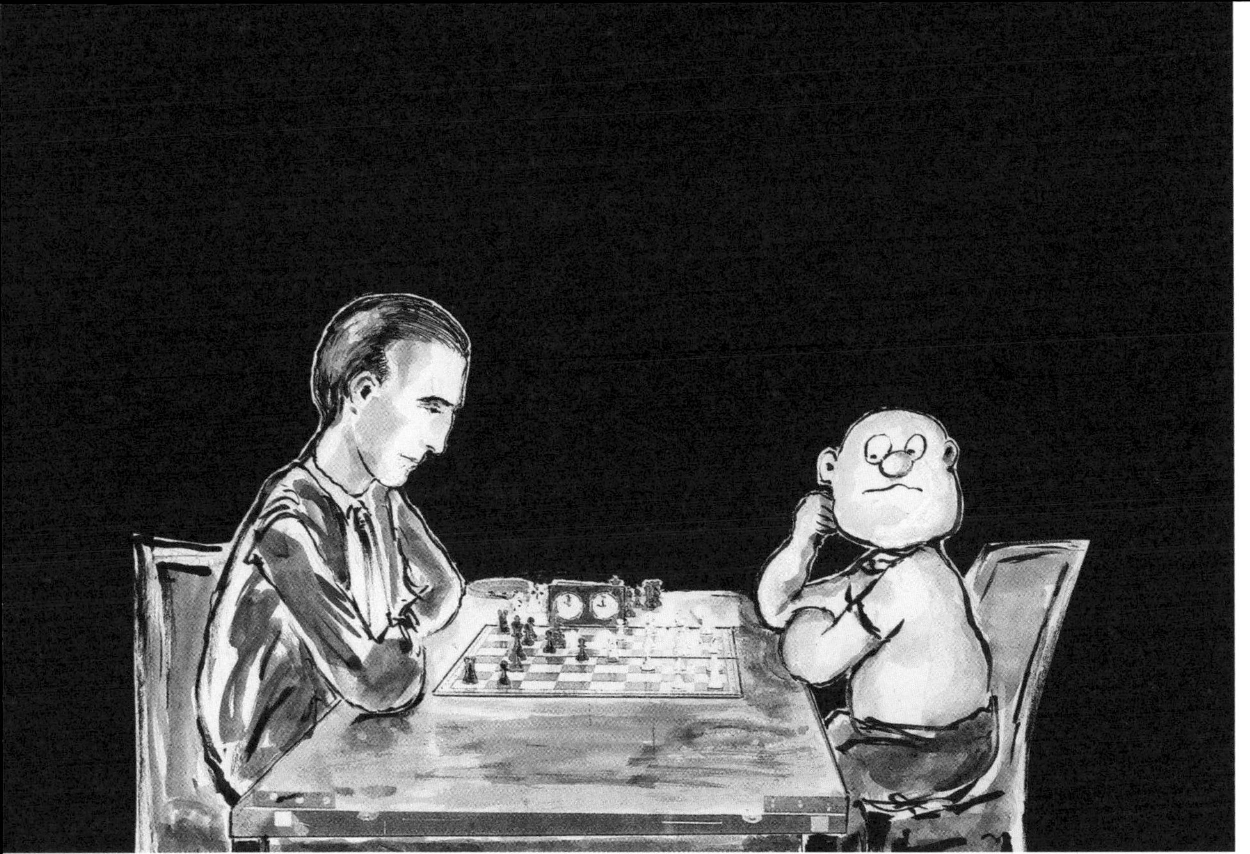

As the only one out of over 2,000 works (by 1,200 artists), Duchamp's urinal was censored. He had titled it 'Fountain.' The polite name didn't prevent the public outrage and heated debate that followed. However, one of the organizers had understood what it was all about: no matter what an artist chooses to submit to an exhibition, this utterly impossible thing is nevertheless the artist's conscious contribution to the exhibition. Because it is he, and no one else, who has chosen to show it. Therefore, the 'thing' has become his artwork.

In this case, Duchamp had changed the urinal's original function. It was no longer intended for urination. The present 'fountain' had a different purpose and a different meaning. Perhaps it wasn't as fine a sculpture as many sculptures in bronze, marble, wood, etc. But it was just as much a sculpture, and that was the most important thing, even though it was a 'readymade.'

A 'readymade' is the term for an object originally made for a completely different function than the one it would have if it was displayed in an exhibition or another art context.

The original urinal that Duchamp had exhibited got lost. Or perhaps it broke. However, the artist quickly obtained a replacement: a urinal identical to the original, which he turned upside down and adorned with the same signature.

But don't expect to become famous if you also go out and buy an old urinal, turn it upside down, sign it, put it on a pedestal – and then exhibit it. By doing so, you've merely shown that you think Duchamp's idea is worth imitating. But you haven't thought of an original idea yourself. And that's what matters in the art indebted to Duchamp: thinking original thoughts that no one has had before.

After Duchamp, art was never quite the same again.

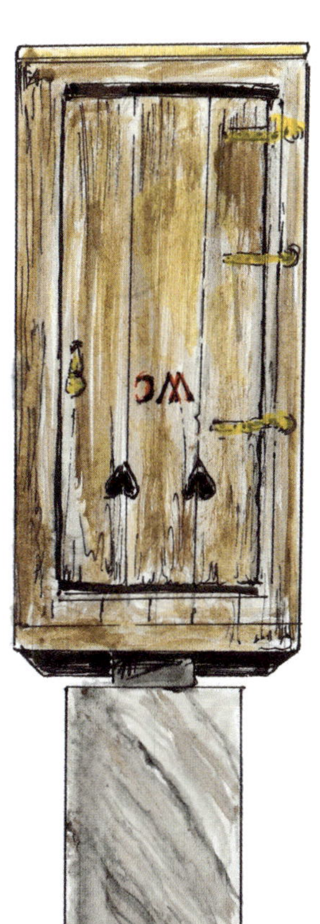

Artistic horseplay

Artists can usually agree on a name, no matter how mad and disgruntled they are. But the name 'Dadaism' nevertheless emerged purely by chance as the label for a particular style. During World War I (which raged from 1914 to 1918), a group of visual artists and writers found themselves in Switzerland, which had declared itself neutral in all future wars since 1815. Therefore, Switzerland became a refuge for revolutionaries, anarchists, pacifists, nihilists, and deserters. (Revolutionaries believe in revolution, anarchists don't believe in governmental power, pacifists don't believe in war, nihilists don't believe in anything at all, and deserters, well, they are people who have fled the front).

They all had in common that – due to the bloody war – they had lost faith in progress and their fellow humans. They also believed that the established art had failed. Therefore, this small group of writers and artists wanted to create a new kind of art.

In Zurich, in February 1916, they founded a literary scene and a small theatre, 'Cabaret Voltaire', where they also organized art exhibitions. But they didn't have a name. The name 'Dadaism' arose when they randomly flipped through the pages of the large French dictionary 'Larousse'. They landed on the word 'dada', which is French for hobbyhorse or stick horse, and the word stuck as a label for this provocative, shocking, and revolutionary movement, which later spread to other cities like Cologne, Berlin, and New York.

According to the dadaists, old art – the one in museums – was pure past. Dadaism also became a kind of past, around 1922. But before that, it managed to influence other contemporary rebellions, such as Surrealism.

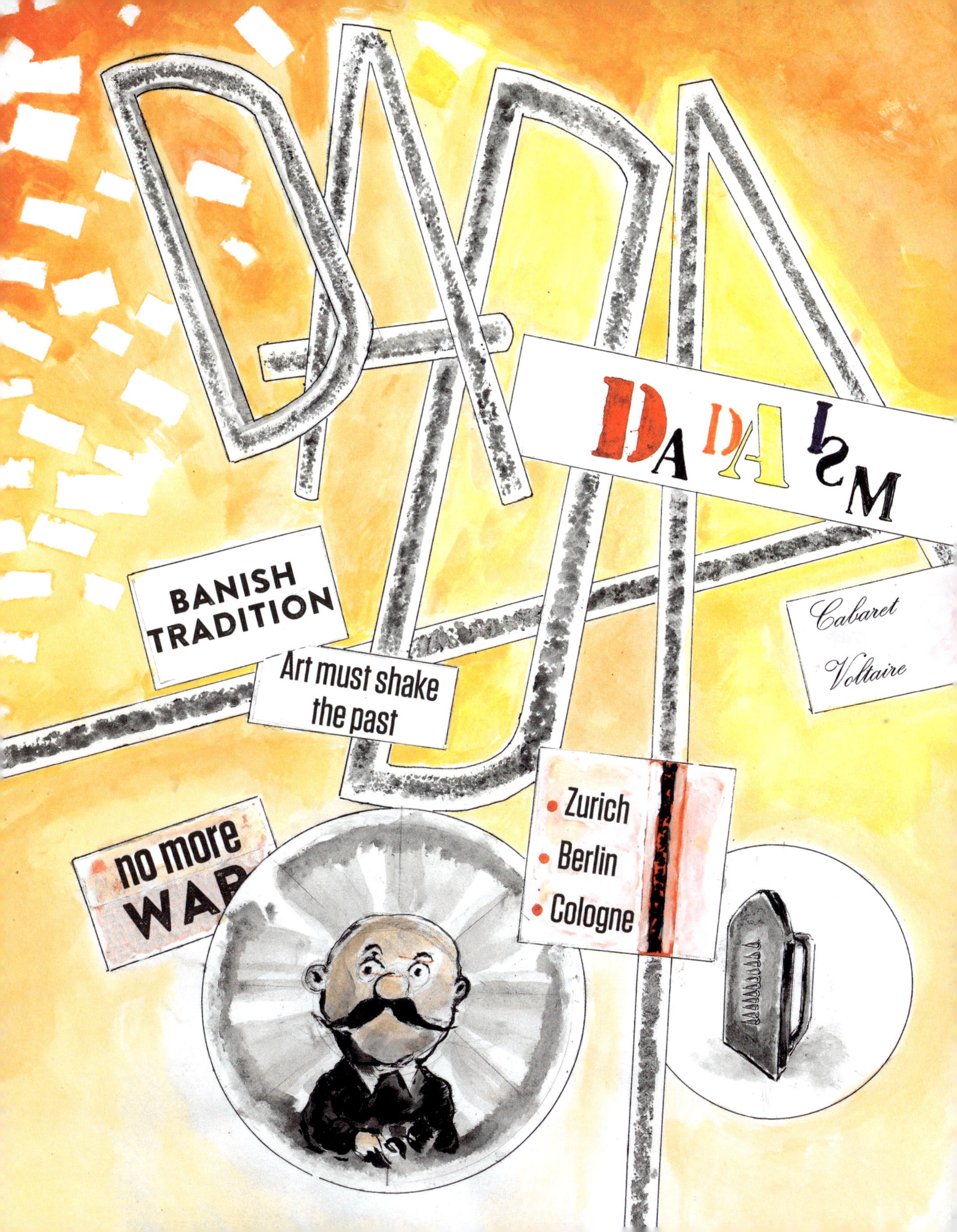
DADA
DADAISM
BANISH TRADITION
Art must shake the past
no more WAR
Zurich
Berlin
Cologne
Cabaret Voltaire

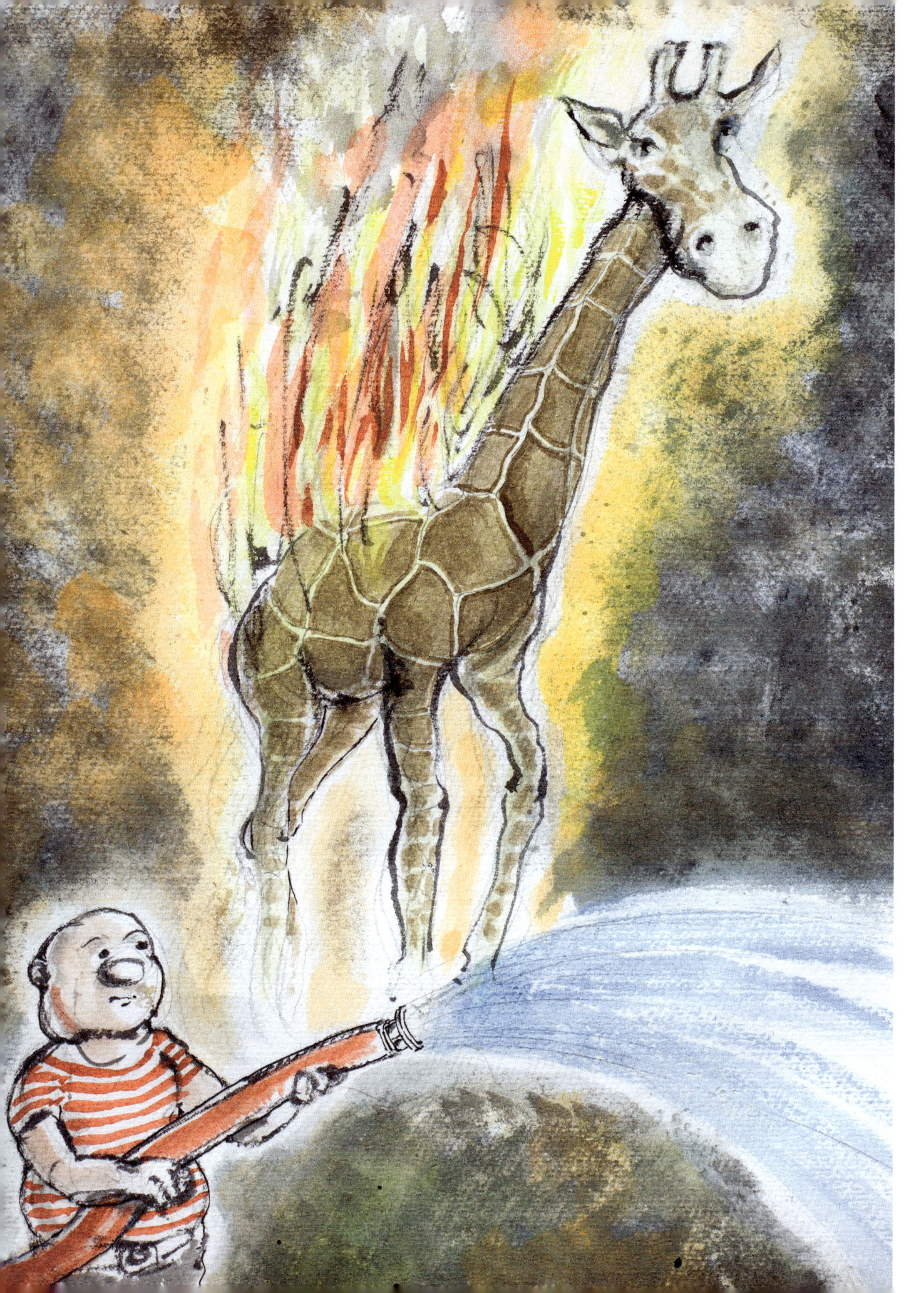

From sewing machines to burning giraffes

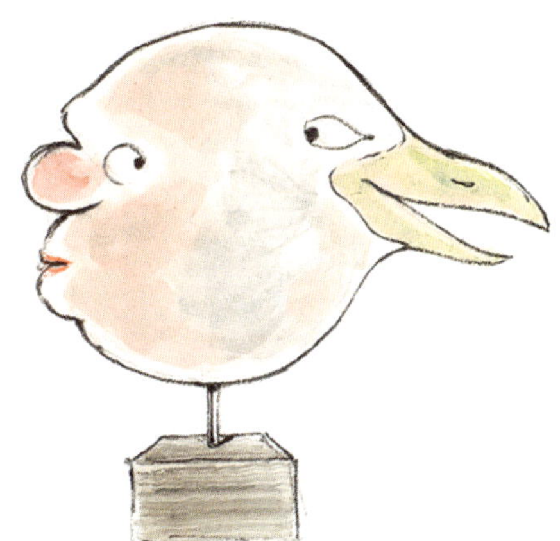

'As beautiful as the chance encounter of a sewing machine and an umbrella on an operating table'.

Doesn't that sentence sound a bit eerie? And mad? It certainly looks mad when you try to draw what it describes. What can an umbrella possibly have to do with a sewing machine? And especially on an operating table, a place where animals or humans are normally operated on? But that's precisely the point of the sentence: it shouldn't make any sense at all. For we have reached Surrealism, where imagination is allowed to take the place of reason. And that's actually the whole point.

The strange sentence about the encounter between the sewing machine and the umbrella was written in 1870 by a French poet who called himself Count Lautréamont.

Fifty years later, a group of French poets and artists began to question whether Naturalism was the whole truth about nature, including human nature. For there existed a world beyond reality – or above it. One that could only be dreamed of or fantasized about. But was no less important for that reason.

Count Lautréamont's real name was Isidore Lucien Ducasse. Lautréamont was just something he called himself, and his poems were no less peculiar for it. The surrealists thought that Lautréamont's words were like fuel for the imagination. But they could also make good use of Sigmund Freud's ideas. Freud was a psychoanalyst who had researched human dreams and subconscious ideas – all that which was not controlled by reason.

Now, dreams, nightmares, and our imagination were to have free rein, and they did in Surrealism. In Surrealism, an artist was not bound by reality, which meant it was possible, for example, for a surrealist to combine a man's head with that of a bird. And it was also possible to set fire to a giraffe, at least when doing so in a painting. This was done by the Spanish surrealist Salvador Dalí (1904–1989), who became the most famous of the surrealists.

It's to remind us of Dalí that our guide in art has acquired a razor-sharp moustache. It's also to remember Dalí that we've let the clock on the wall melt like soft cheese. For melting clocks became one of the Spanish artist's most famous motifs.

There are many strange and impossible things that Dalí and the other surrealists never did. Like setting fire to a snowman. But we are allowed to do that. For in Surrealism, everything is possible, as long as you depict it in a poem, a sculpture, or a painting.

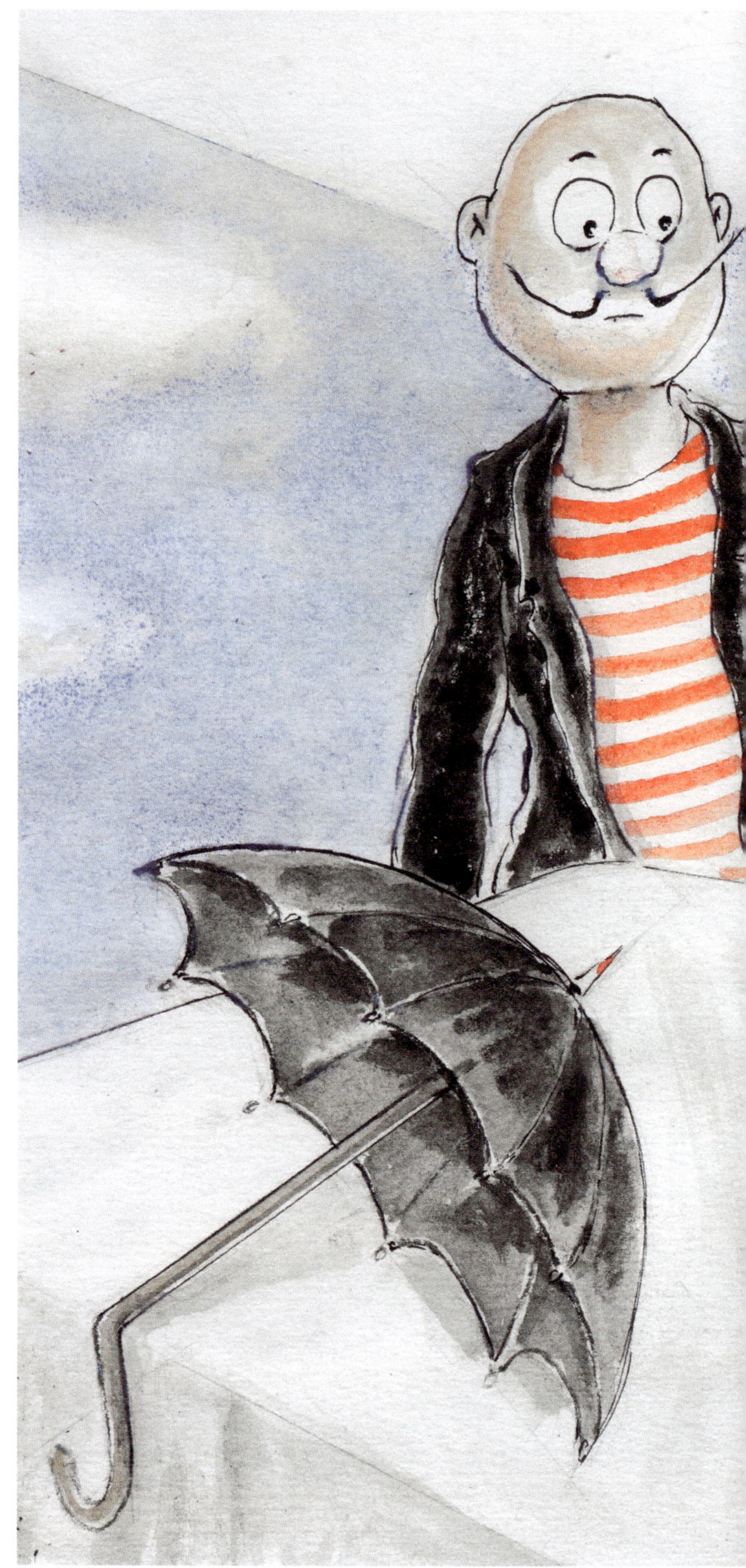

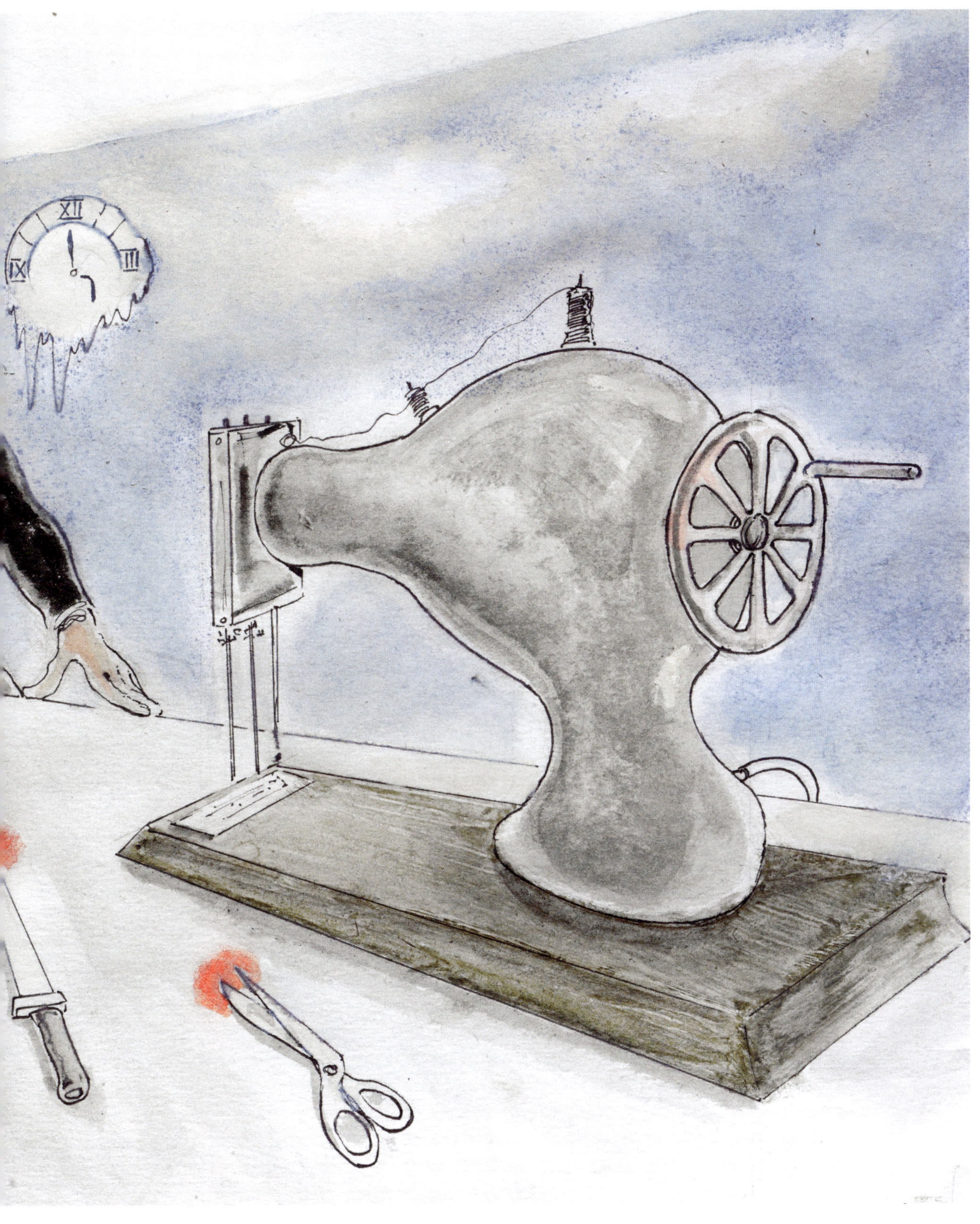

Art without control

When dreaming, it's no longer your reason or consciousness that sets the agenda and determines what you see in your mind's eye. It's the subconscious. The surrealists' spokesman and advocate was André Breton (1896–1966), and it was he who called for a new art and poetry that was not subject to the control of thought. Thought should be freed from the dominance of consciousness, and Automatism was one of the ways art could break loose. With Automatism, the conscious control of hand movements and the influence of consciousness on how a picture is created were abandoned. Instead, the unconscious was allowed to take over. Both the process and its result can resemble action painting within abstract Expressionism.

However, there is a key difference between the two 'free birds' of modern art – Surrealism and Abstract Expressionism. With the latter, there was a selection based on aesthetic criteria. While the artist worked, he seemed to disregard everything. But when he finished his work, he only chose the best pieces, those he liked best. The opposite was true for the surrealists. According to André Breton, the work process was more important than the result.

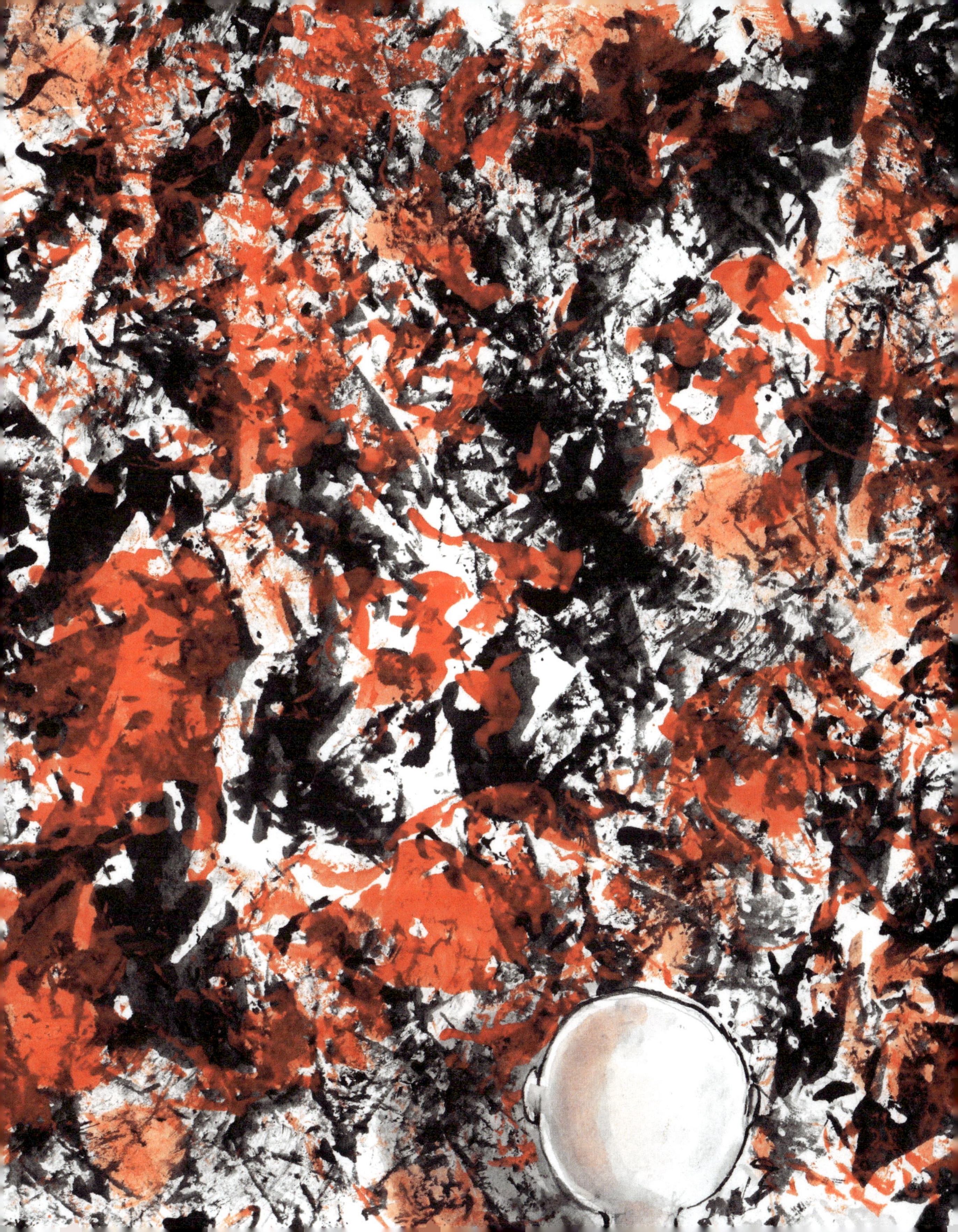

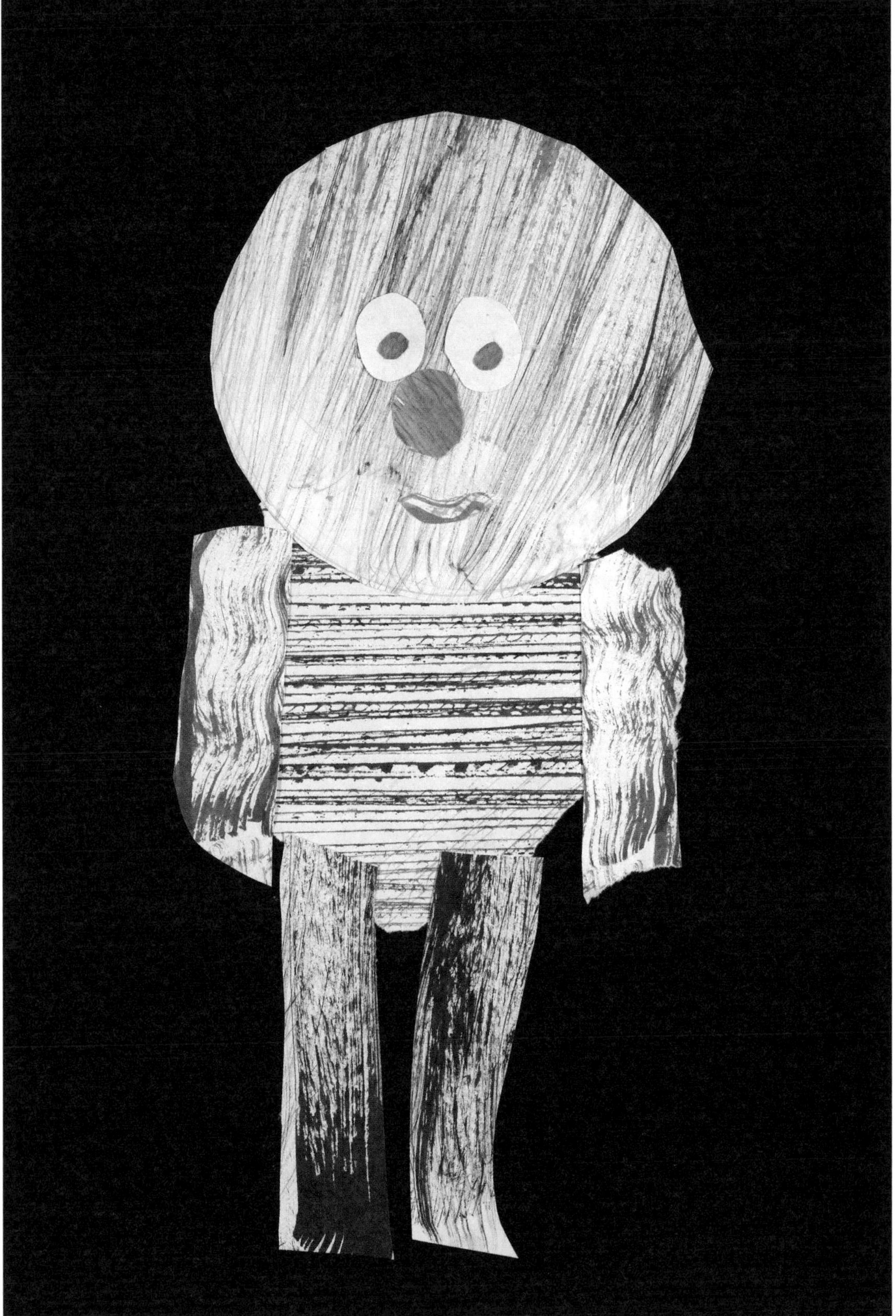

Jean Dubuffet

The brutal art

Sometimes making art can be easier if you haven't received
an education at an art academy with strict teachers or if you
think differently than most due to mental illness. There are
many examples of the need to express oneself in pictures
being just as strong – if not stronger – among patients hospitalized in psychiatric wards. This type of art is often regarded
as rawer, more immediate, and spontaneous.

That was the background for the French artist Jean Dubuffet
(1901–1985) calling this type of art 'raw art' (in French: Art
Brut). Dubuffet was inspired by this so-called outsider art
when he exhibited his new works in 1946 after a long break.
It was roughly the same time that a group of Northern European artists also became interested in children's drawings,
non-Western cultures' art, and art by the mentally ill. We
know them under the name Cobra, which we'll discuss later
in this book. Dubuffet distinguished between this type of art
and what he called 'chameleon or parrot art', because it – like
chameleons – took on the colour of its surroundings or – like
parrots – repeated others without understanding anything of
what was being said. That is, art that merely imitated other
art. For an artist, it was more important to be sincere and
original than to be skilled, he believed.

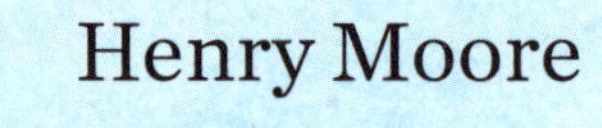

A resting body

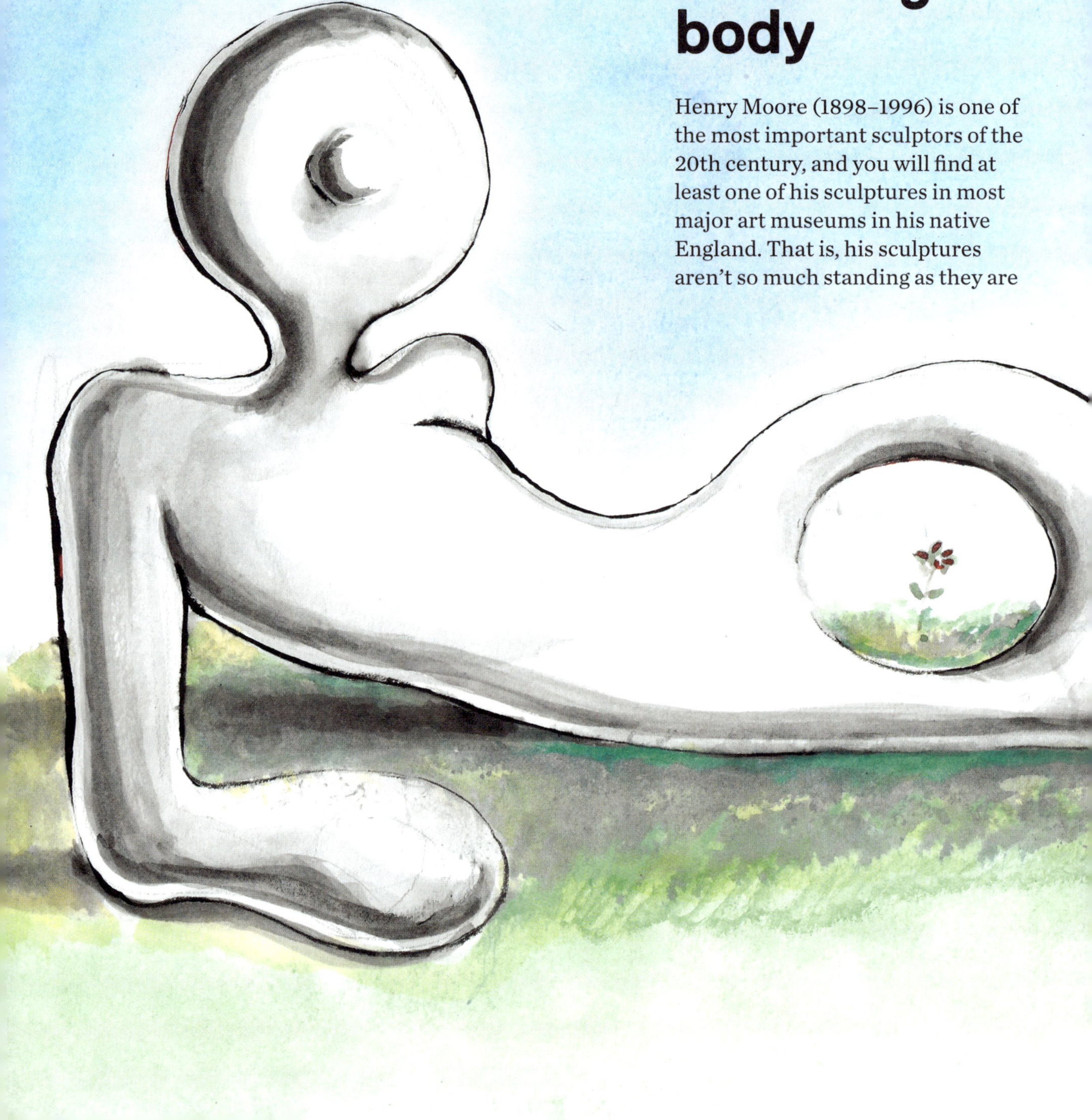

Henry Moore (1898–1996) is one of the most important sculptors of the 20th century, and you will find at least one of his sculptures in most major art museums in his native England. That is, his sculptures aren't so much standing as they are

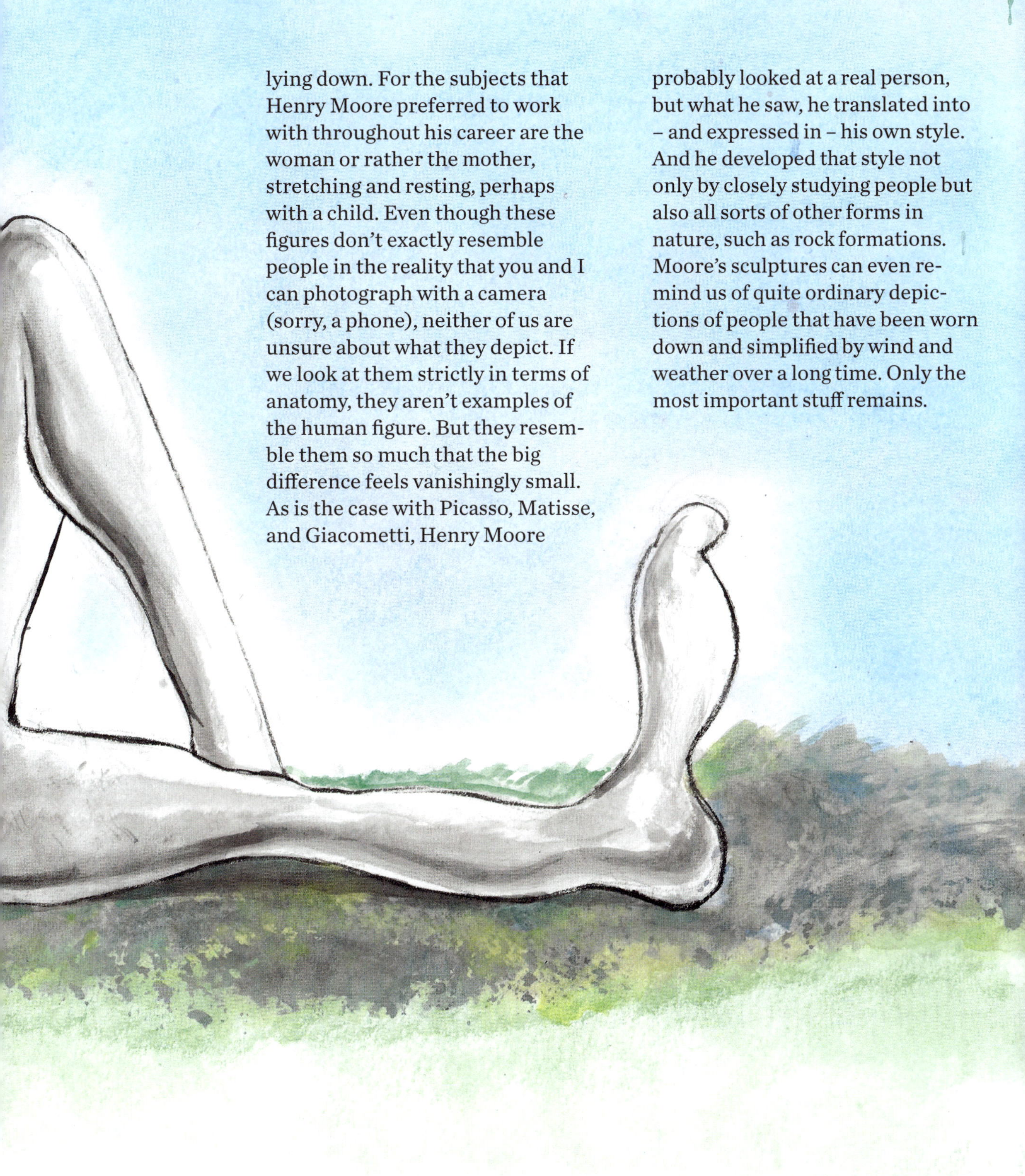

lying down. For the subjects that Henry Moore preferred to work with throughout his career are the woman or rather the mother, stretching and resting, perhaps with a child. Even though these figures don't exactly resemble people in the reality that you and I can photograph with a camera (sorry, a phone), neither of us are unsure about what they depict. If we look at them strictly in terms of anatomy, they aren't examples of the human figure. But they resemble them so much that the big difference feels vanishingly small. As is the case with Picasso, Matisse, and Giacometti, Henry Moore probably looked at a real person, but what he saw, he translated into – and expressed in – his own style. And he developed that style not only by closely studying people but also all sorts of other forms in nature, such as rock formations. Moore's sculptures can even remind us of quite ordinary depictions of people that have been worn down and simplified by wind and weather over a long time. Only the most important stuff remains.

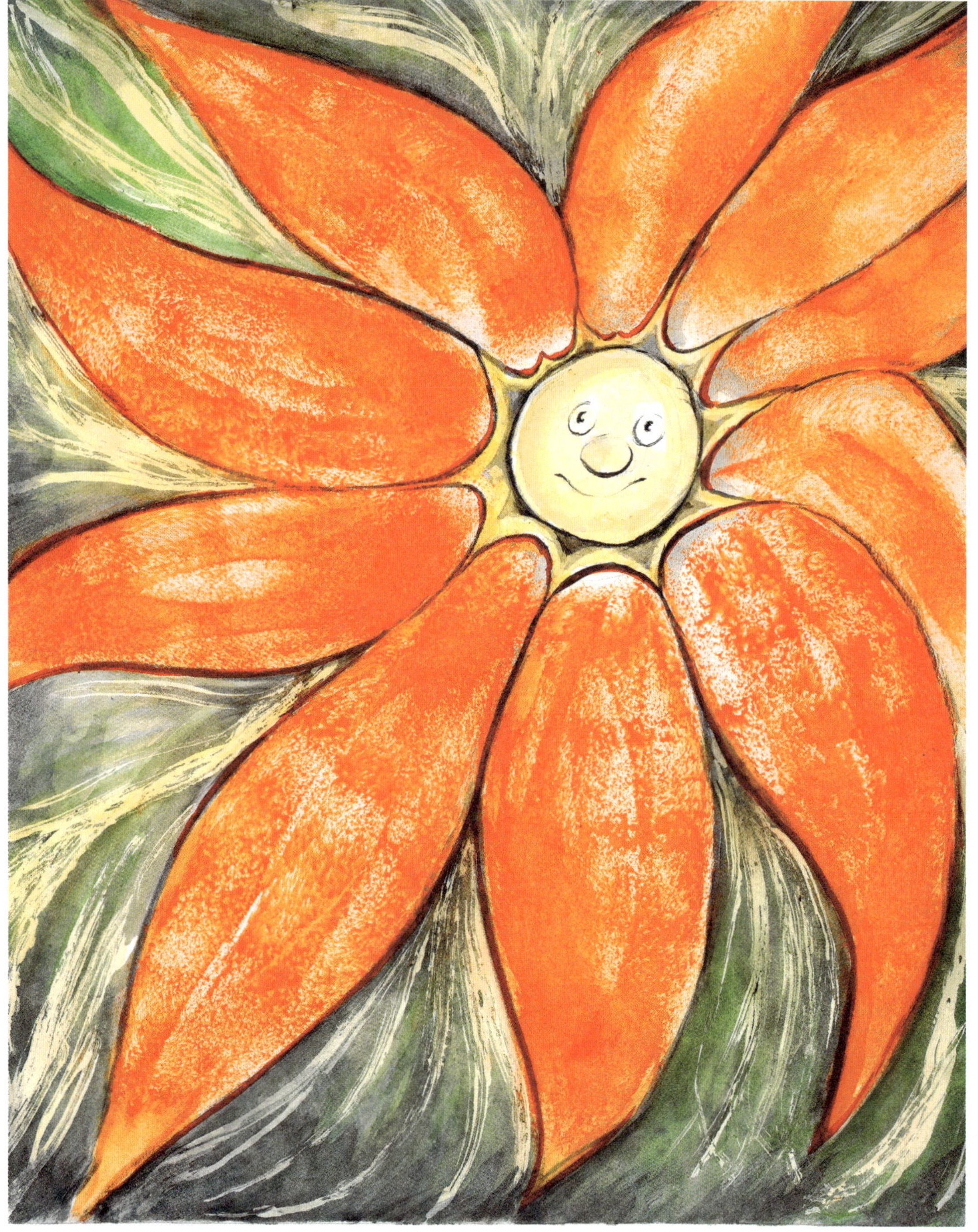

Georgia O'Keeffe

Say it with flowers

The American Georgia O'Keeffe (1887–1986) stood out from most artists of her time simply by being a woman. She only gained recognition for her work late in life, so it was fortunate that she lived to be 98. These three circumstances of her life are actually connected. For if she hadn't been a woman, it probably wouldn't have been long before someone started to respect her as a significant artist. But if she hadn't lived that long, she would never have experienced her own breakthrough. It wasn't until there was a growing interest in female artists that her works came into the spotlight.

In 1983, Georgia O'Keeffe published her autobiography – and not a moment too soon! By then she was 96 years old and had been painting for seventy years. O'Keeffe's first abstract watercolours date back to 1915 and show that even at this early stage of her development, she was not inferior to the male modernists. In fact, she was a pioneer in American modernism. At that time, she had already known and dated the art dealer and photographer Alfred Stieglitz for several years, and he believed in her talent. As the years went by, and impressions from, among others, New Mexico and the landscapes and vegetation of the southwestern USA accumulated, nature began to invade her abstract pictures. Her style was never naturalistic. But despite her abstractions of nature, there was never any doubt about the subject of her pictures, whether it was landscapes, bones, or flowers.

She became most famous for her flower motifs, which she simplified until they were almost abstract. It was a motif also cultivated by Emil Nolde. But Georgia O'Keeffe's interpretations got much closer to the leaves of the flower and turned them into stylized close-ups. Her flower portraits could even be said to have a strong erotic appeal. For flowers don't have their many colours for no reason. The need to be pollinated!

It moves, but it's not a snake

When you hear the word 'Cobra', you might think of venomous snakes, especially those that spread fear and terror in India. But in art history, 'Cobra' is a group of painters and poets from Denmark, Belgium, and the Netherlands, who in 1948 joined forces to form their own movement.

At first, they could easily frighten people like the snake, as they were not afraid to experiment or improvise, meaning to work without having made a plan in advance. For when you cultivated the spontaneous, apparently you could better involve your subconscious in the process. For the spontaneous artist, it was always important to produce a result that not even the artist himself could foresee. The painters associated with Cobra for longer or (often) shorter periods were mostly abstract expressionists.

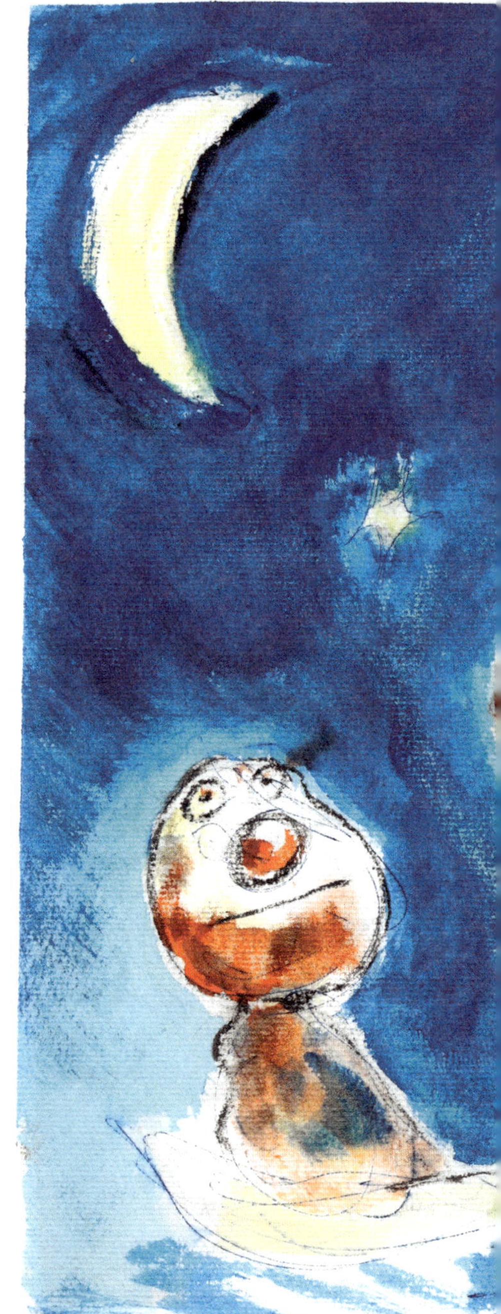

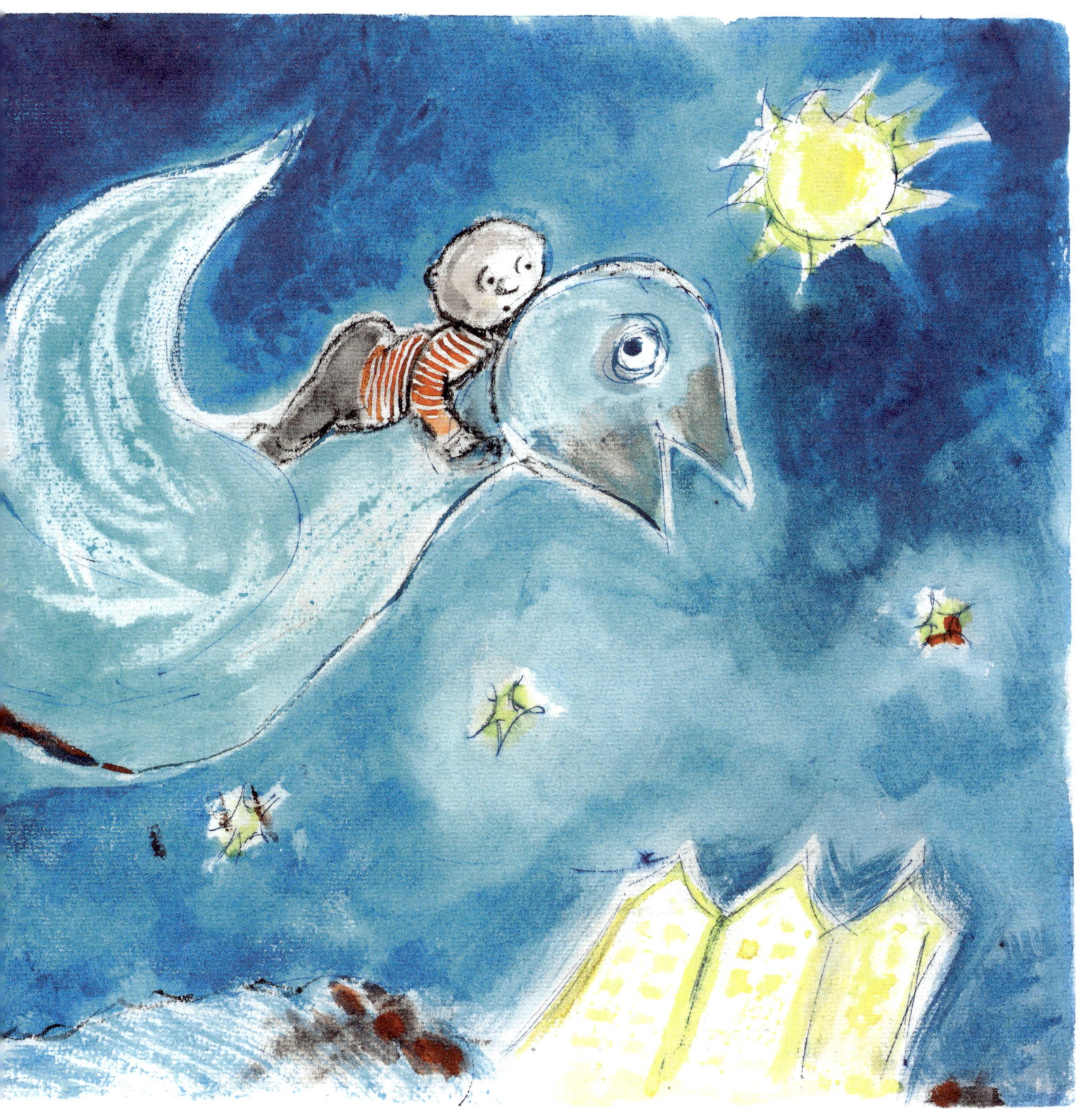

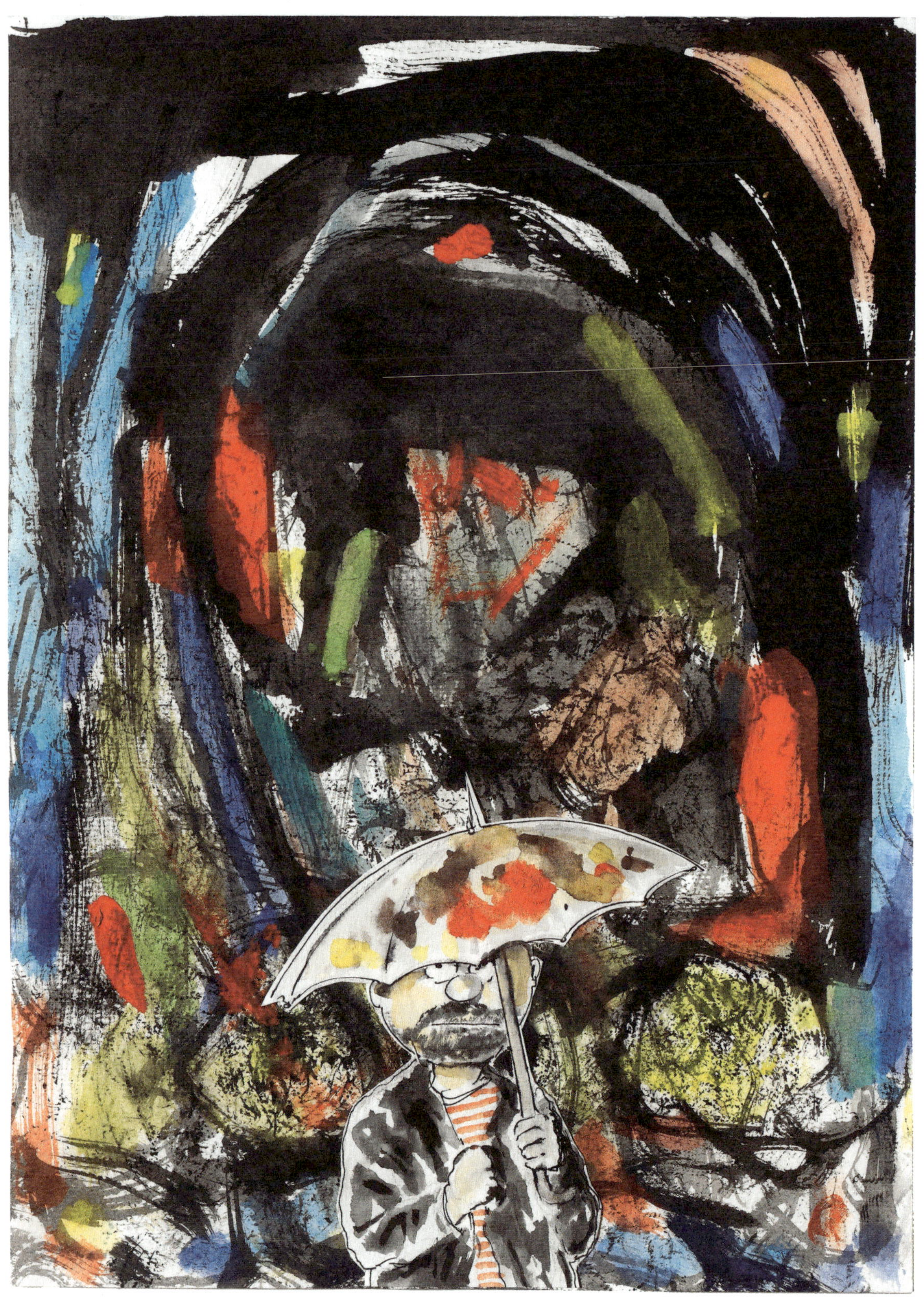

The name of the group has its own explanation. It is a combination of the initials of the three countries' capitals: **Co**penhagen, **Br**ussels, and **A**msterdam. Among the group's many Danish members, one in particular can't be overlooked: Asger Jorn (1914–1973).

Unstoppable

Asger Jorn once said that a kick in the behind is a step forward. He spoke from experience, for he had experienced much adversity, especially in Denmark, where he had received several kicks from, among others, art museums and critics. That was a contributing factor to why he preferred to stay abroad, where he achieved more than any other Danish painter before him.

Jorn helped establish the Cobra movement in 1948, and it was him more than anyone who made the international contacts for 'this movement without a programme', as it was called. However, Cobra also became a movement without funding. In 1951, the solidarity ended, and Jorn was admitted to a sanatorium with tuberculosis. When he was discharged, he continued to paint and write, perhaps even more freely than before. Jorn was unstoppable.

When Jorn painted, it was with a kind of anarchy. There were no rules; each painting had to be created spontaneously, and without the artist – in this case Jorn – feeling bound by how he had painted his previous works. Each painting was its own challenge, its own exploration of the possibilities of form and colour. 'You can't sneak up on the picture without it noticing', Jorn once wrote. By this, he meant that one stroke always leads to the next. A picture has its own life once it has been set in motion, and it isn't certain that the artist can stop or ever finish it.

A painting with plenty of action

Movement in art can be created in more than one way and no one claims that everything has to be painted with a brush. With the brush, you only use the movements of your hand. If, on the other hand, you want to use your whole body when you work, the picture has to be big. This gives the artist room to express himself more freely. Then he can, for example, drip paint onto the picture, directly from a paint can with a hole made in it. He can also whip his canvas with strings dipped in paint.

The latter creates the effect you see here. Such a picture is abstract. It doesn't depict something the artist has seen. Instead, the picture has become a kind of 'thing', something that has arisen in a particular way and therefore must have a particular appearance. If such a painting tells a story, it is the story of its own creation. The American Jackson Pollock (1912–1956) was the most important of these action painters.

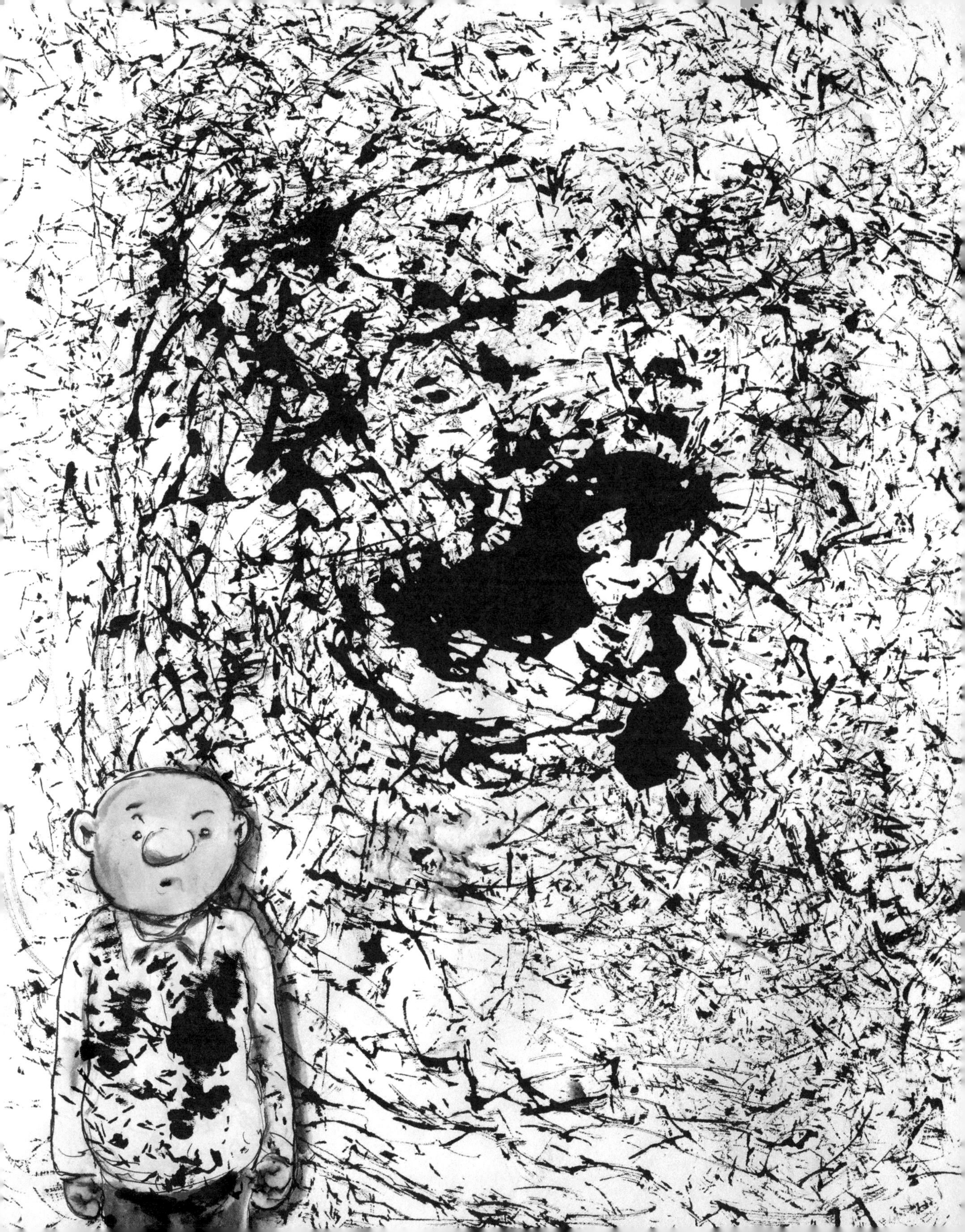

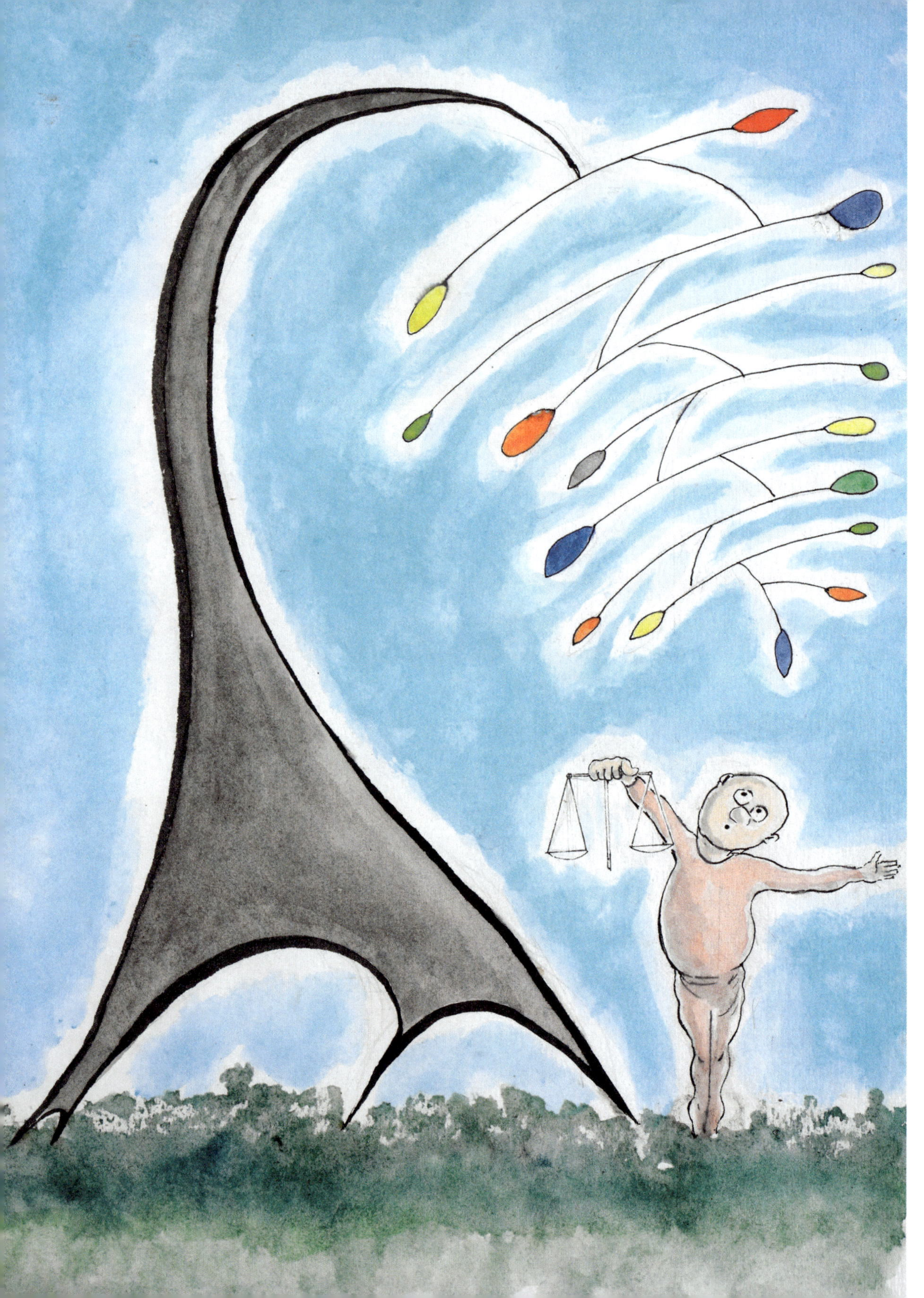

A balancing act

It was the French artist Marcel Duchamp who coined the term 'mobile' to describe sculptures that could move. However, it was the American sculptor Alexander Calder (1898–1976) who created the first works deserving of the term. Just as a mobile phone is a phone you can carry with you when you move around, in art, a mobile is a sculpture whose entire purpose is to move. Its parts can be made of materials like plastic, wood, veneer, or metal plates, and they can be painted in different colours. But the important thing is that all the parts in a mobile are loosely connected to each other, for example, with wire, so if someone blows or pushes them, they move. You may be familiar with the principle from the mobiles you can hang up at home. Calder was trained as a mechanical engineer before deciding to become an artist, and initially, he got the mobiles to move by connecting them to a motor.

After 1934, Calder's mobiles mostly relied on the small movements that a gust of wind could evoke. When the different parts of such a mobile began to rotate and move, the overall appearance changed and distributed light and shadows in a new way. This made the mobile a particularly lively sculpture. Calder called them 'drawings in four dimensions'.

In addition to the mobiles, Calder made so-called 'stabiles', often in steel. These are sculptures that do not move. But otherwise, they resemble the mobiles in their formal language and, like them, do not depict anything specific.

Back to basics

What makes this statue unusual for its time, namely the beginning of the 20th century? The answer is: the fact that it depicts a man.

Most of the sculptures made in Europe in the years between the two world wars were made by men. But they just don't depict men. They depict women, almost always without a stitch of clothing, and their forms are round and appear as soft as a form can appear when cast in bronze. Because that was the preferred material.

The most important of these sculptors was the Frenchman Aristide Maillol (1861–1944). Although he was quite an old man at 83 when he died, it happened in something as violent as a car accident. Perhaps his death was the only dramatic thing in his life.

Before his death, he had modelled – by commission – a long series of nude female figures, one after the other: lying, sitting, or standing. In the history of art, what is new is often a kind of rebellion against what is older, and in French sculpture, Maillol's figures are a rebellion against the more violent, dramatic, and emotionally charged figures made by his colleague Auguste Rodin.

It wasn't that the two Frenchmen didn't respect each other. When Maillol had his first solo exhibition in 1902, he was praised by Rodin, whom Maillol also looked up to as one of the greatest sculptors of the late 19th century. Maillol just wanted to return to sculptures that, like the statues of the ancient Greeks, were simple, stable, and almost rested in themselves. It must have been a great experience for him to visit Greece, which he did in 1908, because it confirmed for him everything that was important in modern sculpture.

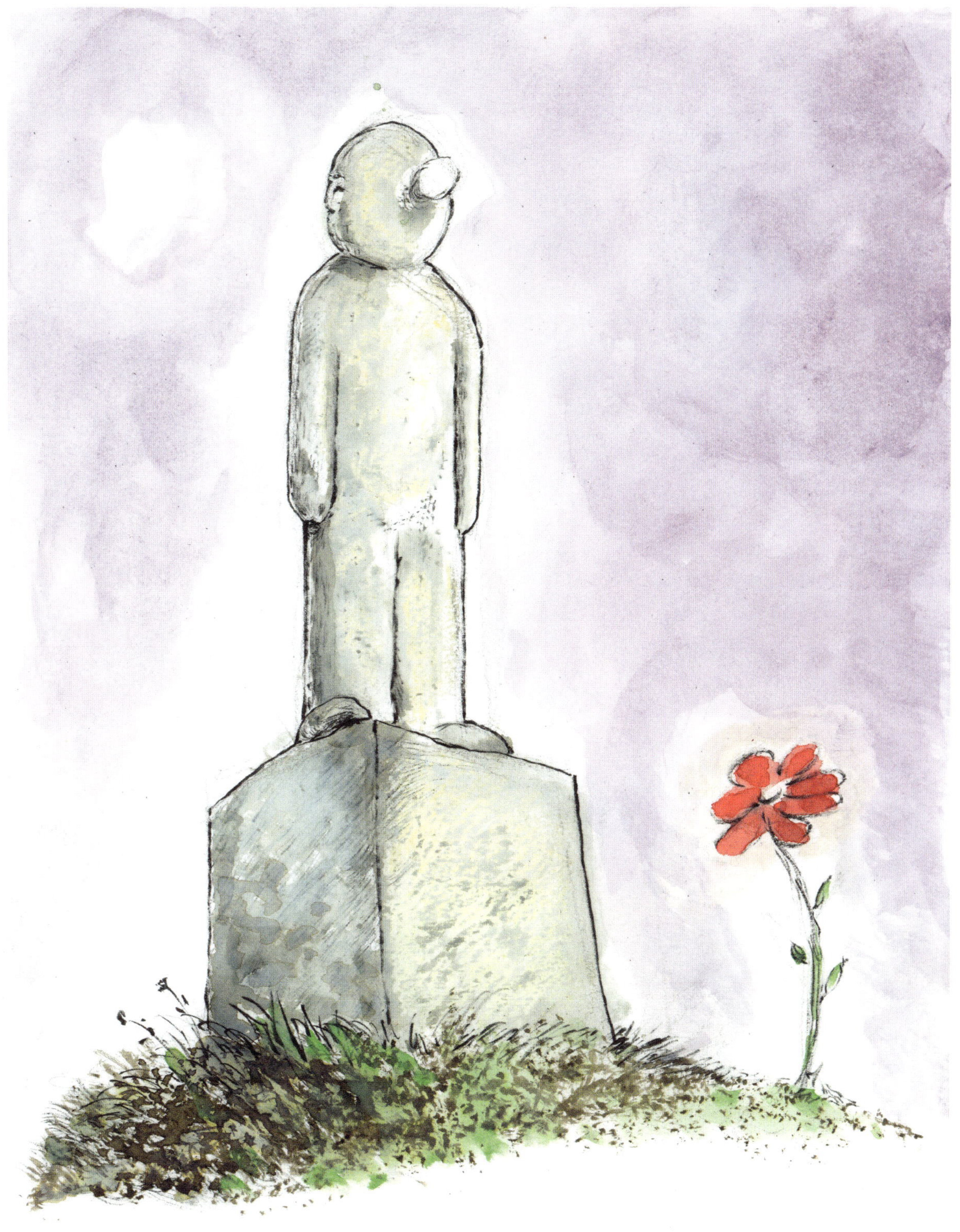

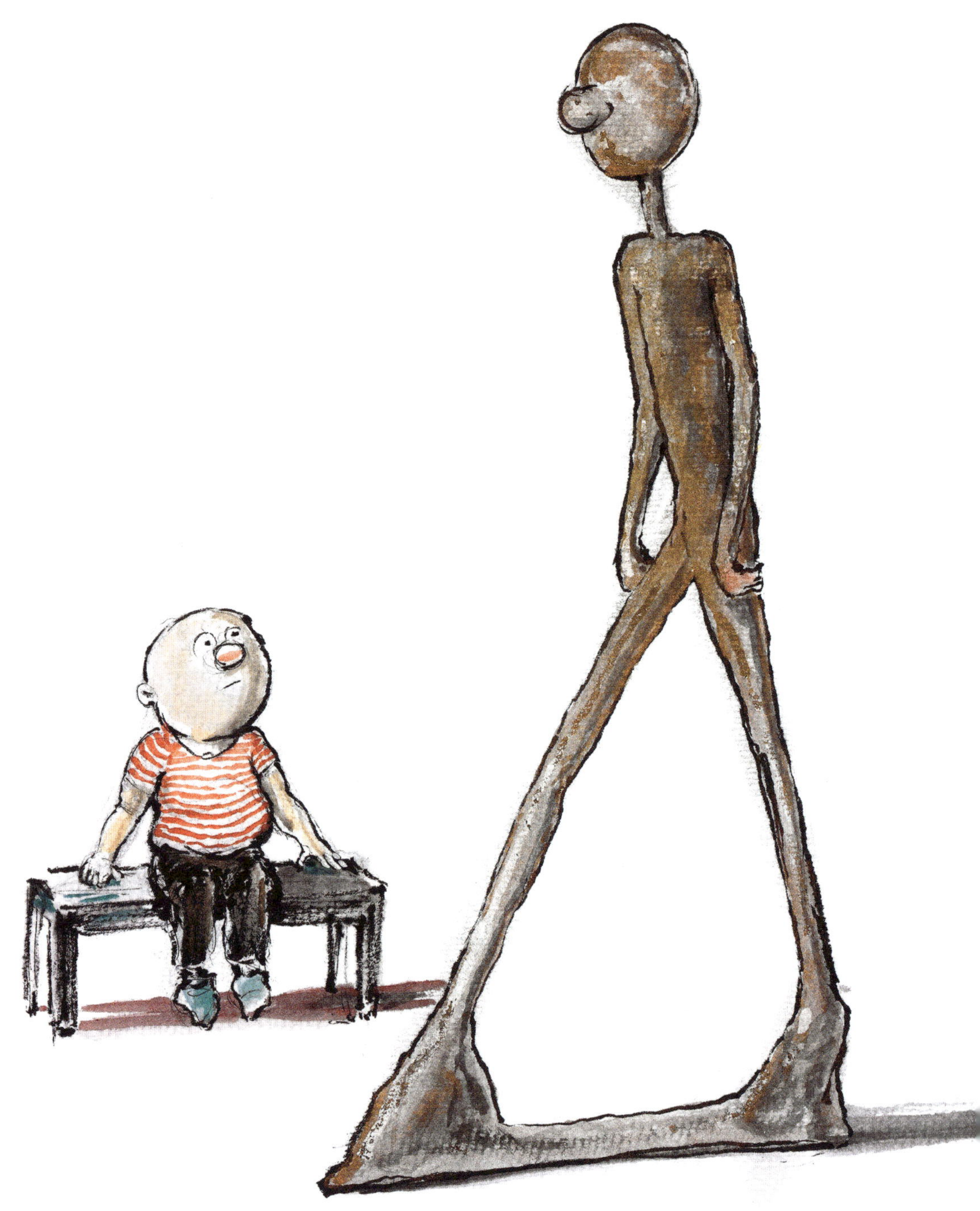

Alberto Giacometti

Skinnier than most

The Swiss artist Alberto Giacometti (1901–1966) was one of the heavyweight sculptors of the 20th century, in the sense of being very important. However, his sculptures themselves are not heavy, as sculptures can't get much skinnier than the figures Giacometti began to make in the years after World War II. Before that time, he had experimented with various forms of expression, including Surrealism. But in the 1940s, the study of models became increasingly important for Giacometti.

His figures have very long bodies, at least as long legs, small heads, and may have been influenced by Egyptian statues, which in turn had influenced archaic Greek sculptures.

Because the sculptures are so extremely slender, it makes no sense to walk around them. Seen from behind, they are almost just a long line in the air. They should be seen from a position like the one our guide in art has taken on the bench: i.e., from the side. Then you can see what Giacometti's figures are up to.

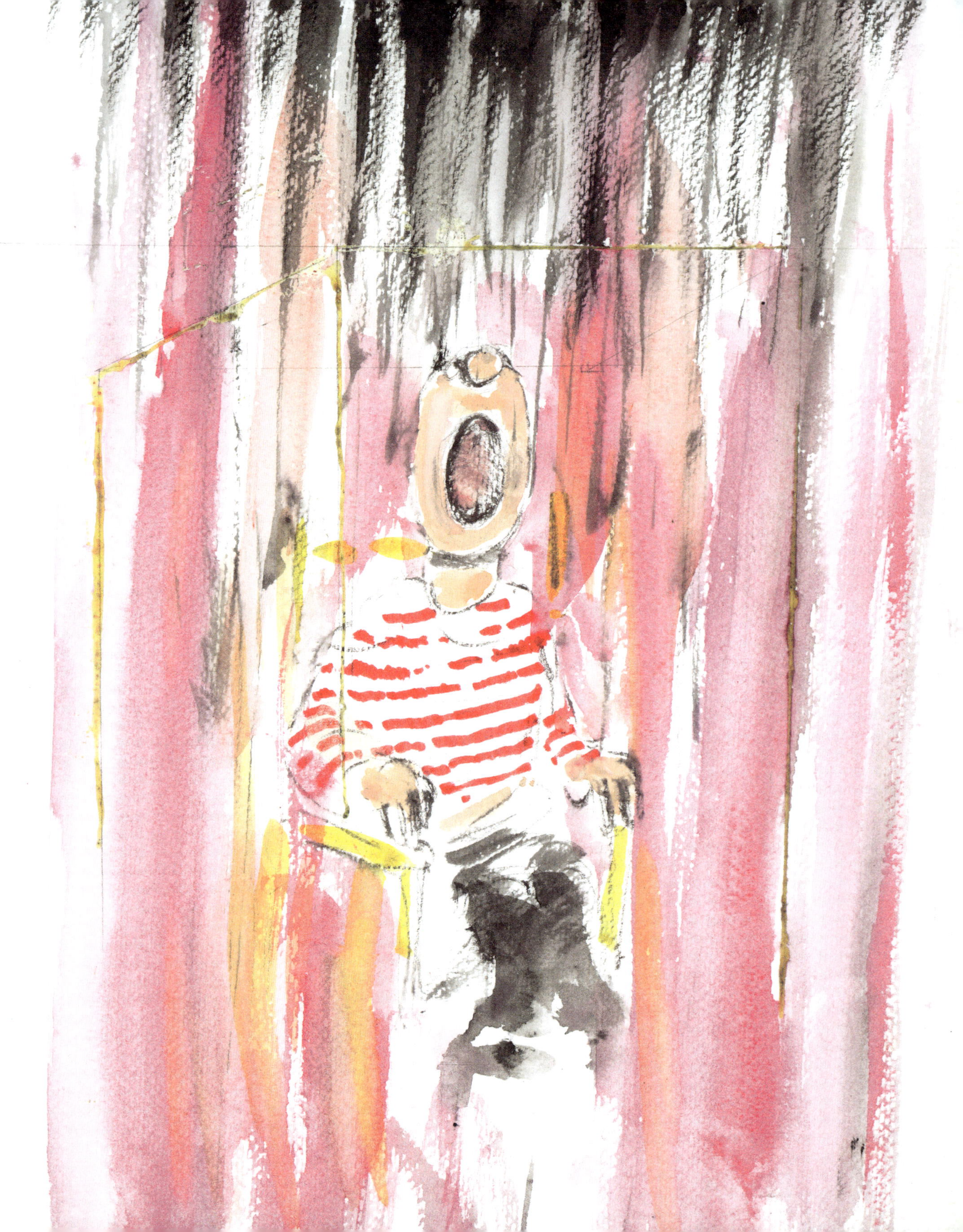

Francis Bacon

Painting for a fearful time

Francis Bacon (1909–1992) was a mature man in his late thirties before achieving success in England. However, when he did break through, his impact was all the more profound. As this loner, originally from Dublin, found the dark path he wanted to pursue with his new paintings, he drew a line through his early production – by destroying it. Bacon's new path was neither easy nor pleasant for his new compatriots to follow. Initially, they were simply shocked by what they saw. But they quickly became convinced that Bacon's paintings represented a new truth, perhaps informed by World War II and the fear of annihilation that so many had lived with. That's why the figures in Bacon's paintings can look so deeply terrified, like our little guide does here.

Bacon drew inspiration for these paintings from a work by the Spanish painter Diego Velázquez. In 1650, Velazquez, during a stay in Rome, painted a portrait of Pope Innocent X, which the model for the painting found far too realistic. Back then, and well into the 1800s, it was expected that a good portrait would beautify and idealize the subject. In Bacon's much later version, the Roman Pope was horrified and screaming, perfectly capturing the spirit of the times.

When the controversial Bacon finally closed his eyes, everyone regarded him as the most significant artist England had produced in the 20th century.

Into the blue

"If one doesn't go to extremes, there's no reason to go at all," the Danish artist Asger Jorn once said. But he wasn't the only one, some went even further. In 1947, the French artist Yves Klein (1928–1962) wrote a symphony called 'Symphonie monotone'. It consisted of one, and only one, tone. Because he thought that was what music was all about.

In the mid-1950s, Klein began painting pictures consisting of only one colour. It started with him exhibiting a series of paintings, each painted in a different colour: green, red, yellow, orange, pink, or blue. The audience thought it was a decoration and were quite pleased. But Klein didn't really like that people loved his paintings. So he decided to make a new exhibition, this time with only blue paintings. Only, it had to be his own blue colour, a genuine ultramarine, which he patented and called 'International Klein Blue'.

According to Klein, colour was the most important element in a painting. In his opinion, the drawing in a picture was just like bars in front of a view. Therefore, he made colour his strongest – and perhaps even his only – card.

His urge for simplification didn't stop here. In 1958, he opened an exhibition in Paris, at the Galerie Iris Clert. It consisted of only one room, where the walls had been painted white. There was nothing else. But it was more than enough to attract attention, spark discussion, and perhaps make him famous. As the first and only one in his time, Klein dared to take art all the way to where it was no longer bound by traditions and conventions. To follow one's own crooked path and then make it all so simple that it doesn't resemble anything seen before takes real courage. And Klein had plenty of that.

Instead of letting yourself be offended, remember that art can also be a kind of research into how to make the impossible possible. For the avant-garde artist, it's crucial to go where no artist has gone before.

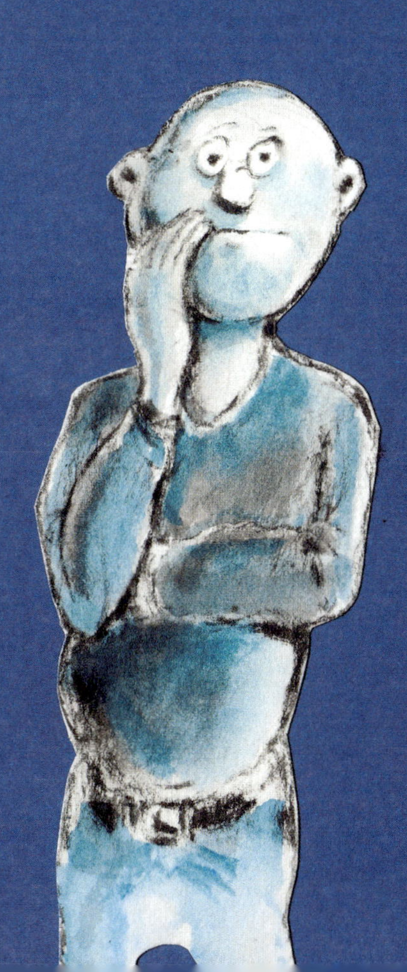

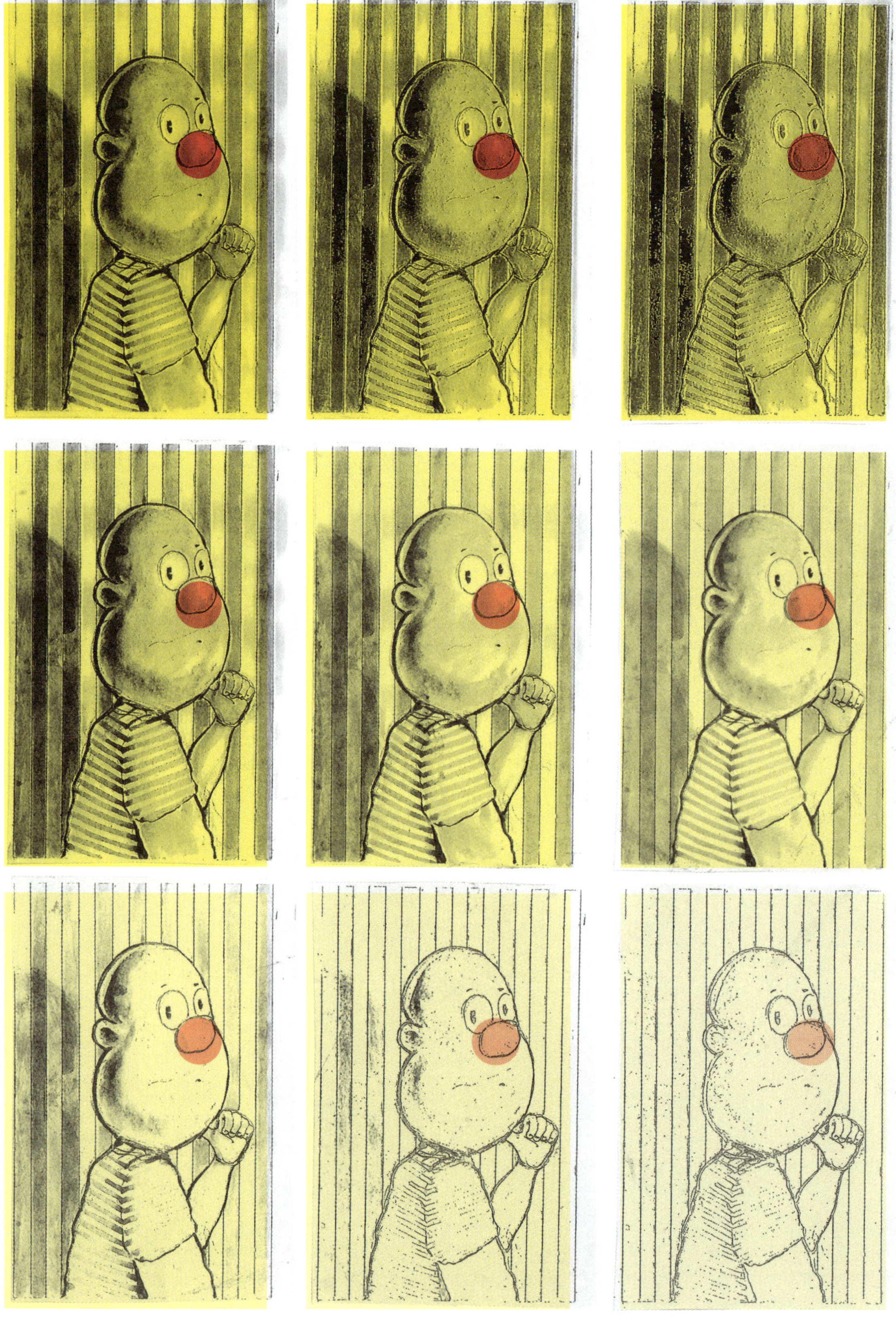

In the future, everyone will be famous

With Pop Art, the art world was invaded by what is most typical of our time – everything that can make us escape from the modern metropolis with all its visual noise (visible stuff can be noisy in its own way). Worst of all are the advertisements, everywhere, and the way they keep repeating the same banal messages over and over to make us buy even more.

The American artist Andy Warhol (1928–1987) was a true master at transforming these simple and banal effects into a new form of art. As a former commercial artist, Warhol knew better than anyone else in the art world that if you want to steal people's attention in a modern culture, all tricks are fair game. The most effective tricks are recognition and repetition, and they go hand in hand. Because once something has been repeated enough times, we also recognize it. And what we recognize the easiest are famous people: movie actors, royals, heads of state, etc.

Andy Warhol once said that in the future, everyone will be famous for 15 minutes. Here, we have given our guide in art the chance to prove Warhol right, which is why his face is repeated so many times, and each time it changes ever so slightly.

An artistic game-changer: comic strips

The comic strip belongs to the culture we call popular culture, and comic strips have been known for more than a century. Just look at the characters 'Katzenjammer Kids', whose story dates back to the 1890s. But it was only with the breakthrough of Pop Art in the 1960s that the comic strip – as a representative of the so-called 'low' art – got the opportunity to inject a bit of life into 'fine art' – i.e., the serious art found in art galleries and major art museums. Pop Art drew its inspiration from the entire modern consumer society, from posters, advertisements, films, and all kinds of packaging with bold signal colours to catch the consumer's eye.

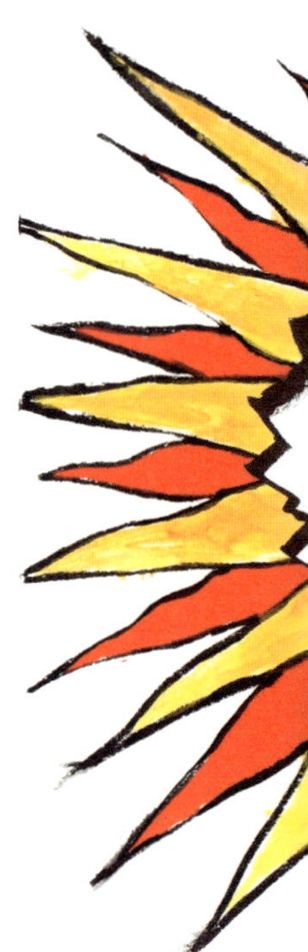

A Pop Art painting could go so far as to mimic the rough screen-printing technique of a comic strip, printed in colours in a newspaper. Here we have tried to show how the American artist Roy Lichtenstein (1923–1997) typically worked. Black, white, and the primary colours red, yellow, and blue dominate, while the figures are usually accompanied by a speech bubble just like in a real comic strip. But the pictures are not small like in a comic strip. They are so large that they must have been made for a large art museum and not for the wall of a private apartment. It didn't take long before any American museum worth its salt had a large Roy Lichtenstein in its collection. For Lichtenstein was one of the leading figures in the generation that put Pop Art in the USA on the hit list of Modernism. However, it was not only in the USA that Pop Art became popular – it was also a hit in London. The fact that this style emerged in New York and London in the 1960s is due to the highly developed civilization of these two cities at a time when many other countries were still reeling from the aftermath of World War II, also artistically. Pop Art did not burn out, but by the 1970s, it was no longer the latest trend.

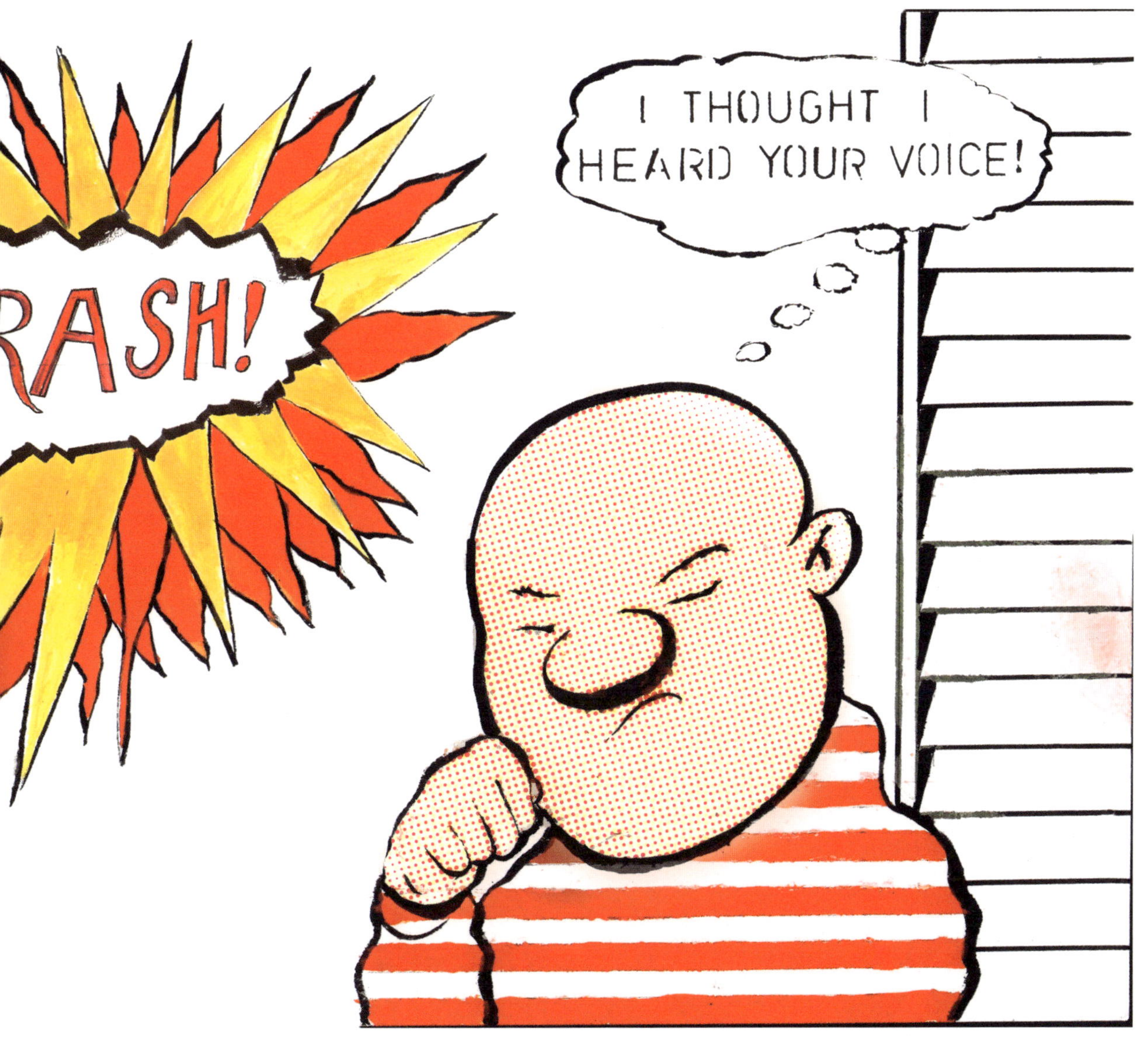

RASH!
I THOUGHT I HEARD YOUR VOICE!

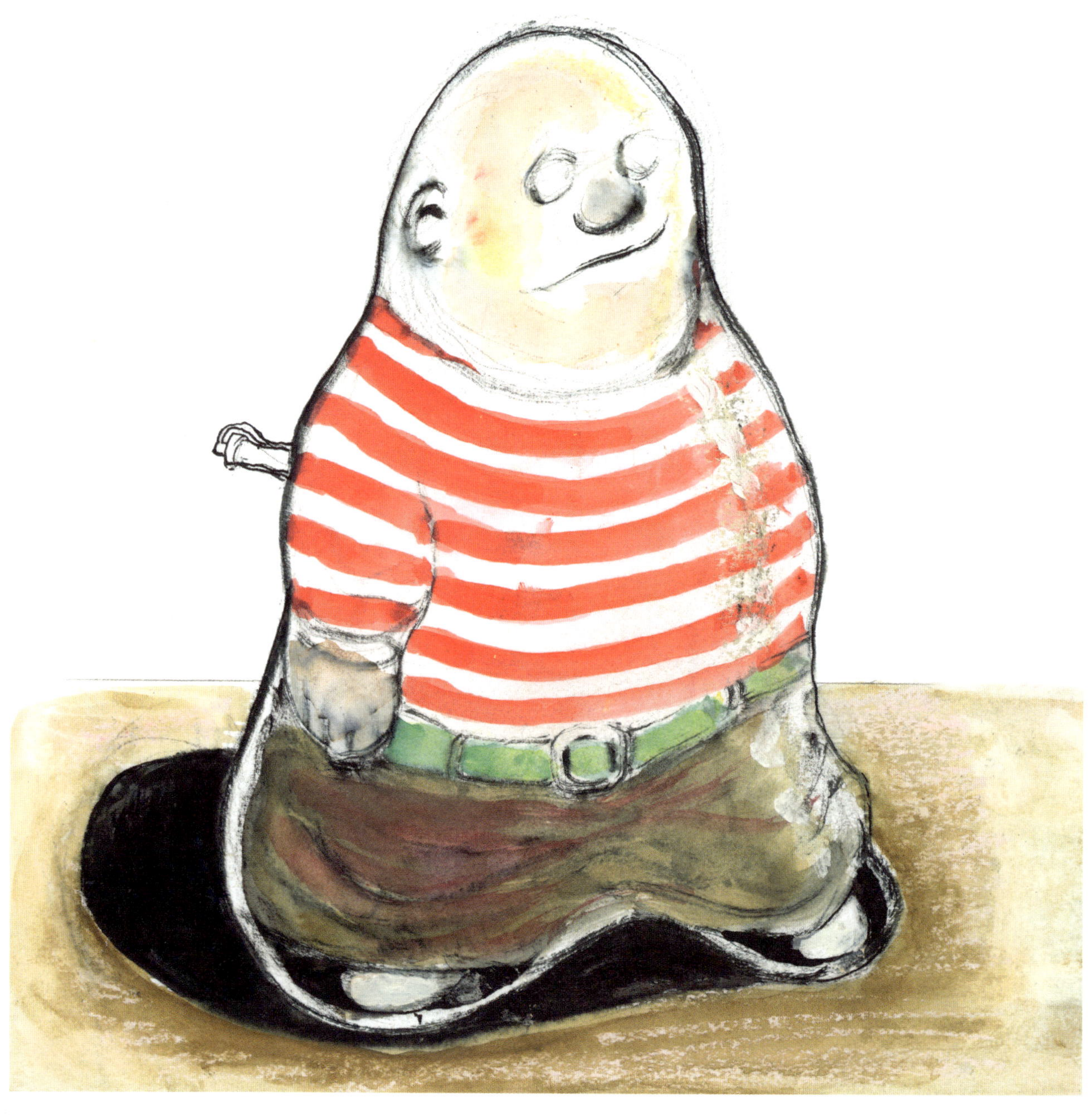

BIG – and soft

Almost any object can be made to resemble a modern Pop Art-sculpture. All you need to do is scale it up and put it in a square or a park where everyone can see it.

This applies to things like a shovel, a saw, a shuttlecock, a clothespin, a lipstick, etc. These are some of the things that Claes Oldenburg (1929–2022) made sculptures of by using the same synthetic materials that so many things from the 1960s were made of, and by making these objects very large. He could choose to make an enormous copy of a cheeseburger or some fries, either in fabric or plastic.

Claes Oldenburg became known as the grand old man of American Pop Art. But originally, he was Swedish and born in Stockholm. He was only seven when his parents took him to the USA. He received his education in Chicago, where his father had been appointed consul. Having had various odd jobs, Claes obtained American citizenship in 1956. In New York, he became acquainted with the latest trends in American art and, based on the knowledge of the development of art that he had already acquired, he got the idea in 1962 for the kind of sculptures that would make him famous in Pop Art: the enormous fast-food sculpture that can do something special: make people smile.

Here you can see what would happen if the artist had done the same to our art guide, i.e., replicated him in plastic and inflated him so that he became as enormous as other Pop Art works. Notice the valve.

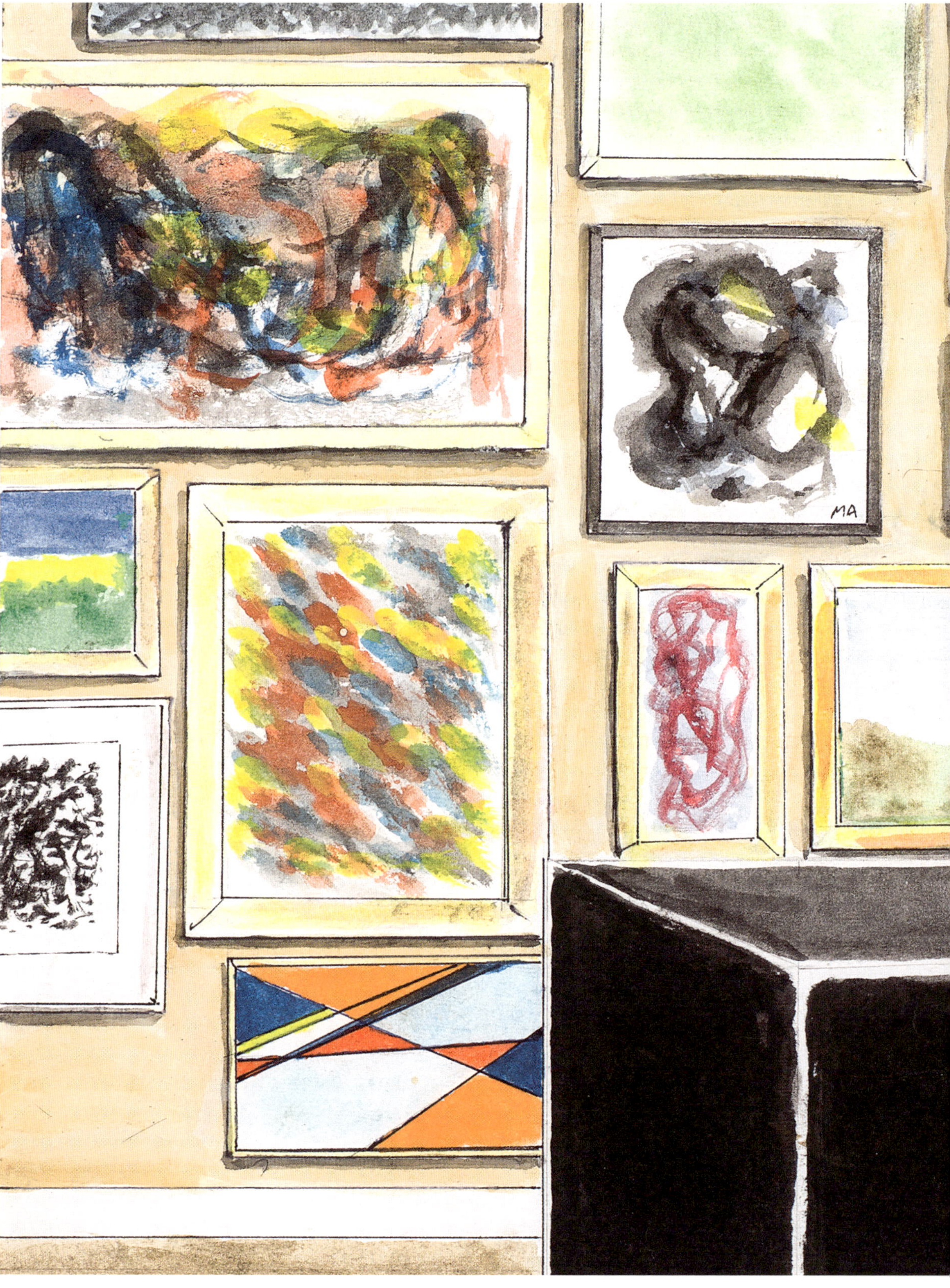

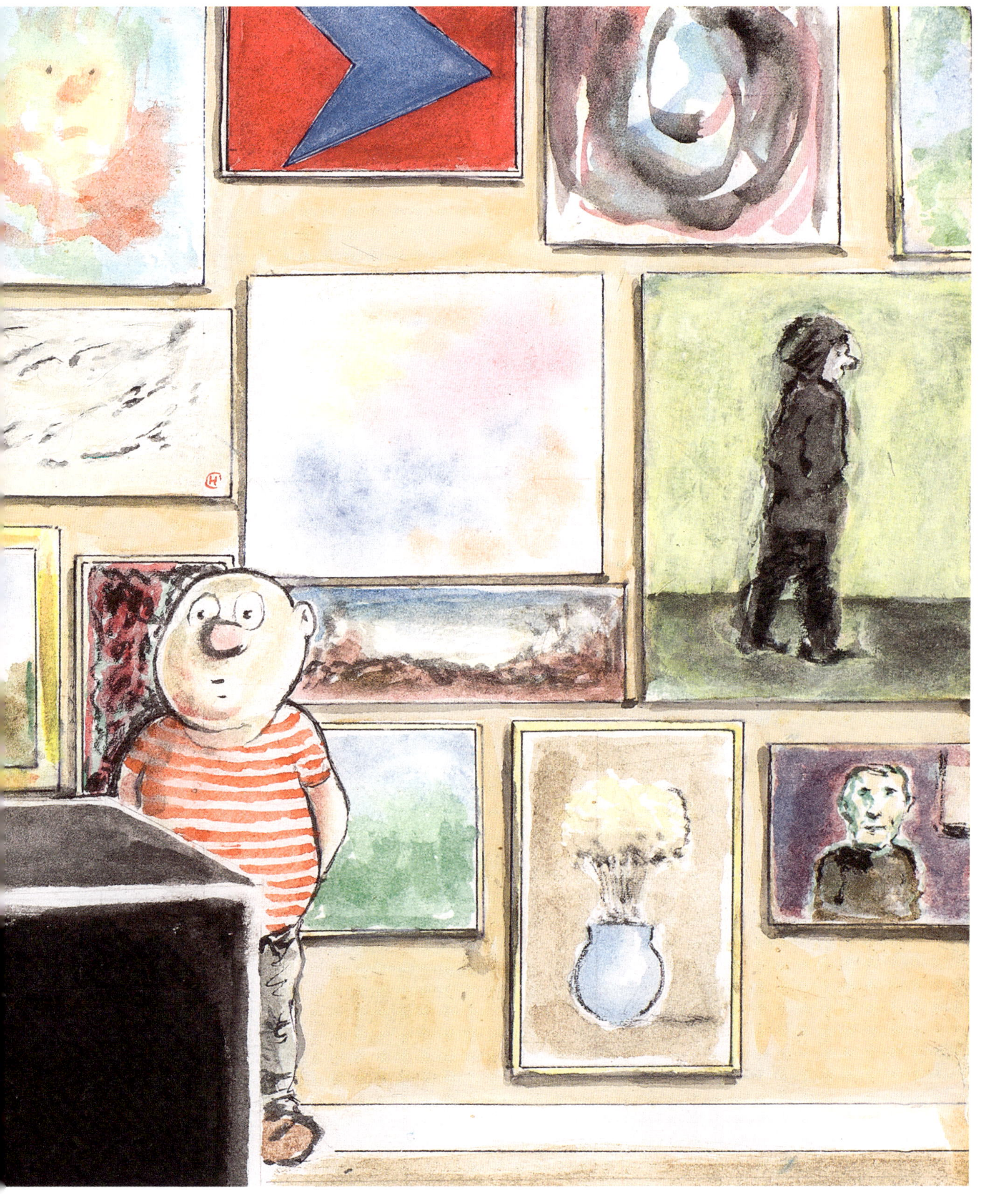

Maximum impact

If you suffer from an overload of impressions, you will naturally start looking for something simple and easy to understand. Because what you can understand catches your eye faster than what confuses you. Minimalism takes advantage of this.

Minimalism emerged as an art movement in the USA in the early 1960s. Some of the most well-known minimalist artists are Americans: Carl Andre (1935–2024) and Donald Judd (1928–1994).

Americans call the movement 'minimal art'. The term tells you that the art is minimized, making it simpler and thus easier to perceive. It even says: 'Less is more'. That's why, in the picture, our guide is looking at the large black cube or block in the middle of the floor. He can better grasp it than all the many paintings, of widely varying sizes and styles, hanging on the wall. They simply confuse the eye with their flickering diversity.

Minimalism was a reaction against expressionist painting, which had allowed the artist to express everything about their feelings, consciousness, etc. Minimalist art does not do that. It doesn't want to be sensitive, expressive, or soulful, and it doesn't pretend to be something it's not. By consisting of simple, geometric shapes, possibly repeated as a series, it can resemble something that could have been manufactured in a factory.

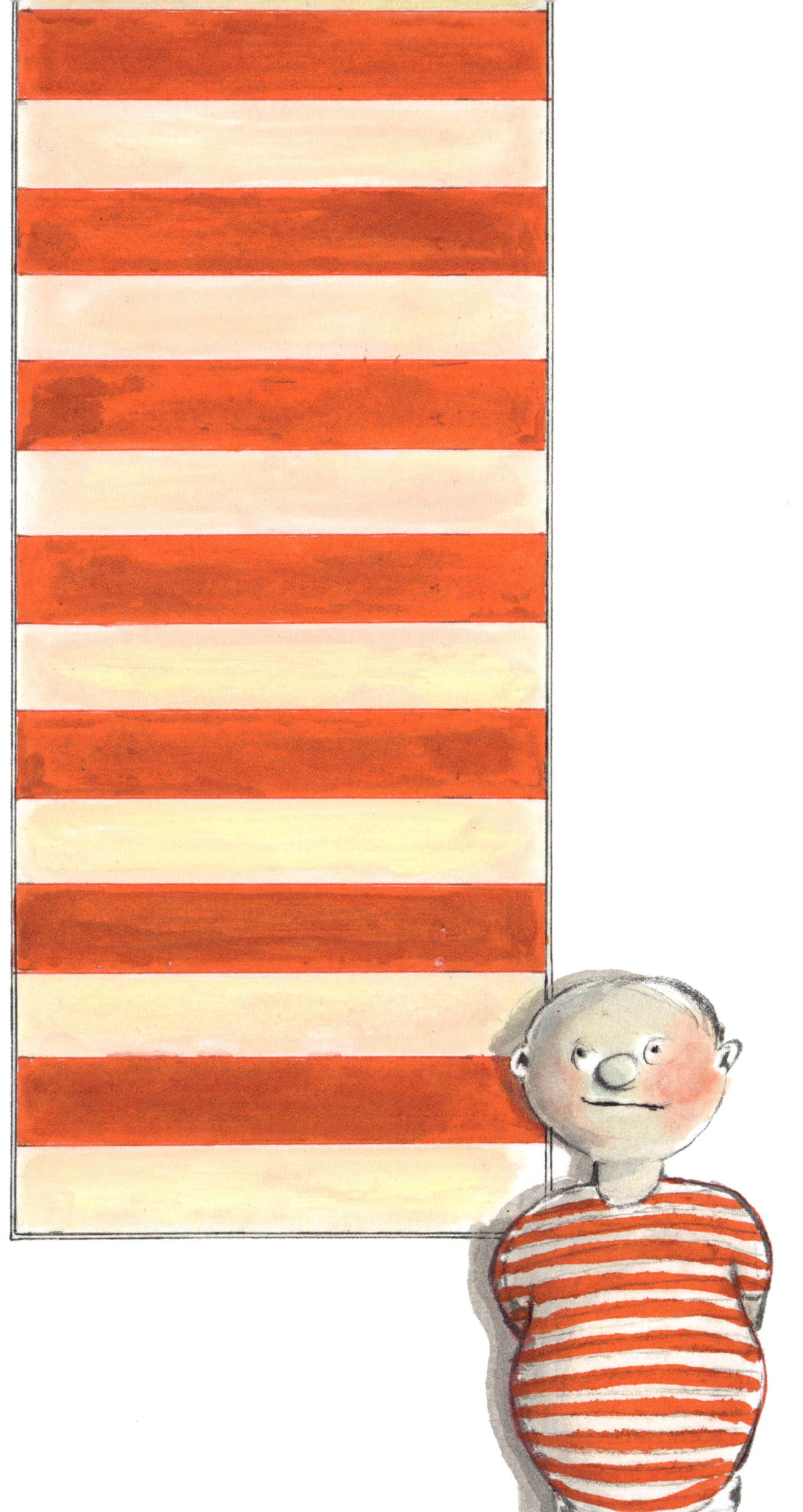

Piero Manzoni

Art
– or hot air?

A prerequisite for something to be called art is, of course, that a genuine artist has made it. But does that mean that everything this artist produces is also art? That's what the Italian Piero Manzoni (1933–1963), one of the most radical artists of the 20th century, believed. In 1959, he created 45 works that he called 'Corpo d'aria', which means 'body of air'. It was a box containing a very large balloon and a stand for the balloon. If one wished for Manzoni to inflate the balloon, the price would increase considerably. In return, one would receive 300 litres of breath from the artist, who wasn't afraid to push the boundaries. And his breath was genuine.

In 1961, Manzoni went a step further and produced ninety cans, which according to a text on the can (in three languages) contained one-third of a gram of the artist's own excrement. He sold them as art. But were they a form of art? And could one be sure that the contents of the can matched what was on the label.

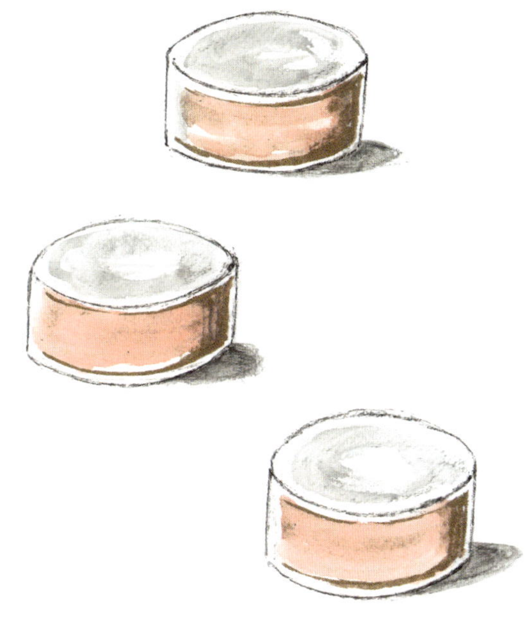

Of course, one could simply open the can and check. But then the little can would lose its value, and this value has only increased over the years. In 2020, such a can of artist's excrement was sold at Sotheby's auctions in Milan for a quarter of a million euros.

With the balloons – and the cans of excrement – Manzoni wanted to ridicule both the art market, collectors, and critics, who often and eagerly talked about an artist's authentic, personal style and could never get enough of it. But nothing is more personal than an artist's breath and his excrement. So in his own controversial way, Manzoni delivered the most personal aspect of his own production, namely, what was inside him – and only him.

Steely sculptor

You can't expect a modern sculptor to use the same materials – copper, marble, wood etc. – as they did in the old days. They have the right to keep up with technological developments, and that's precisely what the American Richard Serra (1938–2024) did. He crafted his enormous sculptures in a material called corten steel. It came on the market in 1964 and has the advantage of being weatherproof. That is, when exposed to rain, sun, and wind, the surface forms a dark reddish-brown layer of rust that is very robust, and this colour also contributes to the overall effect of Serra's constructions.

Therefore, these sculptures can easily stand being outdoors, where, due to their size, they almost block your path or enclose you, leaving you with nothing else to see but the sculpture's large surface. The direct physical encounter with such a work is quite different from seeing it depicted in a book.

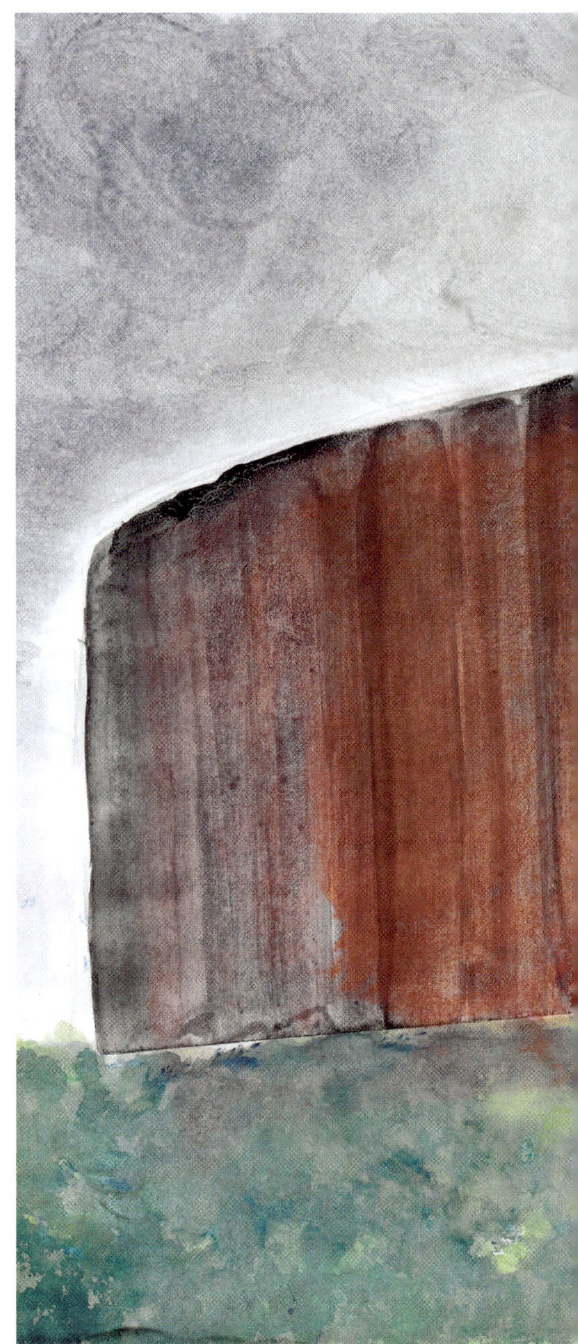

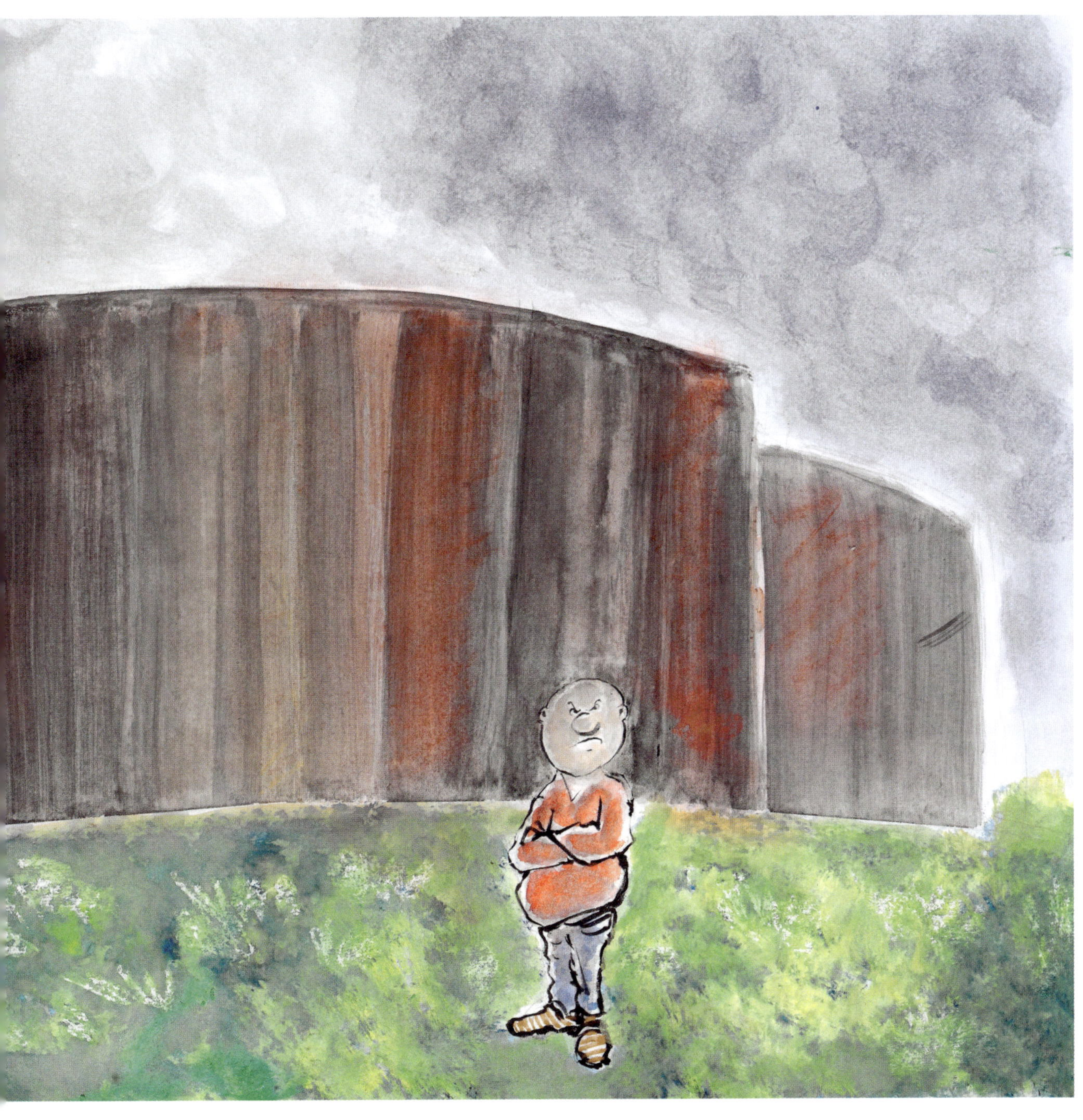

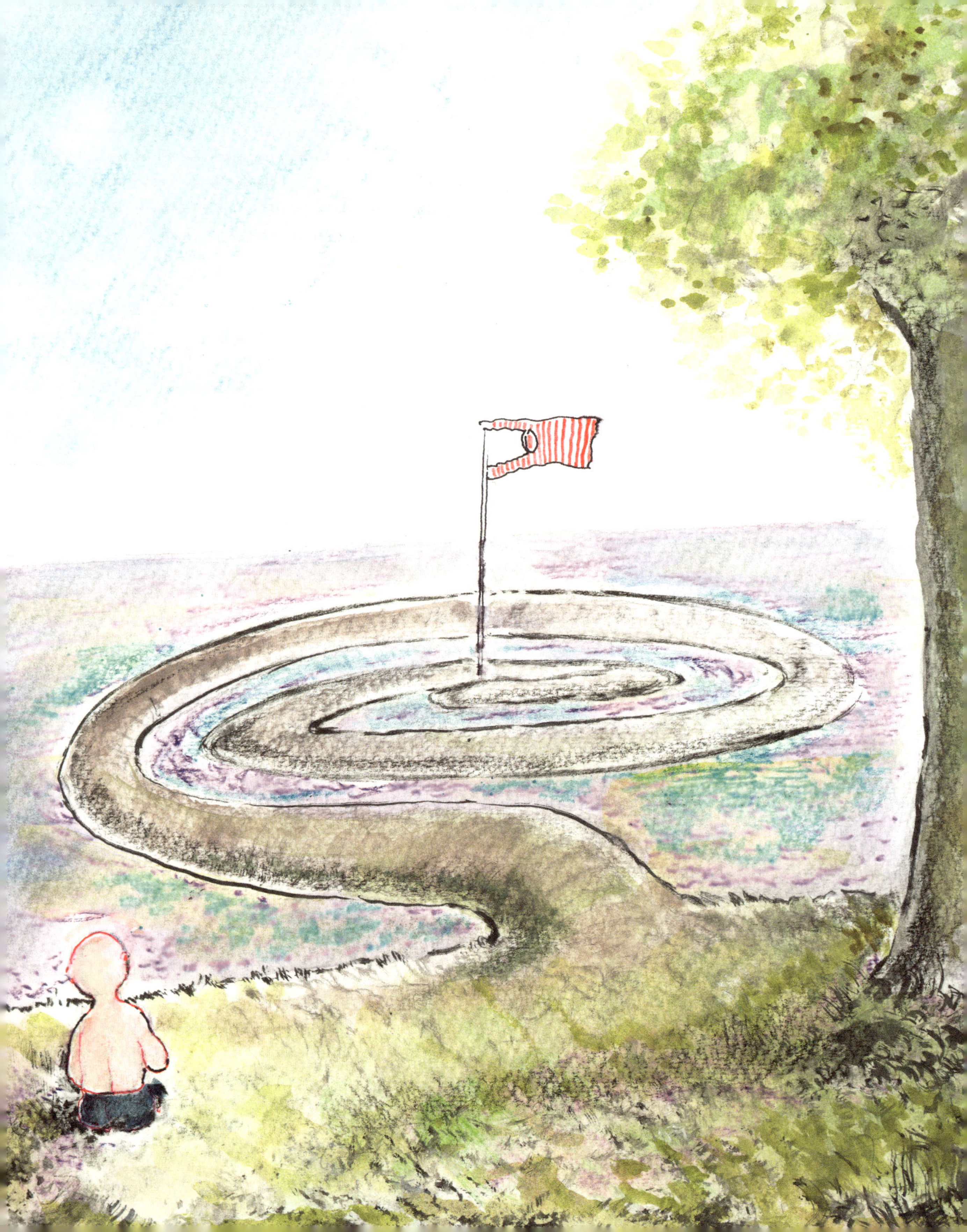

A sculpture that can't be wrapped up

If you included cave art as the beginning, painting was at least 20,000 years old in the 1960s. Sculptures in marble, bronze, and wood had been made by countless artists over time. Therefore, some younger artists felt the need to come up with something entirely new, which also required completely new materials. This gave rise to a series of alternative – i.e., different – forms of expression.

One of them was land art, which also could be called 'earth art'. The materials used were nature's own cheap materials or nature's own waste. In addition to soil, the most common materials were pieces of rock, pebbles, clay, etc. With all this, the artist – and his assistants – could build something resembling small mountains, islands, or landscapes.

Land art was a rebellion against gallery art and 'art as commodity' because the works were impossible to put a price on and even harder to wrap up. Since land art could be expensive to create but not easy to sell, artists sometimes settled for making sketches of their projects.

Thus, land art was a kind of conceptual art (idea-based art), where the underlying idea is more important than the execution itself. Often, land art became a form of happening or performance art because natural forces and precipitation slowly changed the work. The most important land art-artist was the American Robert Smithson (1938–1973), who died in a plane crash while inspecting one of his works from the air.

Poul Gernes

Adding colour to life

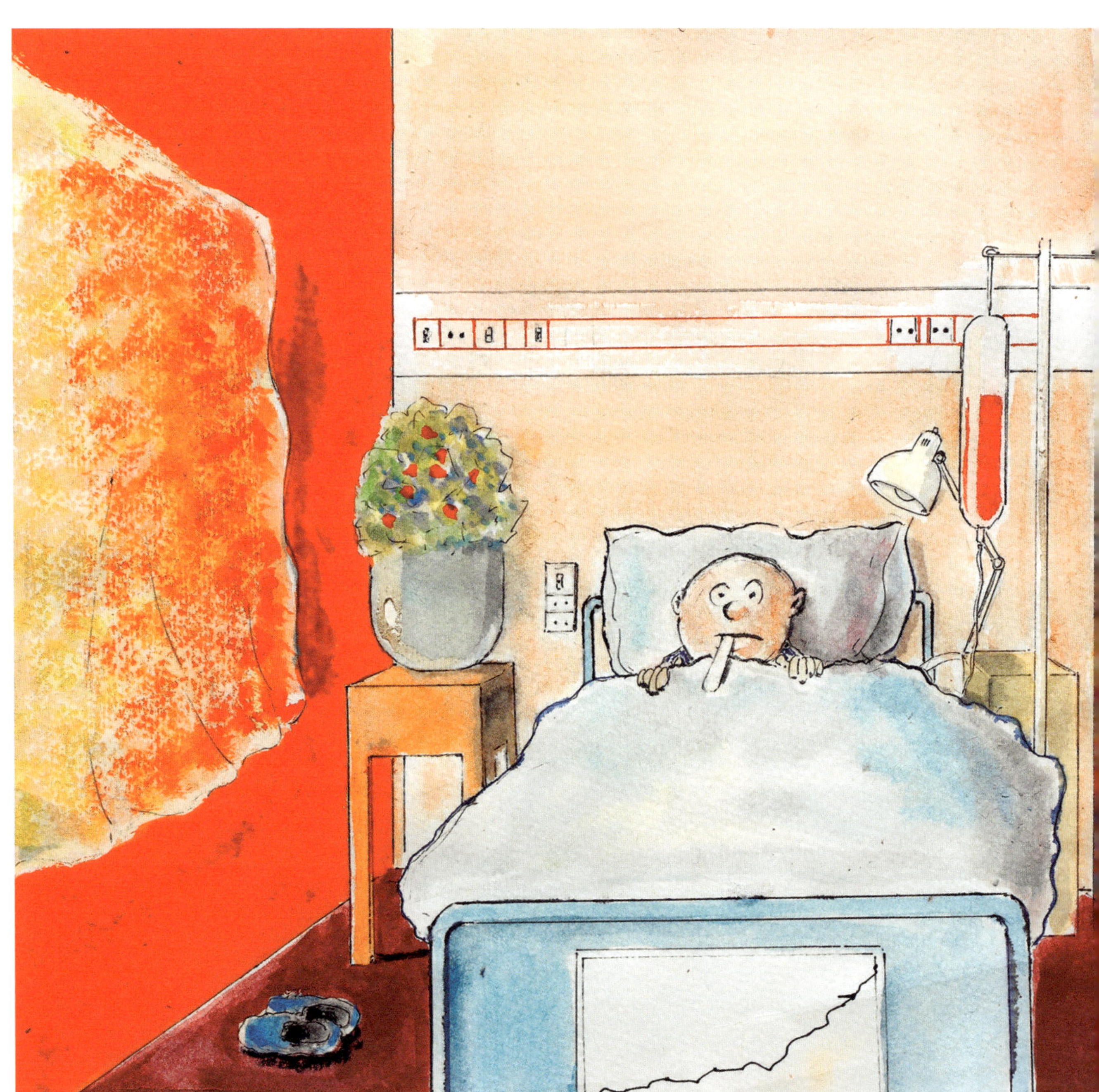

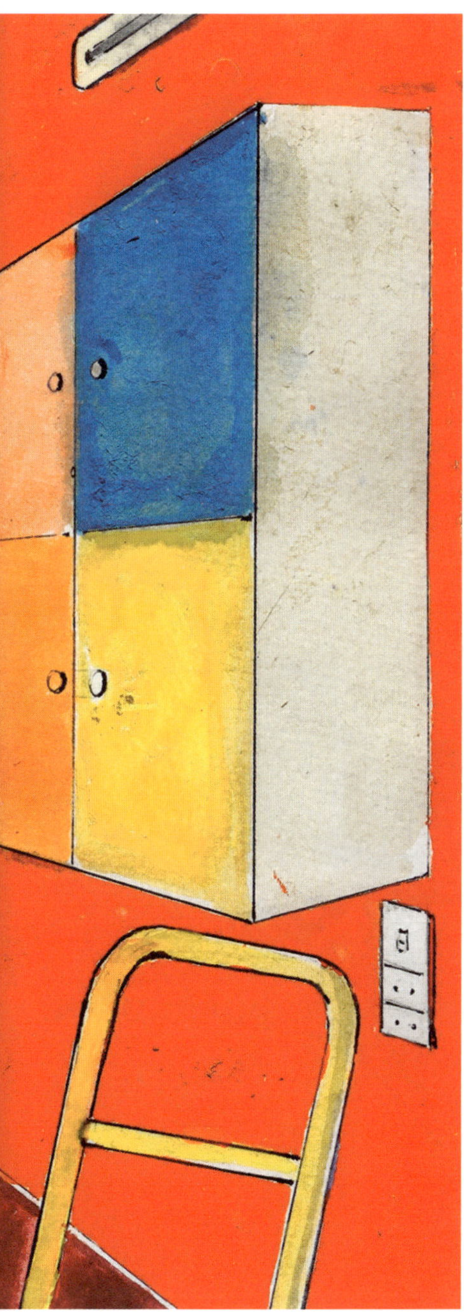

When it comes to capturing your attention, strong hues are a true master. Some colours can even be very stimulating and put you in a better mood. Therefore, the colours we surround ourselves with on a daily basis are not irrelevant, especially if, for example, we are patients in a hospital. A museum of fine arts should also be able to brighten up the landscape with the colours it can paint its facade with.

Danish artist Poul Gernes (1925–1996) consistently thought about adding colours to our lives. In his opinion, it was a misunderstanding that a city's architecture should be colourless – and sad. On that point, this experimentalist was in line with the ancient Greeks, who also – it has been shown – preferred strong and festive colours on their statues and temples. Creating new sculptures did not require expensive materials or cultivating a style that was unmistakably one's own. Art should in principle be able to be made from anything – and be for everyone. A pile of colourful textiles could become an extraordinary sculpture if one let their imagination run wild and rolled it all up into a big lump, as in the picture.

A key idea of Gernes' was that art should be set free and not hidden away in art museums, where people have to pay admission to see it. While he was alive, he did not exhibit in commercial galleries. He only began doing so after his death when people learned to understand and respect his struggle for the democratization of art.

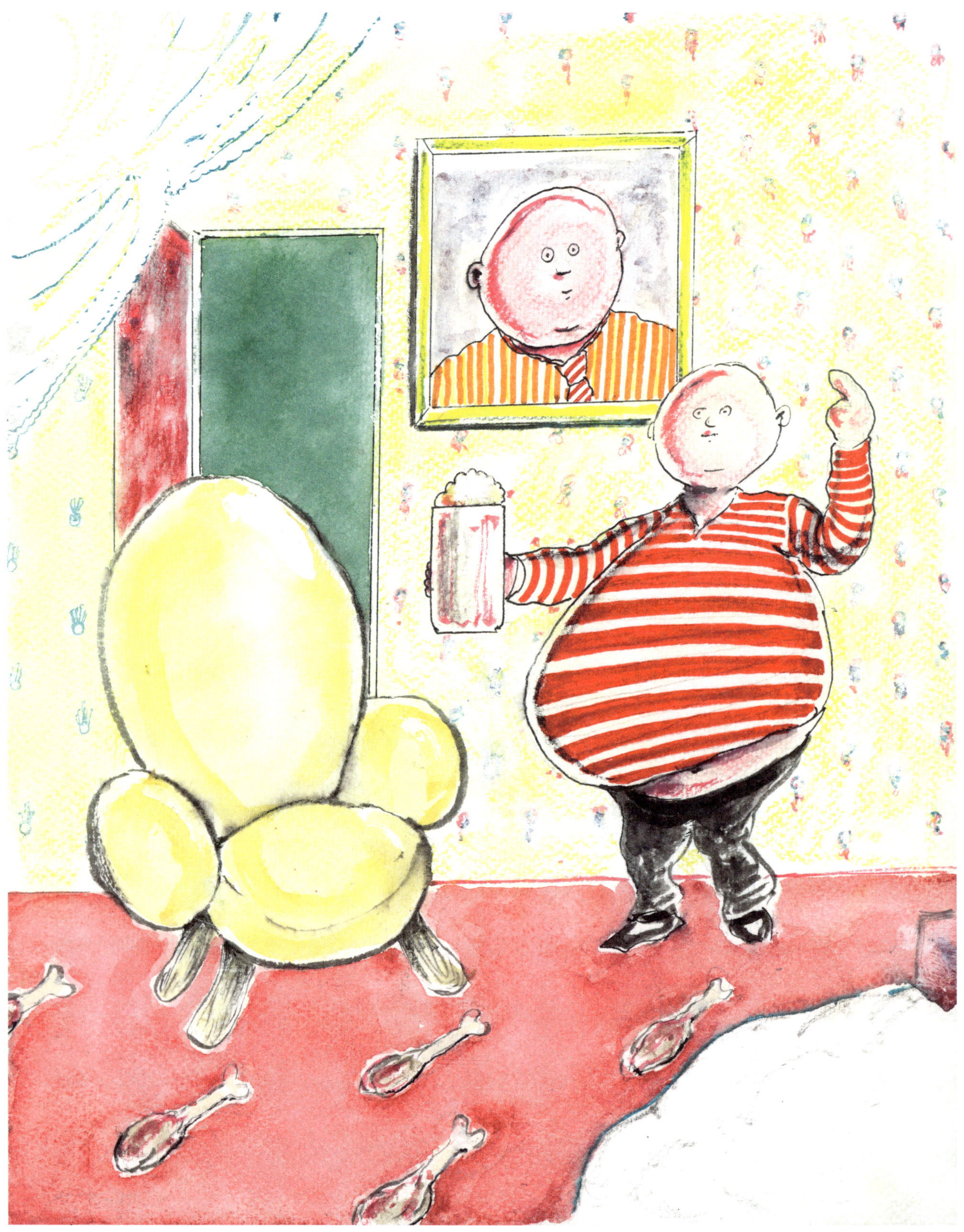

Fernando Botero

Plenty of mass

The Colombian painter and sculptor Fernando Botero (1932–2023) was so popular that a style was named after him: Boterism. This style was characterized by the enormous body volume Botero endowed all his figures with, whether he painted or sculpted them. Moreover, Botero was well-versed in art history, and he often recruited his role models from art's famous classics and used them as inspiration.

But Botero cannot take full credit for introducing obesity into art. The first visible manifestations of artistic obesity can be traced back almost 25,000 years to the Venus of Willendorf. This voluminous Venus has had many successors, especially in the last five hundred years, among artists like Rubens, Renoir, and others. Depending on cultural upbringing, this celebration of human volume can be interpreted as reminders of the power of sexual desire, the abundance of flesh, wealth, and excess, or the opposite: the vulnerability of life.

Perhaps Botero made his figures full-bodied for the same reason the Italian sculptor Alberto Giacometti made his thin as skeletons. Or perhaps it was simply a matter of choosing a style that was unmistakable. Thus, Botero's paintings were not just about obesity. The style itself was rather a fundamental expression of vitality, presence, and existence. Botero wanted to magnify everything, so it appeared enlarged, distorted, or stylized, much like in a funhouse mirror – and not just people, but also the things that surround people in their everyday lives, such as flowers, pots, houses, bricks, etc.

Over time, Botero became very wealthy, but he hailed from a country with few museums. This led him to donate large collections of his and others' artworks to a couple of museums that were particularly close to him. One is located in Medellín, where he was born in 1932. The other is in Colombia's capital, Bogotá. He believed that as many people as possible should have the chance to experience his art.

Christo and Jeanne-Claude

Wrappings

Many people like to wrap up the things they give away as gifts.
Because then the recipient doesn't know what he or she is getting
until the gift is unwrapped. The wrapping increases the excite-
ment and sharpens the anticipation. By making the contents of the
gift a secret, you focus attention on what is wrapped up.

This is the effect that the Bulgarian-born artist Christo, born
Christo Javacheff (1935–2020), exploited in his works. At the
beginning of his career, he wrapped up smaller objects. But as the
years passed, he wrapped up both buildings and bridges. Entire
landscapes in several nations were transformed thanks to him and
his French-born wife Jeanne-Claude de Guillebon (1935–2009),
whom he met after moving to Paris in 1958. In 1964, the couple
permanently settled in New York.

It was because of Jeanne-Claude's organizational talent that the
couple's largest projects – such as wrapping the Reichstag building
in Berlin in 1995 – could even be realized. The work 'Wrapped
Reichstag' was the realization of an old project that Christo had
already conceived in 1971. Covering the German parliament
required 100,000 square meters of synthetic silvery material and
almost 16 kilometres of blue rope. The wrapping in the picture is a
far smaller challenge by comparison. In fact, Christo and Jeanne-
Claude never wrapped up living beings. Instead, they involved
people on a large scale as volunteer helpers to realize their projects. The financing of their major art projects usually happened
by selling hundreds of sketches that Christo produced in connection with his and Jeanne-Claude's preparations. Another important feature was that Christo and Jeanne-Claude's wrappings were
always temporary. In fact, during their careers, they only executed
a single permanent work.

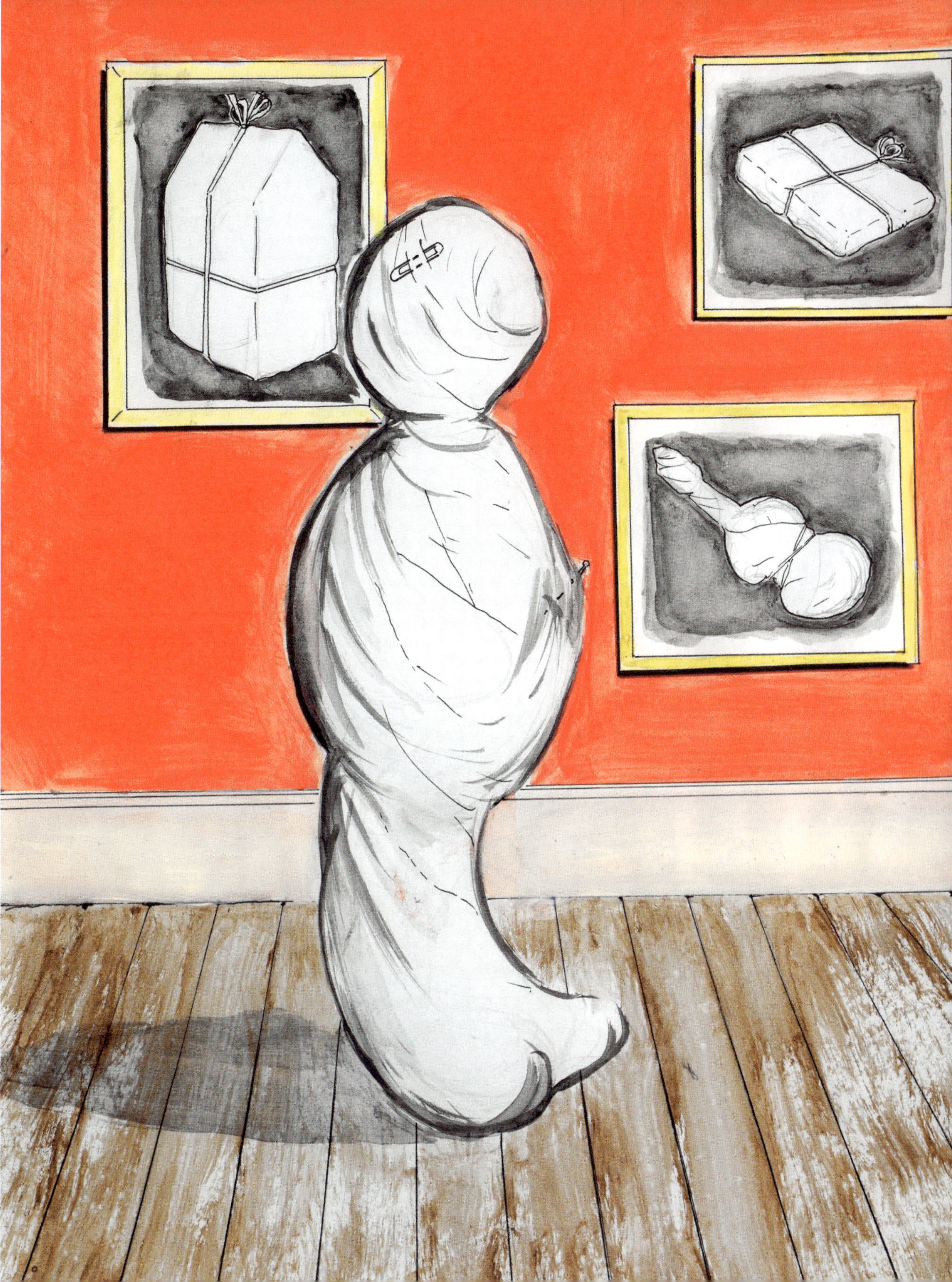

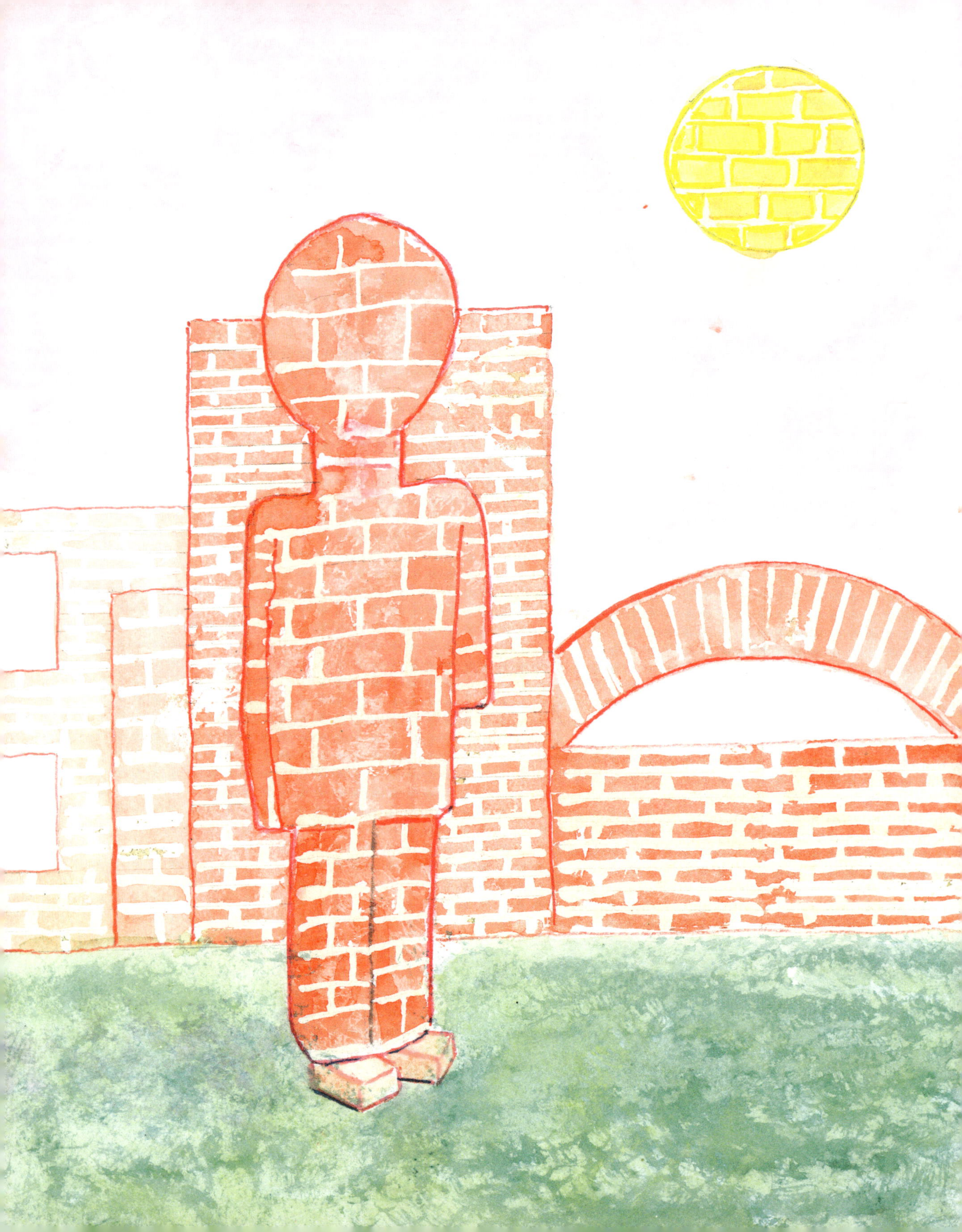

Per Kirkeby

One man
– at least ten
specialties

Change is delightful, even in art. If you're afraid of change and don't dare to move, you will never realize your full potential. The painter who perhaps never dares to make a sculpture, print a piece of graphic art, or write a poem, doesn't know the extent of his artistic talent. As an artist, curiosity is its own reward, and curiosity should start with the artist himself.

For any artist, it is important to express oneself, but it is equally important to evolve. You evolve when you dare to engage with new things. Many musicians paint, and many painters have published collections of poems. In this way, they explore new facets of their talent and may discover what they are really good at – and what they are not so good at. But the most common thing is that artists are people with a strong need to express themselves and communicate with others. After all, art is a form of communication.

The crucial thing is that as an artist, you have something important to say, and there are many ways to communicate an important message. The work – no matter which technique and medium you use – is the way you convey your message, and there is more than one way to express it.

These days, you don't have to choose whether you want to be a geologist, painter, sculptor, graphic artist, architect, poet, writer, filmmaker, or polar explorer. Danish Per Kirkeby (1938–2018) chose to be all of these, almost at once, even though he was primarily an artist. The best thing for an artist is not necessarily to end up in the right niche. The best – in Kirkeby's case – has been to choose from all niches. His many interests and skills have pushed each other and prevented him from stagnating. His sculptures owe their existence to his interest in architecture, in his paintings one can sense his knowledge of geological processes, etc. That's what you see in the drawing, where geological formations surround our guide in art.

You can't just paint out of thin air, as Kirkeby himself has said. There must be something you paint away from, towards, or up to. You can start from 'something' without ending up as a realist. Throughout his life, Kirkeby continued the voyage of discovery through his own possibilities. This has resulted in a very large and diverse production. He created well over a hundred sculptures in brick alone, and his paintings number in the thousands.

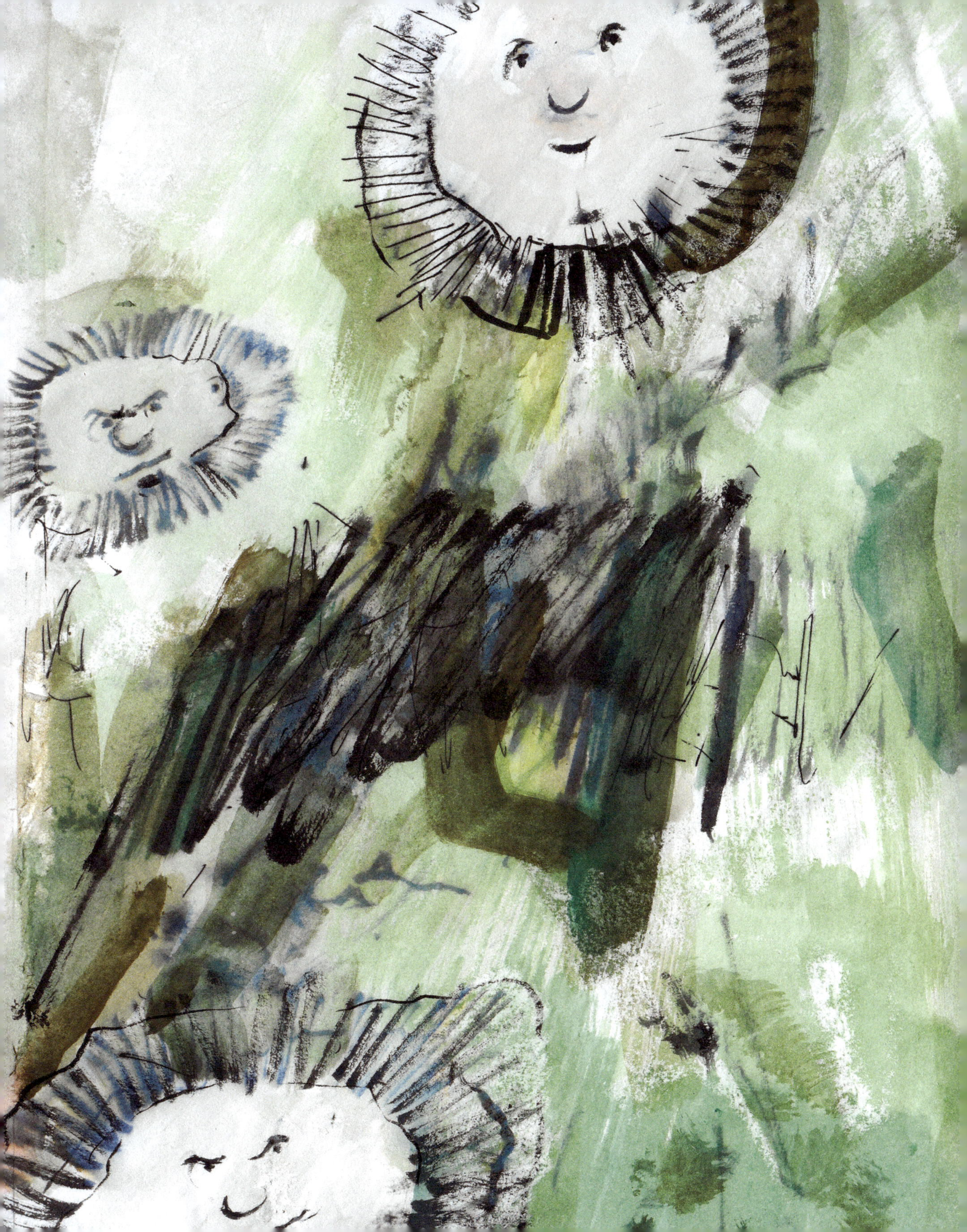

Georg Baselitz

An artist worth turning upside down for

If an artist bends over backwards for the sake of his audience, he's usually not a very good artist. It's a different story, however, if he can get the audience to do it for his own sake, as is the case here. The German neo-expressionist Georg Baselitz (born 1938) has become known as the painter whose subjects are upside down. He is one of the so-called 'Young Wild Ones' in German art, and this wildness spread throughout Europe. People have been wondering whether Baselitz paints his pictures upside down or whether he flips them when they're finished so they end up upside down.

But the most important thing is not how he does it, but why he does it. However, you are not meant to stand on your head to understand Baselitz, as our little guide does here. Because if you do, you haven't understood him. You should think of all this turning-upside-down as a form of abstraction. A picture turned upside down shifts your attention from the subject to the painterly. That's what matters. Then you'll notice the structure, shapes, and colours in the picture better, everything that isn't just representing something, but is something in its own right.

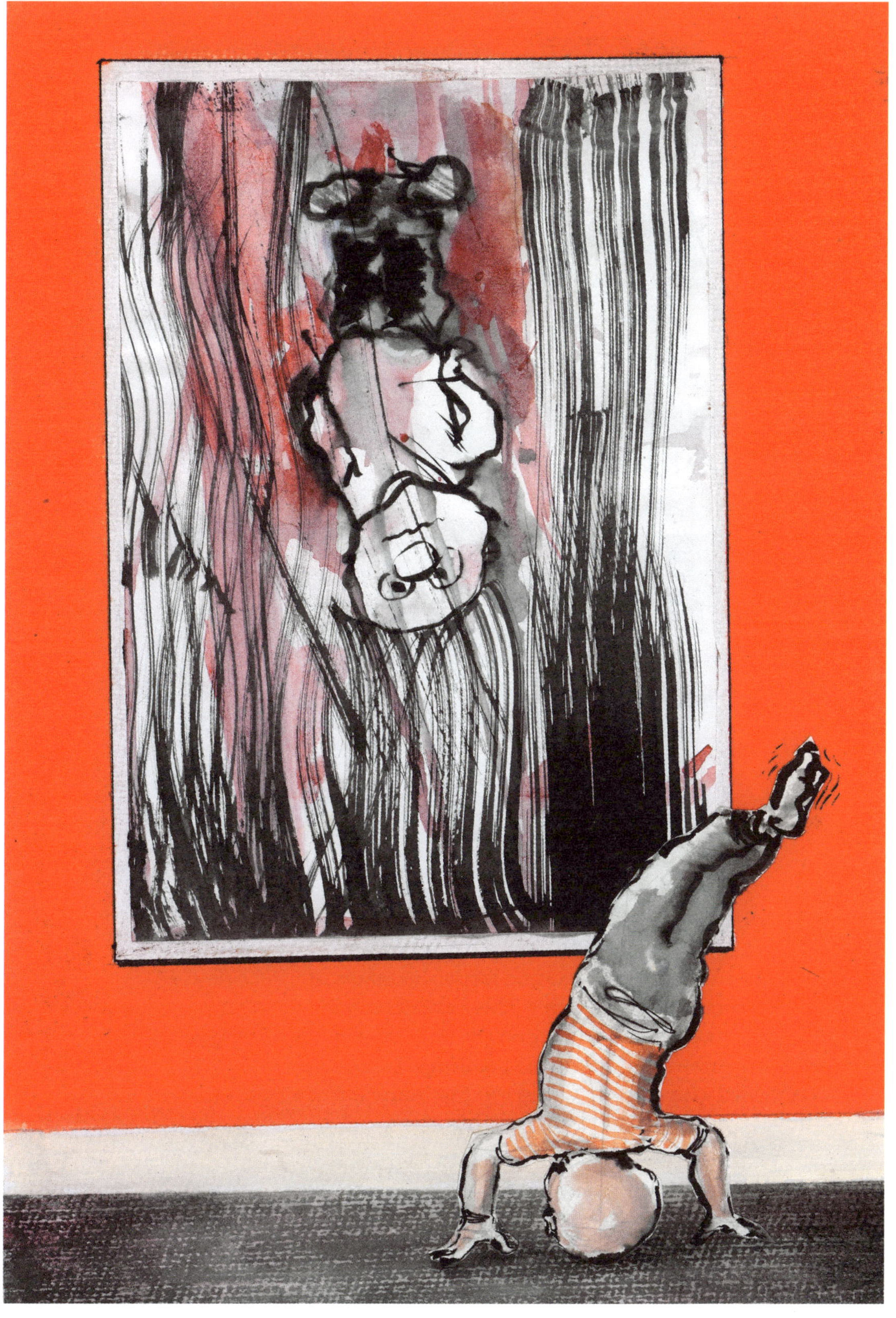

Philip Guston

Here, laughter is allowed

The American Philip Guston (1913–1980) believed that laughter was the best reaction to his paintings. At first glance, his paintings do indeed look funnier than much other American art from the post-World War II era. Most of it is abstract – i.e., without figures of any kind – and Guston began that way too.

Speaking of laughter. Can one laugh at members of the Ku Klux Klan movement when they appear in Guston's paintings with their stitched white hoods? For the Ku Klux Klan was a strong racist movement, and the artist Guston was Jewish.

The message in the painting is political, but in a painterly package. In the illustration, we have continued to expand on Guston's universe and let two members of the clan come to visit a painter. There are already a couple of his portraits hanging on the wall. Do you think they have come to buy the paintings? Or are they dissatisfied with something and want to complain? Undoubtedly the latter.

Our guide – in the small frame on the wall – certainly doesn't look entirely comfortable with the situation.

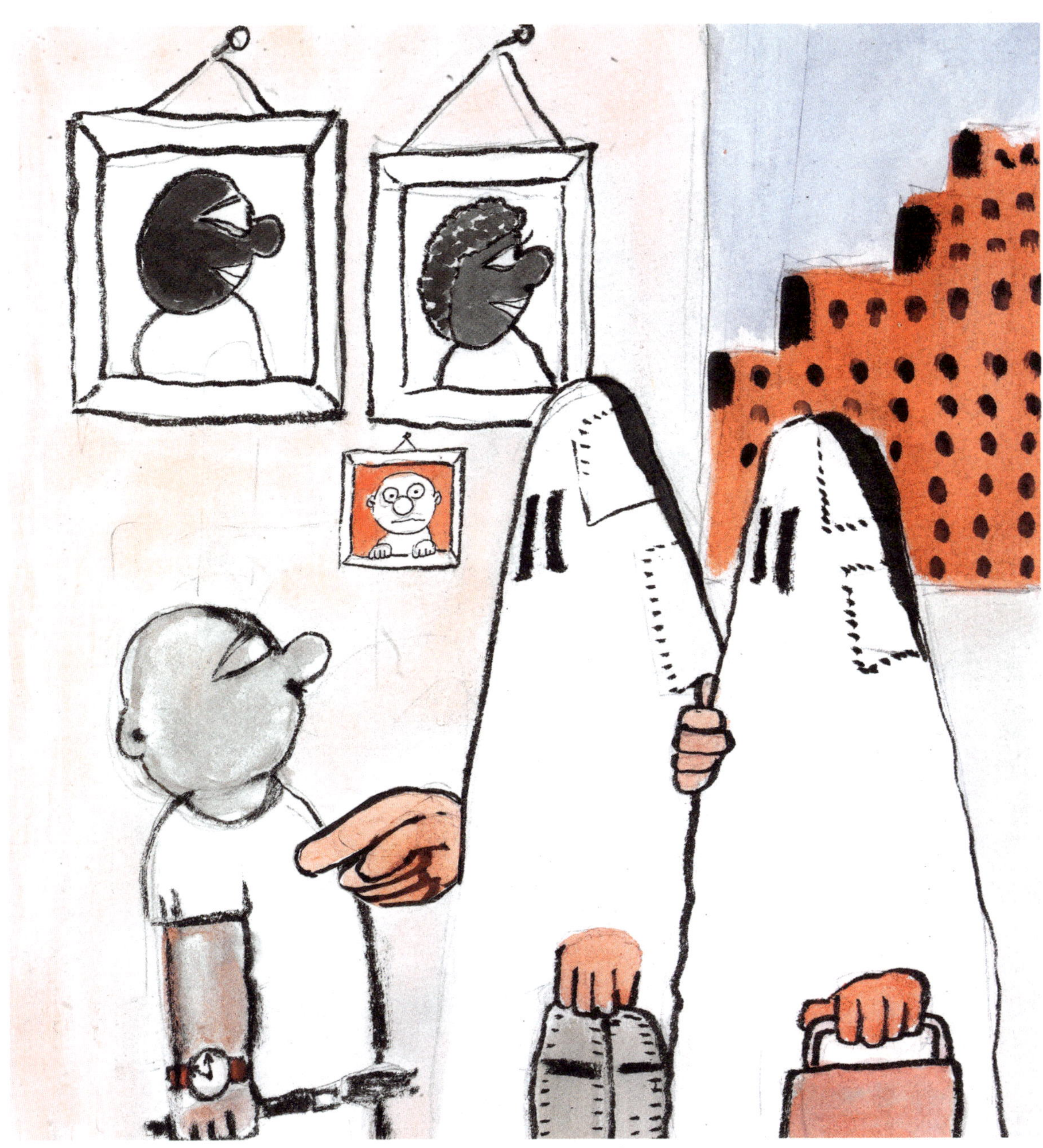

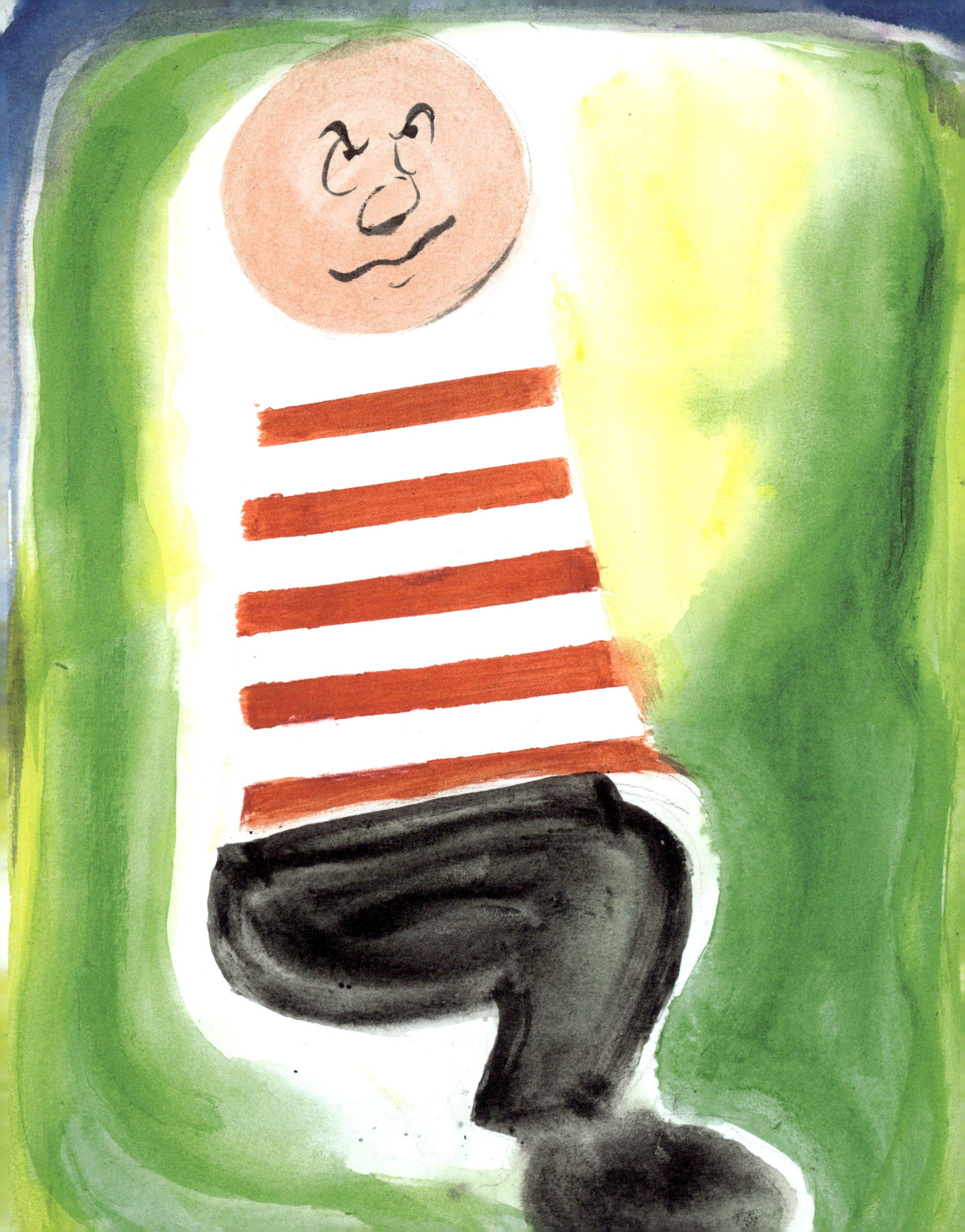

A new Expressionism

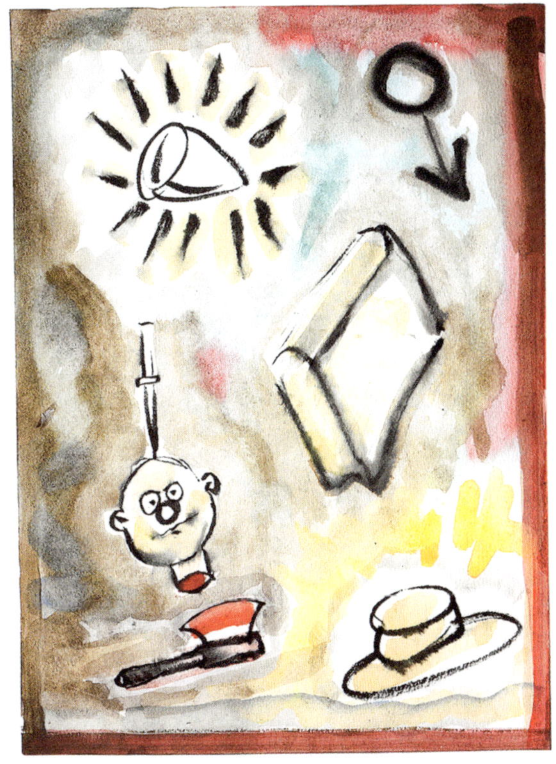

In the 1960s, more and more artists – especially very young artists – became convinced that painting, or visual arts in general, had had its day. In the many thousands of years since cave art, artists had – roughly speaking – painted everything in all sorts of ways: idealistic, romantic, naturalistic, realistic, impressionistic, expressionistic, cubistic, surrealistic, etc. Yes, some artists had even painted images that didn't depict anything. It was almost impossible to paint something that hadn't already been painted. Therefore, many artists turned to other media and forms of expression: conceptual art, minimalist art, photo art, video art, action art, and happenings.

But it didn't last. In the 1970s, the colours on the brushes began to drip once more, and in several places simultaneously, in Germany, Italy, and the USA. Now painting had to happen again, preferably wildly, violently, and as expressionistically as a painter could do it without being an authentic expressionist. The crucial thing was that one dared to put colours and figures on a flat surface, preferably a piece of canvas, and that one hadn't thought too deeply about how to do it. For far too long, painting had behaved far too nicely or passively. Now it was back, and it needed to let loose. Therefore, it was called 'the young wild painting', 'the new wild painting', 'neo-expressionism', or 'trans-avant-garde'. Per Kirkeby and Georg Baselitz were some of the names at the top of the movement.

The body is back in art

As everyone knows, all humans have a body. So there's a good reason why this body has played such a big role in art history.

In the 1960s, some artists created something called body art. This could be, for example, photographs of entirely ordinary bodily functions – but often it involved subjecting one's body to painful things in the name of art. In the 1990s, the body began to return to art, on both sides of the Atlantic. In a few places, it has even been stripped down to the bone. If you ask who the artists use as models for the bodies they exhibit, the answer is often: themselves!

If the goal is to pique the audience's interest with some recognizable shape, the human form is not the worst shape one could choose. In his video projections, the American Tony Oursler (born 1957) limits himself to the human face. These faces he projects so precisely onto a puppet's head that it looks as if the puppet is not just speaking to us but also speaking to our heart and compassion. Here, it's our guide in art who's speaking.

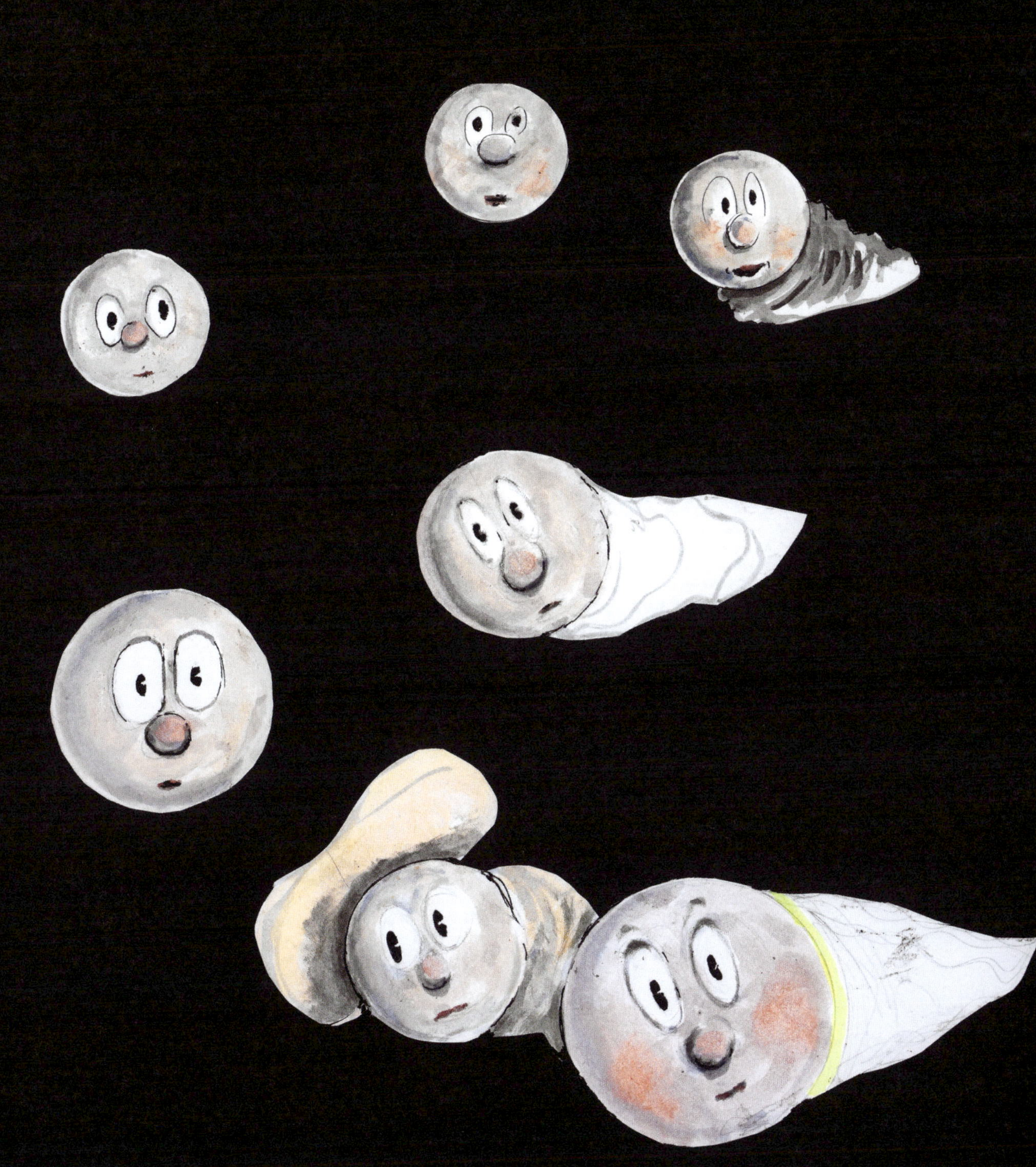

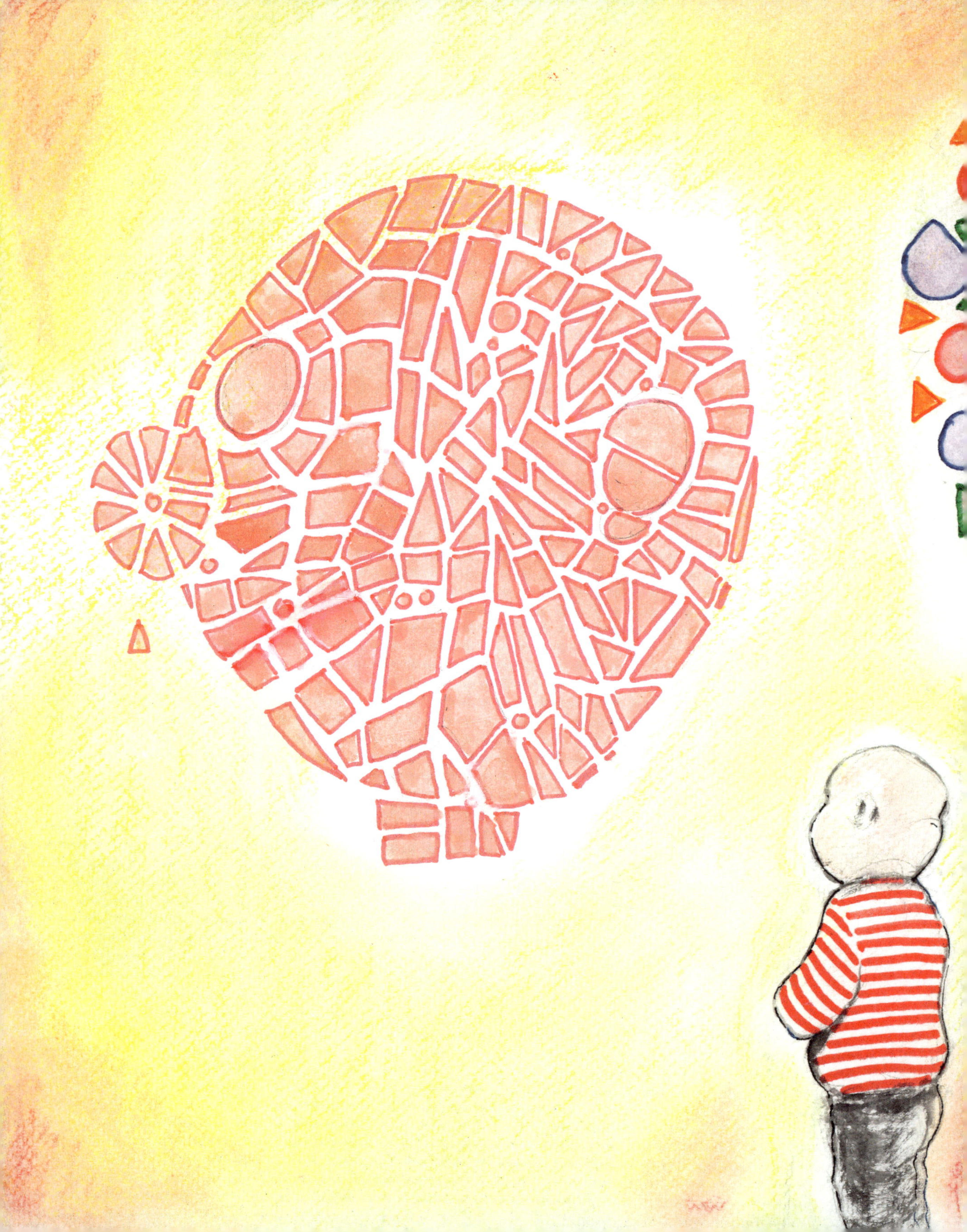

People in a new way

Some artists express what they want to say with words and letters. They are poets. Others do it with, for example, old toys, pieces of furniture, worn-out household items, etc. They are called sculptors. One such sculptor is the Englishman Tony Cragg, who was born in England in 1949 but has lived in Wuppertal, Germany, since 1977.

Just as a sculptural form can be strange and distinctive, so too can the material from which it is made. In his early works, Cragg arranged his waste in patterns, either laid on the floor or attached to a wall. They resembled fragile wall reliefs, and their shape and outline were formed by a multitude of everyday objects in different – or perhaps not so different – colours. It could all have been found at a nearby playground or landfill. So, the building blocks of the sculpture were what the industrial abundance society had left behind, but the artist organized his material so that it formed a meaningful shape, as shown in the illustration. Here, the material forms a portrait of our little guide.

Lately, Tony Cragg has become more 'abstract', although even his most recent sculptures remind us of something we seem to know from before. It is the material that gives the form its final character, whether it is synthetic materials like fiberglass or polystyrene or organic materials like stone, clay, plaster, etc. – or even thousands of dices!

Antony Gormley

And even more people

With a British artist like Antony Gormley (born 1950), we approach our own time. If we were to take stock here, there is, of course, much that has developed since the time of the Sumerians and Egyptians, long before our own era. The materials and conditions for producing art have changed as the major art centres have shifted geographically. Still, there is a common thread running through all these more than five thousand years, and that is the representation of ourselves, namely, humans. But the approach has been highly varied.

In the 1960s, experimental artists advocated a new phenomenon: body art. It is the depiction of humanity that makes a motif recognizable to us. It is also humanity that interests a modernist like Antony Gormley. He is a contemporary of people like Tony Cragg, Tony Oursler and Jeff Koons. Gormley's works tell us about all the ways one can represent one's fellow humans. The way he depicts a human head, arms, stomach, and legs changes with the material and especially the visual language he uses. It can be like a mannequin, fragile and almost transparent, or it can be dense and compact and like cut out in geometric shapes. Standing in front of such a figure, one might think of Cubism – and of the fact that new art – not all art, but much of it – stands on the shoulders of its predecessors.

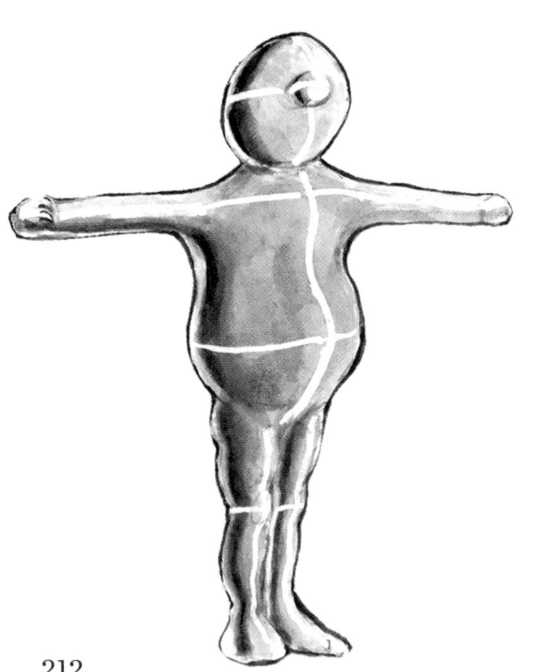

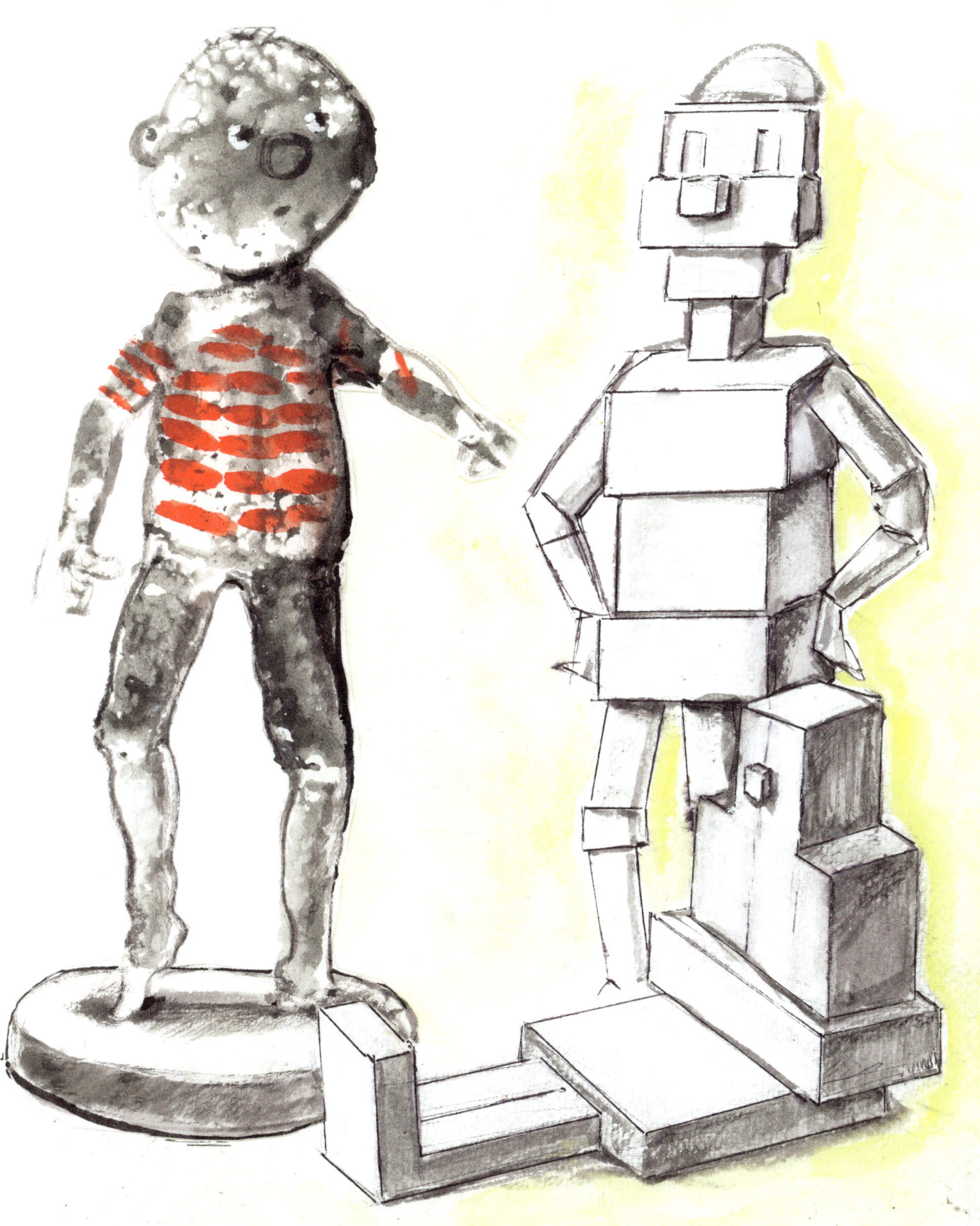

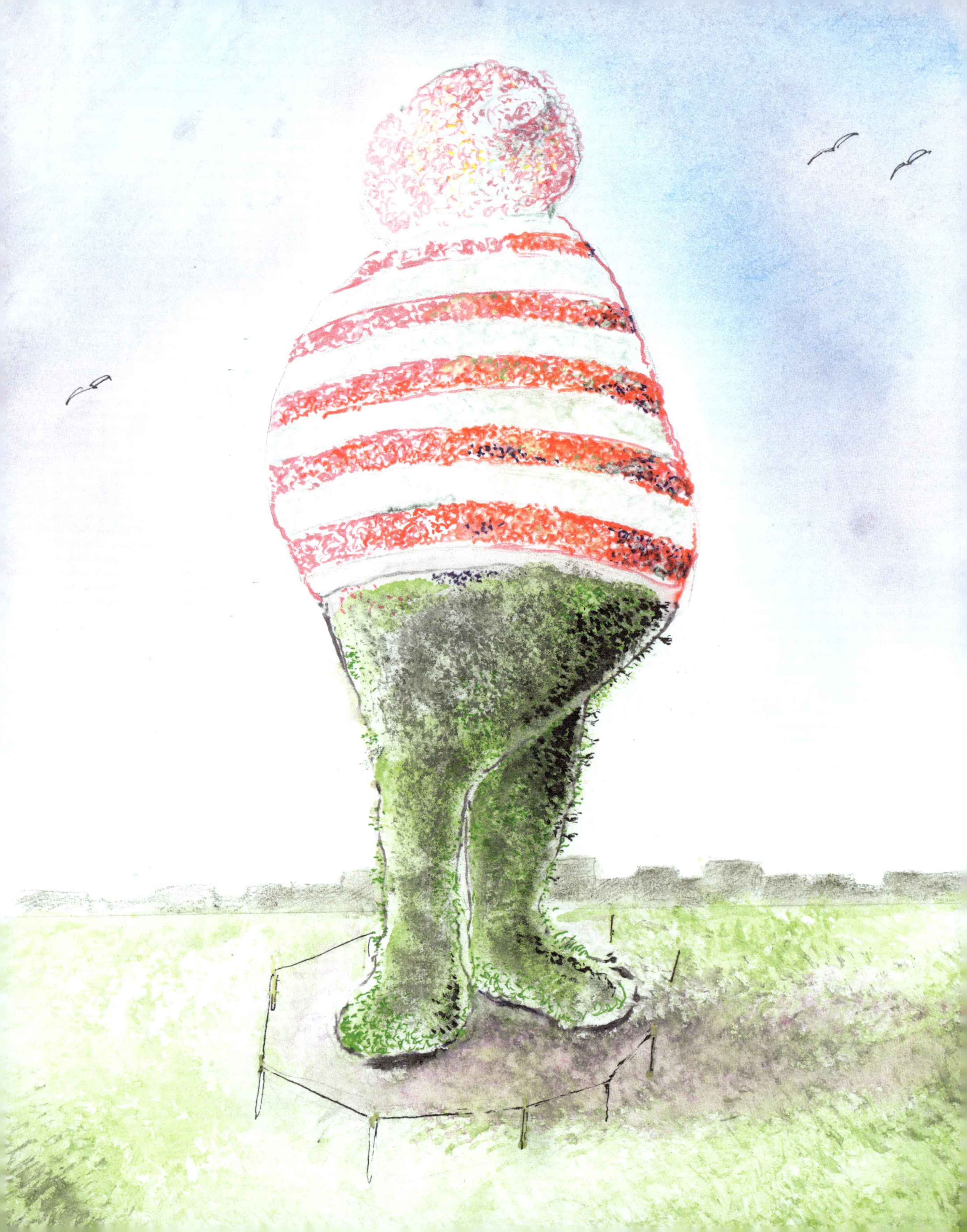

Jeff Koons

The struggle for attention

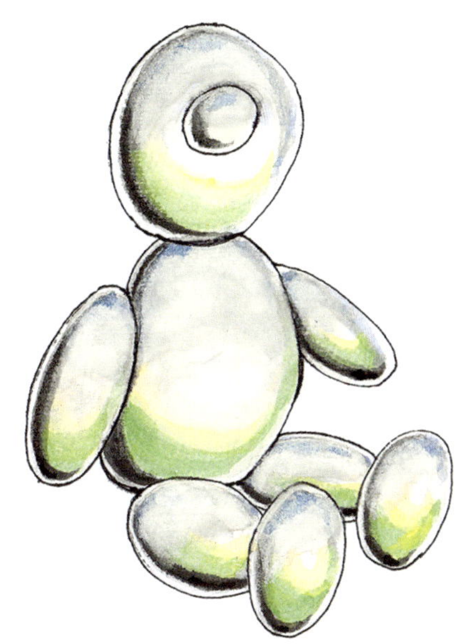

'There is no reality except the one that the media creates. For it is the media that determines our consciousness.' That's what the American artist Jeff Koons (born 1955) has said. Koons is a mega-star, a showman who knows what it takes to capture our attention. He comes from the same country that has produced some of the world's most famous stars in music, film, show business, and politics, and it is the impact on the broad audience that matters to him. The crucial thing to him is to overcome barriers, whether they are created by social, national, or cultural conditions or have to do with generational differences.

Koons wants to give back to art some of the impact that big politics, the economy, and popular music have. Therefore, Koons has brought something that looks like kitsch and souvenirs into the sacred art museum. To him, seduction is the most important thing, as it was for the artists of the Baroque and Rococo periods. They worked for kings and princes and used the most exquisite materials to satisfy the need for the glorification of royal power or the church. It is only in economic and conceptual terms that modern art still lives and thrives in its ivory tower. When it comes to its role models, it is easy to see that it must have long since taken the trip down all the ivory stairs and out onto the cobblestones.

Koons knows how to take people by storm – without batting an eye. He has made representations of dogs in highly polished brass, in which one can almost see one's reflection. Or he has made dogs, using flowers, that are as big as houses (that's why our little guide has also received the same treatment).

Have mercy on the sculpture

Some artists – like Tony Oursler – are not just artists with an international name. They also have a foot in the entertainment industry. Tony Oursler's works are entertaining to an extent that is rare in the serious world of contemporary art. Modern sculptures are usually something we talk about. It's not often that they literally speak to us. And even then, so loudly that nothing else can be heard.

For Tony Oursler, everything comes to life. It addresses and speaks to us in all sorts of ways and with many different kinds of sounds and facial expressions. A typical Oursler-work could be a video recording of a living face, which is projected so precisely onto, for example, a doll's head that it appears as if the doll is speaking to us. Of course, it's a projection. Or an illusion, if you will. A living expression, transferred to a dead object, an organic form of sorts, with the help of light – i.e., electricity – defying all physical laws, appearing lifelike, and appealing to our hearts and compassion.

A work by Oursler works, among other things, through the empathy it evokes in the viewer. If you encounters a humanoid being lying wounded or trapped under a fallen mattress, and this being then looks at you and speaks to you, almost incessantly, your attention and compassion are aroused in a way you never expected.

Oursler has successfully created such animated installation sculptures for the past thirty years. For it all comes alive in such a direct way that no one can be bored. What more can you ask for?

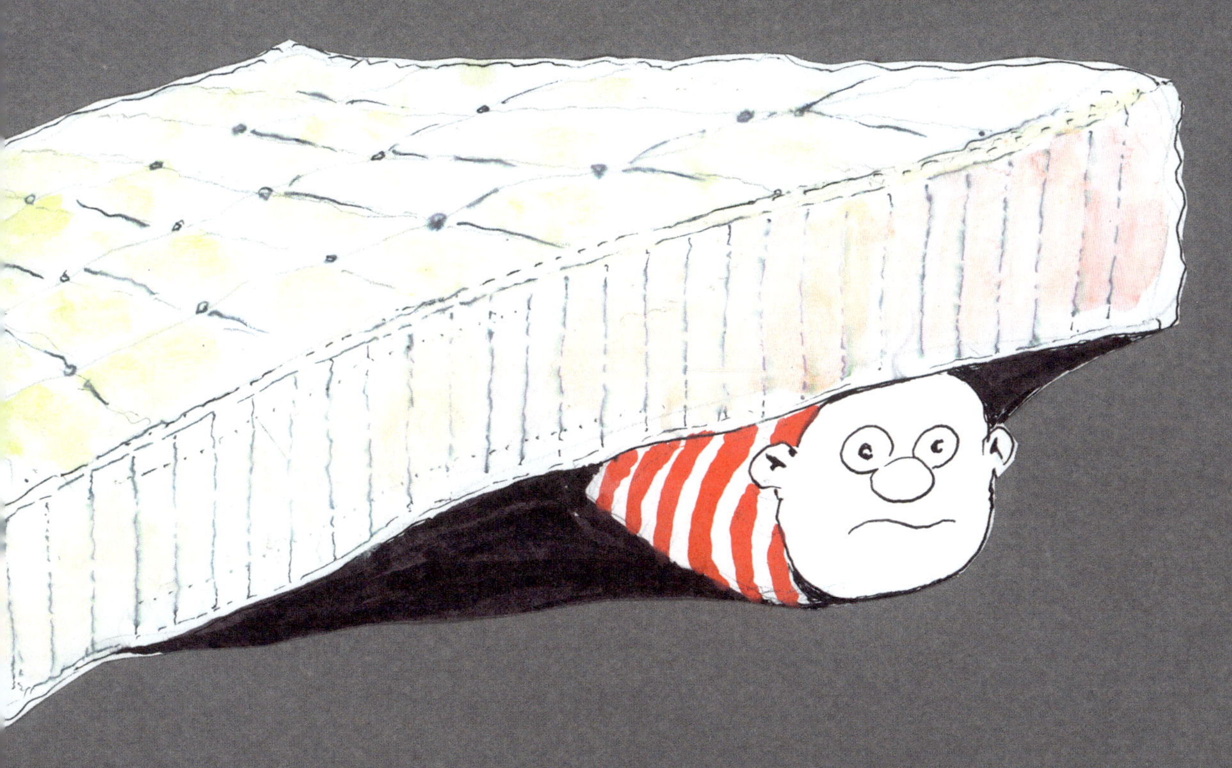

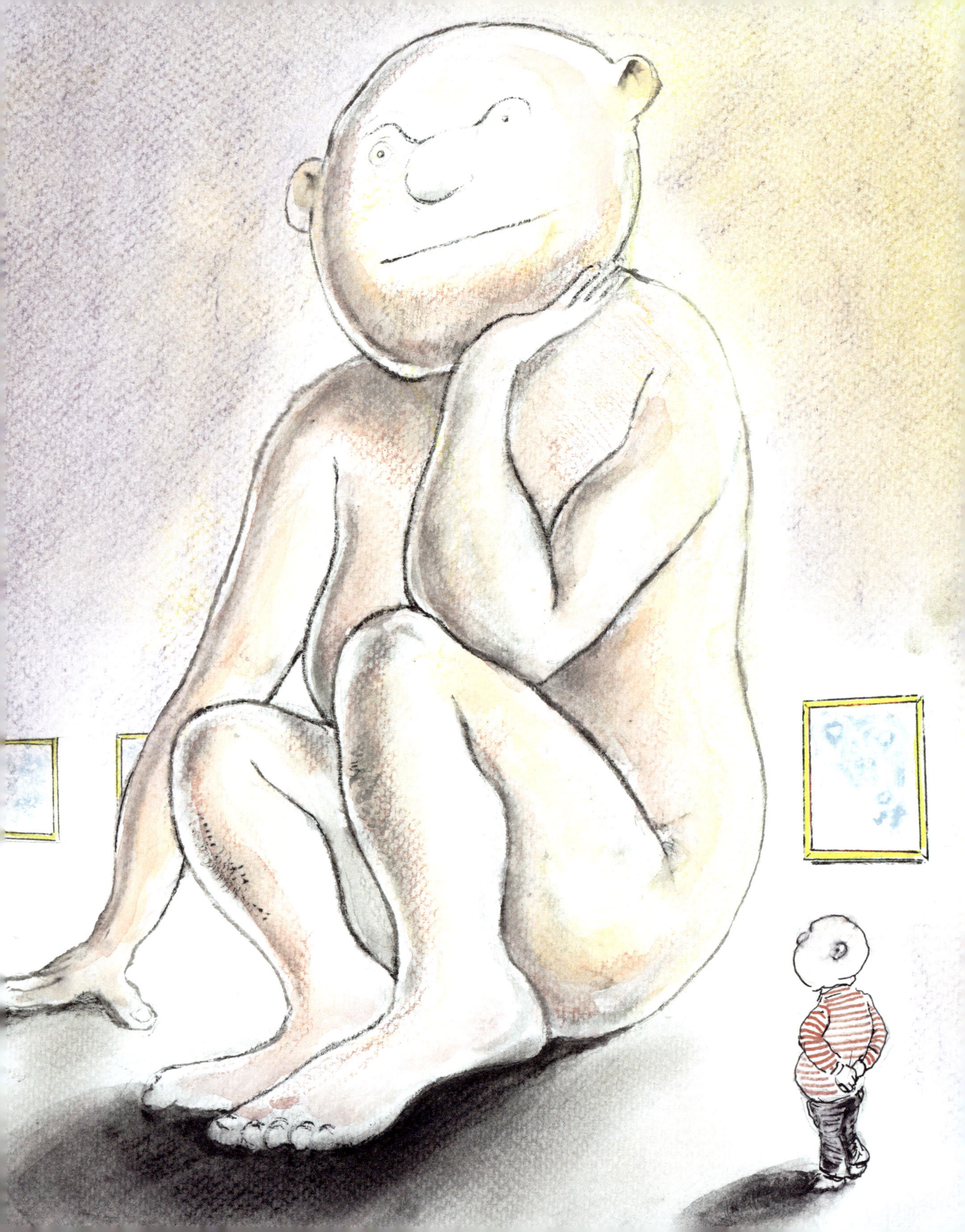

Ron Mueck

It doesn't get bigger or more lifelike than this

When a figure is almost five metres tall, even when kneeling and bending its back, it's impossible to miss. In 2001, the Australian artist Ron Mueck (born 1958) presented such a gigantic sculpture at the Venice Biennale. People were truly astonished, and several museums competed to acquire it despite its enormous size. It ended up in Denmark's second-largest city, Aarhus, where 'Boy', as it's called, has become somewhat of a symbol for the ARoS Art Museum. But the size is not really what matters. For the large format is also found with Jeff Koons, yes, and in the monumental sculptures of the ancient Egyptians. What matters, however, is the lifelikeness of the artificial materials the artist uses to simulate a real human, signalling a new form of hyperrealism. 'Boy' is cast in fiberglass and silicone, but the surface of the figure resembles human skin, complete with fine hair created from fishing line. One can even discern something resembling blood vessels beneath what looks like skin. And 'Boy' looks as if he is very modest and trying to hide, which in this case is rather hopeless.

The amusing thing is that Ron Mueck actually made a breakthrough – at an exhibition in London in 1997 – with a work that was just as unusually small as 'Boy' was unusually large. It was titled 'Dead Dad' and was half life-size, but just as realistic as the artist's later works.

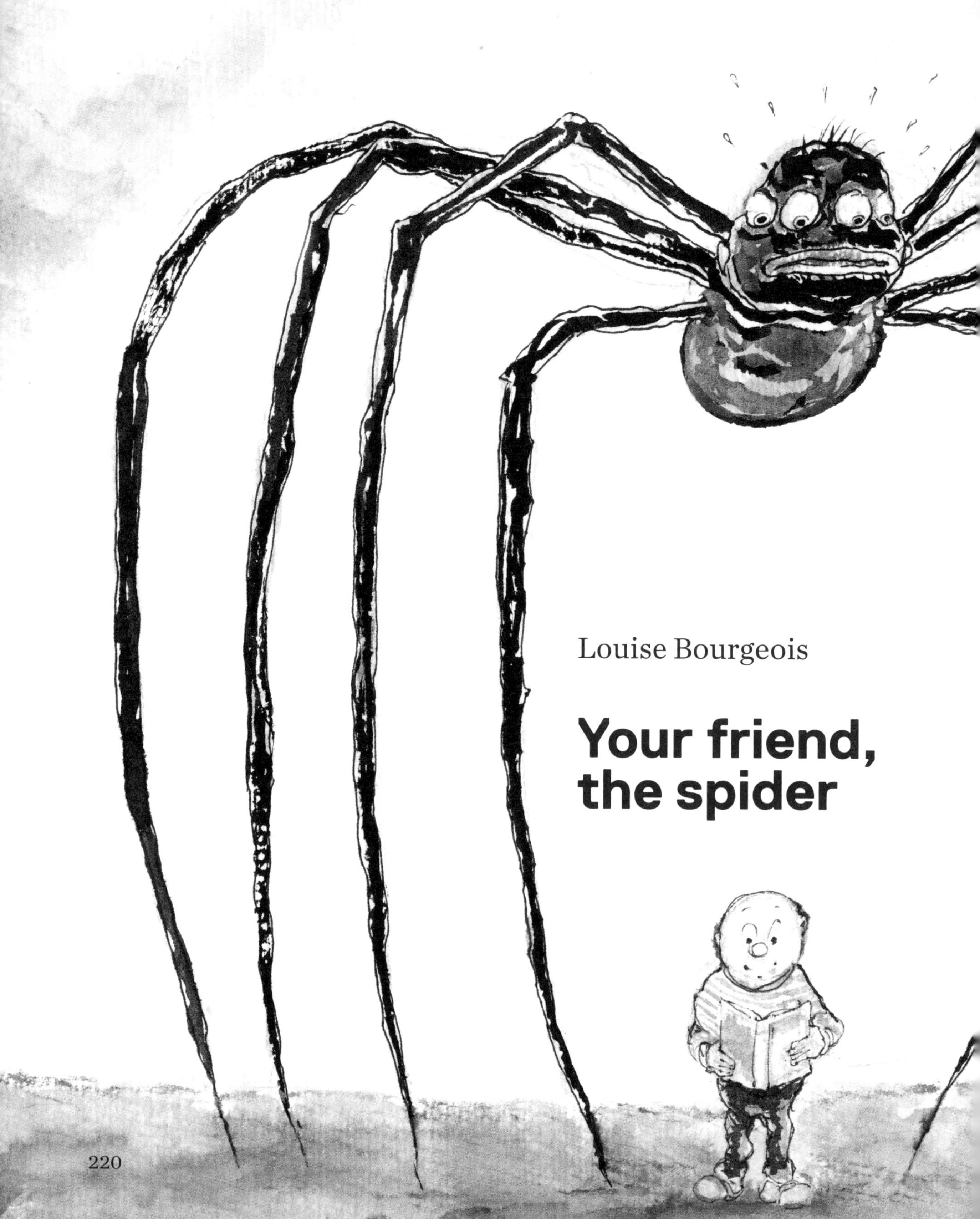

Your friend, the spider

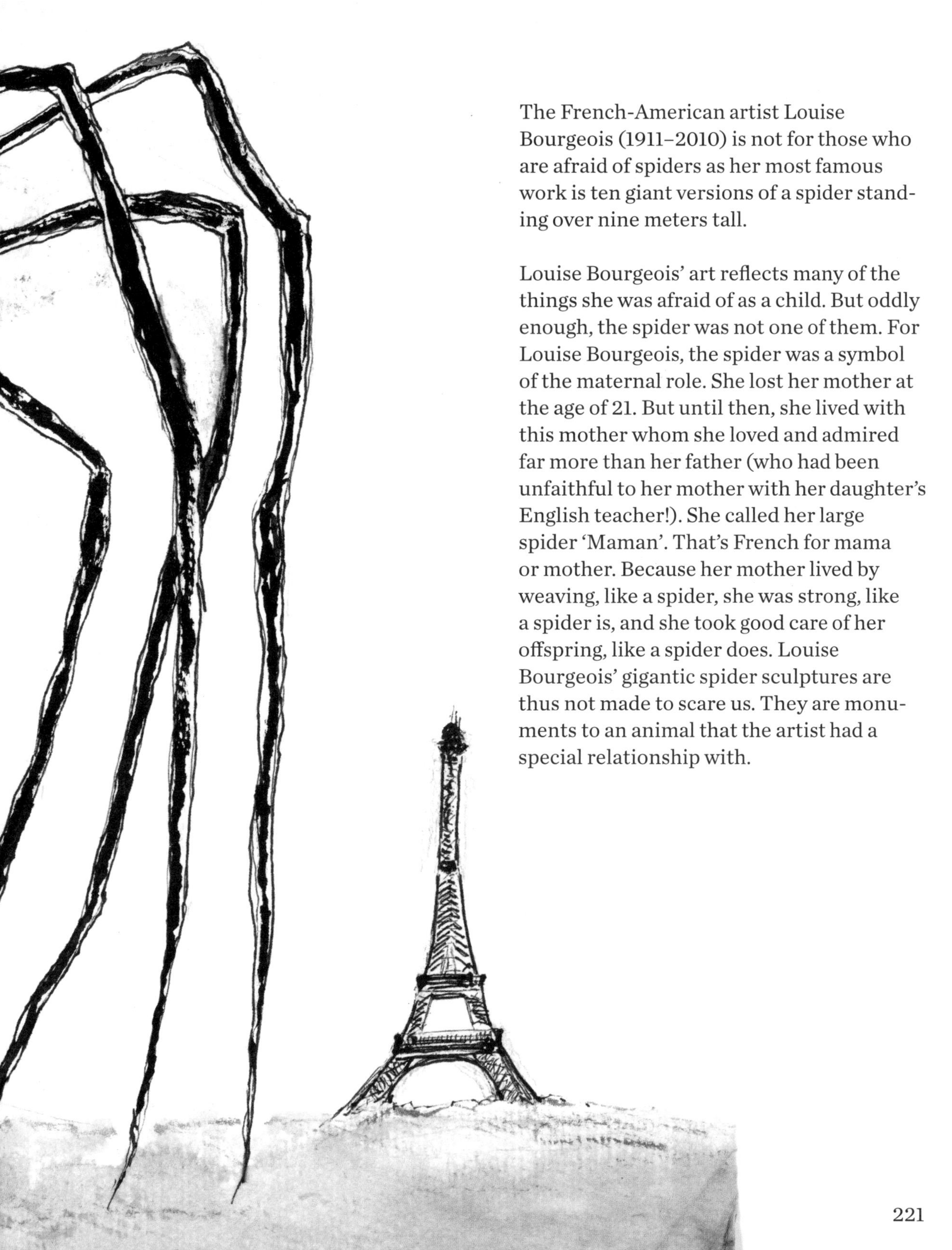

The French-American artist Louise Bourgeois (1911–2010) is not for those who are afraid of spiders as her most famous work is ten giant versions of a spider standing over nine meters tall.

Louise Bourgeois' art reflects many of the things she was afraid of as a child. But oddly enough, the spider was not one of them. For Louise Bourgeois, the spider was a symbol of the maternal role. She lost her mother at the age of 21. But until then, she lived with this mother whom she loved and admired far more than her father (who had been unfaithful to her mother with her daughter's English teacher!). She called her large spider 'Maman'. That's French for mama or mother. Because her mother lived by weaving, like a spider, she was strong, like a spider is, and she took good care of her offspring, like a spider does. Louise Bourgeois' gigantic spider sculptures are thus not made to scare us. They are monuments to an animal that the artist had a special relationship with.

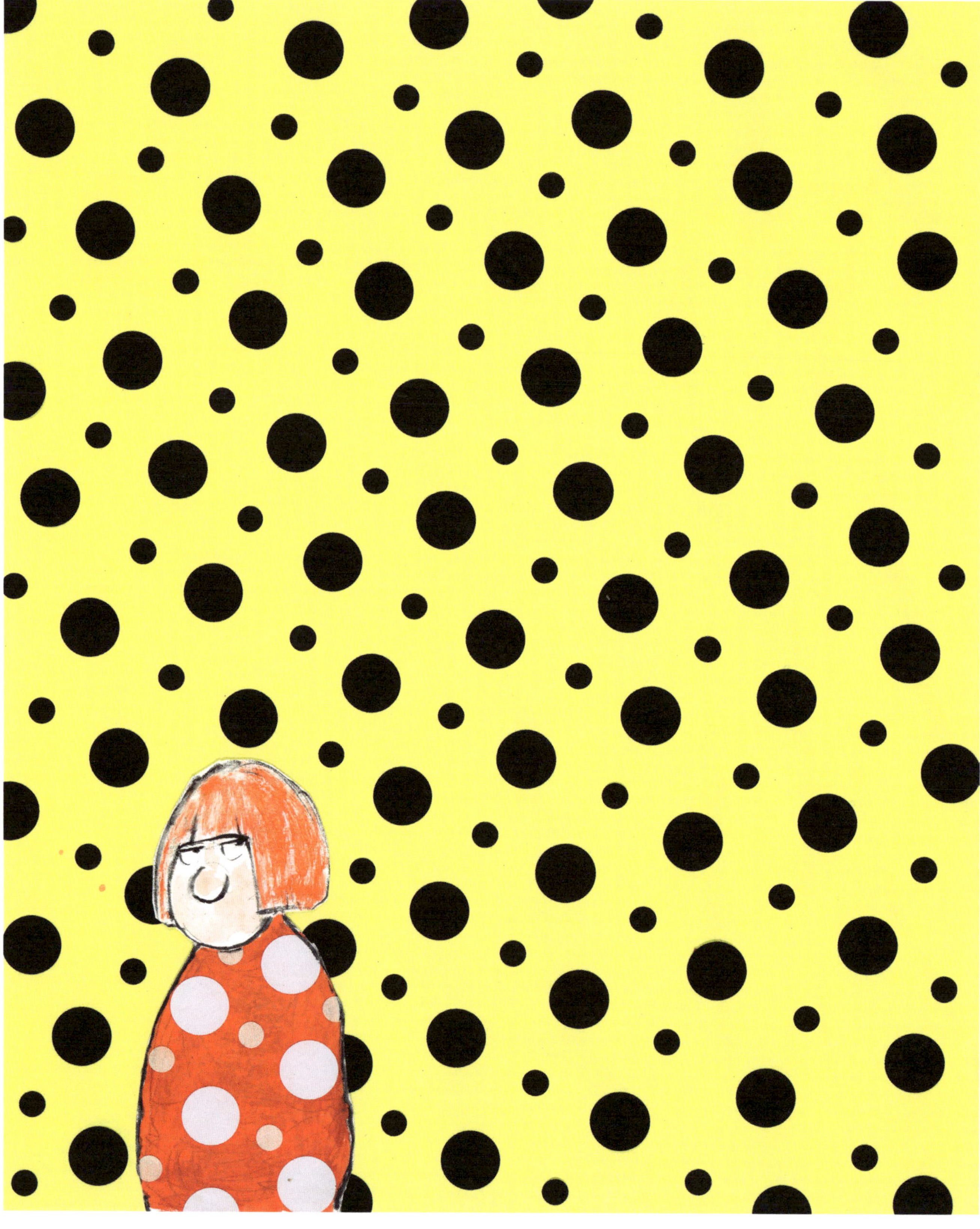

Plenty of dots

Next to Leonardo's Mona Lisa, a polka-dotted work by Yayoi Kusama (born 1929) is probably what attracts the most museum visitors to take selfies. Why? Perhaps because her works seem so decorative. But the Japanese artist doesn't create her dotted works just to embellish the world or entertain her audience. She creates them to combat her anxiety and soothe herself. She once said that if she couldn't make her art, she would have taken her own life long ago. So it's deadly serious.

Kusama first used polka dots in her art in 1939 when she was only ten years old. She has stated that the dots were inspired by some hallucinations she had. When she was 27, she moved to the USA and lived in New York for a number of years, where she connected with several significant American artists. Kusama worked hard and created plenty of art, but it didn't bring her any success. The artist Georgia O'Keeffe tried to support her, even financially. But ultimately, Kusama didn't thrive in the USA. So in 1973, she moved back to Japan. She also wrote surrealist short stories for a while. As an artist, she first gained recognition in the 1990s after representing her country, Japan, at the Venice Biennale in 1993, a major international exhibition held every two years in the Italian city of Venice.

Today, Kusama is known worldwide, and she has had exhibitions at many major museums. However, she is currently hospitalized at a mental health facility in Tokyo – at her own request. Her studio is located near this hospital, and here she continues to work until the day she paints her final dot.

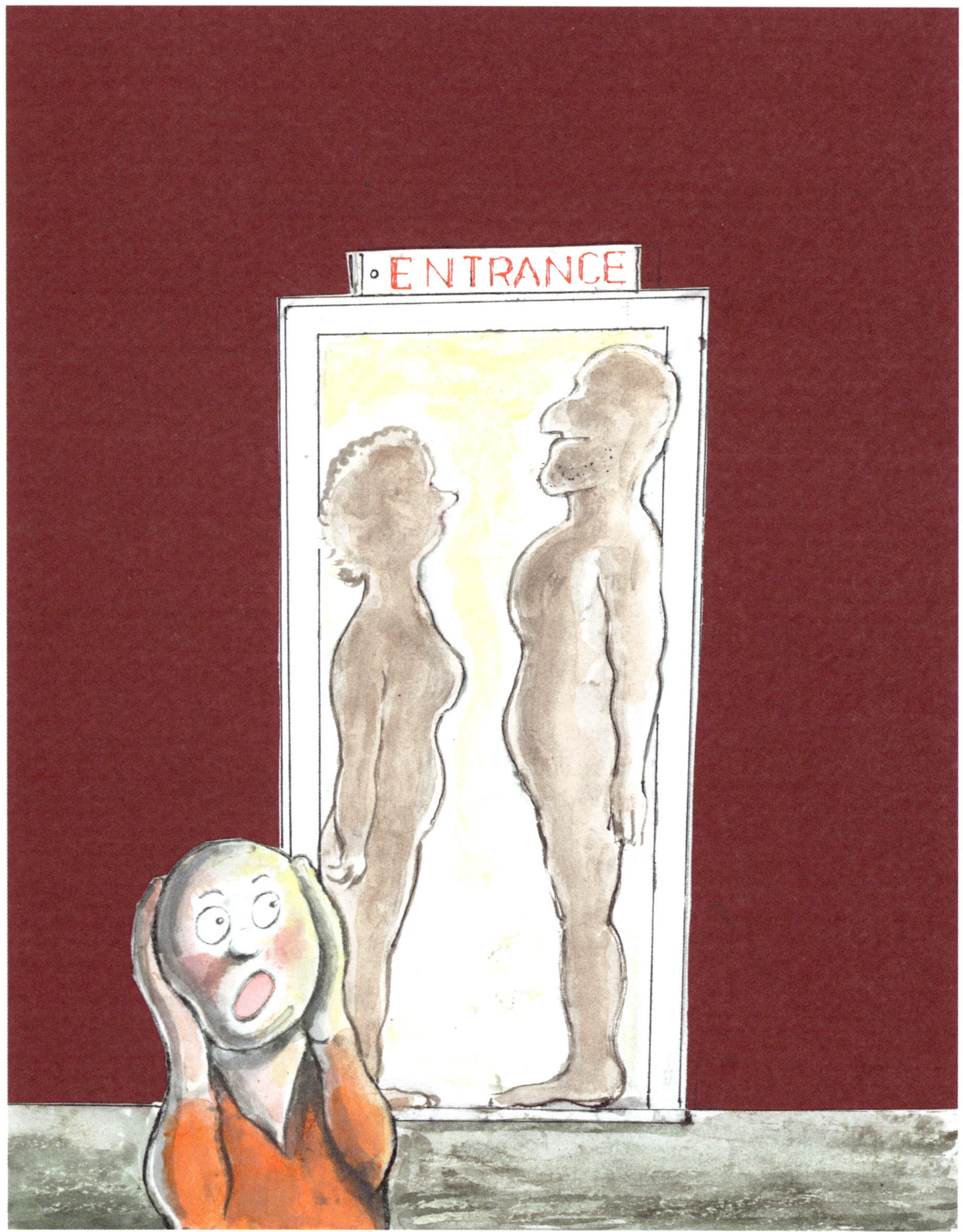

ENTRANCE

Marina Abramović

A bit too close

If you had been in Oslo in 2013 – on the 150th anniversary of the painter Edvard Munch's birth – you might have been among the 270 people who participated in reenacting the Norwegian painter's most famous painting: 'The Scream' (or in Norwegian: 'Skrik'), even in the same landscape that Munch had used as a backdrop.

Here's how it went: You placed your head in a frame and then screamed as loudly as you could, just like the terrified person in Munch's painting. Some of the screams were videotaped. But no one screamed without reason. It was the Serbian artist Marina Abramović (born 1946) who invited all these people to do it.

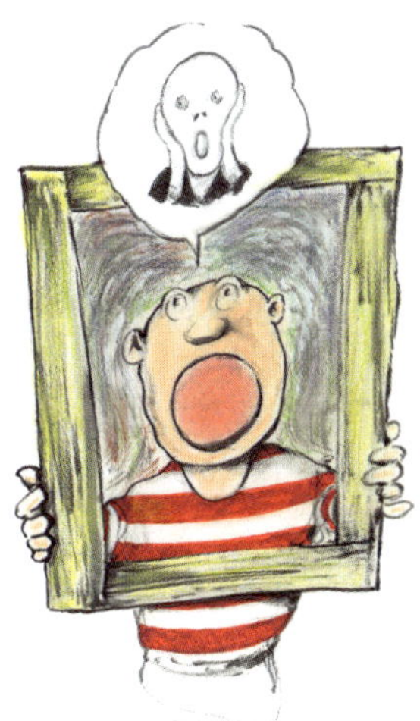

Abramović gets many of these boundary-pushing ideas, and that's what she's become known for. Her art aims to push people to the edge of what they thought they could bear.

While other artists use materials like video, marble, wood, oil paint, etc., in their works, Abramović uses herself and her audience. People and their emotions are the 'materials' she uses in her work.

When Abramović had a major solo exhibition in 2017, which was in Sweden, Denmark, Norway, and Germany, she presented the work 'Imponderabilia', consisting of two naked people – one man and one woman – in a doorway. In the original performance of the work from 1977, it was the artist herself and her partner, the artist Ulay, who stood facing each other. There wasn't much space in the narrow passage. Those who wanted to pass through to see the rest of the exhibition in the next room had to squeeze sideways between the two naked bodies, challenging their modesty. Which way would they prefer to face? Toward the man or the woman? When the work was first performed in Bologna in 1977, the Italian police intervened and stopped it. It speaks to Marina Abramović's daring as an artist.

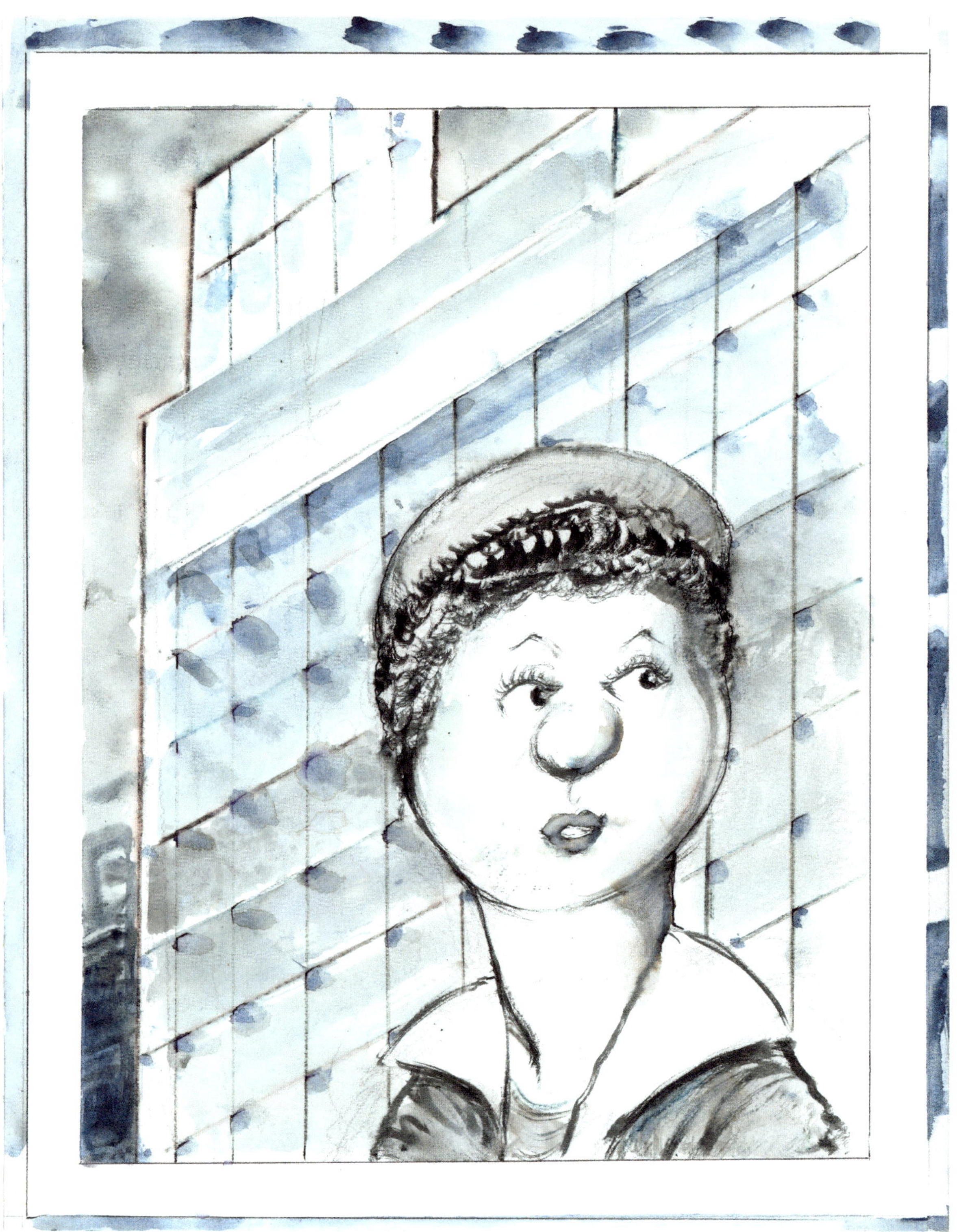

Like in old films

It doesn't attract attention when an actor puts on makeup and disguises themselves to play a role. Because actors often need to do that just to be able to perform their scenes. Each role demands specific clothing, hairstyle, and makeup for the actor. Playing Batman, for example, requires a different costume than if the same person were to play James Bond or Sherlock Holmes.

What's commonplace in the world of theatre and film can be transformed into a very personal artistic project in visual art. That's what the American photographer Cindy Sherman (born 1954) did when she debuted in 1977 with a series called 'Film Stills'. The film medium has always been significant to her, and the images in the series were her reconstructions or stagings of the kind of scenes and situations found in particularly American B-movies from the late 1950s. B-movies mean that the budget for producing these films wasn't very large, so there wasn't enough money to hire the expensive Hollywood stars everyone knows.

B-movies often deal with slim hopes, shattered dreams, and the crime found in a big city. They can have their unique atmosphere and way of telling stories. Cindy Sherman's photographs do too. The recurring figure in her series 'Film Stills' is always herself. Despite their differences, the unknown B-movie actress and the famous artist have something in common. For Sherman directed herself in the role of the female actress, who had been directed in the role by a man. For directors were usually men in the past. Therefore, her images can be interpreted as a feminist critique of the typical male gaze on women, as encountered in particularly older films and artworks. It's called 'The Male Gaze'.

Death didn't stop him

Hard drugs prevented the American graffiti artist Jean-Michel Basquiat (1960–1988) from growing old. At his death, only 27 years old, he was no longer a graffiti artist. But that's how he started – as a street artist – painting on buildings in public spaces where it's usually forbidden to paint. But Basquiat did it so well and convincingly that some people in the art world saw his potential. He was associated with one of New York's leading galleries, and soon the American art scene lay at his feet. He made good contacts and, for a period, painted pictures with none other than Andy Warhol. Basquiat even lived long enough to become one of the most expensive American artists to buy works from.

Basquiat was obsessed with the idea of death. Perhaps that's why skulls so often appear in his paintings, even in the poor copy of one seen here. Death may have put an end to Basquiat's production as his generation's most exciting and innovative expressionist, but it didn't stop his success. In 2020, one of his typical 'skull paintings' sold at auction. The final price for the 'skull' was $110.5 million. The following year – 2021 – was reportedly Basquiat's biggest year yet. That year, Basquiat works were sold for a total value of $2.8 billion! Basquiat fever doesn't stop at the back room of art auctions. Today, you can also get Basquiat on postcards, shoes, bags, T-shirts, etc.

The man who started as an angry, socially critical graffiti artist, painting only in unguarded moments, ended up as a commercial success story.

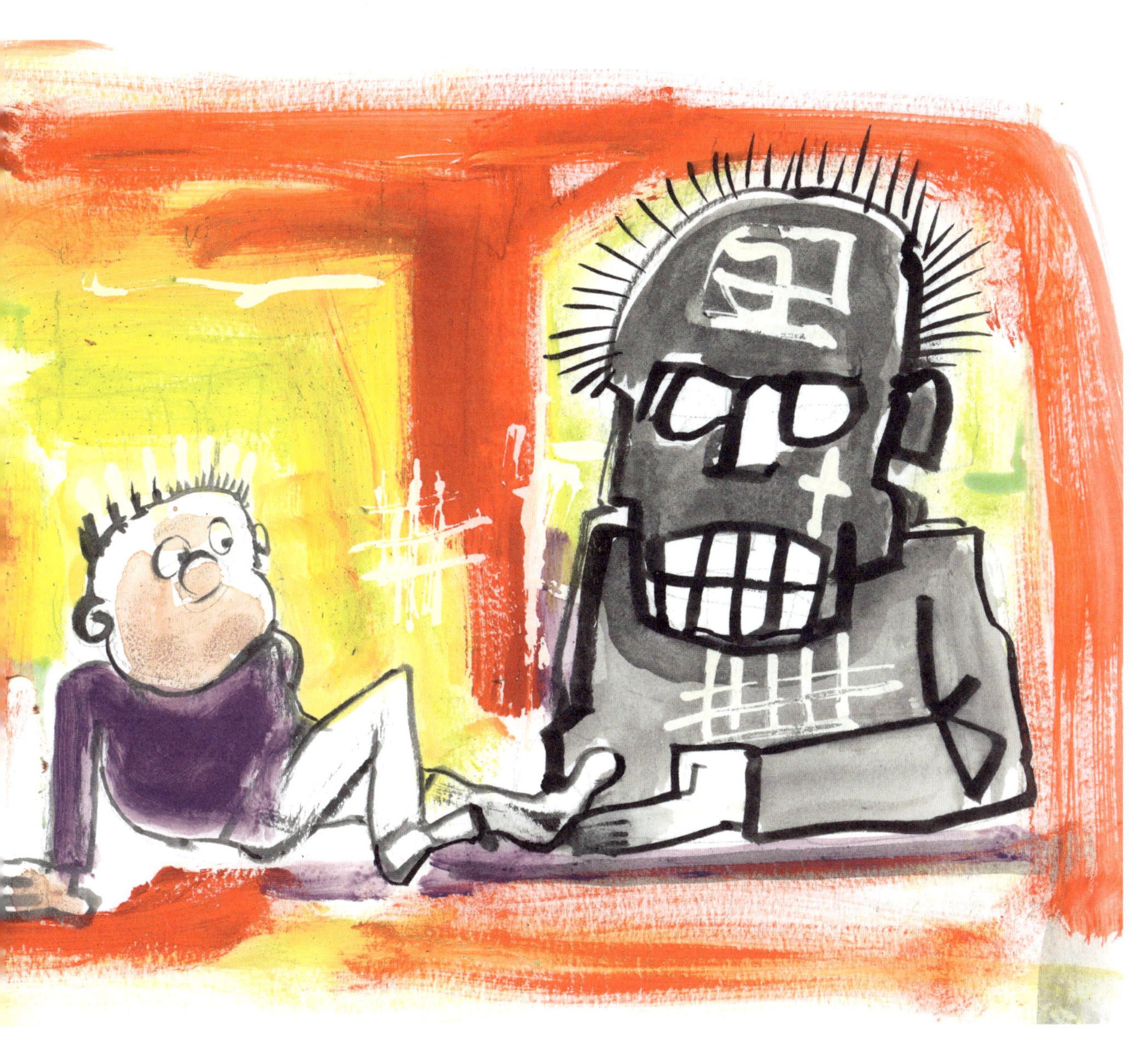

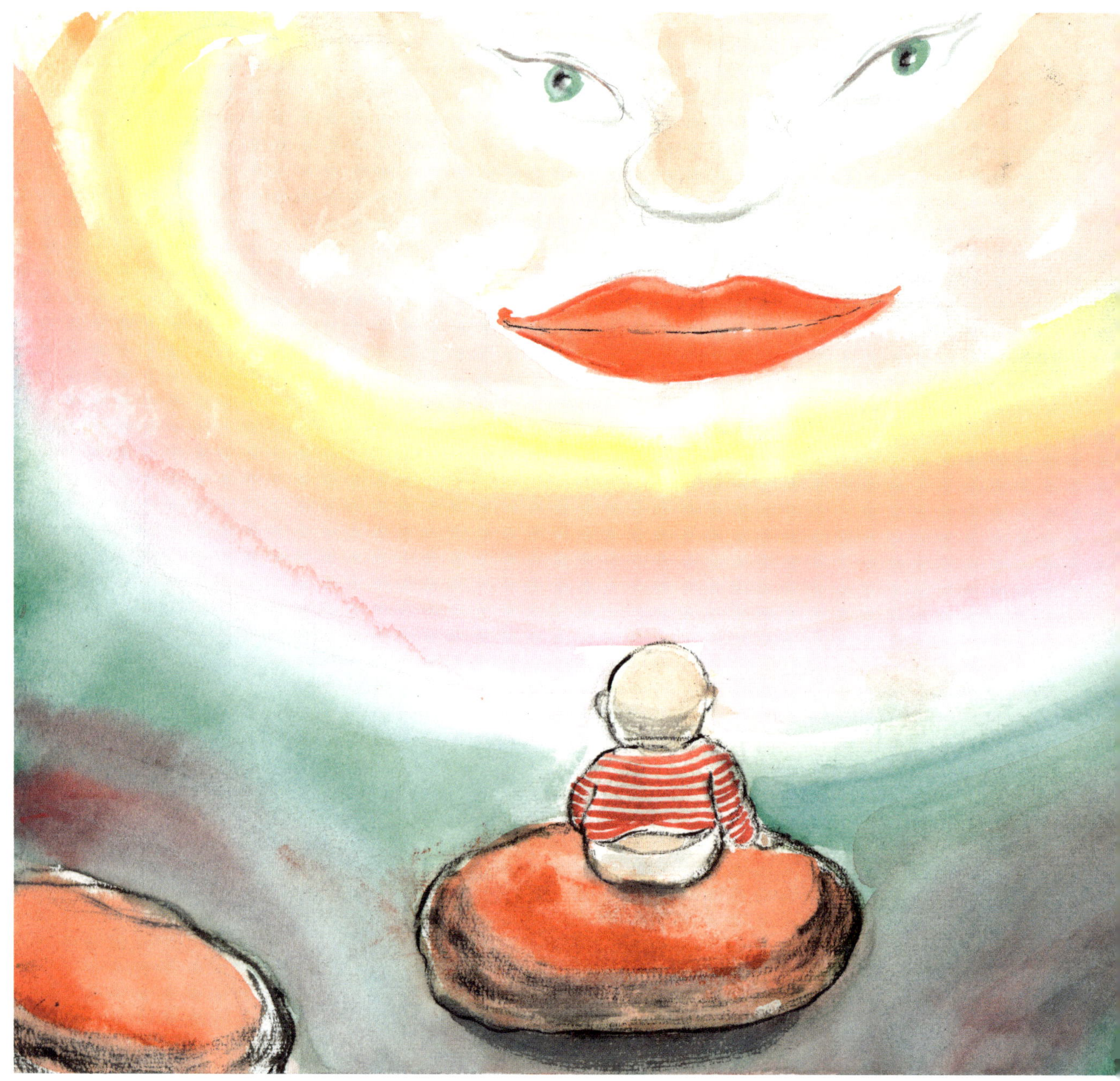

Surrounded by love

The birth certificate actually says Elisabeth Charlotte Rist when the Swiss artist came into the world. When she was twenty, she had her first name changed to Pipilotti, because she had always been fascinated by the children's heroine Pippi Longstocking, who, according to her creator, the Swedish author Astrid Lindgren, loved being free and could overcome the most incredible obstacles. The same is what Pipilotti Rist (born 1962) wants to achieve. As one of her generation's most important video artists, she has exhibited all over the world and, without using words, only moving images, spread a message of love to all who have encountered her works.

Louisiana Museum of Modern Art in Denmark was the first museum in the world to acquire a work by Pipilotti Rist, and the museum has exhibited her video works several times. When she presented 'Homo Sapiens Sapiens' in 2010, visitors could sit or lie down on soft furnishings and look up at a seductive video projection on the ceiling, which, through incredible colour blends, formed figures, faces, eyes, lips, etc.

For Pipilotti Rist, an exhibition should primarily have a social and humanistic purpose, i.e., a purpose involving humanity. The exhibition should break down barriers and unite people of all kinds so that we can better share our emotions and thoughts with each other. She even talks about how through art, we should be able to visit each other's bodies and brains. If we desire it, incredible things will happen. In her video work 'Ever is Over All', a young and very excited woman walks down a street where many cars are parked. One by one, the woman smashes the windows of these cars with a hammer, which is actually a large tropical flower. Then a police officer walks down the same street. 'Oh no! Now the woman will be arrested,' one might think. But it doesn't happen. Instead, the officer smiles at the woman swinging the flower hammer – and walks on. With Pipilotti Rist, love always triumphs. Who other than Pipilotti Rist would think of naming her son after a mountain range. His name is Himalaya.

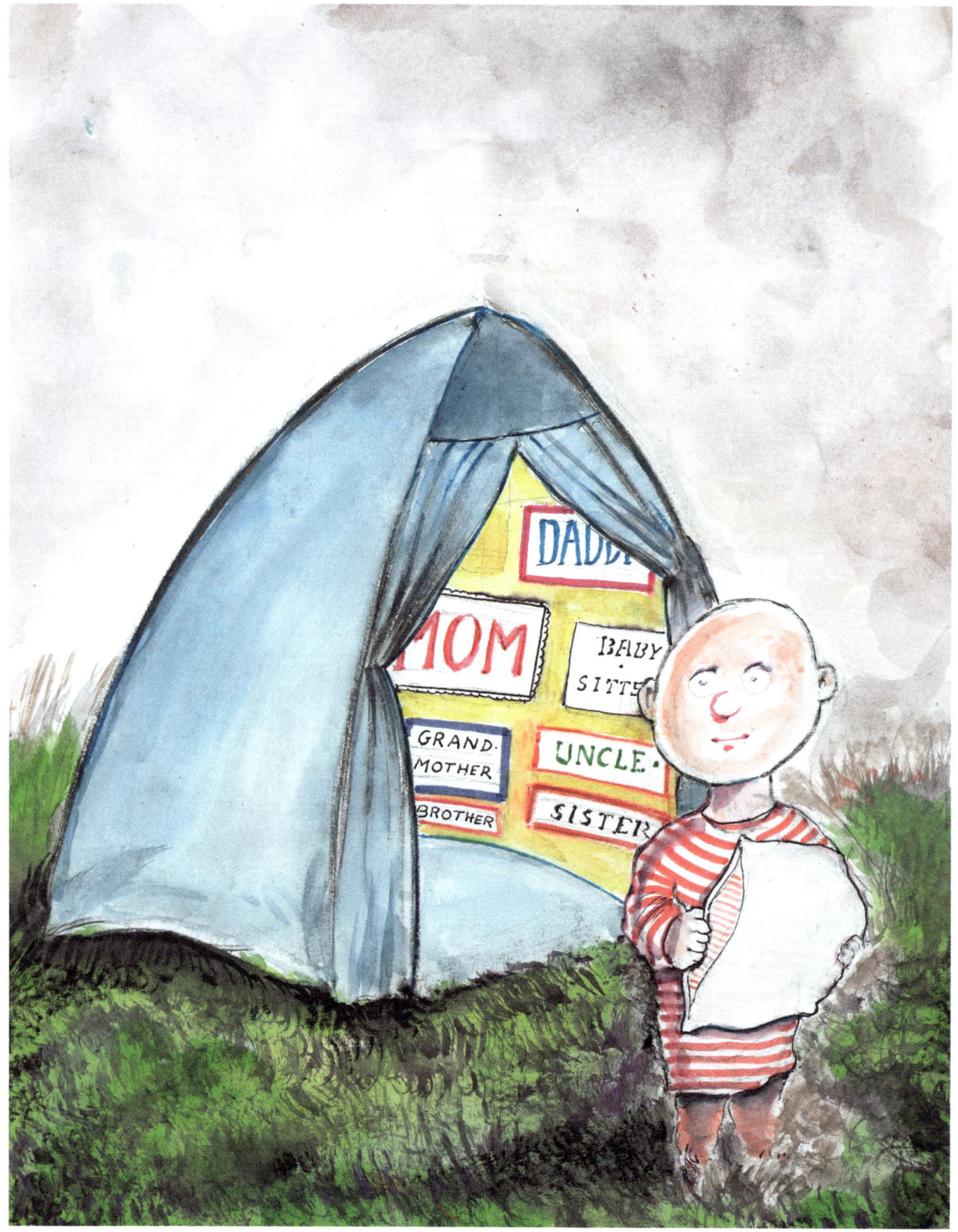

232

Tracey Emin

Bedfellows

Not all artists, like Cindy Sherman, put on makeup, disguise themselves, and try to resemble someone they're not in reality.

There are also those who do the opposite and reveal almost everything about themselves in the works they create and show to others. The autobiographical – what one has experienced oneself, which constitutes one's own experiences – is often the raw material that inspires many contemporary artists.

One of them is the English artist Tracey Emin (born 1963). This world did not treat her well, neither when she was little nor a bit older. When she was thirteen, she was raped, and the experience left deep scars on her mind and became part of the personal material she later used in her art.

Emin's breakthrough as an artist came in 1993 when she was thirty years old. But the work she is best known for, she exhibited four years later at the Royal Academy in London. The work was a tent, the inside of which she had adorned with the names of all the people she had slept with from the year she was born until 1995 when she made the tent.

Tracey Emin therefore titled it: 'Everyone I have ever slept with.' It was mostly names of men she had known and been to bed with. But others were also included. For sleeping with someone is not the same as having sex with them.

So when our guide is to make a tent like Tracey Emin's, our little innocent person must rely on the experiences he himself has had and those he knows himself. The names of the people in his tent are therefore somewhat different from Tracey Emin's. It could be 'Dad', 'Mom', 'Grandma', 'Grandpa', etc. When our little guide grows up, he will probably have to make room in the tent for some more names. If several different people were inspired by Tracey Emin and made their own tent, all these tents would be different, especially in terms of what was written inside them.

Tracey Emin's original work no longer exists. It was destroyed when a famous English art collector's collection burned down in 2004. And to date, the artist has not wanted to create a new version.

An artist with lots of money – and dots

Damien Hirst (born 1965) made waves in 1997 when he exhibited at the 'Sensation'-exhibition in London alongside a group of other young British artists. Among the most sensational works in the exhibition was a 4.2-meter-long shark, submerged in a massive glass display case filled with formaldehyde. The man behind was Hirst. Since then, he has created many versions with other animals, cut into smaller pieces and placed in vitrines and liquid, but never a snake – perhaps because it would require too many vitrines.

Hirst is also known for a series of paintings called spot paintings. They consist of rows of dots in different colours and look as if they were executed by a machine. They are not always executed by Hirst himself, but by his assistants. Around a thousand spot paintings are claimed to have left his studio between 1986 and 2011. Today, Hirst is perhaps the world's richest artist, and his paintings have been called superficial works for a superficial time.

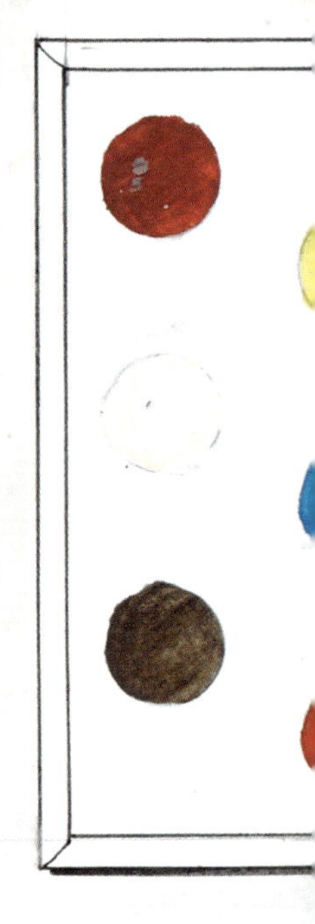

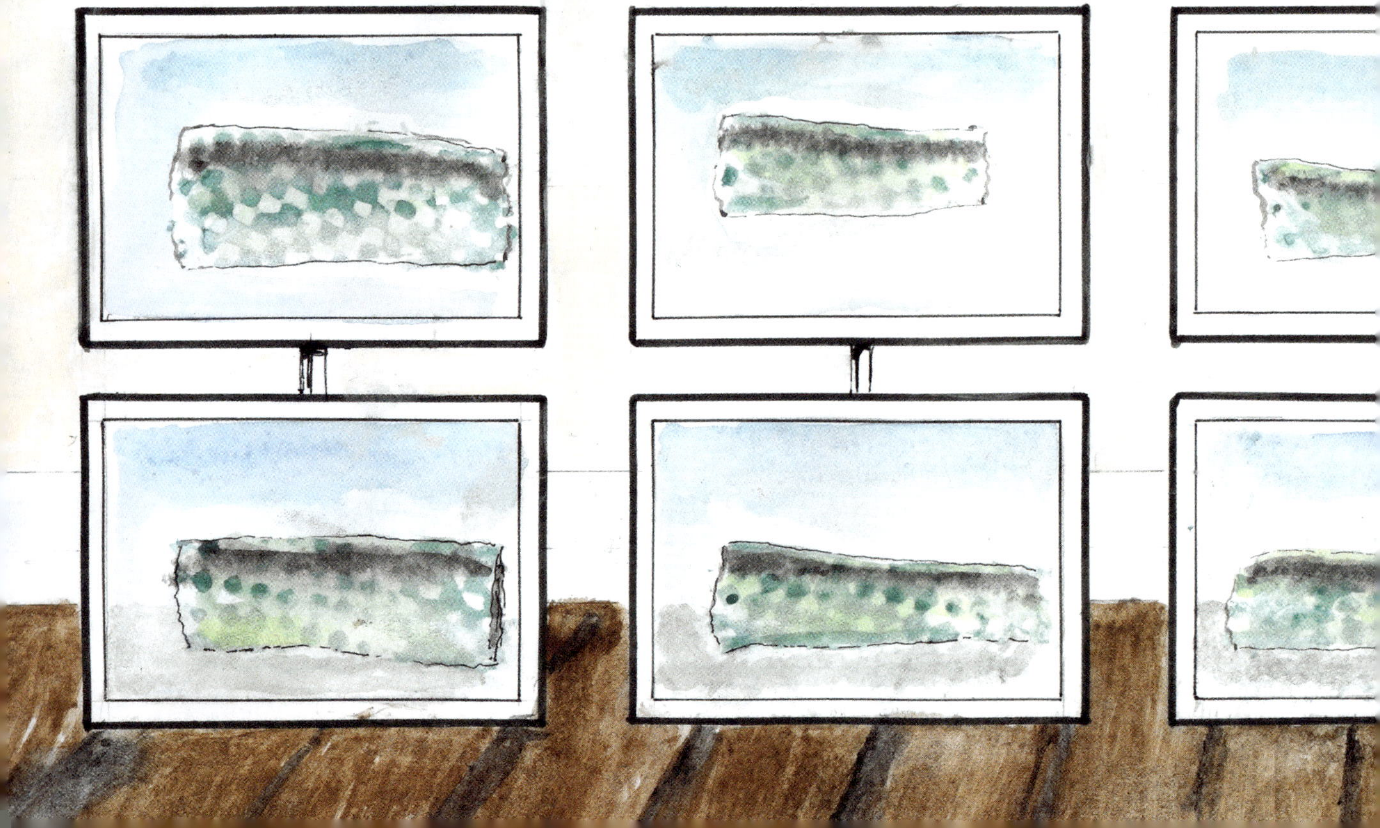

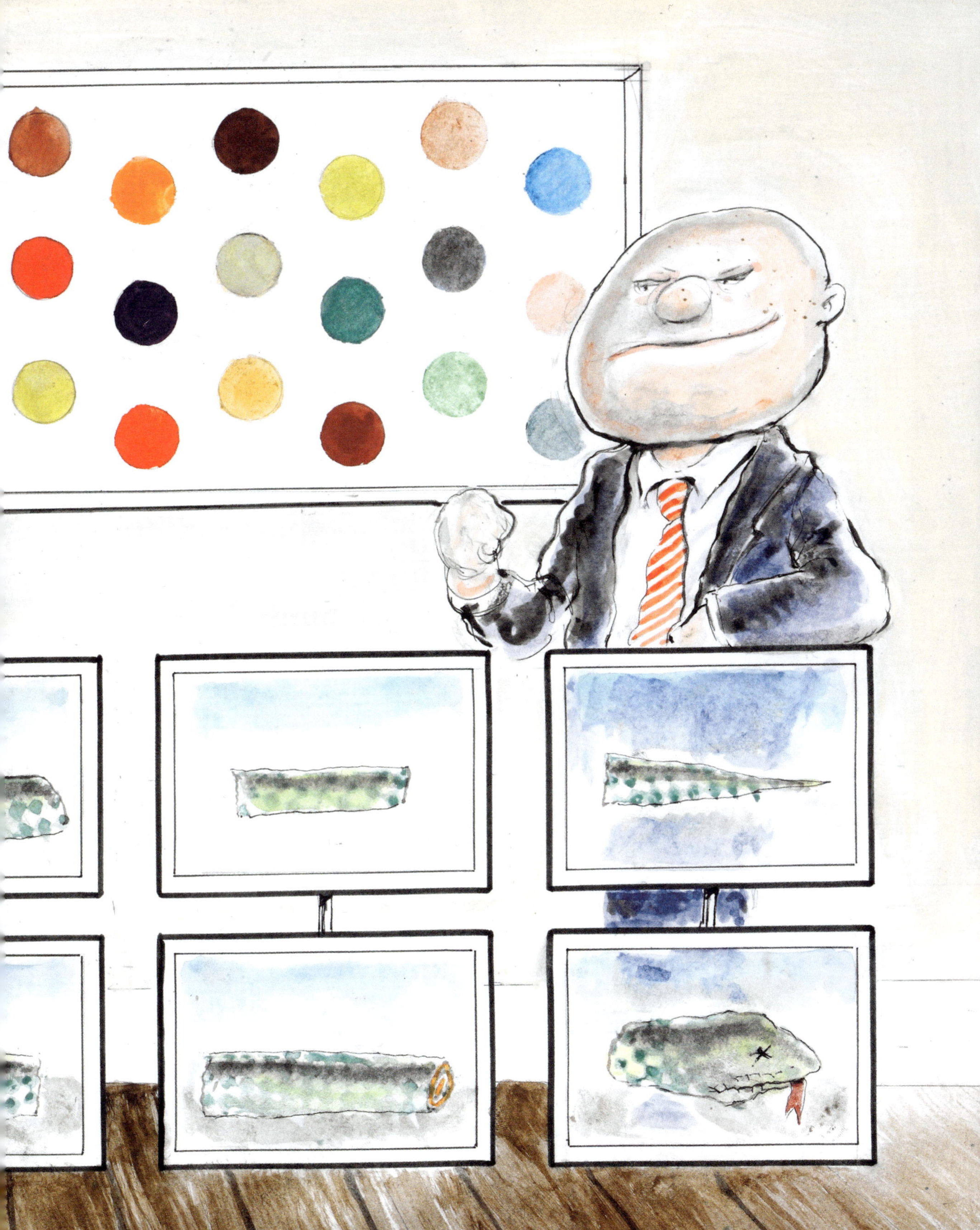

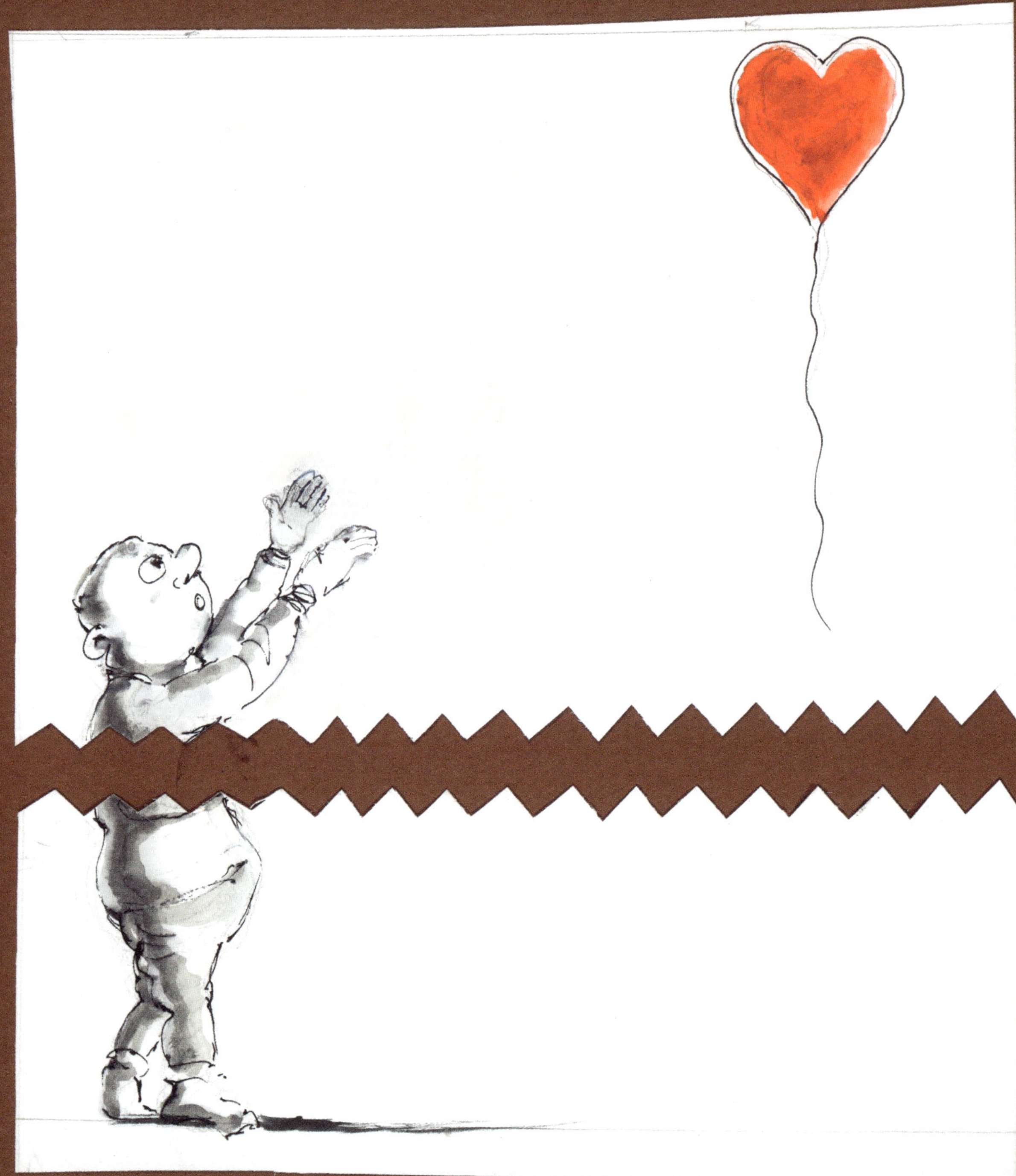

Banksy

The boldest prank

If anyone thinks modern art is strange and completely impossible to explain, here's a story that should confirm that. One of the world's most talked-about artists is an Englishman who goes by the name Banksy. His works, paintings on walls and murals, have often been in the media. Everyone knows what they look like. But no one knows what the artist himself looks like, what his name is, or where and when he was born. And when he receives an award, which has happened more than once, he doesn't show up to accept it. Some believe Banksy was born in Bristol in 1973 and came to London in 2000. But it's not known for sure. However, it is known that he is a former street artist, that he is engaged in politics and social criticism, and that he is opposed to an approach to art that is only about money.

In October 2018, one of his works 'Girl with Balloon' was put up for sale at the auction house Sotheby's in London. It sold for just over a million pounds. But the moment the hammer fell – a sign that the sale was concluded – an alarm went off inside the artwork. At the same time, the work was shredded by a shredding machine hidden in the frame around the artwork. A work that destroyed itself, the prestigious auction house had never experienced before. It was believed that Banksy himself must be behind it, not least because he posted a picture of the shredding machine on Facebook.

The lady who had bought 'Girl with Balloon' was smart enough to keep it, even though she was well within her rights to return the deal because the artwork was destroyed. Later, it was revealed that in October 2021 – three years later – it had been sold again for $25.4 million.

A newspaper called the whole process the boldest prank in art history.

Olafur Eliasson

Nature comes to the museum

Many people live in big cities, and there are more and more of them. In these cities, we live a protected life in apartments and houses with district heating and air conditioning. Here, we don't see much of nature, and therefore we also escape all the things in nature that can hit, overwhelm, or scare us.

Behind the four walls of home, we are not exposed to extreme cold. We also don't experience getting lost in fog banks. We don't risk breaking arms or legs by having to crawl over landscapes of large stones. And the sun is not a force to fear at all. We only encounter it if we choose to face it and therefore go out to the balcony of our home – or even better: out into nature.

In his works, the Icelandic-Danish artist Olafur Eliasson (born 1967) plays on precisely all the natural influences that we don't normally encounter when we inhabit a modern metropolis and have become accustomed to indoor life. Perhaps we have even forgotten or repressed these natural influences. Perhaps it is because of this particular forgetfulness or repression that Olafur Eliasson's works make such a great impression on us when we encounter precisely these influences – in a museum. They certainly change our perception of the museum.

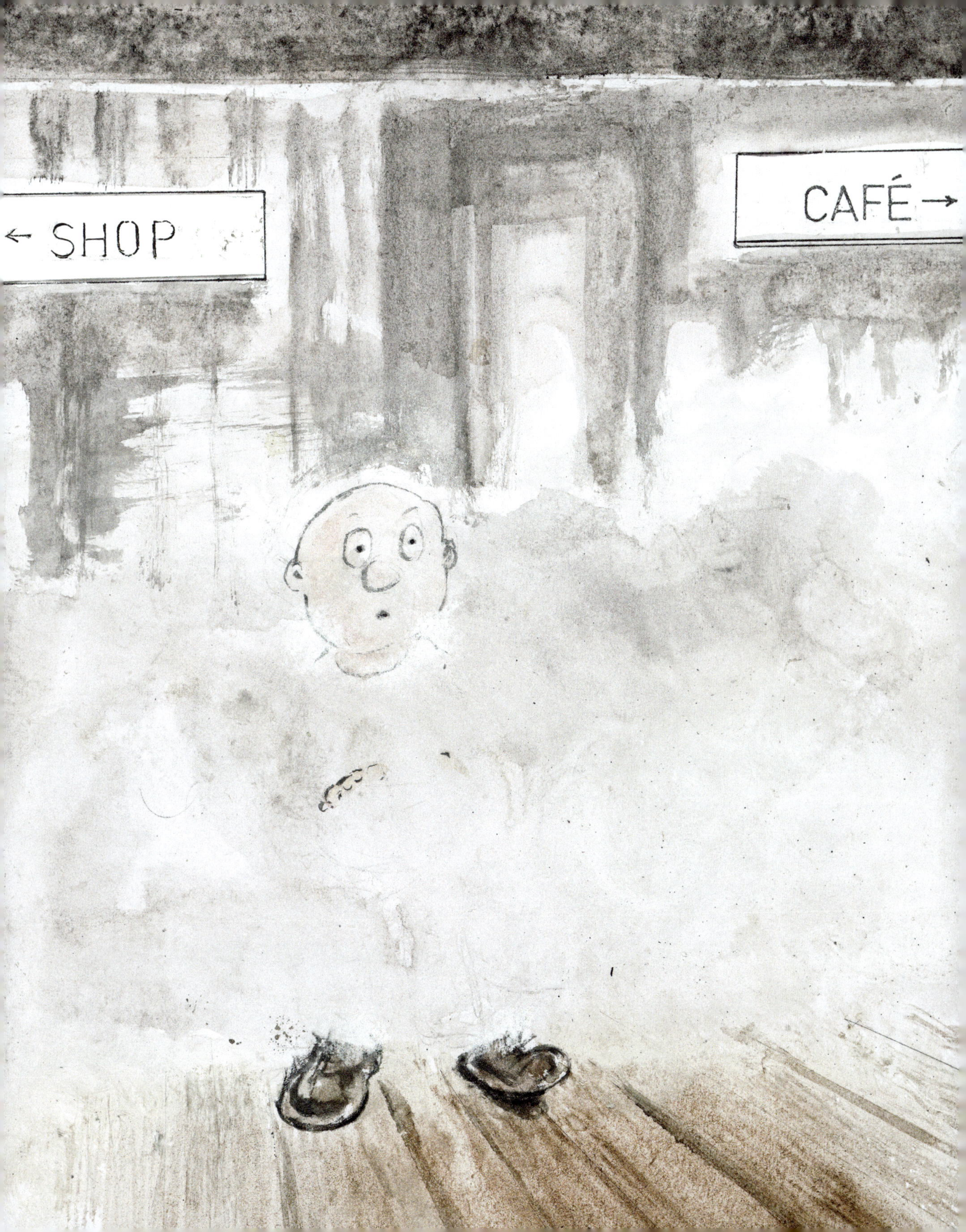
← SHOP
CAFÉ →

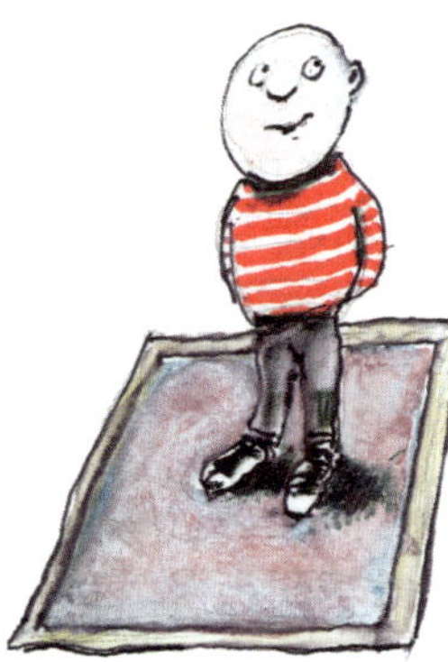

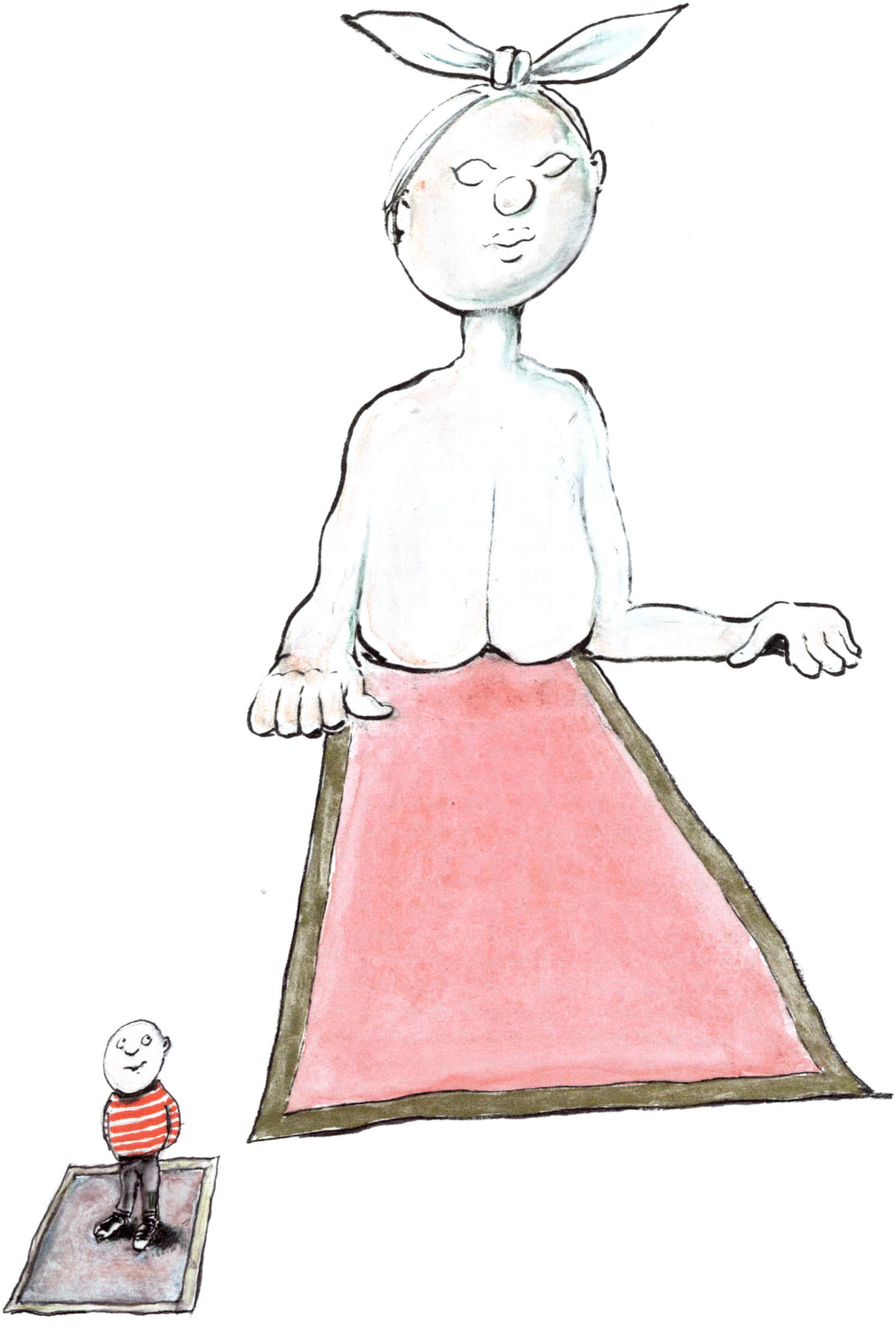

Kara Walker

It doesn't get any sweeter than this

Art history has offered many enormous sculptures of men.
Now it's high time to be introduced to a woman just as large,
created by Kara Elizabeth Walker (born 1969). While the
mighty men you have encountered on some of the preceding
pages have been built of stone, earth, flowers, and synthetic
materials, she, 'A Subtlety' – or 'The Marvelous Sugar Baby',
as she's also called – is made of 80 tons of white sugar to be
precise. So in a way, we're talking about the sweetest sculpture ever made. But the intention behind it is not sweet.

The 75-foot-long reclining female sphinx is the American
artist Kara Walker's monument to all the both burdened and
underpaid coloured women who not so long ago toiled in the
fields extracting sugar from sugar beets, just to satisfy our
sweet tooth. That's why the mighty woman's face is modelled
after a physiognomy known in the South as the 'Southern
Mammy Archetype'.

In 2024, it has been ten years since Walker's work was shown
in a defunct sugar refinery in Brooklyn, New York City, the
'Domino Sugar Refinery'. The material itself – the many tons
of sugar – was donated by Domino Foods. The sculpture was
surrounded by fifteen ushers, five of whom were carved in
sugar, while the other ten were resin sculptures covered in
molasses. When the exhibition closed in July 2014, 130,000
visitors had seen 'A Subtlety' and discussed the political and
social-critical intent behind the entire installation. After-
wards, the sphinx and the surrounding figures were disman-
tled, and the factory building was demolished.

Danh Vo

Light over a New World

The artist Danh Vo was born in Vietnam in 1975 and was just four years old when he, along with his parents, had to flee from the advancing North Vietnamese armies. Landing in Denmark was somewhat of a coincidence. Today, Danh Vo is primarily an internationally recognized artist who, because of his own background, questions the concept of nationality. His perhaps best-known work is 'We the People', which is a 1:1 replica of the Statue of Liberty, a 93-meter-high statue with a pedestal that has stood on Liberty Island at the entrance to New York since 1886. The original title of the statue – created by the French sculptor Frédéric Auguste Bartholdi – is 'Liberty Enlightening the World'.

The colossal statue was a gift from France to the United States in grateful remembrance of the democracy and freedom shared by the two nations. But today, freedom has different conditions, and the changed political climate may be why Danh Vo got the idea to split the replica of the statue into nearly 400 individual parts, which are now scattered around the world. Of course, it was never intended for these parts to be experienced individually. In this fragmented form, they merely resemble other abstract sculptures. Only as a whole do they make sense.
In the drawing, our guide has been allowed to mimic the Statue of Liberty's pose, and for the sake of recognition, he has been accompanied by the symbolic torch that this goddess of enlightenment holds in her right hand.

Danh Vo's background is a key to everything he does. He comes from a former French colony that was long divided and torn apart by a violent war. And he arrived as a child refugee in a country with a completely different language, religion, culture, and history. Therefore, his art pulls you out of the comfort zone that you as an exhibition guest have long taken for granted. Instead, it provides you with the prerequisites for understanding the artist as a human who has experienced, survived, and now unfolds his works under circumstances created by coincidences.

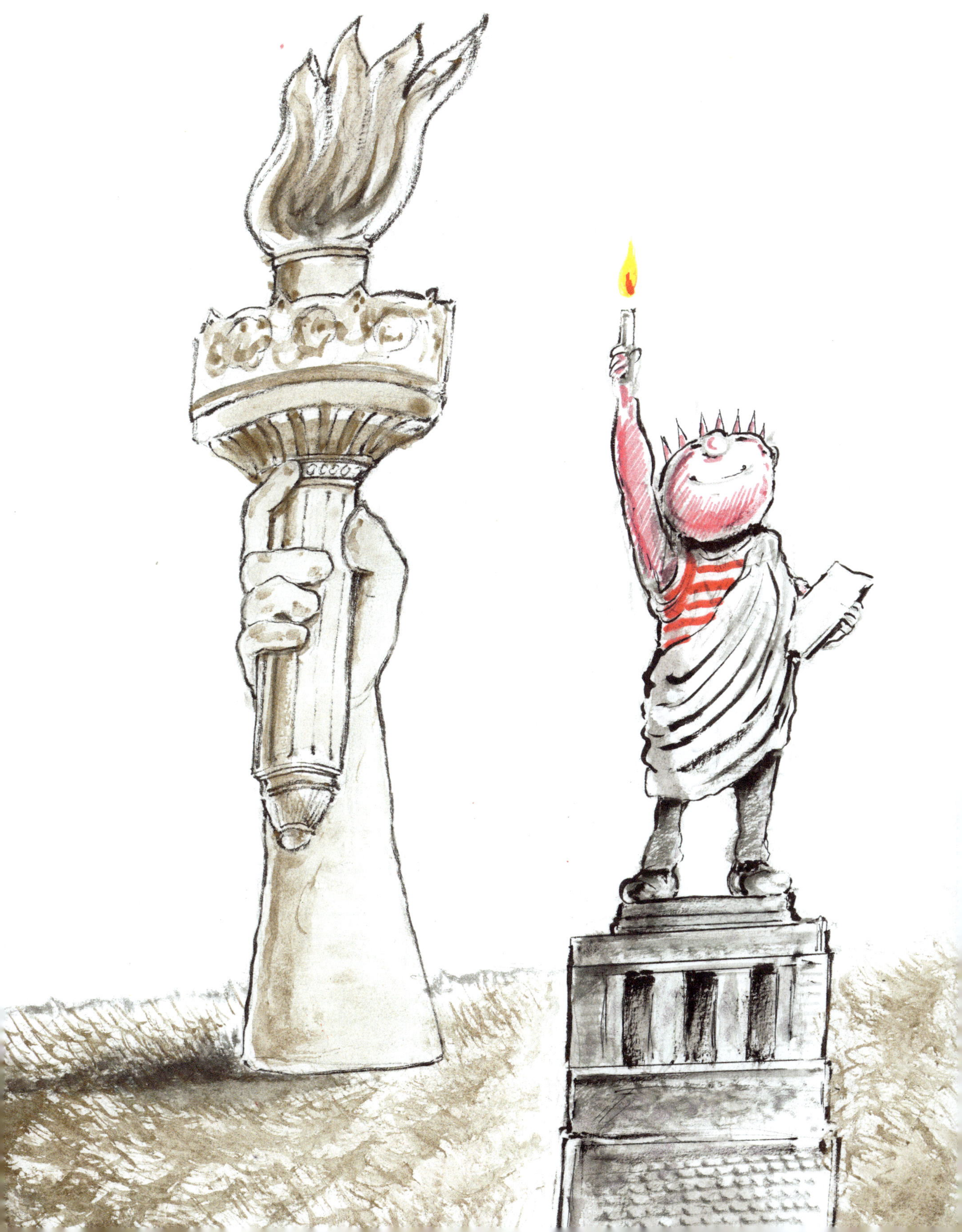

David Hockney

The great liberation

David Hockney (born 1937) was an artistically gifted child prodigy long before he emerged as the most famous English artist of his generation as an adult. Apparently, he can do it all: paint, draw, etch, photograph, design, create illustrations, stage sets – especially for operas – and write books about art, including his own. Although he is comfortable in most modern styles, he was initially associated with Pop Art. But he has never liked being pigeonholed, and

his career has shown how he has always been able to transcend boundaries and incorporate new techniques. He has even become sought after as a fashionable portrait painter.

The journey has taken him from Yorkshire, where he was born, to London, where he was educated, and to the USA. In the early sixties, he moved from New York to Los Angeles, and in the following years until 1967, when he let loose in sunny California, he found with his fascination with water and what movements in water can do to colours in a painting, a typical motif for him: the swimming pool. Regardless of how decorative, perfectionistic, and precise his painting style appears, his art has always been about maximum liberation.

Hockney has understood how to move with the times of technological development, and in recent years, he has attracted attention by incorporating computer technology and digital inkjet painting into his art.

For most of its many thousands of years of history, visual art has been kept on a short leash by the society of which it has been a part. They are connected, and one can always discuss whether it's time that has influenced art or art that has left its mark on the times. It's only in the past couple of hundred years that art has begun to chart its own course. Or so it may seem.

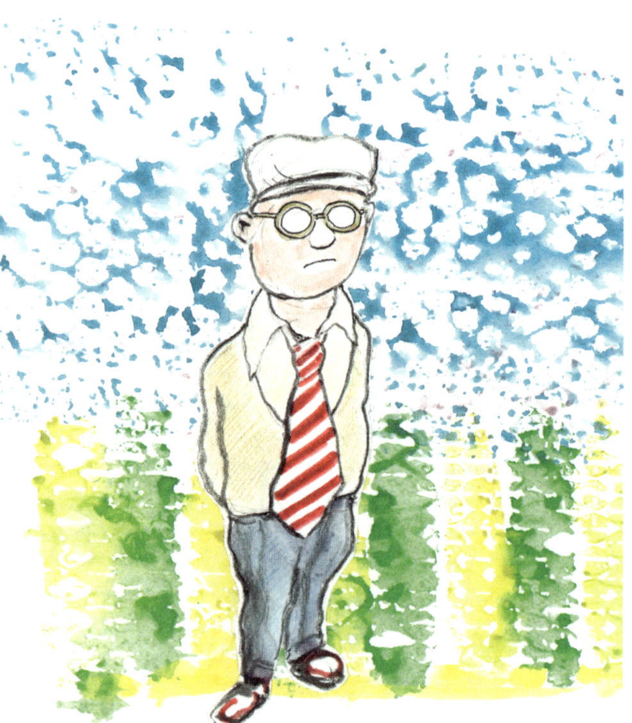

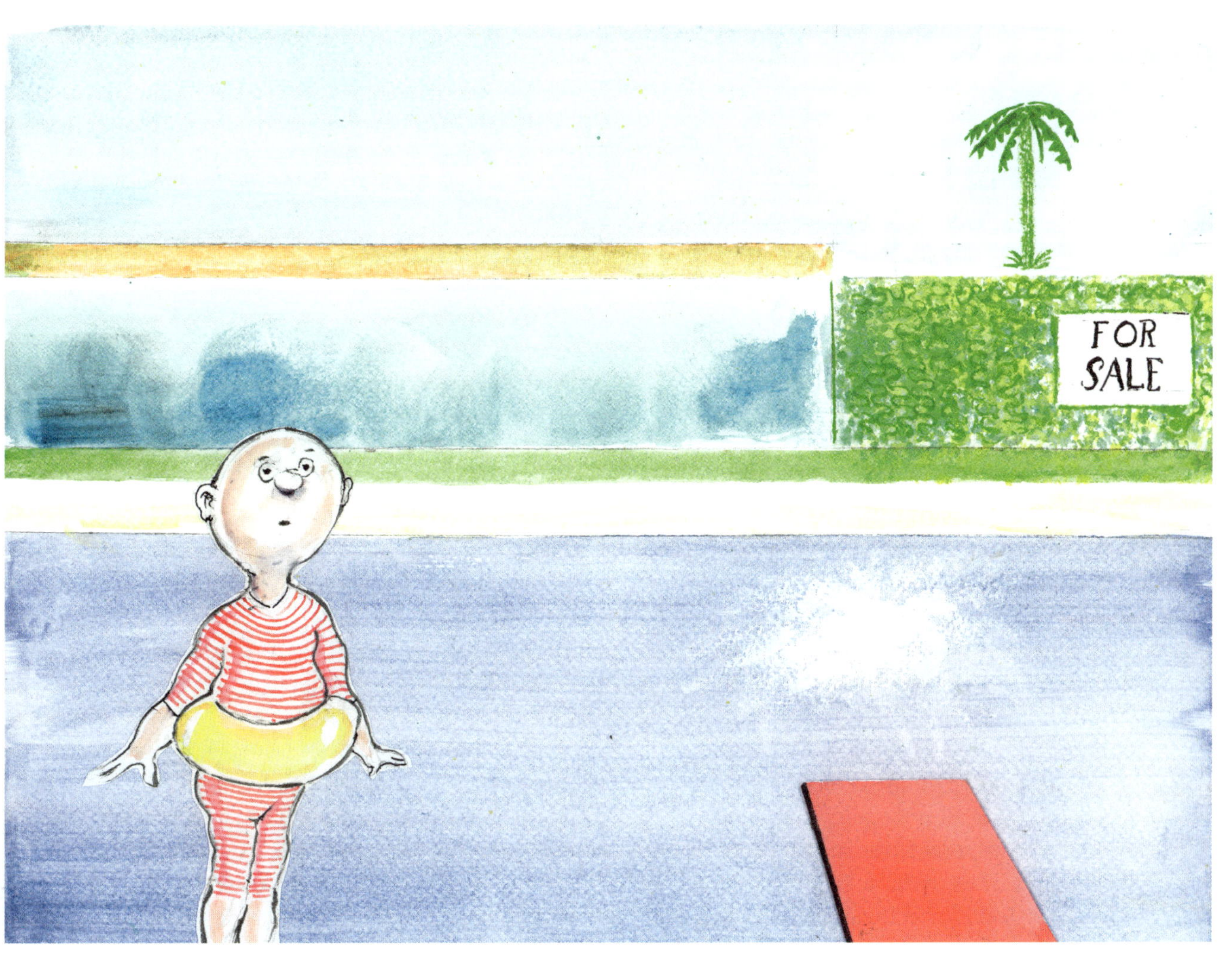
FOR
SALE

Conclusion – and a new beginning

The journey has ended. Roughly – and with quite a few simplifications and omissions – you've gone through the history of art, and now you probably want to see some real works of art. Those are the ones that sell for staggering sums at auctions and hang in art museums. They're also the kind that art historians can write thick books about.

The problem is never finding the art. The problem is being able to grasp it once you've found it. Because when there is enough of it, you can easily lose track, and when you lose track, motivation and desire also vanish. Therefore, it's good advice when visiting a large museum: limit yourself to what first catches your eye. It's usually the controversial stuff.

If you look at the pictures in this book, you'll see that the artist who attracts the most attention is also the artist who has broken away from the pack to create their own expression. That's why art history – especially in modern times – is one long story of rebellion and departure. Only when an event has receded a bit in time and space can you understand why rebellion and departure are often the only way forward.

Unlike athletics, visiting museums isn't about going as far as possible as quickly as possible but about taking the time and peace for attentive immersion. Except for genres like video art, happenings, and mobiles, it's a characteristic of much visual art that it doesn't move. But that doesn't mean it cannot move you if you give it a chance.

But it requires immersing yourself in a work for so long that it eventually unfolds. Therefore: start by asking the questions about a work that you can always answer by just looking, provided you look long enough and attentively at what has caught your interest. How has the artist managed to depict what you see? What do they want? What are their assumptions? And why have they done what they have done?

When you have gotten to know a work so well that you can describe it vividly to others, you've already come a long way. Then the words will carry your experience forward.

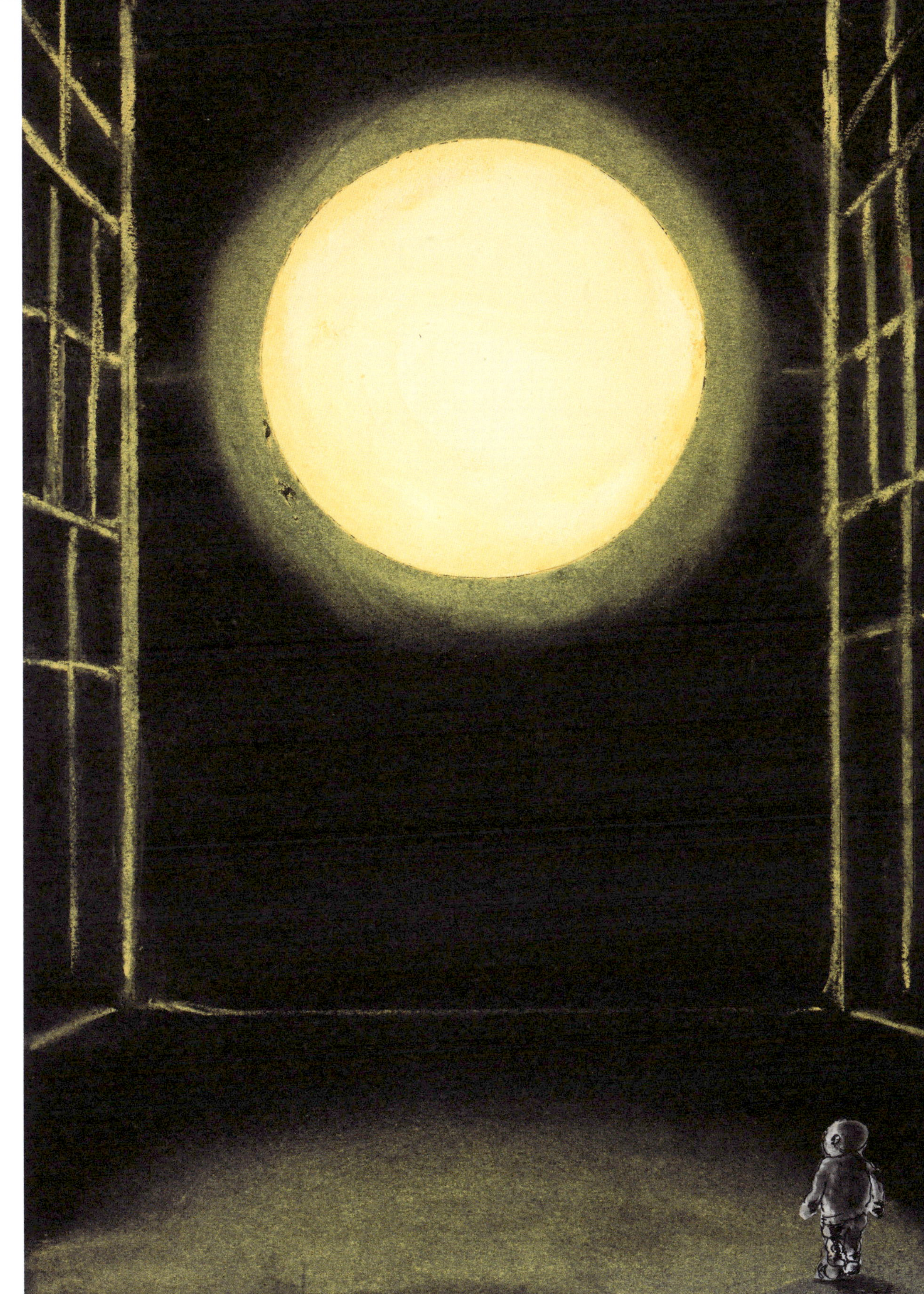

Glossary

Abstract

An artwork is abstract when you cannot see at all what it depicts. But beware! Perhaps the work only shows something that you do not recognize. Abstract artists have disassociated themselves from the 'real world' in such a way that the work becomes its own reality. The verb 'to abstract', which comes from Latin, means to draw from or extract. What is drawn from or extracted is everything that reminds us of the world of reality.

Abstract Expressionism

Used to describe works that are conveyed with strong emotions and which don't represent anything recognizable. Originally used about an anti-naturalistic fraction within early 20th-century German Expressionism, the term was later applied to Cobra. Today, it refers particularly to a group of American artists who emerged in the decades after World War II when New York became the new centre of modern art.

Action art

Artistic form of expression that emerged in the 1950s and 1960s with the intention of breaking down boundaries. This included the boundaries between different art forms such as theatre, art, literature, and music – and the boundaries between art and everyday life, for example, by moving art out of museums and into society or nature.

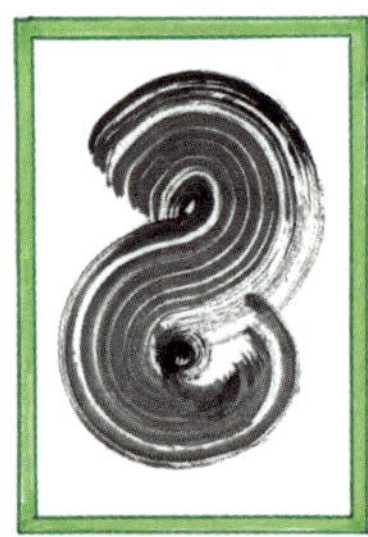

Action painting

An action painting is a painting that clearly shows the mark of its creation, i.e. the artist's process. For this 'action,' the artist can use, for example, balls or strings dipped in paint, or a can of paint with a hole made in the bottom, or they can ride a bicycle or scooter over the painting, as American Jackson Pollock and Danish Asger Jorn did. Action painting is closely related to Abstract Expressionism.

Archaic

Originally meaning 'old', this term is used to describe the strict, stylized style in Greek art between 650 and 480 BCE, which predates the classical period.

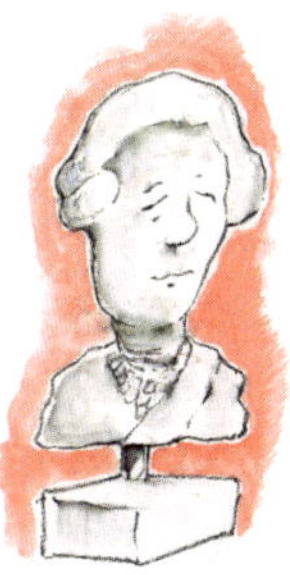

Avant-garde

Originally a French word for a vanguard. The avant-garde is the spearhead of a cultural breakthrough. In the history of modernism in art, avant-garde is used about artists who, in terms of ideas or methods, are at the forefront of an experimental development.

Baroque

Art movement that emerged in Italy in the late 16th century as a reaction against the late Renaissance. Baroque painting is known for its dramatic and emotionally charged depictions, especially of religious subjects. A typical Baroque painting is like a theatrical performance, where the lighting highlights the figures on the stage, at the expense of decorations and scenography. Baroque art was particularly used by the Catholic Church as part of its armament and fight against Martin Luther and the Reformation. The intention was to make people believe in miracles and divine intervention. To achieve this, the contrast between light and shadow was intensified, focusing attention on the main motif. Kings and princes also used artworks, sculptures, and architecture from this period as propaganda to showcase their power and significance when needed.

Bust

A portrait sculpture that only depicts the head of a person, along with a small portion of the upper body. In a museum, a bust is often placed on a tall pedestal or plinth, thus putting it eye to eye with the viewer.

Canon

When the Catholic Church canonizes someone, it declares them to be a saint, meaning a person whom you can invoke as your advocate in Heaven. The term 'canonized' is also used in the context of art, here often referring to a selection of artworks, books, plays or, buildings which are considered particularly important for a country's cultural history. This means they are recognized and accepted as being especially significant.

Colouration

In essence, colouration is simply another word for 'colour'. The term is also used to describe an artist's palette, i.e. the colour scheme that is characteristic of that particular artist. For example, in the case of the Danish painter Vilhelm Hammershøi, his palette is subdued and primarily consists of shades of grey.

Composition

Term for the way in which artists construct the motif in, for example, a painting using individual parts. If a composition is symmetrical, for example, the artist aims for a balance between the right and left sides of the image.

Conceptual art

An artwork where the idea and planning can be more important than the execution of the work. A conceptual artist might only sketch the work they have in mind. If the idea behind the work is strong and original enough, it becomes the expression of the work until it is potentially realized. If conceptual art has a founding figure, it is the Frenchman Marcel Duchamp.

Constructivism

Term for an experimental non-figurative art movement in 1920s Russia, following the Russian Revolution. Today, it is used more generally to describe tendencies within abstract art and modern architecture where the emphasis is on the consistently constructive and technical. It contrasts with Expressionism.

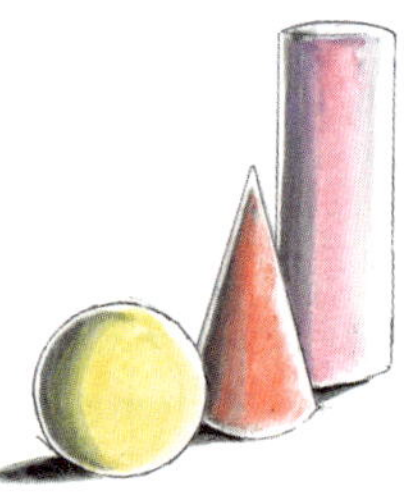

Cubism

A modern art movement that emerged around 1907 in Paris, seeking to approach space in painting in a new way. The cubists rejected linear perspective and didn't believe in pretending that a painting had depth when it was actually flat. In a typical cubist painting, the same object can be seen from multiple sides simultaneously: For example, there are cubist portraits where you can see the subject from the side and front at the same time. The most important painter of Cubism was Pablo Picasso. Cubism had a significant impact on many artistic movements in the 20th century, including Futurism and Constructivism.

Dadaism

European and American movement within modernist art, which emerged in Zurich, Switzerland, in 1916, almost as an ironic anti-art movement. The movement also had branches in Cologne and Berlin, Germany. Dadaism flourished until 1924. The dadaists were against war, unlike the futurists. However, they resembled the futurists in rejecting all traditions within art.

Expressionism

Expressionism is a perception of reality where the expressionist – in clear contrast to the realist – does not seek an exact depiction of what he or she sees. By altering and intensifying the forms and colours observed, the artist tries to express the experienced emotions. For example, if standing in front of a frightening mountain landscape the expressionist would seek to express their fear through the colours they use.

Fauvism

Movement within expressionist art that emerged in France in the early 1900s. The word comes from the French word for wild beasts, *fauves*, which a French critic used in 1905 to describe the movement's painters because they had a particularly vigorous brushstroke and used such wild colours. The fauvists were not concerned with showing the true colours of things – what was more important to them was that the painting became decorative. The most important fauvist is Henri Matisse, who was notorious for painting a picture of his wife where her nose is completely green.

Figurative

If a painting is figurative, it contains figures. Figurative is the opposite of non-figurative. That a picture is figurative does not necessarily mean that it is naturalistic or realistic – i.e., that it resembles reality. It can just as easily be symbolic or surrealistic. There are multiple ways to depict a figure. However, the way you depict the figure reveals which style you are using.

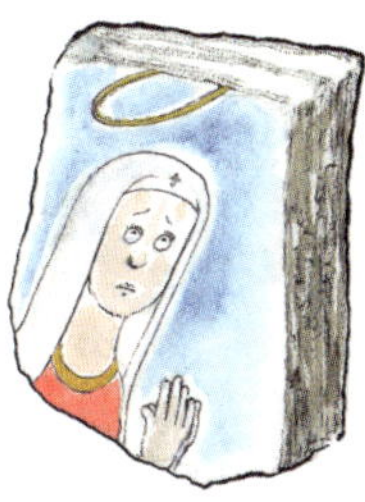

Fresco

Term used for paintings on a wall that has been coated with a freshly applied, still moist layer of plaster. This allows the colour and plaster to form a chemical bond, ensuring the painting's durability. It was especially used during the Renaissance for church decorations, where the artist painted directly on the church wall.

Futurism

Controversial critical movement that emerged in 1909 in Italy and died out before 1918. The name 'Futurism' is derived from *futurum*, the Latin word for future. This explains why the movement distanced itself from museum art – i.e., traditional art – and instead focused on the industrial dynamics that form the basis of modern society. The futurists were enthusiastic about cars and machines, and their artworks typically tried to depict speed and movement.

Genre

In art, the term 'genre' refers to a particular type or style. When we speak of genre painting, the subject matter is drawn from everyday life. Often, such a subject contains a small narrative. You can find this type of painting, for example, in The Netherlands of the 17th century and in Denmark two hundred years later. The word 'genre' comes from the Latin word for 'kind' or 'type,' which is 'genus.'

Gothic

In architecture, the term is used to describe the pointed arch style found in Europe from the mid-12th century and for three to four centuries thereafter. In sculpture, a figure is called Gothic if it (unlike Romanesque) is more dynamic, dramatic, and lacking in symmetry.

Happening

In 1950s and 1960s art, the term 'happening' refers to a new interactive art form where one or more artists use entertaining and engaging elements from film, theatre, music, etc., to blend different art forms and simultaneously break down the boundary between performer and audience.

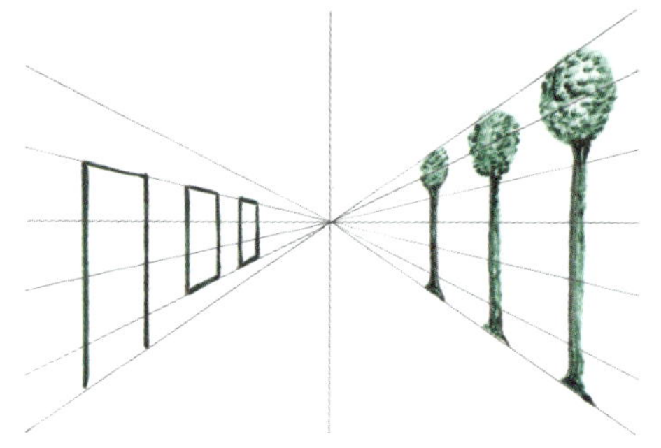

Impressionism

Important art movement from the end of the 19th century, which first exhibited publicly in Paris in 1874. Originally, the group consisted of artists who distanced themselves from the traditional art scene and the prevailing artistic views – views that, for example, prioritized narrative painting, especially history painting, over the depiction of modern society. The impressionists liked to paint outdoors, both landscapes and scenes of the city of Paris. They aimed to represent colours and light as accurately as possible, giving their works a sketch-like quality.

Linear perspective

For a painting (which is flat) to appear deep and spatial (as if it had a third dimension), the artist relies on geometry. This method is also known as linear perspective. The idea is that objects or people are depicted smaller if they are deep within the picture space, and larger if relatively closer to you. The term linear perspective stems from the fact that the perspective effect is built up using lines that converge at the same point. This point is called the vanishing point. Italian artists of the Renaissance were experts in this area.

Land art

Land art is also known as earth art because earth and similar materials are incorporated into the artwork. Land art is constructed in nature using natural materials. It is an artistic intervention in nature, and due to wind and weather, land art pieces often have limited durability.

Mannerism

Artistic style between the late Renaissance and early Baroque. The term derives from the Italian word maniera (manner) and one could regard the new style as a spiritual, emotional and intellectual critique of the calm and rather scientific approach to painting, which had dominated visual art in the 1400th century. In contrast to that, Mannerism produced its own anti-classical conception of form and colour: the human body would often appear elongated, distorted and twisted, and the rendering of colour was no longer based on pure perception.

Medium

In essence, a medium is a channel that someone uses to spread information. For example, we talk about radio and television as mediums. Video and television, for instance, are the mediums utilized by a video artist. However, in the realm of art, painting or drawing can also be a medium, something through which one expresses oneself.

Minimalism

An art movement which emerged in the 1960s in the USA, as a reaction against expressionism and the emotionally charged painting that focused on the artist's personal expression, his or her artistic 'fingerprint'. In contrast, the minimalists aimed to cleanse art of subjective emotions. Therefore, they simplified their works towards pure and clear geometric forms, which were often industrially produced and could, for example, be repeated in series without any apparent difference between them.

Modernism

Or modern art. The term is mostly used for art in the 20th century, which includes all the well-known styles such as Fauvism, Cubism, Surrealism, Automatism, Abstract Expressionism, etc. Towards the end of the 20th century, a new direction in art emerged, called Postmodernism, meaning a movement after

modernism. It criticized Modernism's belief that an artwork must always be a whole. Postmodernism rejected the traditional idea of originality in art. According to this new understanding, an artwork can be composed of quotations from other works and different styles that may seem contradictory at first glance.

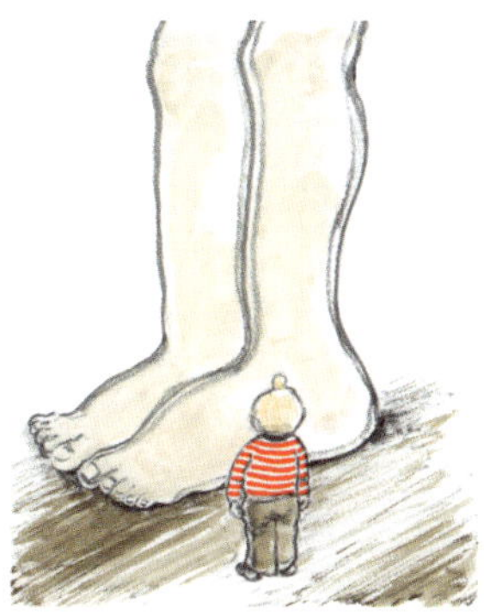

Monumental

A descriptive adjective that indicates that an artwork appears as a monument, meaning particularly grand or imposing. In principle, even a smaller work can have monumental forms.

Naturalism

Naturalism is a term for the artistic pursuit of imitating surroundings, environments, or objects as precisely and credibly as possible. In art history, Naturalism appears mostly in connection with 19th-century art, particularly in France, and primarily in the first half of the century. The terms Naturalism and Realism are often used interchangeably. However, Realism is more socially engaged and appears in visual art later than naturalism.

Neoclassicism

'Classicism' is the collective term for all artworks and stylistic phases that draw inspiration from the art of antiquity. The way in which antiquity perceived and depicted the human figure became a model for many later art movements, from the Italian Renaissance in the 15th century to the French Neoclassicism in the late 18th and early 19th centuries. When speaking of classical art, one thinks especially of Greek art, which later formed the basis for Roman art.

Non-figurative

A work of art is non-figurative when it is without figures, objects or concrete representations. It does not represent anything that you immediately recognize by name. Non-figurative is roughly the same as abstract, but the term is mostly used in relation to abstract art that is concrete.

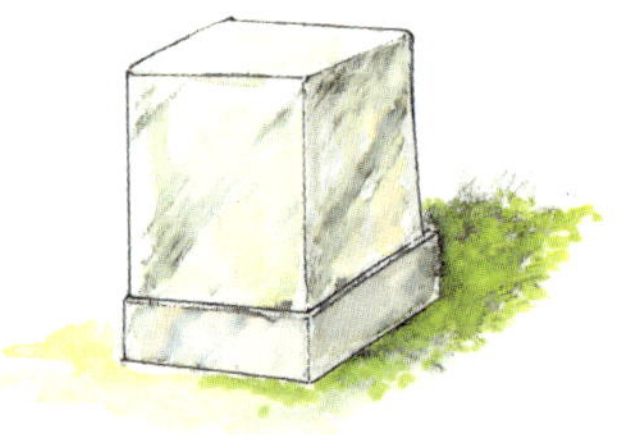

Pedestal

A pedestal is a base for a bust, a statue, a column, or something similar that some-one deems worthy of being raised from the ground. The French word for pedestal is *socle,* which in turn originates from *soccus*, the Latin term for sandal. Just as a person stands (and walks) on sandals, sculptures often stand on pedestals.

Performance

Like happenings, performance art emerged as a reaction against the static concept of works of art, which, unlike, for example, the art of theatre, applied to most of Modernism up until the experimental 1960s. Like theatre, performance art also unfolds in time, meaning it takes place only in the present and in a specific location. If it is to be documented later, for example, in an exhibition, it can be done using video, objects, photography, or writing.

Pop Art

An art movement which took off in the mid-1950s in both the USA and the UK. Pop Art can be inspired by adverts, products in shops and comics. Pop Art is based on all kinds of inspiration from a modern consumer society – as opposed to conventional, so-called 'fine' art.

Primitive

Artworks from the first or oldest stages of development are often referred to as primitive art. According to this view, art produced by indigenous peoples would fall under this label. However, this view is overly simplified; sometimes art may seem primitive to us because we do not understand its premises and the visual language it uses. Primitive art can also be an intentional expression inspired by children's art.

Realism

When it comes to visual art, Realism is a raw depiction of stark reality, often with motifs drawn from the darker aspects of life. The style emerged as a critical counterpoint to Romanticism, which the realists felt adorned its motifs a bit too much.

Relief

An image that is almost three-dimensional, i.e. where something is raised or lifted slightly from the background. In principle, reliefs can be made in any material; the key is that you not just work with the drawing in two planes, but also with depth. You could say that if you cross a drawing with a sculpture, you get a relief.

Renaissance

Renaissance means 'rebirth'. In classical art history, the term especially refers to the revival of the ideas and values of antiquity that gave rise to the Italian Renaissance in the early 1400s. However, there also existed a Renaissance outside of Italy, for example, in the Netherlands.

Rococo

Elegant style period that characterized Europe from 1720–89. You can recognize the style by its curved shapes, light colours, and many ornaments. Artists were inspired by Asian art, and unlike the Baroque style, the Rococo was airy and playful in its expression.

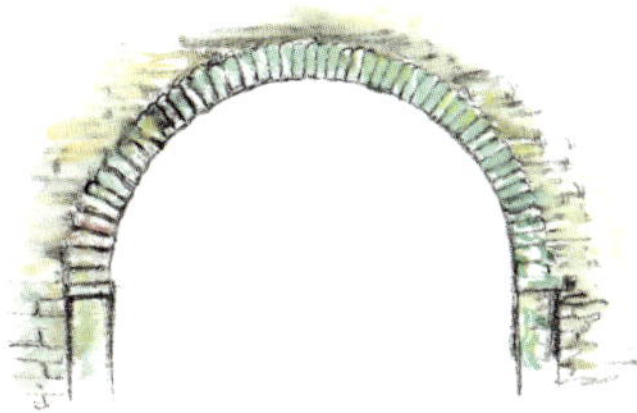

Romanesque

Also known as the round-arch style, this Roman and religiously influenced style is found in church architecture from around 1000 and two centuries onward. In art, the style is heavy, symmetrical, and majestic.

Romanticism

Term for a movement in European culture between c. 1805 and c. 1870. Romanticism emerged as a rebellion against the tendencies in art and culture that were based on science and reason. Romantic art centred on emotion – especially the emotions that can arise when one is out in nature: the sense that nature is magnificent and fierce, and you are small.

Spontaneous

An artist works spontaneously or in a spontaneous manner when they do not create sketches or preliminary studies beforehand but prefer to dive headfirst into the work that will become the finished piece. This is done in the belief that the painting will appear more immediate and powerful in its expression. Many expressionists have worked spontaneously. See also: Action Painting.

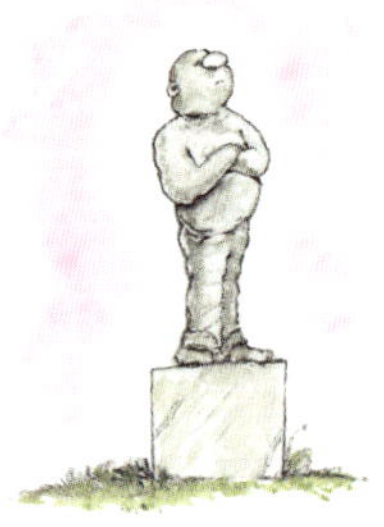

Statue

A statue is a representation of a human figure as a round, full-figure sculpture. Unlike a relief, you can walk around a statue and critically view it from all sides. There are far too many statues of famous men.

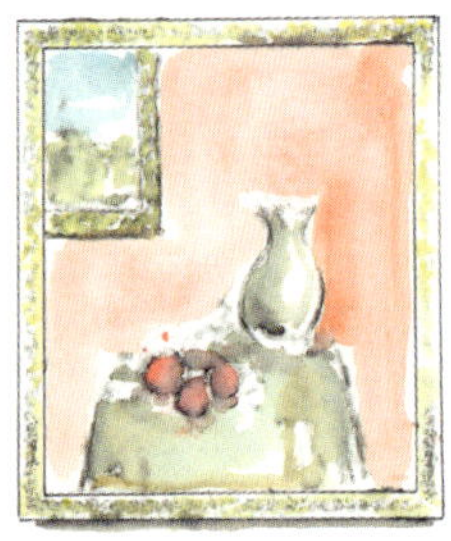

Still life

Term for a depiction of arranged objects, such as fruits, flowers, and porcelain. In French, it is called *nature morte*, which means 'dead nature'. Originally, a still life could indeed serve as a reminder of life's

transience, and sometimes even featured dead animals or skulls. In the 1500s and 1600s, still lifes were a specific genre that many Dutch painters specialized in.

Street art

Street art is the type of art you find in public spaces, and which brightens up even the dreariest street scene with its colours and easily readable forms (often grotesquely enlarged letters). Unlike commissioned public art, street art is created spontaneously and unsolicited by an often anonymous artist. The message in street art can be political or socially critical. When such art is exhibited in a gallery or a major museum (and it does happen!), it should technically be called something else. Banksy is a great example of an artist who has made the transition from the streets to museums.

Stylized

An artist stylizes when they transform a naturalistic form into a more simplified or clearly personal form. Stylization can reveal where the artwork belongs geographically or temporally, or perhaps who the artist is.

Sublime

Something that is elevated and grand in spiritual significance. A landscape painting in Romantic style, for example, is called sublime when it fills you with awe of nature and makes you feel small.

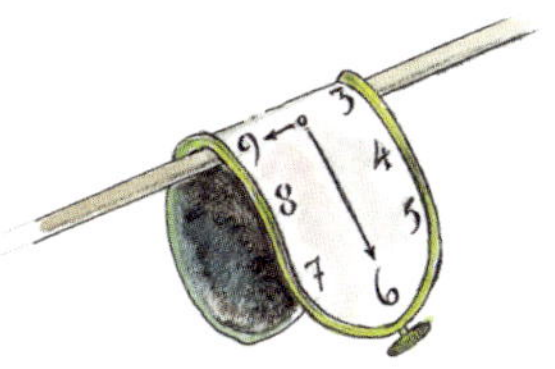

Surrealism

The word actually means 'beyond reality'. It is a term for a literary and artistic movement, which emerged in the 1920s. The surrealists believed that art should not only be about the visible reality. They found it much more interesting to explore the human subconscious and what can be experienced in dreams and the imagination.

Symbolism

Symbolism is a movement in visual arts and literature that began to stir around 1880 and lasted until around World War I. The symbolists felt that the naturalists and realists were too grounded and literal in their understanding of the purpose of art. To the symbolist, the world was not limited to what they could see with their eyes. The world was deep, to quote the German philosopher Friedrich Nietzsche, and it held secrets and meanings that art could hint at.

Index

**The Little Book of Art History
for Children and Curious Grown-Ups**

All illustrations by the author
Editors: Rebecca Vestervang Chong,
Sidsel Kjærulff Rasmussen and Jakob Rabe
Assistant editor: Pernille Gøtze Johansson
Translation: Rebecca Vestervang Chong
Copy editor: Cornelius Holck Colding
Cover and graphic design: Søren Damstedt, Trefold
Image processing: Narayana Press and Garn grafisk

The book is typeset in Replica and Chronicle Text
Paper: 150 g Munken Lynx Rough
Printing: PNB Print
Printed in Latvia 2024
1st edition, 1st print run
ISBN: 978-87-92596-61-1

The first Danish editions of this book were published
with support from The New Carlsberg Foundation,
Arne V. Schleschs Fond, Aage og Johanne Louis-
Hansens Fond, Beckett-Fonden, Politiken-Fonden
and Palle Fogtdal.

Strandberg Publishing A/S
Gammel Mønt 14
DK-1117 Copenhagen
Denmark
www.strandbergpublishing.dk

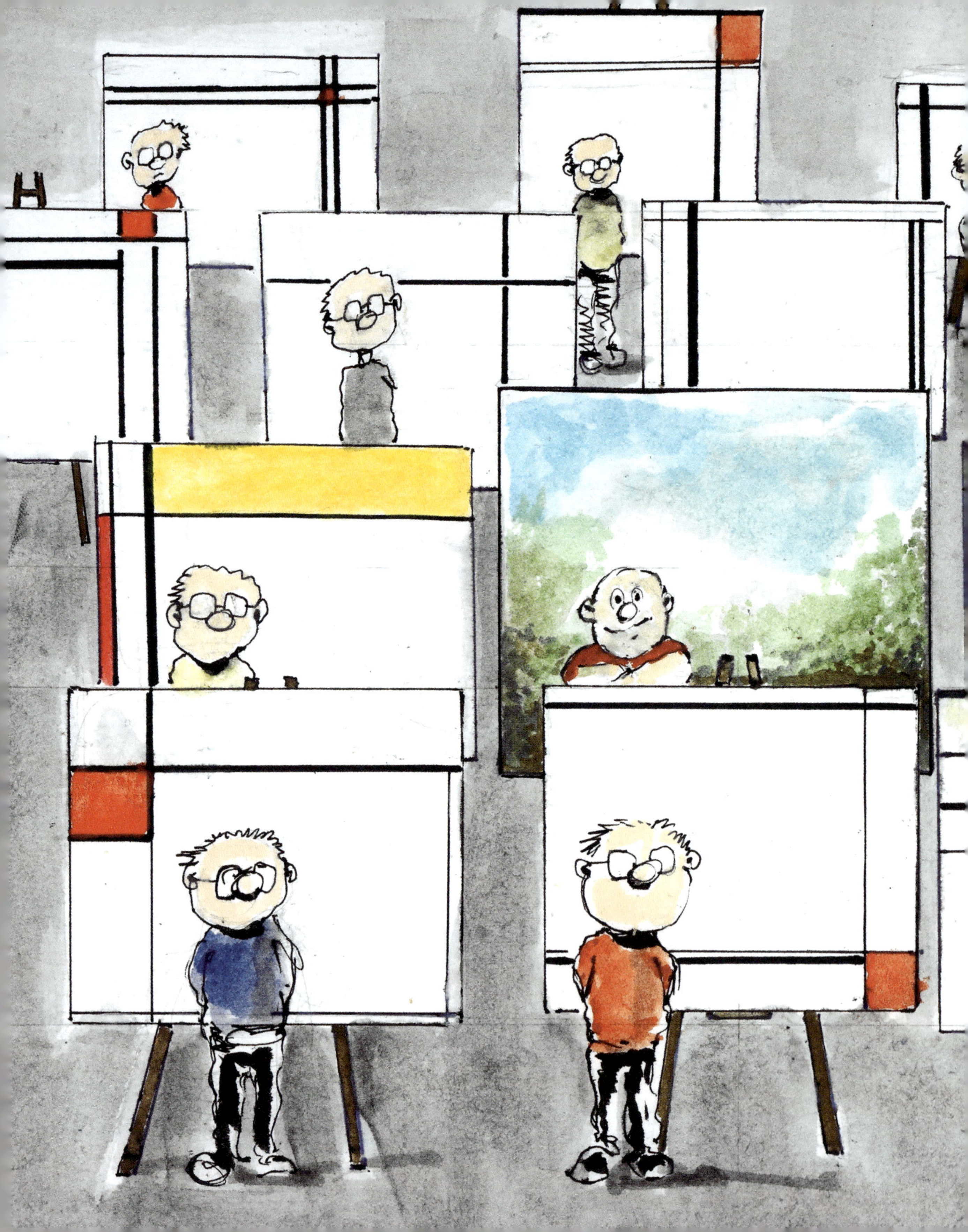